JOHN HENRIK CLARKE AND THE POWER OF AFRICANA HISTORY

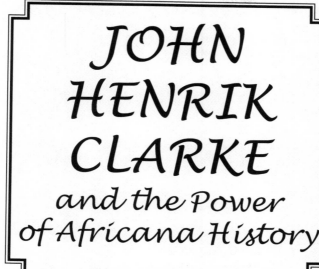

JOHN HENRIK CLARKE
and the Power of Africana History

Africalogical Quest for Decolonization and Sovereignty

Ahati N. N. Toure

AFRICA WORLD PRESS

Trenton | London | Cape Town | Nairobi | Addis Ababa | Asmara | Ibadan | New Delhi

AFRICA WORLD PRESS

541 West Ingham Avenue | Suite B
Trenton, New Jersey 08638

Book design: Saverance Publishing Services

Cover design: Ashraful Haque

Library of Congress Cataloging-in-Publication Data

Toure, Ahati N. N.
 John Henrik Clarke and the power of Africana history : Africalogical quest for decolonization and sovereignty / Ahati N. N. Toure.
   p. cm.
 Includes bibliographical references and index.
 ISBN 1-59221-626-9 (hard cover) -- ISBN 1-59221-627-7 (pbk.)
 1. Clarke, John Henrik, 1915- 2. Clarke, John Henrik, 1915---Political and social views. 3. African American historians--Biography. 4. Historians--United States--Biography. 5. Africanists--United States--Biography. 6. Africa--Historiography. 7. Africa--History--Autonomy and independence movements--Historiography. 8. Black nationalism--Historiography. 9. Pan-Africanism--Historiography. 10. Afrocentrism--Historiography. I. Title.

E175.5.C59T68 2008
973'.04960730092--dc22
[B]
                                   2008031816

To Elders Herman and Iyaluua Ferguson, New Afrikan founders who have charted the course of our freedom. Man and woman of valor, majestic in stature, spirits as strong as steel. Our enemies can never defeat you. We follow in your wake.

To Brother Spartacus R and Sister Pettrige, creators of Global African Peoples' Radio (www.gap-radio.com) You love us dearly and fight for us passionately. You remain undaunted. You see our victory approaching.

To Brother Ezrah Aharone, whose clear grasp of the imperative of Afrikan sovereignty inspires us all.

Contents

Acknowledgments

To truly acknowledge all who contributed to this effort would be an endless list of personalities, circumstances, and events. Because no person is disconnected from a complexity of factors that contribute to his or her forward movement, development, and growth, the list is potentially endless. Nonetheless, out of the limitless possibilities for personal acknowledgments I would like to highlight some of those who stand out in my memory.

Of course, I am grateful for the tremendous support and guidance of those at the University of Nebraska-Lincoln who were readers of this work in its initial stages: Drs. Benjamin G. Rader, Learthen Dorsey, Kenneth J. Winkle of the Department of History and Dr. Michael W. Combs of the Department of Political Science. I am especially grateful to Dr. Rader, who provided invaluable guidance and who offered challenging questions that helped me to clarify some of my ideas and arguments. I also owe a great deal to Dr. Dorsey, whose editorial critiques significantly enhanced my efforts. Much thanks, as well, to the patience and expert stewardship of my editor, Damola Ifaturoti, of Africa World Press.

I am profoundly grateful to my mother, Mrs. Irene W. Torain, and my deceased father, Mr. Joseph Torain, for their inexpressibly rich contribution to my life. My brothers and sister—Jeffrey Niles Torain, Evangeline Suzanne Torain, and Timothy Mitchell

Torain—and their children, my nieces and nephews, have been inextinguishable sources of love, strength, and support.

I have enjoyed invaluable assistance over the years from Dr. James L. Conyers, Jr., of the University of Houston and from his late wife, Mrs. Jackie Conyers. The late Dr. Julius E. Thompson of the University of Missouri-Columbia, with whom I studied for the M.A. degree in Africana Studies at the State University of New York at Albany, was one of my enduring friends and sources of encouragement and support for more than two decades.

I must also acknowledge Dr. Leonard Jeffries and Dr. Rosalind Jeffries for, among other things, their generosity in hosting me in their home during the weekends when I traveled from Albany to New York City to attend the Saturday lectures of the First World Family Alliance in the late 1980s. It was Dr. Leonard Jeffries who introduced me to Dr. Clarke, Dr. ben Jochannan, the Association for the Study of Classical African Civilizations (ASCAC), and the First World Family Alliance. These introductions revolutionized me intellectually, culturally, and spiritually, and set things in motion that eventuated into this study. I owe both Drs. Jeffries greatly.

Among the many to whom I am also indebted is the incomparable Marc A. Soto, Esq. of the Bronx, New York, whose extraordinary hospitality and kindness made my research at the Schomburg Center for Research in Black Culture possible. Marc is a true human being.

I give thanks to the staff of the Division of Manuscripts, Archives and Rare Books at the Schomburg Center for Research in Black Culture, Harlem, New York. I salute Diana Lachatanere, Curator; Andre Elizee, Manuscript Assistant; Steven Fullwood, Manuscript Librarian; Nurah Rosalie Jeter, Manuscript Librarian; Judy Holder, Page; Lisann Lewin, Page. I also offer special thanks and all good wishes to Ms. Diana Graham, Security (Coat Check) at the Schomburg Center.

I also owe many thanks to old friends. I continue to draw inspiration and instruction from Professor Colia L. Clark, who is one of the great, brilliant, and unheralded veterans of our freedom struggle, a true hero of our people, originally of Jackson, Mississippi. I always think with deep affection of Dr. Akwo Elonge of Clark Atlanta University, originally of Cameroon, from where my mother's people were kidnapped several generations ago. Akwo, whether he realized it or not, introduced me to the incomparable beauty of the spirit of Afrika and to the magnificent music of Central Afrika. Finally, I express my appreciation and admiration to Dr. Clyde C. Robertson of New Orleans, Louisiana. He is a true warrior, a true Afrikan, a true brother, and a power house of brilliance, creativity, and commitment.

I give thanks to the intense, guiding love from my Egun, including my paternal great grandparents whom I knew, James and Marie Lambert, and my paternal grandparents whom I also knew, Elisha and Betty Torain. There are also my maternal great great grandparents, great grandparents, grandparents, and great aunts and uncles whom I never knew in this life, but who undoubtedly know me, and decidedly influenced me through the life and love of my mother, including Great Great Grandmother Mandy Jameson, Great Grandfather Jerry Mitchell, Grandmother Irma Wanzer, and Great Aunt Azalene Mitchell Livingston.

I also acknowledge my spiritual elders, whose contribution can scarcely be accounted for in words: Chief Odunfa Bukola Aworeni Popoola of Williamstown, New Jersey; Chief Solagbade Popoola of Lagos, Nigeria; Chief Adebamiji Omonije of Iseyin, Nigeria; Chief Fasina Falade of Los Angeles, California; Chief Ifakunle Dosumu of Bayamon, Puerto Rico; and Baba Ade Ifaleri Olayinka of Brooklyn, New York. I give special reverential acknowledgment to Araba Oluisese Agbaye, Chief Adisa Aworeni Makanranwale of Ile-Ife, Nigeria. I also give special thanks to Chief Jokotoye Bankole of Ile Olukan Arowomole in Ogbomoso, Nigeria, for his incalculable assistance to me.

Finally, I give praise to Ifa, which is supreme. Reverence to Olodumare, to Ori, to Esu Odara, to Orunmila (Eleri Ipin, Ibikeji Olodumare), to Obatala, to Olokun, to the warriors (Esu Odara, Ogun, Ososi, Osun), to all the Irunmole and to all the Orisa. Ase.

Introduction

The Problem

Earl E. Thorpe, in his examination of Afrikan historians of the nineteenth through the mid twentieth centuries, defined the historiographical problem with respect to Afrikan history as one of the neglect of the study of Afrikan people in the United States (and worldwide). This was, he argued, caused by a Euro-American elitism that ignored those members of the human family who did not belong to the European group. The situation has since that time been expanded to a recognition of the paucity of critical examinations of some of the major figures in Afrikan history whose influence in Afrikan cultural, political, and intellectual movement in the United States and in the world—and with particular respect to historical research—has been profound.

There have, of course, been efforts in this regard. Thorpe's *Negro Historians in the United States* (1958), *The Central Theme of Black History* (1969), and *Black Historians: A Critique* (1969) examined the work of both professional academic and non-professional Afrikan historians in two centuries.[1] There are also Darlene Clark Hine's edited work, *The State of Afro-American History: Past, Present, and Future* (1986); August Meier and Elliott Rudwick's *Black History and the Historical Profession, 1915–1980* (1986), which includes a major examination of the work and influence of Carter G. Woodson; and

Benjamin Quarles's *Black Mosaic: Essays in Afro-American History and Historiography* (1988). Another important work is Maghan Keita's *Race and the Writing of History: Riddling the Sphinx* (1998), in which he examines not only the European historical writing about Afrika but Afrikan historical writing about Afrika.[2] James L. Conyers, Jr. has reintroduced the work and thought of two European academy-trained Afrikan historians in two edited volumes: *Charles H. Wesley: The Intellectual Tradition of a Black Historian* (1997) and *Carter G. Woodson: A Historical Reader* (2000).[3] More recent works include W. D. Wright's *Black History and Black Identity: A Call for a New Historiography* (2001); former *Journal of Negro History* editor Alton Hornsby's edited volume titled *Essays in African American Historiography and Methodology* (2004); and John Ernest's *Liberation Historiography: African American Writers and the Challenge of History, 1794–1861* (2004).[4] In addition there are a number of academic essays that explore some aspect of the historiographical question.[5]

Still, the efforts to date have hardly scratched the surface. Some of the major figures who have advanced a historiography of the Afrikan world experience, and who in some instances operated largely outside of the European academy, have had no book-length or even extensive critical treatments of their lives or work. Their names are legion and include William Leo Hansberry, Joel Augustus Rogers, Yosef A. A. ben Jochannan, John G. Jackson, Chancellor Williams, Drusilla Dunjee Houston, J. C. de Graft-Johnson, George G. M. James, and, of course, John Henrik Clarke, among numerous others.

The work on Hansberry provides an example of a slight exception to the rule, possibly in part because of his career as a professor at Howard University. In the 1970s, Professor Joseph E. Harris of Howard University edited two volumes of Hansberry's unpublished research and lecture notes titled *Pillars in Ethiopian History* (1974) and *Africa and Africans as Seen by Classical Writers* (1977). In the first volume, Harris provides a biographical essay titled "William Leo Hansberry, 1894–1965: Profile of a Pioneer Africanist."[6] More recently, Kwame Wes Alford has taken up the mantle of scholarship on Hansberry with a dissertation study completed in 1998, which he is expanding into a scholarly monograph. He has also published scholarly essays examining aspects of Hansberry's life and work.[7] In addition, Alford is the editor/curator of the *William Leo Hansberry Collection, Personal and Private Papers.*

Still, the exceptions underscore the rule. As an example of the rule of historical negligence, Yosef A. A. ben Jochannan (b. 1918), whose research and travel to the Afrikan Nile Valley and whose study in Afrikan antiquity date back to 1939, is perhaps more responsible for the popularization of the awareness of the Afrikan origin of Nile Valley civilization in the Afrikan community in twentieth- and twenty-first-century United States than any other scholar during the period.[8] Yet there has to date been no book-length scholarly research examining either his life or his work. Joel A. Rogers (1880–1966) is perhaps the premier figure responsible for the popularization of the role of Afrikans in European world history. Rogers, who never earned a university degree of any sort, dedicated some fifty years to original research and publication, traveling to Europe and North Afrika and examining and collecting primary and secondary documents and historical artifacts in the French, Portuguese, Spanish, and German languages (in addition to English), in which he had gained fluency. Yet, like ben Jochannan, no scholarly work has been done on this remarkable historian.[9]

Similarly, few have looked at the genesis of Afrikan scholars who were rigorously trained in historical (and often multidisciplinary) methodology and interpretation outside the confines of the European academy. John Henrik Clarke, the subject of this work, is a case in point.[10] He emerged from a tradition of independent Afrikan historical scholarship located in indigenous institutions such as the Schomburg Collection at the 135th Street Library of the New York Public Library system, the Harlem History Club, the Ethiopian School of Research History (and later Charles C. Seifert Library), and private research collections and initiatives developed by such luminaries as Arthur A. Schomburg, Willis N. Huggins, Charles C. Seifert, and William Leo Hansberry. John G. Jackson, who worked closely with Huggins in the Harlem History Club, jointly published with Huggins a survey text on Afrikan civilizations in 1937 and went on to publish at least six other major texts on Afrikan and western Asian antiquity between 1939 and 1990.[11] Clark himself would eventually go on to produce well over 150 publications on primarily historical subjects, including books as well as introductions and book chapters, journal articles, pamphlets and monographs, book reviews, magazine and newspaper articles, published interviews, and audiovisual recordings in the form of motion picture and video documentaries or speeches, sound recordings in the form of long playing records, audiocassette tapes, and compact discs.

Despite the volume of his output, there are few critical, scholarly secondary sources examining his life and work. One of Clarke's former undergraduate students, Barbara Eleanor Adams, has authored two texts, *John Henrik Clarke: The Early Years* (1992) and its revised and expanded version titled *John Henrik Clarke: Master Teacher* (2000), which are autobiographical oral histories of Clarke's life from childhood to his return to New York City from a stay in Ghana in the late 1950s and including transcriptions of selected speeches.[12] Added to this genre of literature are Clarke's personal secretary Anna Swanston's self-published *Dr. John Henrik Clarke: His Life, His Words, His Works* (2003), Kwaku Person-Lynn's edited volume *First Word: Black Scholars, Thinkers, Warriors, Knowledge, Wisdom, Mental Liberation* (1996), which includes a chapter on Clarke titled "John Henrik Clarke: Historian, Educator, Author, Editor, Lecturer"; and Person-Lynn's "On My Journey Now: The Narrative and Works of Dr. John Henrik Clarke, The Knowledge Revolutionary," which was published in a special 2000–2001 edition of *The Journal of Pan African Studies*.[13] Also in this genre is an edited volume by Benjamin P. Bowser and Louis Kushnick with Paul Grant titled *Against the Odds: Scholars Who Challenged Racism in the Twentieth Century* (2002). Their chapter on Clarke, which replicates the autobiographical oral history approach noted above, is titled "Portrait of a Liberation Scholar: John Henrik Clarke."[14]

The edited volume by James L. Conyers, Jr., and Julius E. Thompson titled *Pan African Nationalism in the Americas: The Life and Times of John Henrik Clarke* (2004) departs from this autobiographical oral history approach, instead reproducing a selection of twenty-one of Clarke's published book chapters and essays from such publications as the *Negro Digest/Black World, Freedomways, Journal of Afro-American Issues, Western Journal of Black Studies, Journal of Human Relations, Présence Africaine, Phylon,* and *Journal of Negro Education* from 1961 to 1996.[15] The essays are organized under the rubrics of "Black Nationalism," "Africana Biography and Intellectual Studies,"

"Africana Historiography," "Narratives," and "Pan Africanism." In a
further departure, under the rubric of "Critical and Reflective Essays
on John Henrik Clarke" are three original and previously unpublished essays, one of which is by this author and titled "John Henrik
Clarke and Issues in Afrikan Historiography: Implications of Pan
Afrikan Nationalism in Interpreting the Afrikan Experience in the
United States."[16] James L. Conyers, Jr.'s essay "John Henrik Clarke
and Africana History: A Bibliographical Essay" is more of a biographical essay drawing from "selected essays written by Clarke and
The Oral History Biography of John Henrik Clarke, written by Barbara
Adams."[17] A third essay, written by the late Raymond R. Patterson and titled "John Henrik Clarke's Rebellion in Rhyme," examined Clarke's first and only book of poetry, which was published in
1948.[18] These three essays comprise the principal critical secondary
examinations of Clarke's life and work to date.

Aside from this, memorializing reflections offering skeletal
biographical data appeared in academic journals, newspapers, and
other publications before and following Clarke's death on 16 July
1998.[19] Tonya Bolden's *Strong Men Keep Coming: The Book of African
American Men* (1999) featured a discussion of Clarke. There is a 1993
essay by Gloria J. Braxton titled "John Henrik Clarke: A Doyen
of African History," and an eleven-page essay written in 1998 by
Larry F. Crowe and published by the Kemetic Institute in Chicago
titled "Reflections on the Life of Dr. John Henrik Clarke: January
1, 1915 to July 16, 1998." Until 2007, Jared A. Ball had apparently
written the only graduate study of the late scholar. It was a master's
thesis completed in 2001 at Cornell University's Africana Studies
and Research Center, at which Clarke was a distinguished visiting
professor in the early 1970s. The study is titled "Still Speaking: An
Intellectual History of John Henrik Clarke."[20]

Sources

Regardless of the dearth of critical secondary source material
noted above, Clarke's personal papers, covering the years 1937 to
1996, two years before his death, are housed in the archives of the
Schomburg Center for Research in Black Culture in New York City,
one of four research libraries in the New York Public Library system.

The papers comprise 42.4 linear feet of materials in thirty cartons and nineteen boxes and are organized into twelve series: (1) personal, (2) World War II, (3) correspondence, 1940–1996, (4) lecture notes, 1954–1979, (5) course outlines, 1961–1983, (6) HARYOU-ACT, (7) editing and publishing, (8) writings, (9) organizations, (10) consultancy, (11) subject file, and (12) other authors.

The present study is based on an examination of those papers, with a special focus on materials in the personal, correspondence, lecture notes, course outlines, HARYOU-ACT, editing and publishing, writings, organizations, and consultancy series. The author examined Clarke's personal correspondence with, among others, Langston Hughes, Julian Mayfield, J. C. de Graft-Johnson, Adelaide Cromwell, Basil Davidson, Cheikh Anta Diop, Hoyt Fuller, Ezekiel Mphahlele, Gwendolyn Brooks, Shirley Graham Du Bois, William Leo Hansberry, Elliott Skinner, E. U. Essien-Udom, Calvin and Eleanor Sinnette, William Marshall, Alex Haley, and Alioune Diop. The author also explored Clarke's Africana Studies course syllabi for his teaching at the Department of Black and Puerto Rican Studies at Hunter College and the Africana Studies and Research Center at Cornell University, as well as materials he developed for teaching and education at the Heritage Teaching Program of HARYOU-ACT in the mid to late 1960s.

The author also examined materials related to Clarke's organizational affiliations and activism, including the African Heritage Studies Association, the Fair Play for Cuba Committee (1960), the Afro-American Scholars Council (1972–1979), the Organization of Afro-American Unity (OAAU), *Freedomways* magazine, the Harlem Writers Guild, the African-American Institute based in New York City, and the Institute of the Black World based in Atlanta, Georgia. In addition, the author read materials pertaining to Clarke's research projects, including the 108-episode WCBS television project on Africana history in 1969, his efforts in the 1950s to create a newsletter detailing information about anticolonial movements in various parts of Afrika from his contacts there, and Clarke's book reviews from his nationally syndicated newspaper and magazine column "African World Bookshelf."

In addition to archival materials, this study also draws upon selected videotaped and audiotaped speeches Clarke delivered in community forums in the 1980s through the 1990s, selected published materials written by Clarke in the form of books, journal essays, and book chapters, published and unpublished writings of Clarke's principal instructors, journalistic sources, and critical secondary sources treating principally the nineteenth and twentieth centuries to draw out an intellectual and cultural context in which to situate Clarke's ideas, philosophy, and historiography.

The Purpose of the Study

The research inquiry here is not a biographical study of the eighty-three-year-old life of John Henrik Clarke, nor does it touch upon his literary career as a poet, short story writer, and literary critic, which predates his career as a professional academic historian. Rather, not burdened by a primary interest in chronology and narrative, this study conceptually and philosophically explores Clarke's development of Afrikan world history by examining his intellectual influences, his approach to teaching Afrikan world history, his notions regarding Afrikan agency and Afrikan humanity, his explorations of themes of Pan Afrikanism and national sovereignty, his ideas concerning the relevance of Afrikan culture in historical perspective, and his legacy in Afrikan intellectualism and culture, including his contribution to the Afrocentric paradigm that is the core of the discipline of Africana Studies/Africalogy. In addition, the study frames this analysis within the scope of three central issues.

First, the problem of white supremacist historiography and the related problem of the limited access of Afrikans to the European academy provide the context for a certain kind of Afrikan scholarship that developed in the early twentieth century. Clarke's example and that of some of his colleagues demonstrates that Afrikans launched independent historical research and training initiatives to produce scholars who could advance the work of reconstructing Afrikan history for Afrikan people in the twentieth century. This story has not been told. Indeed, this tradition of independent Afrikan scholarship and community educational initiatives continues in the twenty-first century work of scholars such as Runoko Rashidi of San Antonio, Texas[21]; Ashra and Merira Kwesi of Dallas, Texas[22]; and

Kwaku Person-Lynn of Los Angeles, California, who has an earned Ph.D. from the University of California-Los Angeles.[23]

Critical to this examination is the exploration of the definition and prioritization of the uses of Afrikan history. Clarke's presentation demonstrates that a priority of history was to serve as an interpretive narrative that tells Afrikans, as he often said, "Where they have been and what they have been, who they are and what they are, where they still must go and what they still must be." For Clarke, the exigencies of oppression and colonization required not simply a narrating of the past, but an interpretation of what that past means for the present and the future. In its essence it constituted a reenvisioning to power. Clarke was a leader among Afrikan scholars who were in the forefront of providing history's meaning to their people beyond the trivialization of individualized accomplishments that distinguished single personalities in terms that could be translated into middle class models of success. Their work involved, rather, the explanation of the whole of a people, their history as a collectivity, their personality, their character, and their destiny as a nation. As Clarke's colleague, the eminent Senegalese scientist, Egyptologist, and historian Cheikh Anta Diop observed: "It matters little that some brilliant Black individuals may have existed elsewhere. The essential factor is to retrace the history of the entire nation. The contrary is tantamount to thinking that to be or not to be depends on whether or not one is known in Europe."[24]

Second, there has been a problem of focus in this matter of Afrikan historians and historiography in the United States. It involves an elitist privileging of the persons and perspectives of those Afrikan academics and intellectuals who have generally espoused the position that the teleology of Afrikan struggle has been toward integrating into the American cultural mainstream. This perspective has so dominated the historiography of the Afrikan experience in the United States that it has tended to dismiss Afrikan intellectuals, scholars, and activists who have embraced Pan Afrikan nationalism, which constitutes, in part, the envisioning of a global and national destiny that does not include European presence or overlordship. Typically, exponents of Pan Afrikan nationalism are said to be reactionary, motivated principally by anger, frustration, or disappointment with European "discrimination" and not by any self-directed vision of cultural identity or national destiny. From this perspective, the nationalist and Pan Afrikan nationalist movements are defined as aberrations from the primary goal of acceptance and assimilation into the Euro-American nation. Such a view is not only a distortion of the Afrikan experience that diminishes Afrikan agency, but it has tended to dismiss a universe of social history that has been guided by a decidedly independent ethos, and that has exhibited itself throughout the tenure of Afrikans in the United States.[25]

Third, there is the need to examine the Afrikan perspective on the issue and place of history in the lives and culture of Afrikan people, particularly those held captive in the European world. Historians like Clarke and ben Jochannan saw their lives and work as organically and inextricably interconnected with the lives, interests, and struggle of Afrikan people. Thus, their vision of scholarship dramatically differed from the dubious notion of "pure research." For Afrikan historians like Clarke, historical inquiry was certainly a craft entailing the pursuit of accuracy, of truthfulness, of knowledge, and characterized by a certain methodological rigor, as well as an expansiveness of consciousness that embraced global perspectives and interrelationships. At the same time, historical inquiry also had a practical motive that was cultural, political, economic, and even implicitly military. For historians like Clarke, the context for Afrikans in the United States was colonial domination and psychological warfare. The rediscovery and reconstruction of Afrikan world history had as its task to strengthen Afrikans psychically to regain the confidence, cultural vision, and intellectual and organizational tools to reclaim their independence from European dictatorship. Thus, and significantly, although Afrikans were physically situated in the United States, scholars like Clarke did not culturally or historiographically center them there.

Clarke, then, emerges as one of the foremost theorists of Afrikan liberation and the uses of Afrikan history as a foundation and grounding for liberation. Under Clarke's formulation, liberation is defined not simply as freedom from European domination but fundamentally as the restoration of Afrikan sovereignty. Clarke's presentation of history went, therefore, beyond its mere chronicling to its interpretation; it explored its political and cultural meaning for Afrikan destiny, for the Afrikan present and the Afrikan future. In short, he offered a philosophy of history. He explores history's utility in moving an oppressed and subordinated people from a position of subjugation on multiple levels—political, cultural, economic—to full status as a self-sustaining, self-defining, self-directed, free and independent people on a global stage.

The Value of the Study

The value of the study is that it examines a subject that has remained largely unexamined: the exploration of indigenous Afrikan intellectualism in the United States through the example of a major figure in Afrikan cultural and intellectual history. Part of the significance of this phenomenon is seen in the fact that Clarke was a seminal influence in the founding and development of the discipline of Africana Studies/Africalogy in the European academy in the United States. Although he was a leader among European-trained Afrikan academic intellectuals who joined or who were already engaged in the European academy beginning in the 1970s, his education and training were, for the most part, outside of the European academy. Instead, his training is part of a movement for the indigenization of Afrikan academic intellectualism that can be traced back to the early nineteenth century. Indeed, this study of Clarke becomes the launching point for discussions of culture and epistemology in Afrikan intellectualism. The study is also unique because it is the first extensive critical examination of Clarke as an exemplar of indigenous intellectualism in Afrikan culture in the United States.[26]

The study also breaks new ground on a number of fronts in this exploration of the thinking and work of a Pan Afrikan nationalist historian. Among other things, it departs from the assimilationist historical tradition of attributing nationalism among Afrikans in the United States to frustrations and disappointments with the pace and progress of Afrikan assimilation into the European cultural mainstream. Instead, this study examines Afrikan nationalism on its own merits and demonstrates that it arises fundamentally from notions of history and culture that are diametrically opposed to those espoused by assimilationist intellectualism.

Implicit in this analysis is the view that assimilationist intellectualism is a product and manifestation of the success of European cultural oppression and conquest; it is not representative of the Afrikan mainstream, but of what the Africalogist Molefi Kete Asante calls a decentered and inauthentic self.[27] The study, therefore, attempts to clarify the differences between assimilationism and nationalism by exploring the cultural dynamics that separate Afrikans in their aspirations and understandings of the nature of their struggle against subordination in European society. By defining Afrikan oppression in the United States as colonialism, Pan Afrikan nationalist historiography views the assimilationist interpretation of Afrikan history and culture in the United States as comparable to the problem of the *assimilado* or the *évolué,* which were the products of Portuguese and French colonialism in Afrika and the Americas. In clarifying the cultural and colonialist dynamics that inform Afrikan identity formulations in Afrikan intellectualism in the United States, the study transcends racialized understandings and characterizations of the debate among Afrikans. The question of nationality, then, culturally framed, assumes center stage as an interpretive framework.

The study is, therefore, a conscious effort to explicate the Pan Afrikan nationalist worldview and to interpret assimilationist thought from the Pan Afrikan nationalist conceptual lens. Its use of language reinforces Clarke's conceptual approach to heighten the clarity of the issues offered from a Pan Afrikan nationalist analysis. Indeed, the use of language and its epistemological implications is a matter of some significance in postmodernist discourse concerning language, reality, and history.[28] While postmodernist discourse assumes an essential disassociation between language and reality, the opposite is the case in Afrikan epistemology, which assumes that the use of language resonates with and evokes the active manifestation of the reality that language signifies.[29] In other words, language and reality are dynamically bound together. This explains Amos N. Wilson's contention that the use of language is a form of power that calls reality into being, for he is drawing upon the Afrikan notion of the generative and productive power of the spoken word or word-force.[30] "When we get ready to create revolution we must *re*define the world, and *re*define words; there's no way around it," he writes. "There is a connection between naming and dominion, between naming and bringing into reality. When we permit another people to name and define, we permit another people to gain dominion and control over us"[31] (original emphasis).

Hence, instead of the use of terms such as *African American, Black American, minority, underprivileged,* and the like (except where directly quoted), this study employs the Kiswahili spelling of Afrika and Afrikan (a common spelling in nationalist and Pan Afrikanist circles) and terminologies such as *Afrikans* and *Afrikans in the United States* to describe and clarify the fundamental cultural definition of Afrikan people in the United States that is advanced by Pan Afrikan nationalist intellectualism.[32] It accords with Clarke's insistence on the centrality of national identification that "relates us to land, history, and culture."[33] This cultural definition is equally demonstrated in the use of such terms as *Americo-Europeans* and *Europeans* instead of *whites,* the latter of which suggests a more racialized identity that ignores the central role of culture and the analysis of colonialism that informs Pan Afrikan nationalist theorizing and conceptualization. One of Clarke's conclusions is that Afrikans in the United States are a nation within a nation searching for a nationality. Thus, unlike Afrikans in the Caribbean and in Central and South America, who had largely, until perhaps very recently, settled upon the nationality of the peoples of the states wherein they reside, Afrikans in the United States are alienated from American nationality. Those who strove to achieve it, Afrikan assimilationists, recognized that it was more of a goal or an ideal than a reality. What is at work in this study is the exploration of a cultural dynamic largely ignored in nearly all historiography about the Afrikan group in the United States.

In addition, and significantly, the study of Clarke, who represents the Afrikan effort to indigenize intellectualism and knowledge production and knowledge validation in the new colonial setting, highlights the significance of the quest for the recovery and reclamation of power and sovereignty as a persistent theme in Afrikan culture and intellectualism in the United States. It shows that Afrikan historical and cultural memory has in various ways resisted domestication and containment by what Afrikan sociologist Clovis E. Semmes identifies as "the metaproblem of cultural hegemony, or the systemic negation of one culture by another."[34] In short, Clarke's work represents the Africalogical quest for decolonization and sovereignty.

An Outline of the Study

Accordingly, chapter 1, titled "John Henrik Clarke and the Afrikan Academy," and chapter 2, titled "The Training of an Afrikan Scholar," explore the concept of an independent Afrikan academy, a concerted effort at the indigenization of Afrikan academic intellectualism and knowledge production in the United States. Despite formidable barriers to university education, certain Afrikan intellectuals (those with and without university degrees) assumed the responsibility for producing knowledge about themselves and their relationship to the world that also involved a process of training informed by research and pedagogical methodologies, theoretical assumptions, and a publication mandate. Clarke, one of the exemplars of this movement for the indigenization of academic knowledge, emerges as a major and highly respected figure in Afrikan culture and movement in the United States and the world. The two chapters explore his prominence in that world and the importance of Harlem as an intellectual and cultural center, as they discuss the four major figures who guided his academic development: Arthur Alphonso Schomburg, Willis Nathaniel Huggins, Charles Christopher Seifert, and William Leo Hansberry. In exploring Clarke's intellectual pedigree, the chapters examine indigenous Afrikan intellectual production from the perspectives of the Afrikan intellectuals themselves. They seek, therefore, to engage Afrikan perspectives and interpretations, to disclose the scholars' motives and their initiatives in reconceptualizing the world in their own terms and the role that their investigation of history played in this effort.

Chapter 3, titled "The Teaching of Africana History," and chapter 4, titled "Africana History: A Weapon of Liberation," explore Clarke's mastery of the subject of continental and diasporan Afrikan history by discussing his teaching at the Department of Black and Puerto Rican Studies at Hunter College and at the Africana Studies and Research Center at Cornell University. It further explores his in-service teaching of Africana Studies and Afrikan world history in the public school systems in the New York City metropolitan area, in community education projects, chiefly the Heritage Teaching Program of HARYOU-ACT, and in Africana Studies and other disciplinary units within universities in New York State and across the United States. The focus here highlights Clarke's mastery of a subject that few in the European academy of that time were adequately prepared to teach. Moreover, the examination of Clarke's teaching extends not only to his development of courses but to the content of his syllabi, his selection of required and supplementary texts, the volume of his use of material in teaching Afrikan world history, and concludes with a discussion of the political implications and underpinnings of his philosophy of teaching in Africana Studies/Africalogy.

Chapter 5, titled "The Force and Implications of Afrikan Agency and Humanity," highlights Clarke's role as a philosopher of Afrikan history and his theorizing of the role that history and culture play in demonstrating a people's humanity and agency in the past that also enables them to become agents in their present and in their quest to overcome colonial and cultural oppression. The chapter situates Clarke's theorizing by exploring the dynamics of Afrikan historical and cultural consciousness in the early nineteenth century through the early decades of the twentieth century in the United States, the struggle of certain Afrikan intellectuals to control the academic knowledge produced about themselves, and the epistemological implications of Afrikan history in reconceptualizing human reality and human possibility in Afrocentric terms for reenvisioning the past, present, and future of Afrikans in the United States.

Chapter 6, titled "The Imperative of Pan Afrikanism and the Quest for National Sovereignty," and chapter 7, titled "Pan Afrikan Nationalism in Action: The Organization of Afro-American Unity and the African Heritage Studies Association," extend the epistemological discussion implicit in the cultural implications of history for a people struggling for decolonization to the question of Afrikan nationality, Afrikan internationalism, and the quest for national sovereignty. Cheikh Anta Diop, who envisioned the political and economic unification of the continent in *Black Africa: The Economic and Cultural Basis for a Federated State* (1978),[35] had worked out a historiography and anthropology of the Afrikan continent in such works as *The Cultural Unity of Black Africa* (1978)[36] and *African Origin of Civilization: Myth or Reality* (1974)[37] that argued for a common cultural origin in the Afrikan Nile Valley. As a diasporan Afrikan, Clarke expanded upon this view to posit a global unification based on a historical understanding of the commonality of cultural, geographical, and biological origin in the Afrikan continent. To underscore the fundamentally cultural nature of Afrikan identity formation under Americo-European colonialism, the chapters contrast and illuminate the debate between Pan Afrikan nationalism and Afrikan assimilationism (a form of Americo-European nationalism) in terms of their respective assumptions about nationality and national destiny. Chapter 7 extends this examination further by illustrating how the philosophical dimensions of Clarke's Pan Afrikan nationalism concretely manifested in two of the many movements in which he was intimately involved: Malcolm X's Organization of Afro-American Unity (OAAU), established in 1964, and the African Heritage Studies Association (AHSA), created in 1969.

Chapter 8, titled "The Dynamics of Afrikan Culture," provides a brief historical discussion of the relationship of Afrikan culture to resistance in the Americas, the continental Afrikan origins of Afrikans in the United States, and their continuity with Clarke's assessment of the meaning of indigenous continental Afrikan culture in the social life of Afrikans in the United States and in their struggle for liberation. Regarding Clarke's assessment, the chapter focuses particularly on his discussion of the relationship between religion, spirituality, culture, human freedom, and the state. Chapter 9, titled "The Clarkean Legacy and Contribution to the Afrocentric Paradigm," offers some critical discussions of Clarke's legacy in Afrikan intellectualism and culture and summary reflections on his contribution to the Afrocentric paradigm in Africana Studies/Africalogy.

Notes

1. Earl E. Thorpe, *Negro Historians in the United States* (Baton Rouge, LA: Fraternal Press, 1958); ibid., *The Central Theme of Black History* (Durham, NC: Seeman Printery, 1969); ibid., *Black Historians: A Critique* (New York: William Morrow and Company, Inc., 1969).

2. Maghan Keita, *Race and The Writing of History: Riddling the Sphinx* (New York: Oxford University Press, 2000).

3. Darlene Clark Hine, ed., *The State of Afro-American History: Past, Present, and Future* (Baton Rouge: Louisiana State University Press, 1986); August Meier and Elliott Rudwick, *Black History and the Historical Profession, 1915–*

1980 (Urbana and Chicago: University of Illinois Press, 1986); Benjamin Quarles, *Black Mosaic: Essays in Afro-American History and Historiography* (Amherst: The University of Massachusetts Press, 1988); James L. Conyers, Jr., ed., *Charles H. Wesley: The Intellectual Tradition of a Black Historian* (New York: Garland, 1997); ibid., *Carter G. Woodson: A Historical Reader* (New York: Garland, 2000).

4.   W. D. Wright, *Black History and Black Identity: A Call for a New Historiography* (Westport, CT: Praeger, 2001); Alton Hornsby, ed., *Essays in African American Historiography and Methodology* (Acton, MA: Copley, 2004); John Ernest, *Liberation Historiography: African American Writers and the Challenge of History, 1794–1861* (Chapel Hill: The University of North Carolina Press, 2004).

5.   M. Sammye Miller, "Historiography of Charles H. Wesley as Reflected through the Journal of Negro History, 1915–1969," *Journal of Negro History* 83, no. 2 (Spring 1998): 120–126; Robert L. Harris, Jr., "Coming of Age: The Transformation of Afro-American Historiography," *Journal of Negro History* 67, no. 2 (Summer 1982): 107–121; Frank J. Klingberg, "Carter Godwin Woodson, Historian and his Contribution to American Historiography," *Journal of Negro History* 41, no. 1 (January 1956): 66–68; John David Smith, "A Different View of Slavery: Black Historians Attack the Proslavery Argument, 1890–1920," *Journal of Negro History* 65, no. 4 (Autumn 1980): 298–311; Dickson D. Bruce, Jr., "The Ironic Conception of American History: The Early Black Historians, 1883–1915," *Journal of Negro History* 69, no. 2 (Spring 1984): 53–62; John Hope Franklin, "George Washington Williams, Historian," *Journal of Negro History* 31, no. 1 (January 1946): 60–90; Edward M. Coleman, "William Wells Brown as an Historian," *Journal of Negro History* 31, no. 1 (January 1946): 47–59; Charles H. Wesley, "W. E. B. Du Bois—The Historian," *Journal of Negro History* 50, no. 3 (July 1965): 147–162; Jessie P. Guzman, "W. E. B. Du Bois—The Historian," *Journal of Negro History* 30, no. 4 (Autumn 1961): 377–385.

6.   Joseph E. Harris, ed., *Pillars in Ethiopian History: The William Leo Hansberry African History Notebook*, vol. 1 (Washington, DC: Howard University Press, 1974); ibid., *Africa and Africans As Seen by Classical Writers: The William Leo Hansberry African History Notebook*, vol. 2 (Washington, DC: Howard University Press, 1977).

7.   Kwame Wes Alford, "A Prophet Without Honor: William Leo Hansberry and the Origins of the Discipline of African Studies, 1894–1939," (Ph.D. diss., University of Missouri-Columbia, 1998); ibid., "The Early Intellec-

tual Growth and Development of William Leo Hansberry and the Birth of African Studies," *Journal of Black Studies 30, no. 3 (January* 2000): 269–293; ibid., "William Leo Hansberry and African Studies Beginnings in the United States," in *Contemporary Africana Thought, Theory and Action: A Guide to Africana Studies*, ed. Clenora Hudson-Weems (Trenton, NJ: Africa World Press, 2007), 89–103.

8. Yosef ben Jochannan's works comprise some forty-two volumes in Spanish and English on various aspects of Africana history and culture since 1939. Among them are: *African Origins of the Major "Western Religions"*, vol. 1 of *The Black Man's Religion* (New York: Alkebu-lan Books Associates, 1970); *Black Man of the Nile and His Family* (New York: Alkebu-lan Books Associates, 1970, 1971); *Africa: Mother of Western Civilization* (New York: Alkebu-lan Books Associates, 1971); (with George E. Simmonds) *The Black Man's North and East Africa* (New York: Alkebu-lan Books Associates, 1971); *Cultural Genocide in the Black and African Studies Curriculum* (New York: Alkebu-lan Books Associates, 1973); *A Brief Chronology of the Development and History of the Old and New Testament: From Its African and Asian Origins to Its European and European-American Revisions, Versions, etc.* (New York: Alkebu-lan Books Associates, 1973); *The Myth of Genesis and Exodus and the Exclusion of Their African Origins*, vol. 2 of *The Black Man's Religion* (New York: Alkebu-lan Books Associates, 1974); *The Need for a Black Bible*, vol. 3 of *The Black Man's Religion* (New York: Alkebu-lan Books Associates, 1974); *Understanding the African Philosophical Concept Behind "The Diagram of the Law of Opposites"* (New York: Alkebu-lan Books Associates, 1975); *Influence of Great Myths of Contemporary Life: Or, the Need for Black History in Mental Health: A Sociopolitical and Anthropological Student's and Researcher's Edition* (New York: Alkebu-lan Books Associates, 1986); *Our Black Seminarians and Black Clergy without a Black Theology* (New York: Alkebu-lan Book Associates, 1978); *The Saga of the "Black Marxists" versus the "Black Nationalists": A Debate Resurrected*, vols. 1–3 (New York: Alkebu-lan Books and Education Materials, 1978); *In Pursuit of George G. M. James' Study of African Origins in "Western Civilization" (1980); They All Look Alike! All of Them?*, 4 vols. (New York: Alkebu-lan Books and Education Materials Associates, 1980–1981); *We the Black Jews*, vols. 1 and 2 (New York: Alkebu-lan Books and Education Materials Associates, 1983); *The African Mysteries System of Wa'Set, Egypt, and Its European Stepchild: "Greek Philosophy"* (New York: Alkebu-lan Books and Educational Materials, 1986); *Abu Simbel-Ghizeh: Guidebook/Manual* (New York: Alkebu-lan Books and Educational Materials, 1986); and *From Afrikan*

Captives to Insane Slaves: The Need for Afrikan History in Solving the "Black" Mental Health Crisis in "America" and the World (Richmond, VA: Native Sun Publishers, 1992).

9. Joel A. Rogers's works include *As Nature Leads: An Informal Discussion of the Reason Why Negro and Caucasian Are Mixing in Spite of Opposition* (Chicago: Printed by M.A. Donohue & Co., 1919); *The Ku Klux Spirit: A Brief Outline of the History of the Ku Klux Klan Past and Present* (New York: Messenger Pub. Co., 1923); *From "Superman" to Man* (New York: Lenox Pub. Co., 1924); *The Real Facts about Ethiopia* (New York: J.A. Rogers Publications, 1936); *Your History From the Beginning of Time to the Present* (Pittsburgh, PA: The Pittsburgh Courier, 1940); *Sex and Race: Negro-Caucasian Mixing in All Ages and All Lands*, vol. 1: *The Old World* (New York: J. A. Rogers Publications, 1940); *Sex and Race: A History of White, Negro, and Indian Miscegenation in the Two Americas*, vol. 2: *The New World* (New York: J. A. Rogers Publications, 1942), *Sex and Race: Why White and Black Mix In Spite of Opposition*, vol. 3 (New York: J. A. Rogers Publications, 1944); *World's Great Men of Color*, vols. 1 and 2 (New York: J.A. Rogers Publications, 1947); *Nature Knows No Color-Line: Research into the Negro Ancestry in the White Race* (New York: 1952); *100 Amazing Facts about the Negro: With Complete Proof: A Short Cut to the World History of the Negro* (New York: H. M. Rogers, 1957); *Africa's Gift to America: The Afro-American in the Making and Saving of the United States* (New York: J.A. Rogers Publications, 1959); and *The Five Negro Presidents: According to What White People Said They Were* (New York: Helga M. Rogers, 1965).

10. William D. Wright, who is critical of Clarke's Afrika-centered historiography in *Black History and Black Identity*, nonetheless acknowledges Clarke, along with ben Jochannan, as "professional historians." See Wright, *Black History and Black Identity*, 50, 123–128. At the time of the book's publication, Wright was professor emeritus of history at Southern Connecticut State University.

11. John G. Jackson's *Introduction to African Civilization* (New York: University Books, 1970); *Man, God, and Civilization* (New Hyde Park, NY: University Books 1972); *Christianity before Christ* (Austin, TX: American Atheist Press, 1985); and *Ages of Gold and Silver and Other Short Sketches of Human History* (Austin, TX: American Atheist Press, 1990) are full book-length works. *Ethiopia and the Origin of Civilization: A Critical Review of the Evidence of Archaeology, Anthropology, History and Comparative Religion, According to the Most Reliable Sources and Authorities* (New York: Blyden Society, 1939); *Pagan Origins of the Christ Myth* (New York: Truth Seeker, 1941);

Black Reconstruction in South Carolina (Austin, TX: American Atheist Press, 1987); and *The Golden Ages of Africa* (Austin, TX: American Atheist Press, 1987) are pamphlets of less than fifty pages.

12. Barbara Eleanor Adams, *John Henrik Clarke: The Early Years* (Hampton, VA: United Brothers and Sisters Communications, 1992); ibid., *John Henrik Clarke: Master Teacher* (Brooklyn, NY: A&B Publishers Group, 2000).

13. Anna Swanston, *Dr. John Henrik Clarke: His Life, His Words, His Works* (Atlanta, GA: I Am Unlimited Publishing, 2003); Kwaku Person-Lynn, ed., *First Word: Black Scholars, Thinkers, Warriors, Knowledge, Wisdom, Mental Liberation* (New York: Harlem River Press, 1996); ibid., "On My Journey Now: The Narrative and Works of Dr. John Henrik Clarke, The Knowledge Revolutionary," *The Journal of Pan African Studies: A Journal of Africentric Theory, Methodology and Analysis* Special Issue, 1, no. 2 (Winter–Fall 2000) and 2, no. 1 (Spring–Summer 2001): 219–220.

14. Benjamin P. Bowser and Louis Kushnick (with Paul Grant), ed., *Against the Odds: Scholars Who Challenged Racism in the Twentieth Century* (Amherst and Boston: University of Massachusetts Press, 2002). The scholars featured in the volume include Clarke colleague and erstwhile mentor John G. Jackson, Afrikan classicist Frank Snowden Jr., John Hope Franklin, St. Clair Drake, Robert C. Weaver, Hylan Lewis, Kenneth B. Clark, Herbert Aptheker, and W. E. B. Du Bois.

15. James L. Conyers, Jr., and Julius E. Thompson, ed., *Pan African Nationalism in the Americas: The Life and Times of John Henrik Clarke* (Trenton, NJ: Africa World Press, 2004).

16. Ahati N. N. Toure, "John Henrik Clarke and Issues in Afrikan Historiography: Implications of Pan Afrikan Nationalism in Interpreting the Afrikan Experience in the United States," in *Pan African Nationalism in the Americas: The Life and Times of John Henrik Clarke*, ed. James L. Conyers, Jr., and Julius E. Thompson (Trenton, NJ: Africa World Press, 2004), 1–19.

17. James L. Conyers, Jr., "John Henrik Clarke and Africana History: A Bibliographical Essay," in *Pan African Nationalism in the Americas: The Life and Times of John Henrik Clarke*, ed. James L. Conyers, Jr., and Julius E. Thompson (Trenton, NJ: Africa World Press, 2004), 23, 21–34.

18. Raymond R. Patterson, "John Henrik Clarke's Rebellion in Rhyme," in *Pan African Nationalism in the Americas: The Life and Times of John Henrik Clarke*, ed. James L. Conyers, Jr., and Julius E. Thompson (Trenton, NJ: Africa World Press, 2004), 35–40.

19. Robert L. Harris, Jr., "Dr. John Henrik Clarke, 1915–1998," *Journal of Negro History* 83, no. 4 (Autumn 1998): 311–312; Richard Newman, "John Henrik Clarke," *Transition*, no. 77 (1998): 4–8; "In Memoriam. John Henrik Clarke 1915–1998," *Journal of Blacks in Higher Education*, no. 21 (Autumn 1998): 14; Robert McG. Thomas, Jr., "John Henrik Clarke, Black Studies Advocate, Dies at 83," *New York Times*, 20 July 1998, A13; Robin D. G. Kelley, "Self-Made Angry Man," *New York Times Magazine*, 3 January 1999, SM17; Robin D. G. Kelley, "Dr. John Henrik Clarke, The Peoples' Scholar," *Black Issues Book Review*, 1, no. 5 (September/October 1999): 15; Herb Boyd, "In Memoriam: Dr. John Henrik Clarke (1915–1998)," *Black Scholar* 28, no. 3/4 (2001): 50–52; Bruce Karriem, "John Henrik Clarke: A Man for All Seasons," *New York Amsterdam News*, 23 July 1998, 12; Al Sharpton, "Dr. John Henrik Clarke," *New York Amsterdam News*, 23 July 1998, 13; David N. Dinkins, "John Henrik Clarke's Legacy Will Continue to Enrich Us," *New York Amsterdam News*, 23 July 1998, 13; Obituary, *New York Times*, 22 July 1998, A17; Nell Painter, "John Henrik Clarke, 1915–1998," *Crisis* (September/October 1998): 40.

20. Tonya Bolden, *Strong Men Keep Coming: The Book of African American Men* (New York: John Wiley and Sons, Inc., 1999); Gloria J. Braxton, "John Henrik Clarke: A Doyen of African History," *African World* 1, no. 1 (November/December 1993): 33–34; Jared A. Ball, "Still Speaking: An Intellectual History of John Henrik Clarke" (Master's thesis, Cornell University, 2001); Larry F. Crowe, "Reflections on the Life of Dr. John Henrik Clarke: January 1, 1915 to July 16, 1998" (Chicago: Kemetic Institute, 1998). Of course, this study derives from my graduate study, "John Henrik Clarke and the Power of Africana History: A Historiographical Examination of the Thought and Work of a Pan Afrikan Nationalist Historian" (Ph.D. diss., University of Nebraska-Lincoln, 2007).

21. See http://www.cwo.com/~lucumi/runoko.html.

22. See http://www.kemetnu.com/.

23. See http://www.drkwaku.com/.

24. Cheikh Anta Diop, *African Origin of Civilization: Myth or Reality*, ed. and trans. Mercer Cook (Westport, CT: Lawrence Hill, 1974), xvi.

25. See comments by John Henrik Clarke, "We See Ourselves in New Ways," *New York Times*, 15 June 1969, D19–20.

26. See comments by Clovis E. Semmes, "Foundations in Africana Studies: Revisiting *Negro Digest/Black World*, 1961–1976," *Western Journal of Black Studies* 25, no. 4 (2001): 195–201.

27. Molefi Kete Asante, "The Afrocentric Idea in Education," *Journal of Negro Education* 60, no. 2 (Spring 1991): 170–180; ibid., "The Ideological Significance of Afrocentricity in Intercultural Communication," *Journal of Black Studies* 14, no. 1 (September 1983): 3–19; Diane D. Turner, "An Oral History Interview: Molefi Kete Asante," *Journal of Black Studies* 32, no. 6 (July 2002): 711–734; Molefi Kete Asante, "A Discourse on Black Studies: Liberating the Study of African People in the Western Academy," *Journal of Black Studies* 36, no. 5 (May 2006): 646–662.

28. See Joyce Appleby, Lynn Hunt, and Margaret Jacob, *Telling the Truth about History* (New York: W. W. Norton, 1994), 214–217.

29. See, for example, the discussion of the effectiveness of prayers in the Yoruba belief system called Ifa in Fasina Falade, *Ifa: The Key to Its Understanding* (Lynwood, CA: Ara Ifa Publishing, 2002), 625–649.

30. Molefi Kete Asante, *The Afrocentric Idea* (Philadelphia, PA: Temple University Press, 1987), 17, 59–63.

31. Amos N. Wilson, *The Falsification of Afrikan Consciousness: Eurocentric History, Psychiatry and the Politics of White Supremacy* (Brooklyn, NY: Afrikan World InfoSystems, 1993), 22.

32. Gwendolyn Brooks at a certain point in her career chose to use the Kiswahili spelling of *Afrika* and *Afrikans*. See Annette Debo, "Signifying *AFRIKA*: Gwendolyn Brooks' Later Poetry," *Callaloo* 29, no. 1 (2006): 168–181. Examples in academic writing include Rufus Burrow, Jr., "Martin Luther King, Jr.'s Doctrine of Human Dignity," *Western Journal of Black Studies* 26, no. 4 (Winter 2002): 228–239; ibid., "The Afrikan Legacy in Personalism," *Western Journal of Black Studies* 26, no. 2 (Summer 2002): 107–118; Clovis E. Semmes, "Foundations of an Afrocentric Social Science: Implications for Curriculum-Building, Theory, and Research in Black Studies," *Journal of Black Studies* 12, no. 1 (September 1981): 3–17; and Eugene Perkins, "Literature of Combat: Poetry of Afrikan Liberation Movement," *Journal of Black Studies* 7, no. 2 (December 1976): 225–240. The Global Afrikan Congress (GAC), an international nongovernmental organization network that was created by and caters to all continental and diasporan Afrikans, uses the spelling. The organization was created at the Afrikans and Afrikan Descendants World Conference against Racism (AADWCAR) held in Bridgetown, Barbados, in 2002. It offers three reasons for its use of the spelling: (1) "It is a Pan-Afrikan spelling which relates both to the Afrikan continent and the Diaspora," (2) "It reflects the spelling of 'Afrika' in all Afrikan languages," and (3) "It includes the concept of 'ka,' the vital energy which both sustains

and creates life, as expressed in ancient Kemetic (Egyptian) teachings." See http://www.globalafrikancongress.com/about/protocol.htm#Footnote.Even a small liberal arts college, Augsburg College of Minneapolis, Minnesota, has a Pan-Afrikan Center under the auspices its Student Services.

33. John Henrik Clarke, "Africana Studies, A Decade of Change, Challenge and Conflict," Consolidating Africana Studies: Bonding African Linkages, on the occasion of the Tenth Anniversary of the Africana Studies and Research Center, Cornell University, 26–28 September 1980, 2–3.

34. Clovis E. Semmes, "Existential Sociology or the Sociology of Group Survival, Elevation, and Liberation," *Journal of African American Studies* 7, no. 4 (2004): 3.

35. Cheikh Anta Diop, *Black Africa: The Economic and Cultural Basis for a Federated State*, trans. Harold J. Salemson (Westport, CT: Lawrence Hill Books, 1978). It was originally published in French under the title *Les fondements économiques et culturels d'un état fédéral d'Afrique noire* (Paris: Présence Africaine, 1974). Diop, however, writes he first introduced the concept in writing in 1960.

36. *The Cultural Unity of Black Africa* (Chicago: Third World Press, 1978) was originally published in French as *L'unité culturelle de l'Afrique noire: Domaines du patriarcat et du matriarcat dans l'antiquité classique* (Paris: Présence Africaine, 1959) and published in English by Présence Africaine in 1963.

37. Diop's *The African Origin of Civilization: Myth or Reality*, ed. and trans. Mercer Cook (New York: Lawrence Hill, 1974) was a translation of sections of *Nations negres et culture* and *Antériorité des civilisations negres: Myth ou vérité historique?*, which had been published in French by Présence Africaine in 1955 and 1967, respectively.

Chapter One

JOHN HENRIK CLARKE
AND THE AFRIKAN ACADEMY

I think my value in the whole field of teaching history is that
I have prepared during my lifetime, and I have prepared in the
years when no one was thinking anything about black studies,
but I kept on preparing until ultimately the door opened.

—John Henrik Clarke, 1970[1]

He came from a tradition that researched, wrote, and taught
black history outside the academy.

—Robert L. Harris, Jr., 1998[2]

Dr. John Henrik Clarke is one of the original architects of
modern Afrikan-centered scholarship. His work has influenced
more young scholars and activists than that of any other in the
field.

—Kwaku Person-Lynn, 1996[3]

While less than a decade before John Henrik Clarke's death on
16 July 1998 he was being feted by Afrikans of considerable
social stature in the United States as a scholar of enormous merit
and accomplishment, the seventy-nine-year old professor emeritus
and erstwhile chair of Hunter College's Department of Black and
Puerto Rican Studies remained largely unknown to many in the

European academic world.[4] In 1994, four years before his death, Camille Cosby, the wife of famed comedian and actor Bill Cosby, would declare in praise of his influence on her thinking: "To my mind, Dr. John Henrik Clarke is a walking mountain of information and historical perspective that I have both valued climbing and enjoyed contemplating. The study of history, our most important subject, has been changed by his determined questioning of 'traditional' approaches and by his pursuit of history in its truest forms, unlike others." Indeed, she concluded, "His persistence, often alone in the wilderness, and his work for our people continues to garner the tremendous respect of us all."[5]

Two years later, the action film star Wesley Snipes would complete production and narration of a ninety-five-minute documentary film titled "John Henrik Clarke: A Great and Mighty Walk," which was directed by documentary filmmaker St. Clair Bourne.[6] In June 1997, one of the leading research libraries in the United States on Afrikan world history and culture would host the film's premiere. A year before Clarke's death, the Schomburg Center for Research in Black Culture, located on 135th Street and Malcolm X Boulevard in central Harlem, held a spectacular extravaganza in his honor. A multitude of Afrikan celebrities, dignitaries, literati, and others gathered for the celebration of Snipes's monumental film tribute to the life and work of this scholar-activist and his reflections on the history of a people to whom he had dedicated his entire life.[7] In his personal recollections a few years later, Snipes described Clarke as "the Great Oracle," adding "I found the Sacred Oracle, right there in Harlem. His name was John Henrik Clarke."[8]

Even two decades earlier, eminent Afrikans from across the United States recognized Clarke as a tremendously respected scholar of the history of Afrikan peoples around the world. Among them was Alex Haley, author of *Roots* and Malcolm X's amanuensis in the classic twentieth-century Afrikan narrative *The Autobiography of Malcolm X*. Concerning a proposed book project on Afrikan world history, the noted writer once remarked to Peter Schwed, chairman of the editorial board of the New York-based publishing house Simon and Schuster: "If I were looking for someone to teach me a whole lot more than I know about African history, or Black history, the person I'd make tracks to get to would be John Henrik Clarke."[9]

Accolades of this sort were hardly unusual. In anticipation of his retirement from a career as a university professor that spanned nearly two decades, friends in New York City hosted a luncheon tribute to honor the sixty-eight-year old Hunter College professor on Saturday, 17 September 1983 at the Sheraton Centre. The guests and cochairs of the event read like a who's who of the glittering Afrikan elite. The event's honorary cochairpersons were the famed actress Ruby Dee and the award-winning television journalist Gil Noble. Guests included the legendary veteran human rights organizer Ella Baker; internationally renown painter Romare Bearden; actor, singer, and human rights activist Harry Belafonte; former Student Non-Violent Coordinating Committee (SNCC) activist and Georgia State senator Julian Bond, who would fifteen years later become national chairman of the eighty-nine-year-old National Association for the Advancement of Colored People (NAACP); New York State assemblywoman Geraldine Daniels, whose district included Harlem; New York City attorney and politician David Dinkins, who in three years was to become Manhattan borough president and in six years New York City's first and only Afrikan mayor; sociologist, university professor, and social activist Harry Edwards; graphic artist and illustrator Tom Feelings; civil rights activist Jesse Jackson, who would a year later seriously contend for the Democratic nomination for the U.S. presidency; John H. Johnson, Chicago-based publisher of *Ebony* and *Jet* magazines; New York Democratic politician, diplomat, future New York State comptroller, and future gubernatorial candidate H. Carl McCall; former SNCC activist Robert Moses; U.S. representative Major Owens of Brooklyn; dancer, choreographer, and anthropologist Pearl Primus; U.S. representative Charles Rangel, who succeeded the legendary Adam Clayton Powell, Jr., as the U.S. congressman for the village of Harlem; TransAfrica founder and president Randall Robinson; the nationally celebrated rhyming comedian Nipsey Russell; attorney, former New York State and New York City politician, and business entrepreneur Percy Sutton; New York State assemblyman Albert Vann of Brooklyn; former aide to Martin Luther King, Jr., and former Southern Christian Leadership Conference (SCLC) executive director, the Rev. Wyatt T. Walker; and former King lieutenant, former U.S. ambassador to the United Nations, and Atlanta mayor Andrew Young. Among the non-Afrikans represented was Hunter College's president Donna Shalala, who would a decade later go on to become the secretary of health and human services in the administration of the forty-second president of the United States, William Jefferson Clinton.[10]

In contrast to the state of anonymity he may have enjoyed among many European academics, Clarke was widely known and respected among a host of luminaries—artists, journalists, novelists, poets, essayists, intellectuals, political activists, revolutionaries, scholars, and government officials—from across the Afrikan world. His extensive contacts and associations were attributable to a number of factors, but chiefly (beginning in the early 1930s) to his residence and immersion in the literary, artistic, cultural, political, and intellectual life of Harlem in New York City. From this base—already an international entrepot of Afrikan peoples and ideas—Clarke's world expanded to world travel, the editorship of books and literary and intellectual journals; the production of a CBS television series on Africana history; university professorships; and his own considerable contributions to newspapers and literary, political, intellectual, and scholarly publications throughout the Afrikan world.

From quite humble birth in Union Springs, Alabama, on 1 January 1915, and an impoverished childhood and youth in nearby Columbus, Georgia, Clarke's migration to New York City in the early 1930s introduced him to a life of political, intellectual, and cultural ferment that fortuitously connected him to some of the most dynamic currents of movement in the Afrikan world. He had known Ghana's first president Kwame Nkrumah since the 1930s; both in their youths were members of the Pan Afrikanist activist Willis N. Huggins's Harlem History Club. It was also during this time that he became well acquainted with the future first president of Nigeria, Nnamdi Azikiwe.[11] He knew the Trinidadian Pan Afrikanist scholars C. L. R. James and Eric Williams, the latter of whom was to become the Caribbean island's first prime minister. Clarke was also acquainted with the celebrated actor Sidney Poitier as early as the 1950s; both were among a circle of writers, artists, and intellectuals with whom Clarke was intimately associated.[12] Indeed, one of his oldest friendships was with the peripatetic writer, actor, novelist, and political activist Julian Mayfield.

In the late 1940s, he participated in the activities of the Association for the Study of Negro Life and History and drew richly from the mentorship of senior scholars there who included Charles H. Wesley,[13] Lawrence Reddick,[14] Lorenzo Greene,[15] Raymond Pace Alexander,[16] and Benjamin Quarles.[17] Clarke had been friends with the redoubtable Pan Afrikan nationalist revolutionary Malcolm X from 1958, when they first met, until Malcolm's assassination seven years later in 1965. Among other things, he and Clarke collaborated in the authorship of the statement of the basic aims and objectives of the Organization of Afro-American Unity (OAAU), which Malcolm founded following his departure from the Nation of Islam and in emulation of the Organization of African Unity, founded by the independent states of Afrika in 1963. Clarke was also a colleague of the great Senegalese scientist, Egyptologist, historian, and anthropologist Cheikh Anta Diop. In fact, Clarke proved instrumental in getting Diop's *The African Origin of Civilization: Myth or Reality* (1974) and *The Cultural Unity of Black Africa* (1978) translated from French and published in English in the United States.[18]

As with Diop, Clarke acted both officially and unofficially as a literary agent in the United States for numerous continental Afrikan writers and scholars. Among others, he managed to get the Ghanaian academic J. C. de Graft-Johnson's book, *African Glory* (1954), republished in the United States, and he subsequently used the text as required reading in his courses on Afrikan world history. De Graft-Johnson was professor and director of the Institute of Public Education at the University of Ghana at Legon, located just outside the capital city of Accra. Clarke accomplished a similar service for Ezekiel Mphahlele in the early 1970s. Mphahlele, one of South Africa's leading poets, short story writers, and novelists, was, according to Clarke, one of the best-known authorities on continental Afrikan literature among Afrikan writers and critics.[19]

Clarke's friendships and collaborations were numerous and spanned the cultural, academic, journalistic, and political worlds. They included E. U. Essien-Udom, professor and head of the Department of Political Science at the University of Ibadan in Nigeria; Hoyt W. Fuller, managing editor of the Chicago-based Johnson Publishing Company magazine the *Negro Digest*, which later became the *Black World*; Alioune Diop, the founding editor of the prestigious Paris,

France-based Pan Afrikanist publishing house Présence Africaine, which for a time produced one of the premier intellectual journals (of the same name) of the Afrikan world; Ghanaian scholar, nationalist, and Nkrumah mentor (and later political adversary) Joseph B. Danquah; the famed novelist, short story writer, essayist, playwright, and poet Langston Hughes; the equally famed novelist, playwright, and anthropologist Zora Neale Hurston; Harlem Renaissance poet and novelist Claude McKay; novelist, essayist, and human rights activist James Baldwin; the brilliant novelist, essayist, and Harlem Writers Guild member John Oliver Killens; famed actor Ossie Davis; early Namibian political activist Mburumba K. Kerina; and Hollywood actor William Marshall, perhaps best known for his role as a vampire in the 1973 horror film *Scream, Blacula, Scream.*

Significantly, Clarke's notoriety in the Afrikan world was the consequence of his immersion in that world. As Elliott P. Skinner, erstwhile chair of the Department of Anthropology at Columbia University and former U.S. ambassador to Upper Volta (now Burkina Faso),[20] once commented: "I suspect that Professor Clarke has participated in almost every important philosophical, political, social, and cultural movement affecting the lives of Blacks in America."[21] This immersion in an Afrikan world included not only his early career as a student and a literary writer but also later as an editor, lecturer, and university professor of Afrikan world history and the central role he played as a founding influence in the development of Africana Studies in the United States.

It was Clarke's move to Harlem that prepared him for this. Harlem was a center of extraordinary cultural, political, and intellectual activism, and this, in part, emerged from the fact that it was a village within New York City that facilitated the meeting and interaction of Afrikans from many parts of the globe. As an intellectual and academician, Clarke's training took place largely in this environment, although, significantly, very much outside of the European academy, despite the fact he undertook studies at several universities in the United States and Afrika over the years: Columbia University (circa 1930s), New York University (1948–1952), New School for Social Research (1956–1958), University of Ghana (1958), and University of Ibadan (1958).[22]

The substance of his training, however, occurred in the academies of instruction—autonomous and Afrikan-focused—that had by the early 1930s been a few decades old. In an era when few Afrikans enjoyed access to baccalaureate education and when fewer still were admitted to graduate studies at the European universities in the United States, Clarke found himself in an intellectual environment where Afrikans were intent upon constructing the academic and research capacity to pursue their own in-depth teaching, research, and publication on the nature of the Afrikan global experience. It was an imperative for those who "were interested in learning about our suppressed history and culture" and who "were cut off," as a Clarke colleague and mentor, the late and eminent historian John G. Jackson, observed, "from the white dominated and segregated university libraries and research sources."[23] Hence, Clarke's education and training in Afrikan world history emerged from a tradition of Afrikan scholarship that functioned independently of the European academic structure and that emphasized original research, publication, and teaching for principally Afrikan mass consumption.[24] This tradition in the New York City metropolitan area dated back at least to the early twentieth century with the founding in 1911 of the Negro Society for Historical Research in Yonkers, New York.[25]

Indeed, the Negro Society for Historical Research's founding evolved from a growing interest in a more organized and systematic approach to the study, production, and dissemination of Africana history that had begun to coalesce in the late nineteenth century. Although first proposed as early as 1853 as part of the northern Afrikan-led antislavery and democracy movement,[26] this more organized and systematic approach represented an important transition from individualized efforts earlier in the century by such writers as James W. C. Pennington (1807–1870), Robert Benjamin Lewis (b. 1802), William Cooper Nell (1816–1874), James Theodore Holly (1829–1911), William Wells Brown (1814–1884), Joseph T. Wilson (1836–1891), and George Washington Williams (1849–1891). This collective approach witnessed the founding in 1892 of the American Negro Historical Society in Philadelphia and five years later the formation of the American Negro Academy in Washington, D.C., "the most prestigious organization dedicated to encouraging research in black history."[27] One of the important features of this new approach was the establishment of research libraries developed initially by private collectors. Some of these libraries, consolidated in various historical associations into central libraries, contained both primary and secondary source materials consisting of published and unpublished manuscripts, books, essays, prints, art work, and other documents for reading and consultation by its members and for the conduct and presentation of research on various themes in the Afrikan world experience. In some cases, these private and organizational research libraries became, within a few decades into the twentieth century, the basis for research collections at Afrikan colleges and universities or public library systems. Among the better known examples are Howard University's Moorland-Spingarn Collection and the Schomburg Collection of the New York Public Library system, which was eventually to become the Schomburg Center for Research in Black Culture. Thus, the various associations represented a more formalized organization of the Afrikan intelligentsia, which established research agendas for the investigation and promotion of Africana history and culture. This included the presentation of scholarly papers at annual meetings and their subsequent publication, and the hosting of lectures and discussions on various aspects of the global historical and cultural experience of Afrikan people. In short, the associations represented the attempt by Afrikan intellectuals to establish the formalized study of Africana phenomena independently of hostile European, Eurocentric, and white supremacist academic structures. Those who organized and participated in these societies had as their primary mission the assumption of Afrikan control over the research, production, and transmission of knowledge related to the global history and culture of Afrikan people.

In the late nineteenth century members included those few who had managed to earn baccalaureate or graduate educations in Europe, Canada, or the United States, including the rare Ph.D. (such as William Edward Burghardt Du Bois's Harvard University Ph.D. in 1895), or those who had distinguished themselves in such careers or avocations that demonstrated a profound interest in advancing the knowledge of the history and culture of Afrikans in the United States and worldwide.[28] Among the leading intellectuals of the era whose work would indirectly but profoundly influence Clarke was journalist John Edward Bruce, who saw Afrikan history as a powerful tool for intellectual liberation and Afrikan empowerment in the United States. During the 1890s, Bruce was among a generation of Afrikan intellectuals who saw U.S. and continental Afrikan history as means of creating an ethos of nation and cultural solidarity sufficient to sustain collective action to counter European oppression and dictatorship. In writing, however, he sought to translate historical knowledge in ways that were accessible to the average reader, seeing the Afrikan press as "as an affordable and popular medium that effectively reached community readers."[29]

While the late nineteenth century featured a thriving Africana history movement in the United States, it claimed adherents from a wide spectrum of Afrikan thought—from integrationist accommodationism to Pan Afrikan nationalism, which in the late nineteenth century included those who agitated for "political and civil rights, cooperative economic schemes, all-Black towns, missionary uplift, and emigration [to Afrika or to Afrikan settlements and countries in other parts of the Americas] movements."[30] Nonetheless, it was the Pan Afrikan nationalist core that pursued a historiographical focus most consistent with the education and historical training Clarke would enjoy in the 1930s.[31] By the early 1900s, Bruce became a central figure in the Afrikan history movement, and his approach would include the advocacy of continental Afrikan history and the belief championed most notably by the Liberian scholar Edward Wilmot Blyden that "contemporary African culture could play an important role in rebuilding Africa."[32] Bruce's contribution to the Afrikan history movement included activities that typified the efforts of independent Afrikan scholarship outside of the university in the late nineteenth and the early twentieth centuries. Like others, he "published newspaper articles, authored pamphlets and books, delivered numerous speeches, collected evidence, undertook research, and advocated the adoption of Black history courses in Negro colleges and secondary schools." Throughout his life Bruce participated in research societies and he became "a respected bibliophile and active within a network of Black book collectors in Washington, D.C., Philadelphia, and New York." Of further significance is the fact that Bruce and others like him helped to train succeeding generations of scholars and historians to carry on the tradition of independent scholarship. This they accomplished despite the absence of formal academic training, university affiliation, or financial resources that were more readily available, however stintingly, to the very few university-trained Afrikans.[33]

Thus, in 1911, Bruce would partner with the Puerto Rico-born Arthur A. Schomburg, one of Clarke's most important intellectual mentors and professors of Africana history, to create the Negro Society for Historical Research, an achievement one scholar called "a significant step toward professionalizing and popularizing the discipline of African American history."[34] Bruce and his contemporaries, colleagues, and successors believed such institutions were an imperative of Afrikans' ability to independently interpret their global history, wresting it from the control of European historiography, which questioned Afrikan humanity and denied the Afrikan contribution to global human civilization.[35] Four years later, Carter G. Woodson, Harvard University's second Afrikan Ph.D., would establish in Chicago and incorporate in Washington, D.C., the Association for the Study of Negro Life and History. One year later he would launch the association's academic journal, now in the dawn of its ninth decade, *The Journal of Negro History*.[36] Five years later, in 1921, Woodson established Associated Publishers, Inc., to produce historical and other academic monographs.

Table 1.1
Selected Early Africana Historical Research Societies[37]

Organization	Founding Year	Founding City
American Negro Historical Society	1892	Philadelphia, Pa.
American Negro Academy	1897	Washington, D.C.
Negro Society for Historical Research	1911	Yonkers, N.Y.
Association for the Study of Negro Life and History	1915	Chicago, Ill. Washington, D.C.
Ethiopian School of Research History	1920s? / 1930s?	New York, N.Y.
Harlem History Club	1932	New York, N.Y.

By the early twentieth century, metropolitan New York City and Washington, D.C., represented two of the most significant centers of Afrikan intellectual activism in the United States. Although both were centrally involved in the developing Africana history movement, they typified differing intellectual trajectories and featured important contrasts in ideology, academic training and resources, and historiographical focus and interpretation. On the one hand, Washington, D.C., the capital city of the United States and the home of the historically Afrikan Howard University, had long been the city of a more politically conservative, integrationist, bourgeois, and university-degreed Afrikan intelligentsia whose interests were comparatively more Americanist and less internationally focused. By contrast, the Afrikan intelligentsia that emerged in metropolitan New York City was leavened by an increasing international influx of Afrikan activists and intellectuals from the poor, laboring, or lower middle classes in the southern United States, the Caribbean islands, and, to a considerably lesser extent (in terms of numbers and working class background), continental Afrika. Lacking an Afrikan university of its own, and largely barred from local European academic institutions, New York's intellectuals, who tended in the main to be more internationalist, radical, revolutionary, nationalist, or Pan Afrikanist in perspective, concentrated their efforts on creating centers of learning and training that were divorced from segregated European academic institutions. Their academic production was, correspondingly, guided more by an interest in reaching a thinking mass of Afrikan people as opposed to an established academic audience.

These differences account for some of the tensions and conflicts that, despite collaboration, erupted between Bruce and Schomburg's New York-based Negro Society for Historical Research (NSHR) and Woodson's Washington, D.C.-based Association for the Study of Negro Life and History (ASNLH). On the one hand, Woodson's association represented an enormously successful effort by the very few Afrikan intellectuals and scholars trained in the European academy to further historical research on Afrikan people within the context of the European academy and to advance it as a field of academic research and teaching. On the other hand, Bruce and Schomburg's society represented that group of Afrikan intellectuals for whom access to formal university education was never a realistic option and whose greater ideological connections and sympathies were with the Pan Afrikanist and nationalist movements and sentiments of the Afrikan common people.

Thus, notes Schomburg biographer Elinor Des Verney Sinnette, the society "became a stronghold of black nationalist lay historians, many of whom would later espouse the philosophy of Marcus Garvey."[38] Predictably, such views markedly differed from those of most of the members of the older, more prestigious, elitist, and conservative Washington, D.C.-based American Negro Academy, of which both Bruce and Schomburg were members. Further, from its inception the society's members included continental, Central American, South American, and Caribbean Afrikans, some of them persons who would become a focus of Clarke's study, research, writing, and teaching, among them Edward Wilmot Blyden of Liberia and Sierra Leone, and J. Caseley Hayford of the Gold Coast (later Ghana). Indeed, Schomburg once boasted, the "Negro Society for Historical Research ... has succeeded in stimulating the collection from all parts of the world of books and documents dealing with the Negro. It has also brought together for the first time co-operatively in a single society African, West Indian and Afro-American scholars."[39] Not unlike its sister organizations in other cities, one of the society's primary purposes was to document the fact that Afrikans have a history that predates the existence and history of the "proud Anglo-Saxon race," and in doing so to collect books, manuscripts, and other historical data to support claims of the antiquity of Afrikan history and civilization.[40]

Despite similar missions, however, "considerable rivalry and antagonism" plagued relations between the New York-based society and the Washington, D.C.-based association. "Members of the latter considered Schomburg's group too strident in their pro-black attitude and too subjective and unscholarly in their approach to black history and culture." On the other hand, Schomburg had grown increasingly disillusioned with his university-trained colleagues for what he judged to be their social and intellectual snobbery, their unrepentant elitism and distance from the common people, and their unattractive and quite unnecessary craveness or obsequiousness toward European people.[41] Envy of Woodson's greater success in both research publication and in securing critical funding to support his research efforts complicated matters.[42]

Aggravating the growing antagonism between the two groups was also Woodson's apparent refusal to publicly credit the source of a great deal of the research that contributed to his success. "Schomburg had provided [to Woodson] generous access to his private library," yet Woodson was evidently reluctant "to acknowledge Schomburg or the NSHR for providing primary materials and research suggestions that enhanced his publications," observed Bruce biographer Ralph L. Crowder. The benefit of Schomburg's research extended both to Woodson's monographs and his *Journal of Negro History*. Naturally, then, Woodson's silence concerning the critical importance of Schomburg's contributions became a major source of grievance among the society's founders and members.[43] "Over a period of years Schomburg had given Woodson generous access to his collection to select prints and photographs for" Woodson's monograph *The Negro in Our History*, published in 1922, added Elinor Des Verney Sinnette. "Often Woodson would leave Schomburg's home with batches of material, and more than once Schomburg had to remind him to return the borrowed items. Nevertheless, Woodson's brief preface made no acknowledgment of Schomburg's assistance and generosity."[44]

In recollections of the man under whom Clarke studied for the four epochal years of 1934 to 1938 (the year of the elder scholar's death), Clarke praised Schomburg as "the antecedent of the Black Studies Revolution and one of the ideological fathers" of the generations of Afrikan students who participated in the Africana Studies movement.[45] Further, he acknowledged Schomburg as the professor and mentor who of all his teachers exercised the most profound influence on his intellectual development and on his career as a historian of Afrikan world history.[46] Described by the independent Afrikan historian and anthropologist Joel A. Rogers as the "Sherlock Holmes of Negro History" in the former's celebrated and comprehensive two-volume biographical compendium titled *World's Great Men of Color*,[47] Schomburg (1874–1938) grew up in San Juan, Puerto Rico, and in the Virgin Islands before immigrating to the United States in 1891. A Puerto Rican revolutionary nationalist who in his early years in the United States supported the armed independence struggles of both Cuba and his own nation, Schomburg later focused on the struggle of Afrikans in the United States and the effort to rescue Afrikan humanity from the calumniation of white supremacist historiography. He was one of the earliest and staunchest advocates of "the establishment of courses in black history in schools and universities." A founding member of the Negro Society of Historical Research, and member and later president of the prestigious American Negro Academy, Schomburg enjoyed the reputation of a master researcher who referred to the nationalist and liberationist elements of the Africana history movement as "racial patriotism" and who, further, advocated, as early as a 1913 speech, that Afrikans seize the leadership in schools and universities in defining the nature of the Afrikan experience, no longer relying on sympathetic European scholars.

Schomburg's continued emphasis and advocacy of a Pan Afrikanist historiography doubtless exercised enormous influence on Clarke's imagination and historical interpretation. Schomburg's lectures before the American Negro Academy, for example, consistently highlighted the history of Afrikans in other parts of the Americas outside of the United States. Schomburg was a major supporter of the Jamaica-born Marcus Garvey's Universal Negro Improvement Association and African Communities League (UNIA and ACL) movement. While he did not join the UNIA, "he did entertain Garvey in his home, lend him items from his collection, translate letters and documents for him, and contribute articles to Garvey's newspaper the *Negro World*." Garvey, not surprisingly, would later become the focus of one of Clarke's most important historical works, an edited volume produced in collaboration with Garvey's widow, Amy Jacques Garvey, titled *Marcus Garvey and the Vision of Africa* (1974).[48]

Less skilled as a historian, Schomburg's greatest gift was as a researcher and builder of research libraries. Described by one scholar as "one of the Western world's foremost private collectors of books and other materials documenting the history and contributions of Africans and people of African descent,"[49] Schomburg for a time served as the curator of the Afrikan collection at Fisk University, responsible for developing its collection in Africana material.

In later years, Schomburg's research collection, which he sold in 1926 to the New York Public Library, was catalogued as containing 2,932 volumes, 1,124 pamphlets, and many valuable prints and manuscripts. This extensive collection of materials covering Africana history and culture in Afrika, the Caribbean, North, Central, and South America—one of several important research collections in the library system—included original copies of the famed Afrikan mathematician Benjamin Banneker's almanacs from 1792, 1793, 1794, and 1817. The collection also featured important Africana research materials gathered from countries that included England, France, Italy, Russia, Poland, and Spain. As an expert researcher, Schomburg had gained an international reputation in the Afrikan world. Among others, the continental Afrikan statesmen Kwame Nkrumah of the Gold Coast (later Ghana), Nnamdi Azikiwe of Nigeria, and Tom Mboya of Kenya were known to have made good use of his research collection. Prior to its relocation to the 135th Street branch of the New York Public Library, located in central Harlem, even the West Afrikan educator J. E. Kwegyir Aggrey had put in his bid to purchase the collection for Achimota College in the Gold Coast.[50]

By 1912, some twenty-two years before Clarke was to study at the library, Schomburg had collected original manuscripts and publications of some of the most significant Afrikan writers, intellectuals, and activists of the eighteenth and nineteenth century United States. They included signed copies of the poems of Phyllis Wheatley (1753–1784) and two volumes by the Afrikan emigrationist Paul Cuffee (1759–1817).[51] There were also works by nineteenth century writers, historians, and activists such as James W. C. Pennington (1807–1870) and William Wells Brown (1814–1884), and the poets Paul Laurence Dunbar (1872–1906) and Frances E. W. Harper (1825–1911).[52] Naturally, then, when Clarke found himself in New York City in the early 1930s, he came upon a tradition of research and scholarship that had institutionalized itself for slightly more than two decades. It was a tradition of pioneering in original research, the collection of primary source materials, special collections, and independent instruction not attached to government or private university systems. It was, in fact, the creation of an independent Afrikan academy, what Clarke was later to call "the university without walls."[53]

But Schomburg's influence upon Clarke began when he was still a teenager in Georgia, and when he had discovered, quite by accident, a copy of Howard University philosophy professor Alain LeRoy Locke's edited volume, *The New Negro: An Interpretation* (1925), and Schomburg's essay in that volume, "The Negro Digs Up His Past."[54] The discovery of that essay revolutionized his life, then only fifteen years old. "I knew then that I came from a people with a history older even than that of Europe," Clarke recalled four decades later as an adjunct professor in the Department of Black and Puerto Rican Studies at Hunter College of the City University of New York. "It was a most profound feeling—this great discovery that my people did have a place in history and that, indeed, their history is older than that of their oppressors."[55]

In his essay, Schomburg argued that Afrikans in the United States had to adopt an attitude quite different from that of Europeans, for whom history was ostensibly less important. For Afrikans the consciousness of the group's collective historical past was an imperative of repairing the social and psychological damage that affected the group, and persons within the group, as a consequence of centuries of enslavement and human violation. "History must restore what slavery took away," he asserted, "for it is the social damage of slavery that the present generation must repair and offset."[56]

This restoration of historical consciousness, however, is not to be achieved through dubious measures, but through a sober examination of the factual record. Even while an important and ultimate purpose of Afrikan history is what he called "group justification," the pursuit of an authentic Afrikan history "has become less a matter of argument and more a matter of record," he pronounced. "There is the definite desire and determination to have a history, well documented, widely known *at least within race circles,* and administered as a stimulating and inspiring tradition for the coming generations"[57] (added emphasis).

Schomburg advocated that the study of Afrikan history move from "the vagaries of rhetoric and propaganda," to which it had been subjected by white supremacist historiography, and in which it had been kept, in some instances, by overzealous counter argumentation.

Instead, the study of Afrikan history must become "systematic and scientific."[58] A systematic and scientific analysis would render three conclusions about that past, he noted. First, Afrikans were active agents in their own history and in their own successful struggles for liberation. Second, the notion of exceptional Afrikan individual achievers, even as offered by sympathetic historians, has promoted the underlying premise that genius, intelligence, and achievement are divorced from the capabilities and experiences of the masses of Afrikans or the Afrikan group as a collective or as a totality. Third, the continental Afrikan origins of Afrikans in the United States, examined "scientifically," disclose a credible record of achievement for the group and, more importantly, speak to the beginnings and early development of human culture.[59]

Schomburg also discussed the evidences of Afrikan agency within the context of the American experience, noting: "When we consider the facts, certain chapters of American history will have to be reopened. Just as black men were influential factors in the campaign against the slave trade, so they were among the earliest instigators of the abolitionist movement."[60] These, he noted, were "as scholarly and versatile" as any of their noted European counterparts. Moreover, "they carried their brilliant offensive of debate and propaganda" in Europe and Afrika, garnering international recognition "from academic, scientific, public and official sources."[61]

Proceeding in a "scientific" search for the facts of Afrikan contributions to the human experience is necessary so "that the full story of human collaboration and interdependence may be told and realized," Schomburg advanced. A central problem in the European supremacist interpretation of the human experience, he continued, is the "bigotry of civilization," which he charged is "the taproot of intellectual prejudice." This prejudice has advanced "the depreciation of Africa which has sprung up from ignorance of her true role and position in human history and the early development of culture." Nonetheless, the propaganda of Afrikans as peoples without history and culture is being challenged by "a new notion of the cultural attainment and potentialities of the African stocks," he noted, "partly through the corrective influence of the more scientific study of African institutions and early cultural history."[62] As the research in Afrikan human experience proceeds, one result is that Afrikans now see themselves "against a reclaimed background, in a perspective that will give pride and self-respect ample scope, and make history yield for him the same values that the treasured past of any people affords."[63]

Thus it was that Clarke, shortly after having arrived in New York City, sought out the great Arturo Alfonso Schomburg[64] at the 135th Street library and began his first four years of intensive study under Schomburg's expert instruction. The regimen of instruction, Clarke related decades later, included reading extensively in Schomburg's rich research collection, listening to his lectures, and engaging in discussion of both the lectures and the readings he was assigned in pursuit of his knowledge of Afrikan world history.

Moreover, Schomburg's method was to first direct Clarke in reading deeply into European history, to thoroughly understand the contours of the European experience, before beginning his exploration proper of the history of Afrikan people. One of the reasons for this, Schomburg taught, was that Afrikan history constituted, in fact, the missing pages of world history. To thoroughly understand it, one would have to study the history of the European oppressor. This method was critical to learning the reasons Europeans felt it necessary to oppress Afrikans and to remove them from "the respectful commentary of human history."[65] The other reason, Clarke explained, was because "it is not enough to know the history of African people and their role in the world to understand African people; it is also necessary to understand their relationship to all people in the world throughout history and the influence of non-African people on African people."[66] Consequently, when Clarke had completed the bibliography on European history Schomburg had assigned him, "I had a clearer understanding of world history and how the history of African people related to it," he recalled. "I entered the serious study of African history through the study of the history of Europe. I learned that African people were older than the very existence of Europe and that they had had two Golden Ages and were in decline before Europe was a functioning entity or had appeared on the world scene."[67]

In addition to a strong emotional bond between professor and pupil,[68] Schomburg's library provided Clarke with an extraordinary opportunity for reading and studying primary source materials in

Africana history and culture. This pattern of study and research—of consulting experts in the field and of conducting library research in both secondary and primary source documents—would become his standard approach to historical investigation. "The Schomburg Collection was like an extension of my home; so very few nights passed without at least one conversation with Arthur Schomburg," he remembered. "Through him, I had the opportunity of reading a large number of unpublished manuscripts that he had collected, especially some of the diaries and letters of 19th and 20th century Black writers."[69]

Thus it was that during the years he studied with Schomburg, Clarke also studied in the personal research library of the Jamaican historian and anthropologist Joel A. Rogers (1880–1966), another important figure in the tradition of independent Afrikan scholarship, whose collection Clarke assessed in 1982 as "qualitatively one of the best private libraries on people of African descent in existence. Much of his library material was highly selective reflecting his research and extensive travel."[70] Clarke had known Rogers "since about 1935, having met him before Rogers went to Ethiopia as a correspondent [for the *Pittsburgh Courier*] covering the Italian-Ethiopian War. I visited him many times and had the privilege of using his library and looking at his extensive notebooks."[71]

In his lifetime Rogers devoted some fifty years to independent research and publication. One of the most prolific writers of his time, he gained fluency in German, French, Portuguese, and Spanish, and conducted exhaustive research in primary and secondary documents and in historical artifacts in those languages in Afrika, Europe, and the United States. His work combined history and anthropology, exploring the origins of the human race, the role of Afrikans in world history, and the genetic mixing of Afrikans and Europeans in the historical experience. He rejected the doctrine of Afrikan inferiority and sought to establish not only that success was not an exclusively European preserve, but that enslavement was not an inherently Afrikan fate or condition.[72]

Clarke's early training under Schomburg, then, became a well-established methodology. Some two decades later, when he would travel for the first time to the Afrikan continent for a three-month summer stay, Clarke visited the library of the British Consulate in

Accra, Ghana, to study its documents and to discuss with various British officials the political history of Ghana and British colonialism in the country. He also visited, consulted, and researched in the personal library of the erudite Ghanaian nationalist Joseph Danquah (1895–1965),[73] a major political figure in the country and a former school teacher and political mentor (and later political adversary) to Ghana's president Kwame Nkrumah, regarding the nation's political and cultural history. Danquah was a leading authority on the recent and ancient history of the peoples of Ghana, and Clarke read extensively in his personal library and held numerous conversations with him concerning that history.[74] Besides Danquah, he similarly consulted other leading Afrikan and European academics, intellectuals, and political figures in Ghana. They included J. C. de Graft-Johnson, J. W. de Graft-Johnson, Nii Kwabena Bonne II, K. A. Busia, Moses Danquah, Amanke Okafor, J. D. Fage, Magnus J. Sampson, and George Padmore.[75]

Indeed, Clarke deeply and extensively studied the history, culture, politics, and social life of Ghana and West Afrika from numerous sources not available in the United States. His methodology included personal observation and travel, social immersion, formal and informal interviews, and, as related above, both library and archival research. In his travels to and from Ghana, for example, he researched West Afrikan history in libraries in London, England; Barcelona, Spain; Paris, France; and Brussels, Belgium. In Ghana he studied documents on West Afrika at the Ghana National Archives in Accra and consulted the library of Ghana University College at Legon and the Afrikan collection in the library of Achimota College in Accra. Officials at Achimota College, it will be remembered, had decades earlier sought to purchase the Schomburg collection in New York. In addition, Clarke traveled to other parts of Ghana, conducting research at Prempeh College and at Kumasi College of Technology, both in Kumasi. He also collected Nkrumah's speeches. In Nigeria, to which he also traveled, Clarke conducted research at the Lagos Museum and Library and at the library of the University College in Ibadan, where the Nigerian historian K. Onukwa Dike hosted him.[76]

He also took the opportunity for social immersion and travel to gain a more informed understanding of West Afrikan cultural, social, and political realities. In Ghana he lived among the Ga people in the Jamestown section of Accra, taking opportunities to attend their ceremonies and to participate in the activities and rhythms of daily life. He also regularly visited Ghana's national parliament, its courts, and its market places and traveled to nearly all regions in the country, visiting, among other places, "all the coastal towns, small Kingdoms and old Forts, such as Elmina Castle, Fort Amsterdam, Fort William, Cape Coast Castle and other sights indicating the early European contact with the Gold Coast, now Ghana."[77]

As a correspondent for Nkrumah's newspaper, the *Evening News*, headquartered in Accra, he also attended the first congress of the Parti du Regroupement Africain (PRA), which met in Cotonou, Dahomey (now Benin), from 25–27 July 1958. With more than 1,000 delegates from twelve French-controlled territories in West and Central Afrika, it was an assignment that gave him an extraordinary opportunity to examine Afrikan political activity outside of British-controlled areas. At the congress Clarke met and conversed with "most of the political leaders of French Africa." Formed from nine of the major political parties in March of that year, the PRA was intended "to create a larger and more effective force in the rapidly changing political atmosphere." The Senegalese poet and statesman Leopold Sedar Senghor, who was the party's leader, would two years later assume the presidency of an independent Senegal. Two other major parties declined the merger but sent observers—the African Democratic Rally (RDA), headed by the future president of Cote d'Ivoire, Felix Houphouet-Boigny (who, like Senghor, would come to power in two years), and the African Independence Party (PAI).[78]

Before returning to Ghana, Clarke also traveled to Lome, Togoland, where he interviewed Sylvanus Olympio, who headed the Togolese Unity Committee, the major political party in the territory, and who would for three short years assume the leadership of an independent Togo before his assassination in 1963. Clarke also traveled to Cote d'Ivoire's capital, Abidjan, and to important cities in southwestern, middle, eastern, and northern regions of Nigeria, including Ile-Ife, Benin, Enugu, and Kano.[79]

Based on these experiences, Clarke managed to secure publication of some of his research the following year. An account of his experience of a Ga funeral appeared in the Paris-based journal

Présence Africaine in French.[80] He also published in succeeding years some travel accounts and historical essays of his experiences in Ghana and Nigeria and his research on West Afrika in Afrikan-controlled academic and intellectual journals. These included "Ancient Nigeria and the Western Sudan" (1960) in *Présence Africaine*, "Old Ghana" (1960) and "New Ghana" (1960) in the *Negro History Bulletin* (published by the Woodson-founded Association for the Study of Negro Life and History), "Africa and the American Negro Press" (1961) in the *Journal of Negro Education* (published at Howard University), "Third Class on the Blue Train to Kumasi" (1962) in *Phylon* (founded by W. E. B. Du Bois and published at Atlanta University), and "The Morning Train to Ibadan" (1962) and "The Search for Timbuctoo"(1964) in the *Journal of Negro Education*.[81]

Hence, Clarke's relationship with Schomburg is instructive because it underscores essential features of this independent Afrikan tradition of historical training and scholarship, which can be seen in terms of its approach to research and pedagogical methodology, theoretical assumptions, and publication mandate. Indeed, this tradition—especially of that school of Afrikan scholarship that was Pan Afrikanist and Afrikan nationalist in orientation, or what today would be called Afrika-centered—manifested several important characteristics. These included a focus on the development of research libraries and specialized collections in Africana history and culture; extensive library research and emphasis on the use and investigation of both secondary and primary source materials; the consultation of sources in research, historiography, and scholarship typically suppressed in the European academy; a teaching methodology that featured close associations and mentorship between professors and students, and that included lectures, discussion, and directed readings; an emphasis on the international dimensions of Afrikan history in relationship to the history of other peoples in the world, including most especially Europeans; a Pan Afrikanist focus that underscored the importance of examining the international experience of Afrikans in various parts of the world and their interconnection; the notion of Afrikan agency as the historiographical starting point for historical interpretation; research publication distributed through Afrikan-controlled vehicles accessible to Afrikan audiences (such as newspapers and magazines) or otherwise addressed to an Afrikan reading public; and Afrikan nationalism and a cultural orientation that consistently expressed skepticism in varying degrees toward assimilation, Europeanization, and Christianization, instead emphasizing Afrikan culture as an exemplar for Afrikan human development and the reconstruction of Afrikan society across the globe.[82]

Table 1.2
Features of the Independent Afrikan Academy

Research Methodology
- Focus on the development of research libraries and specialized collections
- Extensive library research
- Emphasis on the use of both secondary and primary source materials
- Consultation of sources typically suppressed in the European academy

Pedagogical Methodology
- Close associations and mentorship between professors and students
- Lectures, discussion, and directed readings
- Emphasis on the international dimensions of Afrikan history
- Exploration of Afrikan history in relationship to the history of other non-Afrikan peoples
- Pan Afrikanist examination of the international experience and interconnection of Afrikans globally

Theoretical Assumptions
- Afrikan agency as the historiographical starting point for historical interpretation
- Afrikan nationalism and Pan Afrikanism
- Skepticism of assimilationism, Europeanization, and Christianization
- Indigenous Afrikan culture as the basis for modern Afrikan human development and society

Publication Mandate
- Research publication distributed through Afrikan-controlled vehicles accessible to Afrikan audiences

This Afrikan tradition of independent scholarship is clearly reflected in the substance of Clarke's work. In his career, Clarke did not principally address himself to Europeans, although a critical aspect of his scholarship was the mission, established earlier in the twentieth century, of wresting control from Europeans of the production of knowledge about the global Afrikan world. This was true of his lectures, writings, research, and message, which were directed to Afrikans. Accordingly, the teleology of his historiography, which was avowedly Afrika-centered (which is to say Pan Afrikanist and Afrikan nationalist), envisioned an epistemology of the past and the future that anticipated the discontinuation of the presence and domination of European people in the lives of Afrikans in the United States and the world. Perhaps after W. E. B. Du Bois, Clarke was one of the most influential Afrikan scholars in the twentieth-century United States. In relationship to the volume and range of publications, his influence on Afrikan historiography (particularly in Africana Studies), his facilitation of the publication of the work of Afrikan intellectuals and scholars from across the Afrikan world, his connection to or participation in Afrikan world movements, his activism among Afrikan academicians, his training of students and scholars (both university and nonuniversity affiliated academic professionals), his impact on the emerging discipline of Africana Studies in the late twentieth century, and his ability to bridge both the worlds of the European academy and the popular avenues of Afrikan education that reached the masses of the people—he is perhaps one of the foremost Afrikan scholars ever produced in the twentieth century.[83] Equally at home in the classrooms of Ivy League universities or in the public forums of educational community organizations like Harlem's First World Alliance or East Orange, New Jersey's Afrikan Echoes, Clarke was a distinguished graduate of an aggressive and independent Afrikan system of scholarly education undercapitalized in terms of institutional structures and unsanctioned by European academic credentials.

Notes

1. John Henrik Clarke, "A Search for Identity," *Social Casework* 51, no. 5 (May 1970): 261.

2. Robert L. Harris, Jr., "In Memoriam: Dr. John Henrik Clarke, 1915–1998," *Journal of Negro History* 83, no. 4 (Autumn 1998): 311.

3. Kwaku Person-Lynn, ed., *First Word: Black Scholars, Thinkers, Warriors, Knowledge, Wisdom, Mental Liberation* (New York: Harlem River Press, 1996), 3.

4. One rather enormous exception to this was in the European-dominated field of African studies, a field of study with which he had been intimately involved since at least the early 1960s. Clarke's role in the leadership of the Afrikan scholarly challenge to European control of the African Studies Association in 1968 and 1969 meant that his presence had been powerfully felt some two decades earlier.

   With respect to Clarke's chairmanship of the department, I refer to the James L. Conyers, Jr., letter to the author, 13 March 2003 and to the James E. Conyers, interview with the author, 21 March 2003. James E. Conyers, former assistant director of Africana Studies at Kean University of New Jersey, and a member of the anthropology faculty in the Department of Sociology and Anthropology, reports that Clarke was a personal friend of his family and one with whom he studied and by whom he was mentored since childhood. He notes that Clarke chaired the Department of Black and Puerto Rican Studies at Hunter College from 1 July 1979 to 30 June 1980, when Clarke stepped down from the position because he believed it was "a clerk's job" and felt his time was better served in the classroom.

5. Camille O. Cosby, letter to the Trustees of the Phelps-Stokes Foundation, 14 November 1994, John Henrik Clarke Papers, Schomburg Center for Research in Black Culture (hereafter JHCP, SCRBC). In the dedication of a brief autobiographical account titled *My Life in Search of Africa* (Chicago: Third World Press, 1999), Clarke wrote: "To Drs. Bill and Camille Cosby with appreciation for their help and encouragement which came at a time in my life when it was most needed."

6. See Clifford Thompson, "St. Clair Bourne: Documenting the African-American Experience," *Cineaste* 26, no. 3 (Summer 2001): 34–35. Bourne, writes Clifford, has directed and produced more than forty films in his career. Besides Clarke, they have included documentaries on such personalities as Paul Robeson, Langston Hughes, Imamu Amiri Baraka, and Gordon Parks.

7. Victoria Horsford, "John Henrik Clarke Royal Treatment at Movie Gala Preview," *New York Amsterdam News*, 7 June 1997, 5.

8. Wesley Snipes, Foreword to "On My Journey Now: The Narrative and Works of Dr. John Henrik Clarke, The Knowledge Revolutionary," ed. Kwaku Person-Lynn, *The Journal of Pan African Studies: A Journal of Africentric Theory, Methodology and Analysis* Special Issue, 1, no. 2 (Winter–Fall 2000) and 2, no. 1 (Spring–Summer 2001): 109, 111.

9. Alex Haley, letter to Peter Schwed, 28 August 1978, JHCP, SCRBC. Haley, who at the time was based in Los Angeles, was discussing the possibility of a book titled *Timetables of African World History*, which was to be edited by Mrs. Arthella Addei. Haley wrote Addei had also invited "my old friend and colleague John Henrik Clarke" and "another outstanding scholar, Dr. Yosef ben-Jochannan." It was a project in which publisher Simon and Schuster appeared to be interested.

10. JHCP, SCRBC.

11. Clarke, *My Life*, 20–21.

12. Ibid., letter to Julian Mayfield, 9 May 1958; JHCP, SCRBC.

13. Ibid., *My Life*, 23–24. In answer to a questionnaire about Charles H. Wesley sent by James Naazir Conyers of Ramapo College of New Jersey, Clarke noted that Wesley and he were friends, colleagues, and fellow academics for thirty years. He described Wesley as a persistent researcher whose work inspired Clarke and who also personally "encouraged me and other young historians in the continuation of our own work." Clarke, questionnaire response to James Naazir Conyers, 18 September 1992.

  Charles H. Wesley (1891–1987), who earned his Ph.D. in history at Harvard University in 1925, served variously as instructor, professor, and chair of the Department of History at Howard University and as dean of the university's graduate school for nearly thirty years before going on to the twenty-three-year presidency of Wilberforce University and its successor, Central State University, in Wilberforce, Ohio. Wesley also served as president of the Washington, D.C.-based Association for the Study of Negro Life and History from 1950 to 1965. He was the author or editor of more than twenty books on subjects in Africana history. See *Contemporary Authors Online*, Gale, 2002, http://www.galenet.com/servlet/GLD/form?origSearch =true&o=DataType&n=10&l=1&docID=txshracd2588&secondary=false& u=CA&u=CLC&u=DLB&t=KW.

14. Ibid. Lawrence Reddick (1910–1995), who earned a Ph.D. in history at the University of Chicago in 1939, had a multifaceted career. In addition to his

academic career as a historian, he was also director of Opportunities Indus-trialization Center Institute, based in Washington, D.C., from 1966–1968, and coordinator of the institute's national policies and programs from 1968–1970. He served as history professor at several historically Afrikan universi-ties, including Kentucky State College, Dillard University (New Orleans, La.), Atlanta University, Alabama State College, and Coppin State College (Baltimore, Md.). He also taught at Temple University (Philadelphia, Pa.), and at City College and the New School for Social Research (both in New York City). From 1939–1948 he served as curator of the Schomburg Col-lection of the New York Public Library. He was the author of several books on history and education. See *Contemporary Authors Online*, Gale, 2002, http://www.galenet.com/servlet/GLD/form?origSearch=true&o=DataType &n=10&d=1&docID=txshracd2588&secondary=false&u=CA&u=CLC&u= DLB&t=KW.

15. Ibid. Lorenzo Greene (1899–1988), historian and civil rights activist, was a professor at Lincoln University in Jefferson City, Missouri, for thirty-nine years, during which time he also served as chairman of the Department of Social Science. He was an authority on Afrikan history in the United States. One of his best known works is *The Negro in Colonial New England, 1620–1776* (1942). See *Contemporary Authors Online*, The Gale Group, 2000, http://www.galenet.com/servlet/GLD/form?origSearch=true&o=DataType &n=10&d=1&docID=txshracd2588&secondary=false&u=CA&u=CLC&u= DLB&t=KW.

16. Ibid. Raymond Pace Alexander (1898–1974), a Philadelphia attorney, civil rights activist, and member of the board of directors of the Association for the Study of Negro Life and History, served in various capacities throughout his career. They included private practice, political and judicial posts in the city of Philadelphia, and diplomatic appointments for the United States gov-ernment. See *Contemporary Authors Online*, Gale, 2002, http://www.galenet. com/servlet/GLD/form?origSearch=true&o=DataType&n=10&d=1&docI D=txshracd2588&secondary=false&u=CA&u=CLC&u=DLB&t=KW.

17. Ibid. Benjamin Quarles (1904–1996), who earned his Ph.D. in history from the University of Wisconsin in 1940, was a member of the executive council of the Association for the Study of Afro-American Life and History from 1948–1984. During his thirty-five-year academic career, from 1934 to 1969, he served in various teaching and administrative capacities at Shaw Univer-sity (Raleigh, N.C.), Dillard University (New Orleans, La.), and Morgan State University (Baltimore, Md.). He was the author or editor some thir-

teen books on Africana history. Among his best known works is the survey history titled *The Negro in the Making of America* (1964). See *Contemporary Authors Online,* Gale, 2003, http://www.galenet.com/servlet/GLD/form?or igSearch=true&o=DataType&n=10&l=1&docID=txshracd2588&secondary =false&u=CA&u=CLC&u=DLB&t=KW.

18. Diop's *The African Origin of Civilization: Myth or Reality* (New York: Law-rence Hill, 1974) was a translation of sections of *Nations negres et culture* and *Antériorité des civilisations negres: Myth ou vérité historique?,* which had been published in French by the Paris-based Afrikan publishing house Présence Africaine in 1955 and 1967, respectively. *The Cultural Unity of Black Africa: The Domains of Patriarchy and Matriarchy in Classical Antiquity* (Chicago: Third World Press, 1978) was originally published as *Unité culturelle de l'Afrique noire: Domaines du patriarcat et matriarcat dans l'antiquité classique* (Paris: Présence Africaine, 1959). See also John Henrik Clarke, letter to Hoyt W. Fuller, 11 March 1974, JHCP, SCRBC.

19. Clarke, who had agreed to find an American publisher for Mphahlele, finally secured an agreement with his publisher Hill and Wang of New York for a collection of "Zeke's" essays along with an essay titled "Voices in the Whirlwind." On May 19, 1970, Clarke had sent Hill and Wang Mphahlele's manuscript, its full title "Voices in the Whirlwind—An Essay of Poetry and Conflict in the Black World." See John Henrik Clarke, letter to Lawrence Hill and Arthur Wang, 13 May 1970; ibid., letter to Lawrence Hill and Arthur Wang, 28 June 1970; Arthur Wang, letter to John Henrik Clarke, 4 December 1970; John Henrik Clarke, letter to Ezekiel Mphahlele, 20 January 1970, JHCP, SCRBC. John Coleman de Graft-Johnson, *African Glory: The Story of Vanished Negro Civilizations* (London: Watts, 1954; Toronto: George J. McLeod, 1954; New York: Praeger, 1955, 1966).

20. Thomas A Johnson, "Blacks Present Views on N. E. T.," *New York Times,* 1 December 1970, 73.

21. Elliott P. Skinner, letter to Tilden J. LeMell, 24 April 1973, JHCP, SCRBC.

22. John Henrik Clarke, Curriculum Vitae, JHCP, SCRBC. While the CV is not dated, an examination of its contents reveals it was written sometime during or after 1977. See also ibid., letter to Henry Allen Moe, 30 October 1951, JHCP, SCRBC. Moe was at the J.S. Guggenheim Memorial Founda-tion of New York City, to which Clarke was writing in application for a fellowship.

23. Eric Cyrs, Benjamin P. Bowser, Herbert Parker, and Elder James Cage, "A World Libertarian: John Glover Jackson," JHCP, SCRBC.

24. A similar intelligentsia developed in late nineteenth and early twentieth century Yorubaland in southwestern Nigeria, according to Toyin Falola in his study titled *Yoruba Gurus: Indigenous Production of Knowledge in Africa* (Trenton, NJ: Africa World Press, 1999). Falola's study examines the emergence of an intelligentsia in Yorubaland that evolved with literacy in the written Yoruba language, that functioned outside of university or academic circles and institutions, and that aimed its production of historical knowledge to popular and even localized Yoruba consumption. As with Afrikans in the United States, elements of cultural nationalism and solidarity were important factors in the historiography this intelligentsia developed concerning the Yoruba experience.

25. See James D. Anderson, *The Education of Blacks in the South, 1860–1935* (Chapel Hill: The University of North Carolina Press, 1988), 5–7. Of relevance is the fact that this ethos of the creation of independent, Afrikan-run institutions of learning—even at the primary and secondary level, and however undercapitalized—predated and succeeded the Civil War and the U.S. constitutional abolition of the legality of individual ownership of persons in United States law. Anderson explains the Afrikan approach to education and literacy at the end of the Civil War was characteristically informed by the "values of self-help and self-determination" and "an ethic of mutuality" in which they rejected not European assistance but European superintendence and dictation.

26. Charles H. Wesley, "The Need for Research in the Development of Black Studies Programs," *The Journal of Negro Education* 39, no. 3 (Summer 1970): 264. Wesley notes that "Proposals were made, as in one at Rochester, New York, in 1853, 'to collect facts, statistics and statements, all laws and historical records and biographies of colored people and all books by colored authors.' It was added that there would be 'for the safe keeping of these documents a library, with a Reading Room and Museum.'"

27. Elinor Des Verney Sinnette, *Arthur Alfonso Schomburg: Black Bibliophile and Collector: A Biography* (New York: The New York Public Library and Detroit: Wayne State University Press, 1989), 38, 39; Charles H. Wesley, "Racial Historical Societies and the American Heritage," *The Journal of Negro History* 37, 1 (January 1952): 27; ibid., "The Need for Research," 267; Ahati N. N. Toure, "Nineteenth Century African Historians in the United States: Explorations

of Cultural Location and National Destiny," in *Black Cultures and Race Relations*, ed. James L. Conyers, Jr. (Chicago: Burnham, 2002), 16–50.

28. One historian who devoted considerable attention to this issue was Charles H. Wesley. His examinations include "The Reconstruction of History," *The Journal of Negro History* 20, no. 4 (October 1935): 411–427; "Racial Historical Societies," 11–35; "Creating and Maintaining an Historical Tradition," *The Journal of Negro History* 49, no. 1 (January 1964): 13–33; and "The Need for Research," 262–273.

29. Ralph L. Crowder, "John Edward Bruce and the Value of Knowing the Past: Politician, Journalist, and Self-Trained Historian of the African Diaspora, 1856–1924" (Ph.D. diss., University of Kansas, 1994), 32–33.

30. Ibid., 34.

31. In short, Pan Afrikan nationalism is concerned with Afrikan national sovereignty, Pan Afrikan unification on a global scale, and, as a necessary condition of the foregoing, independence from European hegemony, including European settler states established as outposts and extensions of continental Europe. See chapter 6 for a deeper exploration of Pan Afrikanism, Afrikan nationalism, and historiography.

32. Crowder, "John Edward Bruce," 35. Crowder also discusses the fact that Bruce enjoyed childhood associations with the abolitionist Henry Highland Garnet and the Pan Afrikan nationalist Martin Robison Delany in the 1860s. These associations profoundly influenced his Pan Afrikanist and nationalist views. Later, in adulthood, his collegial associations with Alexander Crummel and Edward Wilmot Blyden proved a significant element of his ideological leanings.

33. Ibid., 35–36, 208–209.

34. Ibid., 35, 36.

35. Ibid.

36. Carter G. Woodson, "Ten Years of Collecting and Publishing the Records of the Negro," *The Journal of Negro History* 10, no. 4 (October 1925): 599–600. The journal's name is now *The Journal of African American History*.

37. Wesley, "Racial Historical Societies," 11–35; ibid., "The Need for Research," 262–273; Sinnette, *Schomburg*, 38, 39; Crowder, "John Edward Bruce," 35–36, 208–209; Woodson, "Ten Years," 599–600; Romare Bearden and Harry Henderson, *A History of African-American Artists: From 1792 to the Present* (New York: Pantheon Books, 1993), 247–250; Runoko Rashidi, "Notes on Black Scholars of the Moors in John G. Jackson's Life," in *Golden Age of the Moor*, ed. Ivan Van Sertima (New Brunswick, NJ: Transaction Publishers, 1992),

89–92; Clarke, *My Life*, 17; ibid., "The Influence of Arthur A. Schomburg on My Concept of Africana Studies," *Phylon* 49, nos. 1, 2 (Spring/Summer 1992): 7.

38. Sinnette, *Schomburg*, 42.

39. Crowder, 236.

40. Sinnette, *Schomburg*, 42–43, 123, 126.

41. Ibid., 126, 185.

42. Ibid., 62.

43. Crowder, "John Edward Bruce," 207–208.

44. Sinnette, *Schomburg*, 126. See also Tony Martin's discussion of some of the tensions between Schomburg and Woodson in his chap. 7, titled "Carter G. Woodson and Marcus Garvey," in Tony Martin, *The Pan-African Connection: From Slavery to Garvey and Beyond* (Dover, MA: The Majority Press, 1983), 104. Martin notes that Schomburg used the pages of Garvey's *Negro World* newspaper to review Woodson's *The Negro in Our History* and to dismiss the text as unsuitable for high school use because of what he called factual and interpretative errors and the lack of primary sources. While the dispute has a personal dimension, the issues the critique underscores—primary sources, interpretative validity, and factual errors—speak to the maturity of the research methodology of the Afrikan academy.

45. Clarke, "The Influence," 8.

46. Ibid., "Arthur Schomburg, Teacher: A Memoir," *The Black American* 18, no. 34, p. 20, JHCP, SRBC. Clarke stated that Schomburg, "more than anyone else, was responsible for my choice of a profession and lifetime commitment as a teacher of African world history." In "A Search," 261, Clarke also acknowledged: "It was he who is really responsible for what I am and what value I have for the field of African history and the history of black people the world over." See also Clarke, "The Influence," 4, and his discussion of Schomburg in Barbara Eleanor Adams, *John Henrik Clarke: Master Teacher* (Brooklyn, NY: A&B Publishers, 2000), 69–74.

47. J. A. Rogers, *World's Great Men of Color*, vol. 2 (New York: Macmillan, 1972), 449.

48. John Henrik Clarke and Amy Jacques Garvey, ed., *Marcus Garvey and the Vision of Africa* (New York: Vintage Books, 1974). In Clarke's early years in Harlem, he recounted, he was also a member of the Garvey movement's youth group. See Adams, *John Henrik Clarke*, 66; and Person-Lynn, "On My Journey Now," 134.

49. Sinnette, *Schomburg*, 195.

50. Ibid., 3, 9, 16–17, 38, 44, 48, 55, 89, 92, 123, 126, 141, 154, 195, 200.

51. Cuffee was the spelling used at that time for the Akan name Kofi, the name given to a male child born on Friday. Kofi was Cuffee's father's name, which indicates his father most likely came from Ghana. Perhaps one of the first Afrikans in the United States on record to have changed his European-imposed name to an Afrikan one, Cuffee discarded the last name of Slocum, which belonged to his enslaver, for his father's first name. See Joseph E. Holloway, "Africanisms in African American Names in the United States," in *Africanisms in American Culture*, 2nd ed., ed. Joseph E. Holloway (Bloomington and Indianapolis: Indiana University Press, 2005), 86.

52. Sinnette, *Schomburg*, 3, 9, 16–17, 38, 44, 48, 55, 89, 92, 123, 126, 141, 154, 195, 200.

53. Adams, *John Henrik Clarke*, 73; Anna Swanston, ed., *Dr. John Henrik Clarke: His Life, His Words, His Works* (Atlanta, GA: I AM Unlimited, 2003), 96.

54. Arthur A. Schomburg, "The Negro Digs Up His Past," in *The New Negro: An Interpretation*, ed. Alain Locke (New York: Arno Press and The New York Times, 1968; originally New York: Albert and Charles Boni, 1925), 231–237.

55. Clarke, "The Influence," 5; ibid., "A Search," 262. On 1 May 1970, Clarke also recalled: "I knew then that I came from an old people and that I was older than my oppressor, that I was older than Europe and that my people dated back to the very dawn of history and that we were the senior people of the whole world. I knew then what my pursuit in life would be and that would be to define history as it relates to my people, and to convert history into an instrument of liberation. That is the mission of my life and that is the only legacy I care to leave." See ibid., "New Perspectives on the History of African Peoples," Louisiana Educational Association, 1 May 1970, 3, JHCP, SCRBC.

56. Schomburg, "The Negro Digs," 231.

57. Ibid.

58. Ibid., 231–232.

59. Ibid., 232.

60. Ibid., 234.

61. Ibid., 235.

62. Ibid., 237.

63. Ibid.

64. Arthur Alphonso is an Anglicization of Arturo Alfonso. It appears Schomburg was known by both the Spanish and Anglicized versions of his name.

65. Clarke, "The Influence," 5.

66. Ibid.

67. Ibid., 6. See also ibid., "A Search," 263, where Clarke recalled: "I began to study the general history of Europe, and I discovered that the first rise of Europe—the Greco-Roman period—was a period when Europe 'borrowed' very heavily from Africa. This early civilization depended for its very existence on what was taken from African civilization." In Person-Lynn, "On My Journey Now," 133–134, Clarke also recalled: "He taught me the comparative approach to history. How to compare Afrikan history with other history. He taught me to read European history. He said by doing that, 'You're going to understand Afrikan history better. The more world history you know, the better. You can put Afrika into proper focus if you have good knowledge of world history.'"

68. Ibid., 8.

69. Ibid., "Schomburg," 20.

70. Ibid., letter to Helga R. Andrews, 1 February 1982, JHCP, SCRBC.

71. Ibid. Andrews was J. A. Rogers's widow.

72. Ahati N. N. Toure, "Rogers, Joel Augustus," in *Encyclopedia of the Harlem Renaissance*, vol. 2, ed. Cary D. Wintz and Paul Finkleman (New York: Routledge, 2004), 1070–1072.

73. Joseph Boakye Danquah, *The Ghanaian Establishment: Its Constitution, Its Detentions, Its Traditions, Its Justice and Statecraft, and Its Heritage of Ghanaism*, ed. Albert Adu Boahen (Accra: Ghana Universities Press, 1997), xvii, xxii.

74. John Henrik Clarke, "Reflections & Observations ... Ghana Remembered 'Then and Now.'" Seventeenth Annual Conference, 25 July–1 August 1993, National Council for Black Studies, Accra, Ghana (25 July 1993), 10, 12–14, JHCP, SCRBC. Of the British Consulate, Clarke remarked its library "contained some of the best old documents and literature on Ghana, including earlier works of Caseley Hayford, the political father of twentieth century Ghanaian politics; the works of Joseph P. Danquah; and the documents relating to the various attempts at federation within Ghana, the Ashanti federation and the Fanti Federation."

75. Ibid., letter to Henry Allen Moe, 13 October 1958, JHCP, SCRBC.

76. Ibid. See also John Henrik Clarke, "African World Civilization: 19th Century to the Present." Seventeenth Annual Conference, 25 July–1 August 1993, National Council for Black Studies, Accra, Ghana (27 July 1993), 3, JHCP, SCRBC.

77. Ibid., "Statement of Plans for Research; Reference: "Africa without Tears," n.d., 1–2, JHCP, SCRBC.

78. Ibid., 2–3, JHCP, SCRBC. The proposed book was a more journalistic and travel-oriented effort. According to Clarke, it was intended to "observe and comment on many aspects of African life that are generally overlooked by the tourist and the flying journalist, such as: the day by day life in the African village, the changing status of the African market women and other petty traders, food, and the dire lack of hotel accommodations in the small and sometimes large cities in West Africa, the Customs and Immigration Services, run mostly by Africans, the role of the Syrians and other Middle Eastern people in the business structure of West Africa, and a capsule history of the countries through which I traveled."

79. Ibid., 2. Ali A. Mazrui, Introduction to *UNESCO General History of Africa*, vol. 8, *Africa since 1935*, ed. Ali A. Mazrui and C. Wondji (Berkeley: The University of California Press; Oxford: James Currey; Paris: UNESCO, 1993, 1999), 13–14.

80. "La célébration d'une veillée funèbre dans la tribu Ga du Ghana." *Présence Africaine* (December 1958–January 1959): 107–112.

81. "Ancient Nigeria and the Western Sudan," *Présence Africaine* nos. 32–33 (1960): 11–18; "Old Ghana," *Negro History Bulletin* 23, no. 5 (February 1960): 116–117; "New Ghana," *Negro History Bulletin* 23, no. 5 (February 1960): 117–118; "African and the American Negro Press," 30, no. 1 *Journal of Negro Education* (Winter 1961): 64–68; "Third Class on the Blue Train to Kumasi," *Phylon* 23, no. 3 (3rd Quarter 1962): 294–301; "The Morning Train to Ibadan," *Journal of Negro Education* 31, no. 4 (Autumn 1962): 527–530; "The Search for Timbuctoo," *Journal of Negro Education* 33, no. 2 (Spring 1964): 125–130.

82. See also the discussion of an Afrikan intellectual tradition in Jared A. Ball, "Still Speaking: An Intellectual History of John Henrik Clarke" (Master's thesis, Cornell University, 2001).

83. This observation was first mentioned to me in a discussion with Professor Ronald J. Stephens, chair of the African American Studies Department, Metropolitan State College of Denver.

Chapter Two

THE TRAINING
OF AN AFRIKAN SCHOLAR

During my period of growing up in Harlem, many black teachers were begging for black students, but they did not have to beg
me. Men like Willis N. Huggins, Charles C. [Seifert], and Mr.
Schomburg literally trained me not only to study African history
and black people the world over but to teach this history.
—John Henrik Clarke, 1970[1]

I am quite confident that no present-day scholar has anything
like the knowledge of this field (prehistory of Africa) that
Hansberry has developed. He has been unable to take the Ph.D.
degree ... because there is no university or institution ... that
has manifested a really profound interest in this subject.
—Earnest A. Hooton, Chair, Department of Anthropology,
Harvard University, 1948[2]

The nature of Afrikan subjugation in the United States precluded
any meaningful access to both undergraduate and graduate education in the European academy throughout most of the twentieth
century. This fact was made startingly plain three years before the
dawn of the twenty-first century. "At this point, it is useful to review
the progress that blacks have achieved over the past three decades,"
observed editors of *The Journal of Blacks in Higher Education* in a 1997
essay examining Afrikan progress in university education in the United

States. "In constructing our Index, we begin with statistics for the year 1970. Prior to this period very few blacks in the United States had the advantage of higher education. As a result, there are very few detailed statistics on black student participation prior to that period."[3]

Consistent with this finding was a study published in 1946 titled *Holders of Doctorates among American Negroes: An Educational and Social Study of Negroes Who Have Earned Doctoral Degrees in Course, 1876–1943*. In it Harry Washington Greene identified at least 296 Afrikans had earned master's degrees between 1875 and 1943,[4] while at least 343 had obtained baccalaureate degrees during the same period.[5] The majority of the baccalaureate degrees, 187, were earned at thirty-seven Afrikan universities, while the remaining 156 were awarded at sixty-four European or "mixed" institutions.[6] By contrast, in 1940 there were 12,866,000 Afrikans in the United States.[7] As for the Ph.D. and equivalent degrees, Greene reported that in the sixty-eight years from 1875 to 1943 some 381 Afrikans earned doctorate degrees in the United States, Canada, and Europe. "The Ph.D.—an original German product—has been conferred in America since 1866. Yale University was the first to award a Ph.D. degree and likewise the first so to honor a Negro."[8] Significantly, only fourteen Afrikans had earned doctorate degrees in the thirty-nine years between 1875 and 1914, one year before Clarke's birth in Union Springs, Alabama. By 1934, twenty years later and one year after Clarke had come to New York City to begin advanced studies with Arthur A. Schomburg, a mere 107 had earned doctorates.[9] By contrast, in 1930 there were 11,891,000 Afrikans in the United States.[10] One of those few who had earned the extraordinarily rare Ph.D., Willis Nathaniel Huggins (1886–1940), would become one of Clarke's four most influential professors and intellectual mentors.[11]

Table 2.1

U.S. Afrikans Earning Degrees in the United States, Canada, and Europe, 1875–1943[12]

Baccalaureates	343
Masters	296
Doctorates	381

Described by one scholar as a "brilliant writer and ardent Pan-Africanist," Huggins was a social studies teacher in the New York City public school system at the predominantly European Bushwick High School in Brooklyn. According to Clarke, Huggins was also at that time the only Afrikan teacher in the city's public school system. Born on 7 February 1886, in Selma, Alabama, he earned a B.A. from the University of Chicago, an M.A. from Columbia University, and a Ph.D. in education from Fordham University in 1932, one year before Clarke had arrived in New York City. As of 1943, eleven years later, Huggins remained the first and only Afrikan to have done so. The fact that Fordham is a Catholic institution of the Jesuit order, founded in 1841 as the first such institution in the northeastern United States,[13] suggests an explanation for the subject of his dissertation: "The Contribution of the Catholic Church to the Progress of Negroes in the United States." Huggins's major field of research interest was education, history, and the philosophy of education.[14] Still, the direction of Huggins's scholarship hardly followed the track of European historical orthodoxy.

Table 2.2
Number and Percentage of U.S. Afrikans Earning Baccalaureate Degrees at European or "Mixed" and Historically Afrikan Colleges and Universities in the United States, 1875–1943[15]

Historically Afrikan Colleges and Universities		
Percentage	Number	Number of Institutions
54.5	187	37
European and "Mixed" Colleges and Universities		
Percentage	Number	Number of Institutions
45.5	156	64

An example is found in an essay he published in the Saturday, 28 January 1939 edition of the *Chicago Defender*, titled "How Wrong is Hitler? On the History of Jews, Black Folk and 'Aryanism'?" Commenting on the absurdity of Nazism and its white supremacist doctrine of "political Aryanism," Huggins noted the irony of a historical record that indicated the early Aryan language groups "stemmed from the black Dravidians who occupied southern India in remote times. The two peoples [Aryans and Dravidians] mingled freely. Thus, the so-called Indo-European movements around 2,500 B.C. were basically migrations of a Negroid folk which pooled itself in southern, southeastern and southwestern Europe, around 2,000 B.C." Further, the Nazi doctrine was rendered even more ridiculous, Huggins commented, by the fact that the original peopling of Europe—including Hitler's birth place of Austria—derived from Afrikan migrants from the Mother Continent who had settled there tens of millennia earlier. "Indeed black African races, 'The Grimaldi' had already covered most of Europe as early as 20,000 B.C. They left a secondary African base for art in ancient Hellas (Greece), and a primary African base for color, in Austria, Italy, ... Spain and Portugal." In his essay, Huggins argued for a European history of antiquity that was thoroughly and profoundly influenced by the cultural and genetic presence of Afrikan people.[16]

Clarke noted in later recollections that the essay was one in a series by Huggins published in the newspaper, which exercised national influence among Afrikans in the United States. The series explored Afrikan origins of many European practices and symbols associated with Roman Catholicism, historical interpretations of the Judaic portion of the Judaeo-Christian bible in light of Afrikan antiquity, and uncompromising denunciations of Italian military imperialism in Ethiopia, all of which put him at odds with European Jews, Catholics, and Italians in New York City. Clarke suspected his disclosures in the series may have cost him his life.[17]

Table 2.3
Number of U.S. Afrikans Earning Doctorate Degrees, 1875–1914[18]

14

A staunch Pan Afrikanist, a leading authority on Ethiopian history, and an energetic activist who maintained close ties with the Afrikan masses, Huggins was a major pro-Ethiopia supporter during the Italian-Ethiopian war, urging, among other things, Afrikans in the United States to join the struggle against fascist Italy's invasion of Ethiopia. William R. Scott, whose work explores the history of

Ethiopianism and Ethiopian-U.S. Afrikan relations, observed that Huggins was also personally acquainted with several leading Ethiopian officials of the day. In 1935, U.S.-based support groups—principally the Provisional Committee for the Defense of Ethiopia in cooperation with the American League Against War and Fascism—commissioned him to travel to Geneva, Switzerland, to investigate the progress of international discussions at the League of Nations concerning Ethiopia's fate and to register Afrikan and European solidarity in the United States with the Ethiopian cause.[19]

Three years earlier, in 1932, the same year he earned the Ph.D., Huggins founded the Harlem History Club, which some years later became the Blyden Society, named after one of the leading Pan Afrikanist scholars of the nineteenth century, the Caribbean-born Liberian statesman Edward Wilmot Blyden. Huggins's two major works, which he coauthored with protégé John G. Jackson, were *A Guide to Studies in African History: Directive Lists for Schools and Clubs* (New York: Federation of History Clubs, 1934) and *Introduction to African Civilizations with Main Currents in Ethiopian History* (New York: Avon House, 1937).[20]

Table 2.4
Number of U.S. Afrikans Earning Doctorate Degrees, 1875–1934[21]
107

The latter text was further evidence of the approach to research and publication concerning the Africana experience articulated in the independent centers of Afrikan learning. In his preface, among other things, Huggins discussed his research methodology, revealing an approach that Clarke had already adopted under Schomburg's tutelage, and that Huggins clearly reinforced: the use of research libraries and special collections in the conduct of publication research. Thus, in preparing the book, Huggins stated he consulted in France, the Bibliotheque Nationale and the Permanent Museum of the Colonies, both in Paris; in Belgium, the Brussells Museum at Tervueren and the Brussells Mondaneum; in England, the British Museum in London and Oxford University's Bodleian Library; and in Germany, the Berlin Museum. In New York, Huggins consulted

Schomburg for Spanish and Latin American sources. In Washington, D.C., he examined documents in the private library of Dantes Bellegarde, former minister of Haiti to the United States. In Haiti, Huggins, by permission of the Caribbean island nation's president and his cabinet, consulted important government documents and historical papers.[22]

The Pan Afrikanist and internationalist nature of Huggins's subject, as well as the breadth of its scope over time, made such a catholicity of sources necessary. His text explored a survey of human (which is to say, Afrikan) prehistory; a discussion of the histories of ancient Egypt, Libya, and Nubia, including their impact on ancient Palestine; an examination of Afrikans at what he called "the dawn of culture," which involved Afrikan prehistory in Europe, Afrika, and Palestine; Afrikan influence in the ancient cultures of the Aegean Sea, especially Crete and Greece; race mixing in the Nile Valley; both the ancient and more recent political history of Ethiopia, including the imperialist roles of Italy and Great Britain; an exploration of the Islamic influence in West and Central Afrika and the history of the Moorish empire in the western Mediterranean; inquiry into the history of West Afrika and southern Afrika; a discussion of Afrikans in ancient Asia (including western and southern Asia), North Afrika, southern Europe, Oceania, Latin America, the United States, and in the resettlement colonies of Liberia and Sierra Leone; a discussion of the history of Haiti and the British West Indies; and a brief examination of precolonial Afrikan states. Huggins also engaged in discussions of Afrikan historiography, Afrikan art, international relations, and a popular subject of the 1930s—the cultural, historical, and political implications of the use of the term *Negro* as applied to dislocated Afrikans in the European world, including the Americas.[23]

As an expert in the field of education, it is not at all surprising that a critical use of the text in Huggins's view, and one that would be strikingly replicated in Clarke's approach to teaching Africana Studies and Afrikan world history some three decades later, was its pedagogical value. Huggins underscored that the text's worth lies in its utility for teachers in the instruction of high school and university students, as well as those involved in study groups. "The Themes here set forth constitute a series of problems, which have sufficient elasticity, in the hands of the skillful and resourceful teacher, to cover assignments for the school year of thirty-six to forty weeks, with ample provision for supplementary reading." Hence, Huggins dedicated a significant portion of the text to providing bibliographies totaling more than 350 items covering 8 general subject areas introduced in the text; a general bibliography citing more than 400 monographs, government publications, periodicals, pamphlets, newspapers, essays, special collections, and other documents that included sources in French, German, and Italian; an extended discussion of the current state of curricula in Africana studies offered at primarily Afrikan universities in the United States; and other issues in teaching the subject of Afrikan world history.[24]

Further, the matter of Afrikan agency and humanity, as can be seen from a cursory examination of the text's subject matter, was central to Huggins's and Jackson's explication of the global Afrikan experience. "There can be no full picture of the birth and childhood of civilization until Africa has been made to yield up its historical treasures. One of the most important and pressing cultural needs of today is the unbiased explorations of the antiquaries of Africa," they maintained. "A good history of African culture is necessary before it will be possible to work out the equation in which all men are contributing factors."[25] In contradistinction to the prevailing ideology of European supremacy and Afrikan inferiority that pervades the historiography of the human experience in the European academy and European society generally, the "history of Africa, rightly envisioned is a thrilling story. Children need it. They cannot fully understand the world, as it affects them without knowing something, indeed a great deal, of what Africans were in the past and how they have come to their present condition."[26] Without question, Huggins and Jackson concluded, "The more the story of the African is studied, the more wonderful his place in the world scheme is found to be."[27]

Thus it was that Huggins, whom Clarke described as "a master teacher and the first political analyst I had ever met," became Clarke's second professor in Afrikan world history, one of many opportunities that opened up for him after commencing his studies with Schomburg. Clarke recalled that he joined Huggins's Harlem History Club in 1934, where he and other youths listened to his Sunday morning lectures and engaged in "trying to find a definition of African people in history, literally looking on the other side of the 'Slavery Curtain.' To see what kind of people we were before the advent of slavery."[28]

The Harlem History Club under Huggins's leadership provided an experience rich in historical inquiry that spanned the gamut of the Afrikan experience. In addition to the broad array of themes covered in Huggins's *Introduction to African Civilizations* (1937), Clarke's studies there included readings in Afrikan religious history by both Afrikan and European authors, including Edward Wilmot Blyden's *Christianity, Islam and the Negro Race* (1887), a book that exercised "a major influence on my understanding of the impact of African religions on the world."[29] Among numerous other authors, he also studied Huggins protégé John G. Jackson's *The Pagan Origins of the Christ Myth* (1941), *Christianity before Christ* (1938), and *Was Jesus Christ a Negro? and, The African Origins of the Legend of the Garden of Eden: Two Rationalistic Views* (1933);[30] Sir James George Frazer's *Folklore of the Old Testament* (1918),[31] and Gerald Massey's two-volume *A Book of the Beginnings* (1881).[32] Through this study Clarke came to understand that "The social thought of Africans helped to create the three major religions of the world, Judaism, Christianity and Islam." Further, his "studies led [him] to the reading of white European writers who wrote favorably of Africa and African people and who had lost credibility in their own countries."[33]

Moreover, these historical studies in the Harlem History Club not only opened up a deeper exploration of Ethiopian and East Afrikan history and politics, about which Huggins was an acknowledged authority. Huggins's contacts exposed Clarke to a variety of contemporary political movements and personalities across the Afrikan continent, including southern Afrika. In addition to continental Afrikan students and political figures from Nigeria and the Gold Coast—among whom were Nnamdi Azikiwe and Kwame Nkrumah, who were decades later to assume positions as heads of state of Nigeria and Ghana, respectively—"Dr. Willis N. Huggins introduced me to certain aspects of the South African labor movement, especially the career of Clements Kadalie of Nyasaland [now Malawi]," Clarke recalled. "From Clements Kadalie, I would learn the basic history of trade union movements in South Africa." As always, Clarke's historical studies included the investigation of primary source materials. "I read some of the letters between A.

Philip Randolph and Clements Kadalie. I read the old *Messenger*. I read an essay by Clements Kadalie still worth reading, 'The Growth of South African Trade Unionism.'"[34]

Clearly, in the Harlem History Club important elements of the independent tradition of Afrikan scholarship manifested: the investigation of primary source materials; the consultation of sources in research, historiography, and scholarship typically suppressed in the European academy; a teaching methodology featuring close associations between professors and students, which included lecture, discussion, and directed readings; an emphasis on the international dimensions of Afrikan history; a Pan Afrikanist focus that underscored the importance of examining the international experience of Afrikans in various parts of the world and their interconnection; the notion of Afrikan agency as the historiographical starting point for historical interpretation; a cultural orientation that expressed skepticism toward assimilation, Europeanization, and Christianization; and original research and publication geared primarily toward Afrikan consumption. In addition, Huggins's special concern with the pedagogy of Africana history added to lessons well learned by the teenaged Clarke that became evident in his later years as a professional academician.[35]

Another of Clarke's professors during the 1930s, one among the quadrumvirate of scholars who were his principal instructors in the fields of Africana history and what would eventually be called Africana Studies, was Charles Christopher Seifert.[36] Born in the Caribbean on the British island colony of Barbados in 1871,[37] Seifert proved an important influence on Afrikan artists, students, school teachers, and others in the Harlem of the 1920s and 1930s. Among the most renown artists who came under Seifert's influence during that period were the late celebrated painters Jacob Lawrence and Romare Bearden. Two other painters, Earl R. Sweeting and Robert Savon Pious, would become "his dedicated disciples" and work "closely with him to illustrate African history." Known by some as "Professor" for his extensive knowledge of Afrikan world history and his considerable personal library covering the subject, he was the founder and director of the Ethiopian School of Research History, which was located at 313 West 137th Street. Another of Clarke's four principal teachers and mentors—the historian and anthropologist William Leo Hansberry of the Department of History at Howard University, who would in the 1950s go on to lecture at the New School for Social Research in New York City—also taught with Seifert at the Ethiopian School. In addition to artists, university students and school teachers enrolled in Seifert's courses at the Ethiopian School "because it was the only place to learn African history." Respect for his erudition was so great that the Pan Afrikan nationalist leader Marcus Garvey, founder of the Universal Negro Improvement Association and African Communities League (UNIA and ACL), on occasion lived in Seifert's home so as to consult him on various aspects of Afrikan world history and culture and to have ready access to his impressive library. Romare Bearden and Harry Henderson, in their history of Afrikan artists in the United States, observed that Seifert also garnered the respect of academicians because he "simply knew more about African and African-American history than most authorities."[38]

During his youth Seifert was trained in carpentry and construction, and upon coming to New York City he became a successful building contractor, enabling him to invest a portion of his wealth into his lifelong passion—the study, research, and teaching of Afrikan world history and culture. In addition to instruction at the Ethiopian School, he gave an annual lecture series at the Harlem YMCA and lectured in Nashville, Tennessee, to Fisk University students and faculty. Unfortunately, economic difficulties undermined his ambitions for the Ethiopian School, and it became defunct during the Great Depression, a consequence of diminishing contributions from the school's impoverished students and the refusal by the New York City Board of Education to accredit the school as an in-service training center for public school teachers. Thus, in 1939 the Ethiopian School of Research History became the Charles C. Seifert Library. Seifert, nonetheless, continued teaching in small discussion groups until his death a decade later.[39]

While not known for published research, Seifert did in 1938 author a thirty-six-page pamphlet titled *The Negro's or Ethiopian's Contribution to Art*. Consequently, insight as to some aspects of the content of his instruction can be gleaned from an examination of the text.[40] Of Seifert's view of the relationship between art and history, Bearden and Henderson remark:

Believing strongly that pictures could inform and dramatize the past and were an essential technique for informing African-Americans of their heritage, which schools omitted from texts, Seifert converted the basement of his library and school into a studio. There, in the 1930s, the young artists Robert Pious and Earl Sweeting worked on canvases depicting royal court scenes, temple activities, religious and legal courts, caravans, the casting of iron and bronze, and daily life in the ancient African kingdoms. ... Sweeting later assembled his own historical works and painted many scenes that became part of the national collection of Ghana, where he lived for many years.[41]

In his pamphlet, Seifert advanced ideas regarding the importance and impact of Afrikan culture on world culture that would later become central themes in Clarke's writings, lectures, and teaching, and that would, with the emergence of Africana Studies some three decades later, become common knowledge within certain Afrikan intellectual and scholarly circles. Critical to the "Professor's" grasp of Afrikan history was that he made no distinction between continental and diasporan Afrikans; he used the terms *Negro* and *Ethiopian* (a term the ancient Greeks applied to Afrikans of various nationalities) interchangeably, stressing that Afrikans in the Americas were Afrikans without qualification. Hence, he maintained that Afrikan culture was a direct source of influence on both U.S. (American) and continental European societies, and that that influence flowed from Afrikans within those societies as well as from the Afrikan continent. "If it were possible to take the African Negro's cultural wealth out of America, or even Europe, these countries would immediately become barren," he observed.[42] "To-day, no intelligent person who is acquainted with the facts of history, and whose eyes are opened need go to Africa to find African culture, when it may be found profusely spread all over Europe and America, in fact, the whole of the Western world."[43]

Further, Seifert stated that Afrikans were at the beginning of human society and history and, consequently, they were at the center, as a dominant and directing force, of the development of artistic human creativity. "The Negro, or Ethiopian, may be called the metallurgist of the human race," Seifert averred. "It was he who first forged the most important link in civilized man's development from the Stone Age to the Metal Age, and so set him on his real road to progress in every direction."[44]

Significantly, Afrikan influence was seminal in the development of art in ancient Mediterranean Europe and western Asia; ancient Egypt (or Kemet) played a central role in influencing the development of a host of peoples, including the ancient Hebrews, various other peoples of ancient western Asia, the ancient Mediterranean European Greeks and Romans, the Arabs, and modern Europe. Further, that cultural influence was indisputably Afrikan because ancient Egypt was without question an Afrikan culture and an Afrikan state.[45] The Greeks, he explained, were "the first of the white race to have received the first instructions in the art of civilization from the early Egyptians, an African people." This conclusion is contrary to the opinions of the die-hard white supremacists, who "have labored hard to make Egypt white, and cut her off from the rest of Africa, especially Ethiopia, or Negro Africa, but the culture, every bit of it, is the same in origin."[46]

While ancient Egypt assumes particular importance because of its pervasive influence upon the ancient world of Mediterranean Europe and western Asia, Seifert also advanced two important historical positions regarding the significance of Afrikan cultural development that decades later would become fundamental to what would become known as an Afrocentric historiographical understanding of the ancient Afrikan Nile Valley. First, Seifert stated that ancient Egypt benefited from an influx of cultural influences from the interior of Afrika. Second, Seifert explained, ancient Egypt was not the sole representative of high culture in Afrika. To the contrary, cultural advancement and enlightenment could be found contemporaneously within the central Afrikan interior.[47]

Indeed, a few millennia later, Afrikan influence would extend itself into western Mediterranean Europe, Seifert noted, explaining that "the Moorish culture in Spain, was of African origin, and while the Moors finally lost out in Spain to the Spaniards, their culture remained as the intellectual guide for all Europe. It is also, a matter of record that the civilizations of many native African Communities, were on par and in some respect superior to European civilization before the beginning of the slave trade."[48]

Seifert also asserted that Afrika was art's native habitat, that art emerged from Afrika in antiquity principally as a form of religious expression and profoundly influenced its manifestation in cultures outside of Afrika, and that art's contemporary influence continued to reverberate in the modern world. In this vein, he asserted, modern Afrikan art was also reinvigorating modern European art, as the latter, having exhausted itself, returned to the source of its original birth and inspiration.[49]

Such a situation was, perhaps, ironic, Seifert observed, because European chauvinism hid from itself the reality of its own becoming. "If modern so-called civilized man, who is evidently still enjoying much of the rich blessings, which are the gifts of past civilizations, could be reminded often enough that those essential gifts, especially those that elevated him, are the gifts of Black folk, this might act as a check-rein against his bigotry, arrogance and race prejudice."[50]

Table 2.5
John Henrik Clarke's Major Professors and Mentors[51]

Name	Degree	Years of Instruction	Areas of Expertise
A. A. Schomburg (1874–1938) (b. Puerto Rico)	None	1934–1938	History of the Afrikan World, the Afrikan Caribbean, the Afrikan in the U. S. & of Europe
Willis N. Huggins (1886–1940) (b. Selma, Alabama)	Ph.D.	1934–1940	History of Afrikan antiquity, Ethiopia, Afrikan labor movement, Afrikan politics, ancient Afrikan religion and world antiquity
Charles C. Seifert (1871–1949) (b. Barbados, BWI)	None	circa 1934–1941? 1945–1949?	History of Afrikan art, Afrikan antiquity, Afrikan civilization
W. L. Hansberry (1894–1965) (b. Gloster, Mississippi)	M.A./ adv grad studies	1934–1941?, 1957–1958[52]	History of Afrikan antiquity, Afrikan archaeology and anthropology, Ethiopian antiquity, medieval West Afrikan civilizations

Although they presumably were initially teacher and pupil sometime in the 1930s at Seifert's Ethiopian School of Research History,[53] some two decades later Clarke would study with the fourth and last of his major mentors, the Howard University professor of Afrikan history and anthropology, William Leo Hansberry, who, as it happens, was the uncle of the celebrated playwright of *A Raisin in the Sun,* Lorraine Hansberry.[54] The New School for Social Research in New York City (now, since 1997, New School University), founded in 1919 by radical intellectuals animated by the vision of reconstructing American society and with an emphasis on adult education and social reform, invited Hansberry to teach a course on early Afrikan civilizations. By the 1950s Hansberry was a recognized authority in African studies, having established it as a field of study in the academy for nearly four decades, and having created five courses at Howard University's Department of History: (1) "Peoples and Cultures of Africa in Stone Age Times," (2) "Culture and Political History of Nilotic Lands in Historical Antiquity," (3) "Cultural and Political History of Kushite or Ethiopian Lands in the Middle Ages," (4) "Cultural and Political History of the Kingdoms and Empires of the Western Sahara and the Western Sudan," and (5) "Archaeological Methods and Materials."[55] From September 1957 through June 1958, during the fall and spring semesters, Hansberry commuted from Washington, D.C., to New York City, where he lectured to some twenty or more students each Friday. One of them was John Henrik Clarke.[56]

Born in Gloster, Mississippi, Hansberry (1894–1965), like Clarke's other professors, was fired by a sense of mission in disseminating the knowledge of the Afrikan past to Afrikans of the United States and the Afrikan continent. As a consequence of his passionate commitment to the study and teaching of Afrikan antiquity in both historical and anthropological terms, and of his ability to develop the subject as a discrete discipline of academic study at historically Afrikan universities in the United States, he also exercised an enormous influence upon Afrikan scholars and intellectuals in the United States and Afrika. Among the more famous of his students was Nnamdi Azikiwe (1904–1996), who would become Nigeria's first president and who would prove instrumental in creating in 1963 the Hansberry Institute of African Studies at the University of Nigeria at Nsukka in southeastern Nigeria, the region from which the Nigerian head of state originated. In that year Hansberry served as the institute's Distinguished Visiting Professor.[57] As president, Azikiwe praised Hansberry as the one who "initiated me into the sanctuaries of anthropology and ancient African history."[58] Another of Hansberry's more notable students was sociologist and historian Chancellor Williams (1905–1992), perhaps best known for his seminal historiography of the decline of Afrikan civilization in consequence of European aggression titled *The Destruction of Black Civilization: Great Issues of a Race from 4500 B.C. to 2000 A.D.* (1971). Williams studied under Hansberry as a graduate student, matriculating in 1934 into the graduate program in history at Howard University and completing the M.A. degree the following year. "Standing alone and isolated in the field for over thirty-five years, William Leo Hansberry was the teacher who introduced me to the systematic study of African history and, of equal importance, to the ancient documentary sources," Williams noted in recollections years later. "His massive documentation of early Greek and Roman historians and geographers of Africa covered several years of labor, leaving one to wonder how the utterly false teaching that Africa had no written history spread over the world."[59]

There were also peers who recognized the importance of his contribution. A Howard University colleague, Williston H. Lofton, praised Hansberry as the scholar, along with W. E. B. Du Bois and Carter G. Woodson, who "probably did more than any other scholar in these early days to advance the study of the culture and civilization of Africa."[60]

Table 2.6

John Henrik Clarke's Other Early Intellectual Influences (Selected)[61]

Name	Degree	Years of Association	Expertise
John G. Jackson (1907–1993)	None	1934–1993	History & anthropology of ancient and modern Afrika, ancient religion and Afrika, comparative Afrikan and European history
Joel A. Rogers (1880–1966)	None	1935–1966	History & anthropology of ancient, medieval, and modern Afrikan and European world history; and the history of Afrikan & European genetic mixing; comparative Afrikan and European history
R. P. Alexander (1898–1974)	J.D.	1940s–1974	U.S. Afrikan history, civil rights, international law, U.S. judiciary, U.S. politics
Charles H. Wesley (1891–1987)	Ph.D.	1940s–1987	History of U.S. and Afrikans in U.S.; general history of continental Afrika
Lorenzo Greene (1899–1988)	Ph.D.	1940s–1988	History of U.S. and Afrikans in U.S.
Lawrence Reddick (1910–1995)	Ph.D.	1940s–1995	History of U.S. and Afrikans in the U.S.
Benjamin Quarles (1904–1996)	Ph.D.	1940s–1996	History of U.S. and Afrikans in U.S.
Joseph B. Danquah (1895–1965)	Ph.D.	1958–1965	Medieval Gold Coast history, modern Gold Coast/Ghanaian political history; Akan history, law, religion & culture

Hansberry's early interest in ancient history stemmed from his father's influence. While the senior Hansberry died when he was three years old, he had taught history at Alcorn A. & M. College in Gloster. From childhood, Hansberry read his late father's books and developed a fascination with ancient Mediterranean European history. He also developed a deep curiosity concerning the much-neglected role of ancient Afrikan history and culture in the scheme of the human experience. In 1915 he entered Atlanta University as a freshman, but in February 1917, during his sophomore year, he transferred to Harvard University. In the interim, Hansberry had become profoundly influenced by W. E. B. Du Bois's ventures into the research and publication of ancient Afrikan history in *The Negro* (1915), which included chapters on Afrikan kingdoms and empires in antiquity and in the Middle Ages. Surprised but simultaneously fascinated by Du Bois's revelations, he attempted to intensify his independent study through reading the some 193 books, journal articles, studies, and other references listed in Du Bois's bibliography titled "Suggestions for Further Readings." Noting there was "no general history of the Negro race," Du Bois subdivided the reading list into the following subject areas: "The Physiography of Africa," "Racial Differences and the Origin and Characteristics of Negroes," "Early Movements of the Negro Race," "Negro in Ethiopia and Egypt," "Abyssinia," "The Niger River and Islam," "The Negro on the Guinea Coast," "The Congo Valley," "The Negro in the Region of the Great Lakes," "The Negro in South Africa," "On Negro Civilization," "The Slave Trade," "The West Indies and South America," "The Negro in the United States," and "The Future of the Negro Race."[62] Frustrated, however, by the limitations of Atlanta University's inadequately equipped library, Hansberry transferred so that he could delve extensively into Harvard's holdings. In further pursuit of the study of Afrikan antiquity, Hansberry took courses and read independently in Afrikan archeology, anthropology, ethnology, paleontology and also took courses in the history of science, graduating in 1921 with a baccalaureate degree in anthropology. He would return to Harvard years later to earn an M.A. degree in 1932.[63]

Hansberry was deeply committed to the goal of spreading the knowledge of Afrikan ancient, medieval, and early modern civilizations among Afrikans in the United States. After graduating from

Harvard in 1921, he "became deeply concerned over the lack of efforts by black schools and colleges to make use of recent discoveries and studies which confirmed that Africans and their descendants have an honorable, and indeed glorious, past," wrote Joseph E. Harris, who edited two volumes of Hansberry's unpublished research and lecture notes titled *Pillars in Ethiopian History* (1974) and *Africa and Africans As Seen by Classical Writers* (1977). "The time had arrived, in his view, for blacks to affirm their identity by displaying a self-confidence which only a true knowledge of their past could assure."[64] After Harvard, Hansberry took a year-long teaching position at Straight College (now Dillard University) in New Orleans, Louisiana, where, according to biographer Kwame Wes Alford, he established a Department of Negro History and African Studies within the college's social sciences division, and where he introduced an interdisciplinary approach to the study of the Afrikan experience on the mother continent. Indeed, notes Alford, Straight College stood alone in the United States in this regard, as no other college or university at that time taught courses on continental Afrikan history. Alford credits Hansberry as the creator and founder of African studies as an academic field of study at a college or university in the United States.[65]

After a year, however, in 1922, Hansberry took a position at Howard University and its Department of History, where he would be for the next thirty-seven years before retirement in 1959.[66] He founded the Afrikan civilizations section in the department's curriculum and began teaching continental Afrikan history, establishing three new courses: "Negro Peoples in the Cultures and Civilizations of Prehistoric and Proto-Historic Times," "The Ancient Civilizations of Ethiopia," and "The Civilization of West Africa in Medieval and Early Modern Times." The first was a survey course that explored the latest archaeological and anthropological research concerning the cultures of Afrika in the Paleolithic and Neolithic periods, ancient Egypt's predynastic civilization, and Afrika's relations to the eastern Mediterranean and western and southern Asia in the protohistorical and early historical periods. The second was a survey course beginning from about 4000 B.C.E. that covered that area of Afrika encompassing modern Sudan and Ethiopia. Hansberry relied upon Egyptian, Hebrew, and Greek sources and archaeological and anthropological research from several expeditions, including those of the ancient Kushite cities of Napata, Meroe, and Kerma. The third course surveyed political and cultural developments in the medieval western Sudanese empire states of Ghana, Mali, and Songhai, as well as developments in Yorubaland. For this course Hansberry drew from Arab accounts and archaeological and anthropological research from French, German, and English scholarship.[67]

Harris notes that the establishment of these courses in the 1920s was no minor achievement. To effectively teach such courses could only have been possible as the result of a monumental research effort. Looking at Hansberry's work on non-Egyptian Afrikan antiquity, Alford has observed that during the 1930s "Hansberry's courses at Howard existed as the only academic and classroom treatment of this subject in the world."[68] Significantly, Harris remarked in 1974, Hansberry "was able to launch his program with source materials that several universities lack even today." In addition to his extensive use of maps and charts, Hansberry had by 1925, in collaboration with the university's Department of Geology, developed more than 200 slides as illustrations for his courses. His efforts did not go unrewarded. By 1924 some 800 undergraduates were enrolled in his courses.[69]

In the following year, from 3–4 June, Hansberry organized a symposium titled "The Cultures and Civilizations of Negro Peoples in Africa." The symposium, which showcased both the effectiveness and substance of his instruction, featured the presentation of twenty-eight scholarly papers by some of his students who were nationals from the United States, Panama, Guyana, and Colombia. The scope of the examination included subjects that explored "the beginning of the Old Stone Age in the Pleistocene Period to the establishment of African Slave Trade by the Arabs, the Moors, and the European in the Sixteenth and Seventeenth Centuries of our Era."[70]

Five years later Hansberry outlined in a proposal seeking funding for the expansion of his efforts the six basic tenets of his historiographical approach: (1) that Afrika rather than Asia is the probable birthplace of humanity, and that Afrikans are the originators and developers of human culture and civilization; (2) that Afrikan emigration from continental Afrika to Europe and Asia was caused by the expansion of the desert in the Sahara and in Libya; (3) that many of the peoples and cultures of ancient Egypt originated from the continental interior to the South, from equatorial Afrika; (4)

that the peoples of Ethiopia contested with the great western Asian empires of antiquity, notably the Assyrian empire, for first place among the ancient world's leading powers; (5) that the medieval western Sudanese states of Ghana, Mali, Songhai, and Nupe were larger, more effectively organized, and culturally superior to contemporaneous states of the Anglo-Saxon, Germanic, and Slavic peoples of Europe; and (6) that the disintegration of these western Sudanese states resulted from several factors that include the expansion of desertification in the Sahara, Arab invasion of North Afrika and the introduction of Islam and Islamic political systems, and the establishment of Arab, Berber, and European systems of enslavement that targeted and devastated Afrikan peoples.[71]

Interestingly, Hansberry never succeeded in earning the Ph.D. While he did earn an M.A. degree in history and anthropology from Harvard University in 1932 and managed to engage in advanced graduate studies at Chicago University's Oriental Institute (1936–1937) and England's Oxford University (1937–1938), Alford remarks that Hansberry's difficulties in obtaining the Ph.D. degree resulted in part from the fact that he was a greater authority on the subject of Afrikan antiquity than European scholars of his time.[72] Further, the interdisciplinary scope and originality of his research intimidated some would-be Oxonian advisors, who sabotaged his efforts. Moreover, Hansberry pioneered in a field of study that was new, and that suffered from the presumption of Afrikan inferiority among European academicians and those U.S. Afrikans trained by them.[73] Nonetheless, Hansberry spent more than fifty years collecting various materials on continental Afrikan history, accumulating "an impressive personal collection of notes, lectures, speeches, books, articles, pamphlets, and visual aids pertaining to the whole field of African studies."[74]

A general statement of Hansberry's research and teaching on Afrika, and a further elaboration on the six basic tenets of his historiography, can be seen in an unpublished essay Clarke used in his university teaching titled "Africa in Stone Age Times, in Historical Antiquity, and in the Middle Ages." First, Hansberry argued that as late as 1910 it had been held "in academic circles that Africa had played but a very minor role in the early history of the human race," and that, instead, it was the "widely accepted hypothesis that

Asia was the birthplace of man and the cradleland of civilization." It was further assumed that Afrika's earliest peoples and cultures originated from migrations over tens of thousands of years from Asia, peoples who allegedly settled along the coastal regions of the southern shore of the Mediterranean Sea.[75] European scholarship held the rest of Afrika was virtually empty until the very end of the Stone Age period.

"Since 1910, however, it has been abundantly demonstrated that these older points of view are absolutely at variance with the historical facts," Hansberry explained. In the fifty years that followed, "vast quantities of Stone Age remains, covering the entire span of prehistoric man's existence on earth, have been discovered in every part of Africa from Egypt, Libya, and the old Barbary States in the north, to the Cape of Good Hope in the south, and from the Atlantic Ocean on the west, eastward to the Indian Ocean and the Red Sea." He added: "South Africa, Rhodesia, Tanganyika, Kenya, Uganda, the Belgian Congo, and the great basins of the Niger and the Nile—in short, the whole of the interior of Africa—are particularly well represented by such remains." The nature and volume of these findings in human remains, art, and tools have persuaded scholars that Afrika's prehistorical cultures and peoples are indigenous and not immigrants from Asia or Europe. To the contrary, Hansberry observed, "some of the ablest specialists in the history of the Stone Age times think it highly probable that it was from Africa that many of the earliest prehistoric cultures of Europe and Asia were derived." Moreover, he noted, some experts suggest it was from the Afrikan interior that humanity first discovered the manufacture of stone tools and weapons, painting, engraving, sculpture, pottery, and other arts; and that this humanity was Afrikan or Africoid in character.[76]

Further, Hansberry maintained, the evidence of fossilized human remains from this period not only suggests the probability of Afrika as the birthplace of humanity, but "a relatively large number of skeletal remains belonging to Negro and Negroid individuals ... have been discovered at numerous prehistoric sites in widely scattered regions in Europe and Asia." This held true for both the stone and early metal ages. In Asia, locations include Palestine, Anatolia, Arabia, Mesopotamia, Persia, India, Indochina, the Philippines, and the islands of the Indian Ocean and the South Seas. "In Europe, they have been discovered principally on paleolithic or neolithic or aeneolithic sites in the Iberian Peninsula, Italy, Monaco [sic], France, Belgium, Switzerland, Illyria [roughly modern Albania], the Balkan states, and—according to some authorities—in Czechoslovakia, Mecklenburg, Silesia, Denmark and southern Sweden." In addition, paintings, statuettes, and other objects of art found in Crete, Yugoslavia, Bulgaria, the Aegean archipelago, and mainland Greece in proto- and early modern historical times give evidence of an Afrikan presence. The evidence argues that Afrikans migrated to these areas from Afrika, their emigration prompted by significant climatic changes, namely, the expansion of desertification in the Sahara and Libya.[77]

Hence, Hansberry noted, it can be argued that Afrikans "played a profoundly significant part in the ethnic and cultural history of Europe and Asia in earlier human times." Indeed, certain specialists speculate, based on their examination of the evidence, that Afrikans are responsible for introducing higher Stone Age culture to Europe and Asia. Further, certain "world-renowned authorities on human origins have ventured to assert that there are indeed adequate grounds for believing that some of the older Negro and Negroid types of Europe and Asia were the ancestral stocks from which some of the subsequent non-Negroid populations of these two continents were, in part at least, derived." This was accomplished by means of morphological changes resulting from environmental conditions in Europe. Hansberry continued: "An eminent Harvard authority has pointed out that it was in this wise that an ancient dark-skinned and more or less Negroid stock was ultimately transformed into some of the elements making up that great ethnic complex commonly known as the Nordic Race."[78]

Hansberry stated the evidence also suggests the significance of indigenous Afrikan civilization in the historical period, refuting white supremacist presumptions about Afrika that had long been promulgated by European scholarship. In the past century European scholars have found in the river valleys of the Niger, the Zambezi, the Benue, the upper Nile, in the area of Lake Chad, and in the former river valleys of the Sahara "extensive remains of hundreds of wholly ruined and completely abandoned or partly ruined and largely deserted cities and towns which bear witness to the former existence of civilizations of types that are nowadays seldom associated in the popular mind with the 'Dark Continent.'" In both the ancient and medieval periods these "monumental remains of temples, tombs, palaces, public buildings and other memorials of the past" indicate an advanced level of development. There are also written records from indigenous peoples and foreign peoples that, translated into European languages, have now made it "possible to reconstruct in surprising detail the story of scores of large and powerful kingdoms and empires which flourished in the heart of Africa in the days of long ago." These include the ancient kingdoms of Napata, Meroe, and Axum in the region of the upper Nile; the medieval Christian kingdoms of Dongala and Alwan in Nubia and the Ethiopian empire associated by Europe with the mythical Prester John; the medieval states in the region of Lake Chad, including the formidable Kanem-Bornu; and further westward, along the Niger River, the Hausa states, and the empires of Ghana, Mali, and Songhai that "for centuries during the Middle Ages were renowned far and wide as states of vast wealth and unsurpassed power."[79]

Despite the fact they were ruled by "some of the ablest statesmen and most benevolent that are remembered in the recorded annals of man," they were destroyed by the Arab and Berber slave trade in the medieval period and the more recent devastation of the European slave trade, which brought into effect "the decline and fall of civilization in most of these early African states." Consequently, the evidence available on Afrika in the Stone Age, ancient, and medieval periods demonstrates that Afrika "has been throughout the ages the seat of a great succession of cultures and civilizations which were comparable in most respects and superior in some aspects to the cultures and civilizations in other parts of the world during the same period."[80] While the civilizations of Greece and Rome cannot be diminished in significance, nonetheless their experiences, assessed in light of discoveries in Afrikan history, "form but a few fragmentary chapters in the total history of the Human Race."[81]

Hansberry's study of Ethiopia, captured in Harris's edited volume titled *Pillars in Ethiopian History*, provide some additional insights into his historiography of Afrikan civilization. One of the more interesting items in the four-chapter volume, which explored the history of the legendary Queen of Sheba, the role of the fourth century emperor Ezana in the foundation of Ethiopia as a Christian state, and a general history of Ethiopia's early development as a Christian state, was a subject titled "Prester John and Diplomatic Communications with European Powers."[82] Refuting the notion that Afrika remained largely unknown to Europe in the middle ages, Hansberry details the diplomatic outreach of European powers to the Ethiopian state to form a Christian alliance against the threat of the advance of Muslim power into western Europe. The diplomatic communications included letters to and from the papacy of Rome to Ethiopia's rulers beginning in the twelfth century. "If surviving medieval sources are to be believed," Hansberry continued, "it would appear that correspondence between the popes of Rome and the kings of Ethiopia, as well as direct contacts between European and African kingdoms, were much more common in the thirteenth and fourteenth centuries than is usually supposed."[83] Letters sent to Ethiopian kings during this period included those from Pope Alexander IV (1254–1261), Pope Urban IV (1261–1265), Pope Clement IV (1265–1268), Pope Innocent V (1276), Pope Nicholas III (1277–1280), Pope Nicholas IV (1288–1294), Pope Benedict XI (1303–1304), Pope Clement V (1305–1314), and Pope John XXII (1316–1334).[84]

Moreover, European delegations journeyed not only to Afrika, but also to Muslim-ruled Jerusalem in Palestine, where the Ethiopian church maintained a chapel and monastery. Likewise, Ethiopian monarchs sent diplomatic delegations to the papal court in Europe.[85] In the fifteenth century, Hansberry added, "direct relationships between Ethiopia and Europe became very close. Ethiopian ambassadors from Ethiopian King Newaya Krestos visited Venice in 1402, while Ethiopian pilgrims from Jerusalem visited Bologna, Padua, and Rome in 1408. A few years later ambassadors from King Yeshak I sent letters to the rulers of Aragon and France, "urging them to join him in an alliance against the Muslim infidels."[86]

Significantly, Hansberry adds in a discussion of the place of Afrika in the development of ancient European literature, "few names are better known and none is older than that of Ethiopia. Europe's earliest poetry sings of no foreign people quite so romantic; its geography records no country more distant; and its efforts at history memorializes no nation thought more ancient than that designated by this celebrated name."[87] Moreover, the conclusion derived from an examination of the beginnings of European literature reveals that "the very earliest literate communities of Europe were evidently 'Ethiopia conscious.'" Indeed, he maintained, "the name Ethiopia and its derivatives are, as territorial and ethnic expressions, among the oldest living terms known to the geographical and historical literature of Europe," predating the introduction of such terms as *Carthage, Greece, Etruria, Rome, Persia, Babylon,* and *Assyria* by several centuries.[88] Clearly implied in Hansberry's discussion is the position that Afrikan civilization is older than European; its corollary being that Europe is a comparatively younger cultural complex. Further, the implication of his historiography is that what can be characterized as the beginnings of advanced European cultural development is profoundly influenced by the older, and relatively more advanced, Afrikan culture.

Hansberry notes, however, that the Ethiopia to which the earliest European literature referred was not limited to the medieval Afrikan state discussed above. Instead, it served as a more generalized description of the physical appearance of Afrikans, referring to the land where the "sun-burned" or "black-faced" people lived, and that included areas south of ancient Egypt, most notably the Sudan, and portions of western, central, and southern Asia, including Arabia, Mesopotamia, Persia, and India.[89] Nonetheless, Afrikans, or "Ethiopians," were known to the ancient Mediterranean Europeans not only in Afrika but also as conquerors and settlers in "the Aegean lands hundreds of years before Homer's day, and," he continued, "in the centuries immediately following the age in which the great poet lived." Archaeological artifacts, including tombs, pottery, carved stone vases, amulets, stone emblems of divinities, and other objects of art found in and apart from those tombs in Minoan Crete are strikingly similar to artifacts and tombs found contemporaneously in Afrika from the pre- and protodynastic periods, giving support to the conclusion of significant Afrikan settlement in the region. In addition to settlement was the Afrikan influence on European culture. The mass of archaeological "evidence seems to indicate that the links between the Ethiopian regions and Minoan Crete are not only older than the links between Minoan Crete and mainland Greece or Europe," Hansberry explained, "but that it was with the aid of Ethiopians that Cretan culture was first carried to the coasts of Europe, and then inland."[90]

❧

Hansberry's treatment of Afrikan agency in history is consistent with that offered by Schomburg, Huggins, and Seifert. Their collective work shows that an important feature of Clarke's academic training began with the premise that Afrikan agency was critical to the Afrika-centered interpretation of Afrikan history in every era. Further, this interpretation was supported by the philosophical position and methodological approach that stressed the importance of a firm basis in verifiable historical and archaeological evidence. However contrary to the prevailing white supremacist thesis regarding Afrikan agency in history—and, indeed, because of it—all four scholars represented a commitment to the scrupulous investigation and documentation of the evidence supporting Afrikan agency throughout human history. Accompanying the assumption of Afrikan agency was a corollary assumption based also upon historical and archaeological evidence: the anteriority of Afrikan culture to European culture and in world history and culture. In the Afrikan academy, these two historiographical starting points discredited, concomitantly, the credibility, the persuasiveness of European supremacy, reducing it from a form of legitimate knowledge to a vulgar ideological construct intended to reinforce the political, economic, social, and cultural status quo. The fact that these scholars could not pursue this in the European academy—although one of them managed to do so, not without difficulty, in an Afrikan replication of this academy—was axiomatic of the colonialist nature of the Afrikan power position in Americo-European society.

The range and depth of Clarke's training in Afrikan world history, including the depth and breadth of the Afrikan academy's exploration of the relationship of the histories of European and other peoples to the history of Afrikan people, explains the caliber of his teaching and his expertise in Afrikan world history, especially with respect to the seminal role he played in the founding of Africana Studies/Africalogy in the European academy in the United States. Clarke's matriculation in the "university without walls" demonstrated an advanced, rigorous undergraduate and graduate education and scholarly training in an area of study that, in its examination by Afrikan intellectuals and their independent institutions, proved far in advance of anything comparably and contemporaneously explored in the European academy of the United States or Europe. Indeed, the test of his training is seen in his performance within the European academy. The caliber of this education explains why Clarke, over and above academics trained in the European academy, was prepared to offer leadership in the late 1960s through the 1970s in the emerging discipline of Africana Studies/Africalogy on both the graduate and undergraduate levels. This leadership includes his singular role in developing a body of historical knowledge that would become an important part of the foundation of Africana Studies/Africalogy teaching and research. As well, it would be evident in his contribution to the training of Ph.D. candidates in history and other disciplines in the European academy and his guidance of their pursuit of dissertation research that explored an ever-expanding universe of Africana phenomena.[91]

Notes

1. John Henrik Clarke, "A Search for Identity," *Social Casework* 51, no. 5 (May 1970): 263.

2. As quoted by Joseph E. Harris, "Profile of a Pioneer Africanist," in *Pillars in Ethiopian History: The William Leo Hansberry African History Notebook*, vol. 1, ed., Joseph E. Harris (Washington, D.C.: Howard University Press, 1974), 15.

3. "Vital Signs: The Statistics That Describe the Present and Suggest the Future of African Americans in Higher Education," *The Journal of Blacks in Higher Education*, no 15 (Spring 1997): 74.

4. Greene explains the numerical discrepancy between master's and doctoral degrees by observing: "It should be pointed out, however, that all recipients of doctoral degrees did not take the master's, and that, in a few cases, professional degrees such as LL.B., M.D., and S.T.B. are taken into account here and considered at the least as master's degree equivalents." See Harry Washington Greene, *Holders of Doctorates among American Negroes: An Educational and Social Study of Negroes Who Have Earned Doctoral Degrees in Course, 1876–1943* (Boston: Meador Publishing Company, Publishers, 1946), 33.

5.   As regards the numerical discrepancies between doctorate and baccalaureate degrees, Greene notes: "There were also two or more cases of a professional degree having been here adjudged as equivalent to a bachelor's, since the latter degree was not held. And in two cases, an Oxford University Litt. B. was taken after the student had been graduated from college. ... It was impossible to secure complete data on this particular aspect of the problem." See Greene, 36.

6.   Ibid., 33–36.

7.   B. R. Mitchell, ed., *International Historical Statistics, The Americas, 1750–1988* (New York: Stockton Press, 1993), 21.

8.   Greene, *Holders of Doctorates*, 22, 23, 41.

9.   Ibid., 23, 26.

10. Mitchell, *International*, 21.

11. Clarke credited his training in Africana history to major four teachers: Arthur Alphonso Schomburg, Willis N. Huggins, Charles C. Seifert, and William Leo Hansberry. The first three, he stated, "literally trained me not only to study African history and the history of Black people the world over but to teach this history." Indeed, Schomburg "is responsible for what I am and what value I have in the field of African history and the history of Black people all over the world," he disclosed in John Henrik Clarke, ed., *New Dimensions in African History: The London Lectures of Dr. Yosef ben-Jochannan and Dr. John Henrik Clarke* (Trenton, NJ: Africa World Press, 1991), 137. See also ibid., *Who Betrayed the African World Revolution? And Other Speeches* (Chicago: Third World Press, 1994), 117; ibid., "A Search," 263; and ibid., *My Life in Search of Africa* (Chicago: Third World Press, 1999), 14–15, 16.

12. Greene, *Holders of Doctorates*, 22–23, 33–36, 41.

13. See http://www.fordham.edu/general/Orientation/Fordham_at_a_Glance 1625.html.

14. Greene, *Holders of Doctorates*, 31, 100; Runoko Rashidi, "Notes on Black Scholars of the Moors in John G. Jackson's Life," in *Golden Age of the Moor*, ed. Ivan Van Sertima (New Brunswick, NJ: Transaction Publishers, 1992), 90; William R. Scott, *The Sons of Sheba's Race: African-Americans and the Italo-Ethiopian War, 1935–1941* (Bloomington and Indianapolis: Indiana University Press, 1993), 113; John Henrik Clarke, "The Influence of Arthur A. Schomburg on My Concept of Africana Studies," *Phylon* 49, nos. 1, 2 (1992): 8.

15. Ibid., 33–36.

16. Willis N. Huggins, "How Wrong Is Hitler? On the History of Jews, Black Folk and 'Aryanism'?" *The Chicago Defender*, Saturday, 28 January 1939, 13. *The Chicago Defender*, founded on 15 May 1905 by Robert Sengstacke Abbott (1868–1940), was, between the first and second world wars, the single most important Afrikan newspaper in the United States. It enjoyed a paid circulation of more than 230,000 and a readership estimated at between two to five times that number. See Harry Amana, "Robert S. Abbott," *Dictionary of Literary Biography Online*, 2003, http://www.galenet.com/servlet/GLD/form?origSearch=true&o=DataType&n=10&l=1&docID=txshracd2588&secondary=false&u=CA&u=CLC&u=DLB&t=KW. *The Chicago Defender* remains an Afrikan weekly newspaper.

17. Anna Swanston, ed., *Dr. John Henrik Clarke: His Life, His Words, His Works* (Atlanta, GA: I AM Unlimited, 2003), 99–100. Clarke contended that the circumstances of Huggins's death, although officially ruled a suicide, were somewhat mysterious.

18. Greene, *Holders of Doctorates*, 23, 26.

19. Scott, *The Sons*, 48, 51, 112–114.

20. Greene, 31, 100; Rashidi, "Notes," 90; and Scott, 113.

21. Ibid., 23, 26.

22. Willis N. Huggins and John G. Jackson, *Introduction to African Civilizations with Main Currents in Ethiopian History* (Baltimore: Inprint Editions, 1999; originally New York: Avon House 1937), 13–14.

23. Ibid., 3–4.

24. Ibid., 13, 132–154, 162–203, 208–221.

25. Ibid., 43.

26. Ibid., 153.

27. Ibid., 204.

28. Clarke, "The Influence," 7; ibid., *My Life*, 17.

29. Edward Wilmot Blyden, *Christianity, Islam and the Negro Race* (London: W. B. Whittingham, 1887). Blyden lived from 1832 to 1912.

30. John G. Jackson (1907–1993), who, as is evident, emerged from the tradition of independent Afrikan scholarship, was a prolific scholar in his own right. In addition to his collaborations with Huggins, his works include *Was Jesus Christ a Negro? and, The African Origin of the Myths and Legends of the Garden of Eden: Two Rationalistic Views* (New York: Published by the author; Wilson [printer], 1933); *Christianity before Christ* (New York: Blyden Society, 1938); *Ethiopia and the Origin of Civilization: A Critical Review of the Evi-*

dence of Archaeology, Anthropology, History and Comparative Religion, According to the Most Reliable Sources and Authorities (New York: Blyden Society, 1939); *Pagan Origins of the Christ Myth* (New York: Truth Seeker Co., 1941); *Introduction to African Civilizations* (New York: University Books, 1970); *Man, God, and Civilization* (New Hyde Park, NY: University Books, 1972); "Egypt and Christianity," *Journal of African Civilizations* 4, no. 2 (November 1982): 65–80; "Krishna and Buddha of India: Black Gods of Asia," *Journal of African Civilizations* 7, no. 1 (1985): 106–111; *The Golden Ages of Africa* (Austin, TX: American Atheist Press, 1987); *Black Reconstruction in South Carolina* (Austin, TX: American Atheist Press, 1987); *Hubert Henry Harrison: The Black Socrates* (Austin, TX: American Atheist Press, 1987); *Ages of Gold and Silver and Other Short Sketches of Human History* (Austin, TX: American Atheist Press, 1990); *The Mysteries of Egypt* (Chicago Heights, IL: L & P Enterprises, 1990s); and "The Empire of the Moors: An Outline Based on Interview and Summary," *Journal of African Civilizations* no. 11 (Fall 1991): 85–92.

31. Sir James George Frazer, *Folk-lore in the Old Testament: Studies in Comparative Religion, Legend and Law* (London: Macmillan, 1918). Frazer lived from 1854 to 1941.

32. Gerald Massey, *A Book of the Beginnings: Containing an Attempt to Recover and Reconstitute the Lost Origines of the Myths and Mysteries, Types and Symbols, Religion and Language, with Egypt for the Mouthpiece and Africa as the Birthplace* (London: Williams & Norgate 1881). Massey lived from 1828 to 1907.

33. Clarke, "The Influence," 7–8, 16–17.

34. Ibid., *My Life*, 15–16. Asa Philip Randolph (1889–1979) was the founder and president of the International Brotherhood of Sleeping Car Porters from 1925 to 1968. Born in Crescent City, Florida, the brilliant and indefatigable Afrikan labor leader and civil rights activist founded with Chandler Owens in 1917 the socialist *The Messenger: The Only Radical Negro Magazine*, a monthly publication that addressed a panoply of issues affecting Afrikans in the United States. Randolph edited the magazine until 1925. Among numerous accomplishments, Randolph became the first Afrikan vice president of the American Federation of Labor-Congress of Industrial Organizations (AFL-CIO). See *Contemporary Authors Online*, Gale, 2003, http://www.galenet.com/servlet/GLD/form?origSearch=true&o=DataType &n=10&l=1&locID=txshracd2588&secondary=false&u=CA&u=CLC&u=

DLB&t=KW. Clearly, the Afrikan labor movement in the United States was in communication with the Afrikan labor movement in southern Afrika.

35. See John Henrik Clarke, "The Preservers of Afrikan World History," address to New York community audience, circa 1990s, DVD, available from the Nubian Network, http://www.blackconsciousness.com. In this lecture the Hunter College professor emeritus would reflect on his academic training, noting that with respect to source materials, "I would like to take a look at some of the non-Afrikan preservers of our history, and to dispel the idea that all white people have been against our history and against our proper place in history. … as a matter of truth, all the times Europeans were distorting Afrikan history there were groups of Europeans saying 'No. That is not true.'"

36. Ibid., *New Dimensions*, 137.

37. Although Barbados purportedly gained independence from Britain in 1966, and is today considered an independent and sovereign nation within the British Commonwealth, the Central Intelligence Agency's *The World Factbook* notes that the island nation's chief of state is "Queen ELIZABETH II (since 6 February 1952), represented by Governor General Sir Clifford Straughn HUSBANDS (since 1 June 1996)." Barbados's executive government is also not subject to election as "the monarch is hereditary" and the "governor general [is] appointed by the monarch." Further, "following legislative elections, the leader of the majority party or the leader of the majority coalition is usually appointed prime minister by the governor general; the prime minister recommends the deputy prime minister." *CIA World Factbook* on Barbados, available from http://www.cia.gov/cia/publications/factbook/geos/bb.html#Intro.

38. Romare Bearden and Harry Henderson, *A History of African-American Artists: From 1792 to the Present* (New York: Pantheon Books, 1993), 247–250.

39. Ibid., 249–250.

40. Charles C. Seifert, *The Negro's or Ethiopian's Contribution to Art* (Baltimore, MD: Black Classic Press, 1991; originally New York: The Ethiopian Historical Pub. Co., 1938). Seifert was also author of the apparently unpublished works *The True Story of Aesop "The Negro"* (1946) and *The Three African Saviour Kings* (New York: n.d.). In 1954, the Charles C. Seifert Historical Research Association in New York City published a text titled *African Culture and History*. Clarke credits Seifert with authoring two other unpublished books, *The African Origins of the Concept of the Brotherhood of Man* and *Who Are the Ethiopians?* See Swanston, *Dr. John Henrik Clarke*, 90.

41. Bearden and Henderson, *A History*, 250.

42. Seifert, *The Negro's*, 28.

43. Ibid., 35.

44. Ibid., 15, 20–21.

45. Ibid., 21.

46. Ibid., 20.

47. Ibid., 21.

48. Ibid., 28.

49. Ibid., 23, 24, 26.

50. Ibid.19–20.

51. Bearden and Henderson, *A History*, 247–250; Clarke, "The Influence," 4–9; ibid., "A Search," 259–264; Kwaku Person-Lynn, ed., "On My Journey Now: The Narrative and Works of Dr. John Henrik Clarke, The Knowledge Revolutionary," *The Journal of Pan African Studies: A Journal of Africentric Theory, Methodology and Analysis* Special Issue, 1, no. 2 (Winter–Fall 2000) and 2, no. 1 (Spring–Summer 2001): 101–279; Clarke, *New Dimensions*, 137; ibid., *Who Betrayed*, 117; ibid., *My Life*, 14–15, 16; Elinor Des Verney Sinnette, *Arthur Alfonso Schomburg: Black Bibliophile and Collector: A Biography* (New York: The New York Public Library and Detroit: Wayne State University Press, 1989); Seifert, *The Negro's*; Arthur A. Schomburg, "The Negro Digs Up His Past," in *The New Negro: An Interpretation*, ed. Alain Locke (New York: Arno Press and The New York Times, 1968; originally New York: Albert and Charles Boni, 1925), 231–237; Joseph E. Harris, ed., *Africa and Africans as Seen by Classical Writers: The William Leo Hansberry African History Notebook*, vol. 2 (Washington, D.C.: Howard University Press, 1977); ibid., *Pillars in Ethiopian History: The William Leo Hansberry African History Notebook*, vol. 1 (Washington, D.C.: Howard University Press, 1981); Kwame Wes Alford, "The Early Intellectual Growth and Development of William Leo Hansberry and the Birth of African Studies," *Journal of Black Studies* 30, no. 3 (January 2000): 269–293; ibid., "A Prophet without Honor: William Leo Hansberry and the Discipline of African Studies, 1894–1939" (Ph.D. diss., University of Missouri-Columbia, 1998); William Leo Hansberry, "Africa in Stone Age Times, in Historical Antiquity, and in the Middle Ages," n.d., Hansberry Files, 1–4, JHCP, SCRBC; Huggins and Jackson, *Introduction*; William Leo Hansberry, letter to E. Jefferson Murphy, 27 June 1958, JHCP, SCRBC.

52. Clarke's studies were interrupted from 1941 to 1945 by military service during World War II. He was a master sergeant in the Army Air Force. See John Henrik Clarke, letter to Henry Allen Moe, 30 October 1951; ibid., "Contemporary Authors" Biographical Form, n.d.,2, JHCP, SCRBC. In 1954, the Brooklyn unit of the Universal Negro Improvement Association announced that Clarke would be a speaker for a lecture they organized. The announcement indicated that he had studied with Seifert, Huggins, and Hansberry. This was three years before Clarke was to attend the Hansberry lectures at the New School in 1957. As Hansberry lectured at Seifert's Ethiopian School of Research History, according to Bearden and Henderson, *A History*, 247–250, the UNIA announcement suggests the likelihood that Clarke first attended Hansberry's lectures at the Ethiopian School.

53. See note 52 above.

54. William Leo Hansberry, letter to John Henrik Clarke, 2 February 1965, JHCP, SCRBC.

55. Harris, *Pillars*, 18.

56. William Leo Hansberry, letter to E. Jefferson Murphy, 27 June 1958, JHCP, SCRBC.

57. Harris, *Africa and Africans*, xi.

58. Ibid., *Pillars*, 3, 4.

59. Chancellor Williams, *The Destruction of Black Civilization: Great Issues of a Race from 4500 B.C. to 2000 A.D.* (Chicago: Third World Press, 1987; originally Dubuque, IA: Kendall-Hunt, 1971), 361. Also see La Vinia Delois Jennings, "Chancellor Williams," *Dictionary of Literary Biography*, vol. 76, *Afro-American Writers, 1940–1955*, ed. Trudier Harris (The Gale Group, 1988), 196–199. The independent Afrika historian Runoko Rashidi notes that Williams earned a B.A. in education and an M.A. in history at Howard University and a Ph.D. in sociology in 1949 from American University in Washington, D.C. See Runoko Rashidi, "Dedication and Tribute: The Passing of Giants: John G. Jackson and Chancellor Williams," in *African Presence in Early Asia*, ed. Runoko Rashidi and Ivan Van Sertima (New Brunswick, NJ: Transaction, 1995), 19.

60. As cited by Harris, *Africa and Africans*, xxii.

61. Clarke, *My Life*, 23–24; ibid., letter to Helga R. Andrews, 1 February 1982, JHCP, SCRBC; ibid., "Reflections & Observations ... Ghana Remembered 'Then and Now.'" Seventeenth Annual Conference, 25 July–1 August 1993, National Council for Black Studies, Accra, Ghana (25 July 1993), 10, 12–14, JHCP, SCRBC; ibid., letter to Henry Allen Moe, 13 October 1958, JHCP,

SCRBC; *Contemporary Authors Online*, Gale, http://www.galenet.com/servlet/GLD/form?origSearch=true&o=DataType&n=10&l=1&docID=txs hracd2588&secondary=false&u=CA&u=CLC&u=DLB&t=KW.

62. W. E. B. Du Bois, *The Negro* (Philadelphia: University of Pennsylvania Press, 2001; originally New York: Henry Holt, 1915), 273–281.

63. Harris, *Pillars*, 3–5. See also William Leo Hansberry, "W. E. B. Du Bois' Influence on African History," *Freedomways* 5, no. 1 (Winter 1965): 73–82; and *Contemporary Authors Online*, Gale, 2003, http://www.galenet.com/servlet/GLD/form?origSearch=true&o=DataType&n=10&l=1&docID=txs hracd2588&secondary=false&u=CA&u=CLC&u=DLB&t=KW.

64. Ibid., 5. The two texts edited by Harris are *Pillars* and *Africa and Africans*.

65. Alford, "Early Intellectual Growth," 289; ibid., "A Prophet without Honor," 37, 39.

66. Harris, *Pillars*, 18.

67. Alford, "A Prophet without Honor," 223.

68. Ibid.

69. Harris, *Pillars*, 6–7; ibid., *Africa and Africans*, x.

70. Alford, "A Prophet without Honor," 91; Harris, *Pillars*, 7–8; ibid., *Africa and Africans*, x.

71. Harris, *Pillars*, 11–12.

72. Alford, "A Prophet without Honor," 229, 231. See also Harris, *Pillars*, 15. Harris cites a portion of a letter written by Hansberry's former professor and advisor at Harvard University, Department of Anthropology chair Ernest A. Hooton. It reads in part: "I am quite confident that no present-day scholar has anything like the knowledge of this field (prehistory of Africa) that Hansberry has developed. He has been unable to take the Ph.D. degree … because there is no university or institution … that has manifested a really profound interest in this subject."

73. Ibid.," 172–225. See also Runoko Rashidi, "William Leo Hansberry (1894–1965): Hero and Mentor of Dr. Chancellor Williams," in *Egypt: Child of Africa*, ed. Ivan Van Sertima (New Brunswick, NJ: Transaction, 1995), 25–26; Harris, *Africa and Africans*, ix–x.

74. Harris, *Pillars*, ix.

75. Hansberry's mentor and inspiration, W. E. B. Du Bois, had maintained this position in his 1915 publication of *The Negro*. See Du Bois, *The Negro*, 20–25.

76. William Leo Hansberry, "Africa in Stone Age Times," 1–4. The essay was assigned in 29-201 African History and 29-203 African Civilization, which courses Clarke taught during fall 1970, Department of Black and Puerto Rican Studies, Hunter College, City University of New York.

77. Hansberry, 4–5.

78. Ibid., 5–6.

79. Ibid., 6–8.

80. Ibid., 9.

81. Ibid.

82. Harris, *Pillars*, 112–150.

83. Ibid., 125.

84. Ibid., 126.

85. Ibid., 124, 128.

86. Ibid., 141.

87. Ibid., *Africa and Africans*, 19.

88. Ibid., 20, 21.

89. Ibid., 6.

90. Ibid., 24, 35, 44–45. The full discussion can be found on pages 32–63.

91. Person-Lynn, "On My Journey Now," 137. An example is captured in the acknowledgments of Kwando M. Kinshasa, *Emigration vs. Assimilation: The Debate in the African American Press, 1827–1861* (Jefferson, NC: McFarland, 1988), vii. Kinshasa noted that Clarke, "despite his own scholarly commitments and busy schedule, was gracious enough to advise me on the most salient aspects of my voluminous notes. His prodigious knowledge of work in my area of interest saved me inestimable time; his forthright and clear interpretation of the African's experience in the United States gave me enlightened inspiration." Kwame Wes Alford, in his acknowledgments in his dissertation, "A Prophet without Honor," ii, likewise noted that Clarke, one of Hansberry's former students, introduced him to the idea of studying Hansberry during a 1989 lecture in Washington, D.C., and later supported his effort to make the examination of Hansberry's academic and intellectual development the subject of dissertation research. "As a research assistant to Professor Clarke, I received constant advice, counsel, guidance and direction from him at critical junctures during the development of this project. Most importantly, I am indebted to this elder historian for introducing me to the Hansberry family, specifically Hansberry's two daughters, Gail and Kay."

Chapter Three

THE TEACHING
OF AFRICANA HISTORY

This is a most exciting time to live in—a time in which strong people can make meaningful contributions, history-changing contributions. I want to be strong; whether I change history or not, I want to be strong and awake.

—Gwendolyn Brooks in a letter to John Henrik Clarke, 1967[1]

I am still thinking about the Ph.D., and as soon as I have cleared my desk I plan to go into the matter of applying at some of the several schools which have programs that give credit for the work one has already done in life; and, as you know, I have already done work that is more than the equivalent of three Ph.D.'s.

—John Henrik Clarke, 1976[2]

By the late 1960s, the pressure of the citizenship rights movement, combined with the growing Afrikan nationalist demands for self-determination and cultural authenticity, had prompted frantic responses at the university level to accommodate the new insistence upon courses and professors who could teach the history and culture of Afrikan people in the United States. In 1966, for example, Clarke, at his Harlem office at the Heritage Training Program, part of a federally funded antipoverty initiative for the youths of central Harlem, received a letter from James N. Hantula, a teacher of Foreign Studies at the Department of Teaching, State College of Iowa in Cedar Falls, urgently requesting assistance. "Please forward the course outlines you have available as to the teaching of African and Afro-American history. I teach a class in Foreign Studies which focuses upon Africa and Asia and would appreciate any available help in better instructing my students as to the reality of African and Asian history."[3]

Clarke's reputation as an expert on Afrikan world history had been well established, and those in need of his expertise were clamoring for his help. Only two years earlier, Calvin H. Sinnette, M.D., who a year later would be at the Department of Pediatrics at the University College Hospital in Ibadan, Nigeria, had written a letter of recommendation in support of Clarke's application to the directorship of the Heritage Teaching Program. "For over twenty years he has been intimately associated with the creative literary and social thought of the Harlem community. ... As you know, Mr. Clarke has devoted many years of study in the fields of African and Afro-American history."[4] Clarke himself would remark some five years later: "I have related to the serious study of African and Afro-American history since high school, and I've taught the subject on a community level for over 20 years. I've done research in Africa & in the major archives and special collections in this country."[5] By contrast, very few of those who had been trained in the European academy possessed the preparation or the competence to teach the history that restive and aggrieved Afrikan university students were demanding. John Robinson, associate dean of the College of Arts and Sciences at the University of Nebraska-Lincoln, admitted as much in 1971 when he conceded: "At present the history taught is white history, and there are a whole host of ethnic groups it is proper to learn about."[6]

An example of Hantula's dilemma was to emerge in 1968 at the University of Nebraska-Lincoln, where, to meet Afrikan student demand, the College of Arts and Sciences introduced a single survey course titled "The Negro in American Society." The departments of history, English, and sociology jointly taught the course, parceling it out among them in five-week sessions. Further, in teaching its section, the history department opted to divide its responsibilities among six different professors.

While the course's proposed content revealed some sophistication in its conception—it covered historical, sociological, and literary dimensions of the Afrikan experience in the United States, including an examination of the continental Afrikan past—the fact that the initiative was shared by so many individuals and departments discloses the general prevailing ignorance among European academicians concerning Afrikan history and culture in the United States. In 1968, history department chairman Phillip Crowl, who created the course, defended the project by offering that the "interdepartmental approach was the most feasible approach to the make-up of the course."[7] Such a statement regarding its feasibility in actuality revealed that no single professor knew enough about the subject to teach the course competently or in depth. Spread over three departments and a veritable battalion of individuals, the rather embarrassing extent of their collective academic ignorance could, hopefully, be concealed. Clearly, such an enormous mobilization of resources required to teach a single survey course on Afrikan people underscored for those who reflected on such things two essential points. One was that the College of Arts and Sciences, and the university in general, were responding to enormous pressures. The other was that both were virtually incapable of offering more than a single, and somewhat superficial, class on the subject.

By February 1969, one of the professors participating in the effort frankly—although perhaps unwittingly—admitted this. While some, such as sociology professor Jack Siegman, were suggesting the course "opens up the possibility of holding smaller classes and going into more detail in different departments," Robert Knoll of the English department strongly disagreed.[8] There was very little that could be taught about Afrikan history and culture in the United States, in Knoll's view, because it was simply "not a very rich subject." Indeed, he opined, "If you put it into three departments, you would have three thin subjects. Consequently the student would have to take three thin courses to get what he is now getting in a single course." Knoll, further, ridiculed the notion of expanding an Africana Studies curriculum in various departments as "silly." Knoll's statements, however, underscored his ignorance as much as they did his arrogance and bigotry. Despite the fact that 350 students were enrolled in the course, Knoll claimed that it garnered no serious interest, and that it should be temporary, lasting no longer than three to four years. Nor should the university encourage the teaching of courses on Afrikan subjects, he contended. "Not every university should have a black studies program," he declared, while admitting significantly, "We don't have the faculty or experts to teach a black studies program professionally."[9]

Indeed, when the college dropped the course (which had been renamed "Black Experience in America") two years later due to problems of coordination between the three departments, history chairman Crowl admitted the absence of academic competence informed its unwieldy multidisciplinary design. Undoubtedly, part of the problem lay in the fact that Crowl's department had no Afrikan faculty (who presumably would have demonstrated some measure of professional expertise in the subject area), a critical issue in Afrikan student demands.[10] At the time of the course's inauguration, he confessed, "I didn't have a staff member with sufficient background in Negro history to teach a class in it, nor were there funds to get a specialist. So I called on other departments to share the load."[11]

In the matter of academic competence and preparation, however, the University of Nebraska-Lincoln was not alone. In New York City, Clarke found himself urgently courted by administrators at Hunter College of the City University of New York. He was being sought specifically for consultation on the college's new initiative, a Department of Black and Puerto Rican Studies, which was to begin operation in the 1969–1970 academic year. In an April 1969 letter from the office of the college's president, sociology professor Mary H. Diggs informed Clarke that administrators were seeking advice as to how to best develop and implement the new initiative. In a handwritten message at the bottom of the typewritten letter, Diggs urged Clarke to come at least as a consultant for part of an all-day meeting that was to be held to discuss what was needed for the project.[12]

Clarke's success that year as the special consultant and chief developer of the 18-week, 108-episode television history series on WCBS TV, "Black Heritage: A History of Afro-Americans," may have played a role. Premiering in January, the half hour broadcasts aired daily, Monday through Friday from 9:00 to 9:30 a.m., and Saturday from 7:30 to 8:00 a.m. The series generated enormous public attention in New York City. By late March, according to newspaper reports, classrooms in more than forty public schools, colleges, and universities, as well as some community groups, were watching the programs, which were "entirely written, produced, directed and narrated by Black authorities."[13] Clarke himself was pleased that

"Everybody is impressed with the television series ... with the exception of Roy Wilkins who has been attacking me and the other developers of the program with both feet and an extra pair of hands."[14] While the national NAACP executive director, a rabid integrationist, vehemently denounced the series as the product of "the present-day propagandists for Black Separatism,"[15] the National Association of Television and Radio Announcers in August awarded Clarke a citation for meritorious achievement in educational television.[16]

Table 3.1
John Henrik Clarke's Career as Writer, Editor, and Producer, 1947–1983 (Selected)[17]

Year	Role	Project	Medium	Location
1947–49	Book Review Editor	Negro History Bulletin	Journal	Wash., D.C.
1949–51	Cofounder/ Associate Editor	Harlem Quarterly	Magazine	New York, N.Y.
1957–58	Feature Writer	Pittsburgh Courier	Newspaper	Pittsburgh, Pa.
1958	Feature Writer	Ghana Evening News	Newspaper	Accra, Ghana
1959	Editor	African Heritage	Magazine	New York, N.Y.
1961–1970s?	Syndicated Columnist	African World Bookshelf	Associated Negro Press/World Mutual Exchange, International Features	Chicago, Ill.
1962–83	Associate Editor	Freedomways	Magazine	New York, N.Y.
1968–69	Consultant/ Producer/ Board of Directors Member	Black Heritage: A History of Afro-Americans	Television	New York, N.Y.

Further, in addition to his work since 1962 as an associate editor of the influential *Freedomways* magazine, and numerous contributions to scholarly, intellectual, literary, and popular publications on at least three continents,[18] Clarke had already published *The Lives of Great African Chiefs* (1958),[19] *Harlem: A Community in Transition* (1964), the European bestseller *Harlem U.S.A.: The Story of a City Within A City* (1965), *American Negro Short Stories* (1966),[20] and the celebrated *William Styron's Nat Turner: Ten Black Writers Respond* (1968). In 1968, he also received the Carter G. Woodson Award for Creative Contribution in Editing.[21] By October 1969, Clarke's *Malcolm X: The Man and His Times* would be released,[22] and his *History and Culture of Africa* would be published that year. Clarke was also working with Amy Jacques Garvey on what would become *Marcus Garvey and the Vision of Africa*, which would be published five years later.[23]

Table 3.2
*John Henrik Clarke's Honors and Awards, 1968–1977
(Selected)[24]*

Year	Award	Organization/ Institution
1967	Carter G. Woodson Award for Research in Afro-American History	?
1968	Carter G. Woodson Award for Creative Contribution in Editing	?
1969	Citation for Meritorious Achievement in Educational Television	National Association of Television and Radio Announcers
1970	Doctor of Humane Letters	University of Denver
1974–77	Associate in the University Seminar on African-American Studies	Columbia University
1971	Carter G. Woodson Award for Distinguished and Outstanding Work in the Teaching of History	African-American Historical Association
1975	Achievement Award for Outstanding Work in African and Afro-American Studies	Black Studies Union, William Patterson College
1977	Elizabeth Catlett Mora Award of Excellence	National Conference of Artists

Among his many organizational affiliations, he was an active member of the International Congress of Africanists since its founding in 1962, and he had delivered a major paper at its international conference in Dakar, Senegal, in 1967, two years earlier.[25] Moreover, he had had—in addition to his work at the Heritage Teaching Program—prior experience in setting up an Africana Studies program. Twelve years earlier, from 1957 to 1959, he had been involved in the development of the African Study Center at the New School for Social Research, and he had been the assistant to its director from 1958 to 1960. He had also been an occasional lecturer in Africana history there from 1956 to 1958.[26]

Thus, it came as no surprise that a month after Diggs's April 1969 letter, Clarke's involvement had expanded from mere consultant to adjunct professor and chief architect of the new department's Africana Studies curriculum. Hunter College President Robert D. Cross offered the fifty-four-year-old scholar a department position for the 1969–1970 academic year at a salary of $15,000. He was to teach two courses per semester. Cross added: "We are counting very much on the advice you can give us on the developing character of this innovative department."[27] Clarke readily accepted the offer, noting he had agreed to teach a course on continental Afrikan history and another on continental Afrikan culture for the first semester, while he would be teaching two courses on U.S. Afrikan history and culture for the second.[28] He later explained to colleague and friend Adelaide Cromwell Hill,[29] a professor at the African Studies Center at Boston University, what Cross's reference to advice meant. "I will assist in developing this new department in order that it maybe [sic] a model for teaching programs in African and Afro-American history and in Puerto Rican history and culture for the City Universities [sic] of New York," he wrote. "I will also be developing teaching materials in these areas, continuing the kind of work that I started in HARYOU-ACT."[30]

HARYOU-ACT, or Harlem Youth Opportunities Unlimited-Associated Community Teams, was an antipoverty program established in 1964 through a partnership of the City of New York and the national government to address issues of poverty for the youths of central Harlem.[31] Clarke was hired in June 1964 to the Heritage Teaching Program of its Community Action Institute, where he worked until December 1968.[32] As the program's director, he had sole responsibility for developing curricula for most of the teaching programs. He further served as consultant on history teaching materials for both HARYOU-ACT's After-School Studies and Head Start Programs. Among other things, Clarke completed a curriculum guide titled "Harlem, A Dynamic Community," a ten-session orientation course on Harlem that was the first of its kind.[33] But they were Clarke's curriculum guides and bibliographies for the study and teaching of U.S. and continental Afrikan history that were much in demand by the public at large. His work at Hunter College—that is, his teaching and his designing curricula for the study and teaching of Africana history and culture—would be a continuation of what he had established during his four years at HARYOU-ACT.

At the same time that Hunter College was recruiting Clarke, James Turner, director of the Afro-American Studies Center at Cornell University, was also making his bid. Turner, as a graduate student, had first been introduced to Clarke's work at the Heritage Teaching Program in Harlem. Moreover, Clarke had recruited Turner to participate in the successful Black Heritage television series.[34] A mere nine days following Cross's offer, and three days after Clarke had accepted it, Turner was offering Clarke an immediate position as associate professor for a three-year period. Clarke would teach two courses, a lecture course and a seminar in areas of Africana history and literature, and his salary would be in the range of $18,000 a year. "I'd like to emphasize that we would arrange, with your appointment, every opportunity for you to have a maximum amount of time to finish your important writings and research," Turner added. "Because both I and the students view your value as both a teacher and a black scholar, we would draw on the built-in flexibility of the program to arrange assistance for you in clerical and research assistant areas from among the black students in the program."[35] Clarke would come to Cornell University's Africana Studies and Research Center in February 1970 as the Carter G. Woodson Distinguished Visiting Professor of African History. He would resign three years later, in 1973, the same year he would become a full professor at Hunter College.[36] Indeed, by 1972, Clarke was relating to the Nigerian scholar and friend E. U. Essien-Udom that among his various scholarly and organizational activities he was teaching five courses a week: three at Hunter and two at Cornell.[37]

Such a teaching schedule was an accustomed workload for the indefatigable fifty-seven-year-old professor. Seven years earlier, Clarke had remarked to a close friend, the peripatetic writer, actor, and political activist Julian Mayfield, that "With only two teachers I am conducting twelve classes at HARYOU-ACT in the Heritage Program."[38]

In the fall semester of 1969, the launching of Hunter College's Department of Black and Puerto Rican Studies, the department's brochure listed Clarke as an adjunct professor. He was teaching two of the three Afrikan courses offered (the other was in Afrikan literature). One of Clarke's three-credit courses was titled "African History from the Origin of Man to 1600 A.D." Its advertisement read: "African history as a part of world history emphasizing the role that the Africans played in the development of other nations and civilizations." The other three-credit course, titled "African Civilization to 1900," had a brief description that read: "The evolution, interrelationships and influence of elements of African culture for more than two-thousand years." In addition, the department offered three courses in Puerto Rican Studies and a remaining five courses in interdisciplinary areas, eleven courses in all.[39]

With the enormous energy and productivity that had always characterized his approach to creative and scholarly output, Clarke threw himself not only into teaching, but also into developing and introducing a body of new courses at both Hunter College and Cornell University to build the nascent discipline of Africana Studies/Africalogy. A sample of his courses include:

Hunter College

- Fall 1969, African History From the Origin of Man to 1600 A.D.
- Fall 1969, African Civilization to 1900
- Proposed/no date, African History—The Main Currents, from the Origin of Man to the Present

- Fall 1970, African History for Teachers: African History—the Main Currents, etc.
- Fall 1970/Spring 1971, The Teaching of Afro-American History
- Spring 1971, African American History from 1619 to the Present
- Spring 1981, Slavery: A Historical Analysis
- Fall 1983, African-American History I: From Slavery to Emancipation
- No date, African-American History II: From the Reconstruction to the Present
- Fall 1983, African and African-American Resistance Movements in the 19th Century
- Fall 1985/Spring 1986, Dimensions of World History

Cornell University

- Fall 1970 Seminar, Nineteenth Century Resistance Movements: African and Afro-American
- Fall 1970, History of Independent African Nations to 1800 A.D.
- Spring 1971 Seminar, Men and Movements in the Black Urban Ghetto [later introduced at Hunter College]
- Proposed/Spring 1971, The Africans in the Making of the New World, i.e., South America, the Caribbean Islands and the United States
- Fall 1971/Spring 1972 Graduate Seminar, African Heritage: Historiography and Sources; Fall 1971 Seminar, A Study of the Historical Writings of Edward Wilmot Blyden, Sir Harry Hamilton Johnson and George Shepperson; Spring 1972 Seminar, A Study of the Historical Writings of Carter G. Woodson, W. E. B. Du Bois and Basil Davidson
- Spring 1972, Comparative Political History of the African Diaspora[40]

Far from being a thin subject, Clarke's syllabi and study guides demonstrated mastery of a subject of great depth, substance, and complexity. His study guides for the first semester of teaching, supplementary readings to his initial two classes, "African History from the Origin of Man to 1600 A.D." and "African Civilization to 1900," were twenty in number and totaled some 100 pages. In sum, they constituted a veritable textbook on Afrikan history, clearly outlining his conception of the continental experience for that vast period. Clarke indicated the study guides were copyrighted material that formed the substance of a forthcoming book titled *The History and Culture of Africa*.[41] They covered the history of Afrika from the dawn of humankind to the dawn of Afrikan independence in the mid twentieth century: (1) Africa and the Origin of Man; (2) The Beginnings of Organized Societies; (3) Egypt, the Golden Age; (4) The Rise of Kush; (5) Ethiopia; (6) Kush and Egypt: The End of the Golden Age; (7) Africa and the Rise of Christianity; (8) Africa and the Rise of Islam; (9) The Rise of Ancient Ghana; (10) The Rise of Mali; (11) The Rise of Songhay; (12) The Collapse of the Western Sudan; (13) The Slave Trade Begins; (14) West Africa in Turmoil, 1591–1700; (15) Africa and the New World; (16) Extension of the Slave Trade, 1500 A.D.—1700 A.D.; (17) West African States in the Colonial Era; (18) East and Central African States in Transition; (19) Nineteenth Century Resistance; (20) Africa: The Twentieth Century Awakening.[42]

Indeed, in the fall semester of 1973, a brief four years later, during which time Clarke had advanced from adjunct to full professor, the syllabus for one of his first two courses, "African History from the Origin of Man to 1600 A.D.," stretched to forty-nine pages. The required reading list contained thirteen books, all of them by Afrikan authors from the United States, Afrika, the Caribbean, and South America. His bibliography of suggested readings totaled seventy-one books and pamphlets, seventeen of them by Afrikan authors from the United States, Afrika, and the Caribbean. Clarke also listed five unpublished articles by one of his former teachers, the great Afrikan anthropologist and historian William Leo Hansberry of Howard University. He suggested nine other books as texts his students should independently read. Of those, five books, published from 1970 to 1972, were by Clarke's best friend and colleague, the Harlem-based Afrikan historian and Egyptologist Yosef A. A. ben Jochannan.[43]

Clarke's syllabus for his fall 1970 seminar course at Cornell University's Africana Studies and Research Center, "Nineteenth Century Resistance Movements: African and Afro-American," presented a sophisticated examination of contemporaneous Afrikan liberation movements—both armed and intellectual—in the United States and in western, eastern, and southern Afrika from the eighteenth through the twentieth centuries. He explained the course's intent was "to examine in detail the development of resistance movements in Africa and in Black America and to show how these movements related, one to the other, even when there was no direct communication between them." His bibliography for required reading contained twelve books in all: six books on the relevant continental Afrikan history and six books on Afrikans in the United States. His suggested reading list totaled twenty-six books and six volumes of a journal titled *Tarikh*, which covered continental Afrikan historical and political issues.[44]

Through his syllabi and lectures, Clarke was not only exposing his students to the depth and complexity of Afrikan history, its relation to world history, and the organic interrelationship of Afrikan history in the Americas and on the Afrikan continent. He was also preparing them to analyze, interpret, and write logical and academically compelling Afrika-centered history. Thus, his fall 1971/spring 1972 course at Cornell, "African Heritage: Historiography and Sources," was a graduate readings and problems seminar. Its purpose was to explore issues in historical method, inquiry, and interpretation through critically examining the writings on Afrika of six Afrikan and European historians: Edward Wilmot Blyden (1832–1912),[45] Sir Harry Hamilton Johnston (1858–1927),[46] George Shepperson (b. 1922),[47] Carter G. Woodson (1875–1950),[48] W. E. B. Du Bois (1868–1963),[49] and Basil Davidson (b. 1914).[50] "These writers," Clarke explained, "were chosen because of the diversity of their approaches to the history and culture of African people."[51]

The student's task included carefully examining each writer's perspective "in relationship to the time in which they lived and wrote" and assessing their work in light of new evidence that may tend either to support or invalidate their conclusions. The outcome for the student was to develop "new and more creative approaches to African history and historiography" and to employ "new attitudes and research tools that will bring forth new dimensions and insights into

African History and culture." Indeed, "in their research the students are expected to take *an Afro-centric view of history*"[52] (added emphasis). That is, Clarke explained, students were expected to develop a logical and "non-western point of view that is academically defensible." Clarke's bibliography of major works by each of the authors totaled ninety-three in all: twenty-five by Blyden (and another nine about him), twenty-six by Johnston (and another three about him), twelve by Shepperson, six by Woodson, ten by Du Bois (another two about him, and a selected list of thirty-one articles by him on Afrika), and fourteen by Davidson. With the added fourteen books and thirty-one articles, the bibliography totaled 138 items.[53]

Table 3.3
John Henrik Clarke's Required and Suggested Course Readings at Hunter College (New York City), and Cornell University (Ithaca, N.Y.), 1970–1986 (Selected)[54]

Course	Year	Required Books and Other Materials	Suggested Books and Other Materials
Nineteenth Century Resistance Movements: African and Afro-American	1970	12	32
African Heritage: Historiography and Sources	1971–1972	138	
African History from the Origin of Man to 1600 A.D.	1973	13	85
African-American History I: From Slavery to Emancipation	1983	21	68
African History from 1600 A.D. to the Present	1984	6	68
Dimensions of World History	1985–1986	26	11

It is no wonder, then, that Turner, founding chair of the Africana Studies and Research Center at Cornell, was later to remark that the venerable scholar was "one of the principal intellectual and academic mentors in Africana studies." His contribution to the discipline, and to the intellectual development of a generation of scholars, was seminal, and his research and historical insights were original. "Dr. Clarke was instrumental in producing many widely circulated documents and papers on African world history and on African-American history. His papers provided primary reference sources that were not usually available in the established literature, in either world history or American history."[55] Likewise, Columbia University's Department of Anthropology chair Elliott P. Skinner, apparently in a letter of support for Clarke's promotion to full professorship, wrote in 1973 to Tilden J. LeMell of Hunter College's Department of Black and Puerto Rican Studies: "I suspect that Professor Clarke has participated in almost every important philosophical, political, social, and cultural movement affecting the lives of Blacks in America. He thus brings to his lecture a background unparalleled among his contemporaries."[56]

Table 3.4
John Henrik Clarke's Teaching Career, 1956–1988 (Selected)[57]

Years	Appointment	Institution	Discipline
1956–1958	Lecturer	New School for Social Research	Africana history
1957–1960	Developer/ Assistant to the Director	African Study Center, New School for Social Research	Continental African history
1962–1963	Instructor	Malverne High School (Adult Education Division)	Africana history
1964–1968	Director	Heritage Teaching Program, Community Action Institute, HARYOU-ACT	Africana history/Africana studies
1969	Instructor	Head Start Training Program, New York University	Africana history
1969	Lecturer	New School for Social Research	Africana history
1969–1988	Professor (adjunct–full)	Department of Black and Puerto Rican Studies, Hunter College, CUNY	Africana Studies/ Africana history

1970–1973	Visiting Professor	Africana Studies and Research Center, Cornell University	Africana Studies/ Africana history
1979–1980	Chair	Department of Black and Puerto Rican Studies, Hunter College, CUNY	Africana Studies/ Africana history

Fourteen years after he had begun his career at Hunter College, Clarke's syllabus on Afrikan history in the United States to the period of Reconstruction stretched to thirty-four pages. As essential background to the exploration of Afrikan history under the Anglo-American regime beginning in 1619, the first seven lectures in his fall 1983 course for both undergraduates and teachers covered Afrikan encounters with Mediterranean Europe dating from Egyptian antiquity, theoretical discussions on the Afrikan basis of world history, and the motives for the European distortion and excision of the Afrikan role in both world and European history; explored the West Afrikan coastal state contacts with European nations in the fifteenth century; examined the political, economic, and cultural developments in Europe that led to global expansion and conquest; discussed the evidence for the pre-Columbian Afrikan presence and contact with the indigenous peoples in North, Central, and South America, Mexico, and the Caribbean islands; probed Afrikan participation in the Spaniard imperialist penetration of the Americas during the fifteenth and sixteenth centuries; explained the competition among European nations for territorial acquisitions in the Americas and the uses of European labor within Europe that prefigured the exploitation of Afrikan labor and the rationalization of the slave trade; and considered the impact of the destruction of the indigenous populations of the Americas on the European shift to the exploitation of Afrikans to support economic imperialistic operations.[58]

As was typical of his other courses, the sixty-eight-year-old professor's reading lists were extensive. Clarke's required reading list consisted of eleven books and ten pamphlets, all written principally by Afrikan authors in the United States. In addition, his bibliography contained three suggested reading lists, one bibliography that focused on race and racism, and one that focused on Afrikan history before Afrikan captivity under Anglo-American domination. His bibliography in the latter category contained five books. His first suggested reading list contained eighteen books, all save one by Afrikan authors in the United States or the Afrikan continent. His second suggested reading list by European authors contained twenty-two books. He suggested students look at ten books under the category of race and racism, and another thirteen books in a third suggested reading list. Indeed, his entire bibliography, which included notes, was seven pages for a total of eighty-nine books and pamphlets.[59] Clearly, Clarke's more than two-decades long career as a book review editor for the *Negro History Bulletin* and his own syndicated column, "African World Bookshelf," had given him an impressive command of the literature on the subject.[60]

Two years later, and three years before he would retire after nearly two decades of teaching at Hunter,[61] Clarke inaugurated an ambitious two-semester survey course in the emerging discipline, a logical extension of his work in teaching Africana history, titled "Dimensions of World History." Its revolutionary significance lay in the fact that it represented a uniquely Afrikan interpretation of the history of the world. But further, it implicitly asserted that the scope of inquiry of the discipline of Africana Studies knew no bounds, that it was unapologetically appropriating previously-held sacrosanct territory, that Afrikan scholarship and teaching would not defer to traditional European disciplinary boundaries or interpretations within the academy, and that everything—including the history of European and other non-Afrikan peoples—was within its authority to examine, correct, and explain. Indeed, the course signified that the discipline was boldly contesting for intellectual and academic space, asserting its right to epistemologically reorder the understanding of the world experience from its own unique and particular, albeit truthful, Afrika-grounded vantage.

In his fall 1985 syllabus's course description, Clarke noted that the class would present a significant departure from the Eurocentric interpretation of world history that "in most cases, is the story of Europeans and the peoples they conquered." To the contrary, part of "the purpose of this course is to show that much of what we think of as the foundation of World History was firmly developed long before the first nation-state appeared in what would be called Europe." While the course does not intend to "downgrade Europe at all," it does intend to place Europe's role in its proper focus "in relation to World History and the achievements of other peoples and nations. This will be a comparative study of the great ages of history and the role that non-European people played in bringing these into being." Indeed, Clarke remarked in lecture notes to the first session, "we need to consider that we live in a European-conceived intellectual universe. This is a condition that has prevailed in the world for at least five-hundred years and the interpretations of history and all other subjects in the academic community have depended on this fact." He continued, warning his students: "In this course we will be dealing with an approach that might be strange to you. We will begin by dealing with the world before Europe, and most of the course will be focused on the time when the concept of Europe did not prevail over the world."[62]

Clarke announced in his syllabus that some of the main sessions of the two-semester course would include:

- The First Light of Humanity: Civilization Begins
- Africa and Western Asia: The Civilizations of the Great Rivers
- Ancient India and China: Culture, Trade, and Relationships
- The Non-Western Foundations of Western Civilizations
- The Mediterranean World in Ancient Times
- The Impact of the Rise and Fall of the Roman Empire
- The Islamic Challenge to Europe
- The Ages of Darkness and Light: The European Middle Ages and the Rise of the Western Sudan
- The Crusades and the Reawakening of Europe
- Slavery, Racism, and the Rise of the Myth of Western Civilization[63]

The course's second semester promised to examine, "in detail, the impact of the rise of Europe in the fifteenth and sixteenth centuries and its impact on the non-Western world." This period in history, which ushered in the slave trade, colonialism, and the emergence of modern racism, "were the years when Europeans not only colonized the world, they also colonized information about the world. In the next five hundred years, the control of information and images helped the Europeans control the world."[64]

Interesting with respect to Clarke's historiographical approach to world history are his bibliography and sources. Of the twenty-seven books cited as sources for his lectures for the first half of the course, Afrikan authors from the United States, South America, the Caribbean, and Afrika wrote nineteenth of them. The authors included Yosef A. A. ben Jochannan, J. C. de Graft-Johnson, Cheikh Anta Diop, W. E. B. Du Bois, Drusilla Dunjee Houston, John G. Jackson, George G. M. James, Runoko Rashidi, J. A. Rogers, Edward Scobie, Ivan Van Sertima, Chancellor Williams, Eric Williams, and Larry Williams.[65] In the second half of the course, Afrikans from the United States, South America, the Caribbean, and Afrika wrote two of the three required readings, seven of eleven suggested readings, two of five main sources for his lectures, and at least ten of twenty-three materials held on library reserve.[66]

Of note is the fact that this course, like many others Clarke created at the university level, was "designed for ... potential teachers of the subject."[67] But the scholar's concern with the teaching of Africana history, and the teaching and training of teachers, long preceded his work as a university professor.

Notes

1. Gwendolyn Brooks, letter to John Henrik Clarke, 21 June 1967, JHCP, SCRBC.

2. John Henrik Clarke, letter to Julian Mayfield, 26 October 1976, JHCP, SCRBC.

3. James N. Hantula, letter to John Henrik Clarke, 16 February 1966, JHCP, SCRBC.

4. Calvin H. Sinnette, letter to Cyril D. Tyson, 20 August 1964, JHCP, SCRBC. Among other things, Clarke was a cofounder and associate editor of the *Harlem Quarterly*, 1949–1951; research director of the first African Heritage Exposition, 1959; vice president of the Association of the Study of Negro Life and History, 1949–1955. See "Who'sWho in America 38th Edition,"Galley Proof, JHCP, SCRBC.

5. Hunter College Staff Personnel Record, 25 June 1969, JHCP, SCRBC. Note that some of what Clarke called major archives and special collections, such as the Schomburg and Rogers papers, were either developed by Afrikans or were under Afrikan control.

6. Bob Waddell, "Popular Black Studies Course Dropped Because of a 'Lack of Coordination,'" *Daily Nebraskan*, 6 July 1971, 4.

7. "Departments Join, Offer Negro History Course," *Daily Nebraskan*, 7 October 1968.

8. Knoll was eventually to become Varner Professor Emeritus at the University of Nebraska-Lincoln. He was named Nebraska Professor of the Year in 1988, and is said to have had a long and distinguished career of teaching and scholarship at the university. He joined the faculty in 1950 and retired in 1990. He was a Fulbright Professor in Austria and a fellow of the National Humanities Institute. Interestingly, Knoll earned his B.A. from University of Nebraska-Lincoln, and went on to earn his M.A. and Ph.D. from the University of Minnesota. See David Ochsner, ed., *A Century of Achievement: One Hundred Years of Graduate Education, Research, and Creative Activity* (Lincoln: University of Nebraska, 2001), 43.

9. Jim Pedersen, "Interdisciplinary Course Status of 'Negro Culture' Questioned," *Daily Nebraskan*, 21 February 1969, cover.

10. The Afro-American Collegiate Society, led by University of Nebraska Law School senior Wayne Williams, organized specifically to force the university administration to, among its twelve demands, radically increase Afrikan student enrollment, aggressively hire and promote Afrikan faculty, and establish a viable Africana Studies program. Their demands included that "black-oriented courses dealing with areas of literature, culture, history and institutional racism, taught by black professors, be incorporated into the history courses now being taught at the University. ... That the black man's true role in history be incorporated into the history courses now being taught." Williams, Lonetta Harrold, and Ron Lee led negotiations with the UNL administration. Jimmi Smith, a graduate student at the time, notes that the key to the AACS's success was Williams's strategic organizing of the Afrikan student athletes, who engaged in protests and demonstrations, and who threatened to go home when the administration initially refused to meet their demands. Smith recalled it was their threat to quit the university that galvanized the UNL administration to engage in serious discussions and to take some positive action. See Jimmi Smith, interview by Institute for Ethnic Studies, "The History of the Institute for Ethnic Studies," 7 June 2001, IES Archives. See also "Afro Society's Twelve Demands to Bring University Response," *Daily Nebraskan*, 21 April 1969, cover; John Dvorak, "NU Students Protest Administration's Inability to Provide Relevant Programs," *Daily Nebraskan*, 16 April 1969, cover; John Dvorak, "Black Students,

Administration Meet; Regent Talk Scheduled for Saturday," *Daily Nebraskan*, 18 April 1969; "Administration Meets with Black Candidate," *Daily Nebraskan*, 21 April 1969, 3; and "Black Students Skeptical, Will Adopt Wait-and-See Attitude—Williams," *Daily Nebraskan*, 23 April 1969, cover.

11. Waddell, "Popular Black Studies," 4.

12. Mary H. Diggs, letter to John Henrik Clarke, 17 April 1969, JHCP, SCRBC.

13. *New York Amsterdam News*, 29 March 1969, and the *Queens Voice*, 14 March 1969, JHCP, SCRBC.

14. John Henrik Clarke, letter to Calvin H. Sinnette, 8 February 1969, JHCP, SCRBC. Clarke noted the series was in its fourth week.

15. Roy Wilkins, 5-page draft letter to the editor, n.d., JHCP, SCRBC.

16. John Henrik Clarke, "Contemporary Authors" Biographical Form, n.d., JHCP, SCRBC. See also ibid., Curriculum Vitae, JHCP, SCRBC.

17. Ibid., "A Selected List of My Most Important Works from 1939 to the Present Time," n.d., JHCP, SCRBC; ibid., "Contemporary Authors" Biographical Form, n.d., JHCP, SCRBC; ibid., "RE: Curriculum Guide to the Study and Teaching of African and Afro-American History; An Account of Applicant's Career as a Writer and a Teacher," 1966, JHCP, SCRBC; ibid., "Who'sWho in America 38th ed."Galley Proofs, JHCP, SCRBC; ibid., Curriculum Vitae; ibid., Hunter College Staff Personnel Record, 25 June 1969, JHCP, SCRBC.

18. Some of these, dating back to 1939, included *Journal of Negro Education*, *Transition*, *Présence Africaine* (Paris, France), *Journal of Human Relations*, *Negro Digest*, *Africa Today*, *Pan-African Journal*, *Freedomways*, *Phylon*, *Crisis*, *Negro History Bulletin*, *Opportunity*, *New Horizons*, *The Protestant Digest*, *Harlem Quarterly*, *Educational Forum*, *Scribe*, *Points* (Paris, France), *The African Drum* (Johannesburg, South Africa), *Fantasma* (London, England), *The New African* (London, England), *New World* (Georgetown, Guyana), *Midwest Journal*, and *Black Voices*. In addition, Clarke also contributed to various Afrikan newspapers, including the *Chicago Defender*, the *Pittsburgh Courier*, the *Evening News* (Accra, Ghana), and the *New York Amsterdam News*. See Clarke, "A Selected List."

19. This was serially published in the *Pittsburgh Courier*.

20. Clarke wrote of this anthology: "This is the first anthology of American Negro Short Stories to be published, in this or any other country." See Clarke, "RE: Curriculum Guide."

21. Ibid., Curriculum Vitae.

22. W. E. B. Du Bois's widow, Shirley Graham Du Bois, may well have been the inspiration for Clarke's work on Malcolm. Four years earlier, living in Ghana and working in President Kwame Nkrumah's administration in the capital city of Accra, Mrs. Du Bois wrote a letter to Clarke, dated 27 February 1965, seeking his collaboration in producing a work on Malcolm. This was only days after Malcolm's assassination in New York City. Nkrumah was overthrown the following year in a coup d'état backed by the U.S. CIA, and Mrs. Du Bois was forced to flee to Cairo.

23. John Henrik Clarke, letter to Hoyt W. Fuller, 5 October 1969, JHCP, SCRBC; ibid., *The Lives of Great African Chiefs* (Pittsburgh: Pittsburgh Courier Publishing Company, 1958); ibid., *Harlem: A Community in Transition* (New York: Citadel Press, 1964); ibid., *Harlem U.S.A.: The Story of a City Within A City* (Berlin, West Germany: Seven Seas, 1965); ibid., *American Negro Short Stories* (New York: Hill and Wang, 1966); ibid., *William Styron's Nat Turner: Ten Black Writer's Respond* (Boston: Beacon Press, 1968); ibid., *Malcolm X: The Man and His Times* (New York: Collier Books, 1969); ibid., *History and Culture of Africa* (Hempstead, NY: Aevac Inc. Educational Publishers, 1969); ibid., with Amy Jacques Garvey, *Marcus Garvey and the Vision of Africa* (New York: Vintage Books, 1974).

24. Ibid., "A selected list"; ibid., "Contemporary Authors"; ibid., "RE: Curriculum Guide"; ibid., "An Account"; ibid., "Who'sWho"; ibid., Curriculum Vitae; ibid., Hunter College.

25. *The Columbus Times*, vol. 9, no. 16, Fifth week of January 1980, JHCP, SCRBC. See also Clarke, Curriculum Vitae.

26. Clarke, "Who'sWho." See also ibid., Curriculum Vitae.

27. Robert D. Cross, letter to John Henrik Clarke, 14 May 1969, JHCP, SCRBC.

28. John Henrik Clarke, letter to Robert D. Cross, 20 May 1969, JHCP, SCRBC.

29. Hill was the granddaughter of John Wesley Cromwell, a founding member of the prestigious American Negro Academy established in 1897. Cromwell and Arthur A. Schomburg, one of Clarke's most important mentors and teachers, were close friends and colleagues. Thirty years his senior, Cromwell served as a surrogate father to the younger Schomburg. This relationship is an important clue to Clarke's friendship with Hill. See Elinor Des Verney Sinnette, *Arthur Alfonso Schomburg: Black Bibliophile and Collector* (New York

and Detroit: The New York Public Library and Wayne State University Press, 1989), 4, 51.

30. John Henrik Clarke, letter to Adelaide Cromwell Hill, 11 June 1969, JHCP, SCRBC.

31. "History of HARYOU-ACT," JHCP, SCRBC.

32. Hunter College Staff Personnel Record, 25 June 1969, JHCP, SCRBC.

33. *Columbus Times*, January 1980. See also Clarke, "RE: Curriculum Guide."

34. Turner was one among a panel of students who were to discuss in three episodes reflections on past student movements, racism and education, and the future of the Afrikan student movement in the United States. See "Syllabus of Black Heritage: A History of Afro-Americans," Office of Radio and Television, Columbia University, n.d., JHCP, SCRBC.

35. James Turner, letter to John Henrik Clarke, May 23, 1969, JHCP, SCRBC.

36. *Columbus Times.*

37. John Henrik Clarke, letter to E. U. Essien-Udom, 29 February 1972, JHCP, SCRBC.

38. Ibid., letter to Julian Mayfield, 25 August 1965, JHCP, SCRBC.

39. September 1969 brochure for the Department of Black and Puerto Rican Studies, Hunter College, City University of New York, JHCP, SCRBC.

40. JHCP, SCRBC.

41. John Henrik Clarke, *History and Culture of Africa* (Hempstead, NY: Aevac Inc. Educational Publishers, 1969).

42. Ibid., "Study Guides in the History, Civilization, and Culture of Africa, for students in courses 29-201 and 29-203 (African History from the Origin of Man to 1600 A.D. and African Civilization to 1900 A.D.)," Department of Black and Puerto Rican Studies, Hunter College, the City University of New York, 1969, JHCP, SCRBC.

43. Ibid., "African History From the Origin of Man to 1600 A.D.," Department of Black and Puerto Rican Studies, Hunter College of the City University of New York, fall Semester 1973, JHCP, SCRBC. Yosef ben Jochannan's Alkebulan Books Associates, the publishing arm of his Alkebulan Foundation, located at 209 West 125th Street in Harlem, published the five texts, which were listed as follows: *African Origins of the Major Western Religions* (1970); *Africa: Mother of Western Civilization* (1971); *Black Man of the Nile and His Family* (1972); with George Simmonds, *The Black Man's North and East Africa* (1971); and *Cultural Genocide in the Black and African Studies Curriculum* (1972). Among ben Jochannan's forty-two volumes since 1939,

the first three texts are recognized classics in Africana historiography of the Afrika-centered school.

44. John Henrik Clarke, "Nineteenth Century Resistance Movements: African and Afro-American," Africana Studies and Research Center, Cornell University, Seminar Course, fall Semester 1970, JHCP, SCRBC. *Tarikh*, a continental Afrikan history journal published in London by the Historical Society of Nigeria, began publication November 1965.

45. Clarke wrote: "Dr. Blyden was born in 1832 at St. Thomas in the Virgin Islands. In 1847 he went to New York City, hoping to enroll at one of the colleges there, but because of the color prejudice he was unable to enroll in any college. The New York Colonization Society offered him a free passage to Liberia. He arrived in this African country in 1850 and made it his home." John Henrik Clarke, "African Heritage: Historiography and Sources; A Study of the Historical Writings of Edward Wilmot Blyden, Sir Harry Hamilton Johnston, George Shepperson, Carter G. Woodson, W. E. B. Du Bois, and Basil Davidson," Africana Studies and Research Center, Cornell University, fall Semester 1971 and spring Semester 1972, 8–9, JHCP, SCRBC.

46. Clarke wrote: "Sir Harry Hamilton Johnston was considered to be the one man who knew more about Africa than any other European of the nineteenth century. His writings were well written misconceptions and full of contradictions. He was the architect of the colonial approach to Africa so uniquely used by the British. The concept of Africa, as a continent that waited in darkness for other people to bring the light, in many ways was propagated by Sir Harry Johnston." Clarke, "African Heritage: Historiography and Sources," 10.

47. Clarke wrote: "The writings of George Shepperson, a Scottish Historian, represents an enlightened approach to African history and culture. His writings pertained principally to Africa in the twentieth, he has also written a number of articles on nineteenth century Africa particularly the impact of colonial rule on Africa." Clarke, "African Heritage: Historiography and Sources," 11.

48. Clarke wrote: "Carter G. Woodson is considered to be the father of Black History in the United States. Though this claim is somewhat exaggerated, it is true in the main that he founded the Association For the Study of Negro Life and History. Carter G. Woodson formulated the study of the African in the New World and Africans in Africa." Clarke, "African Heritage: Historiography and Sources," 11. Woodson is a central figure in the institutionalization of Afrikan-controlled professional academic vehicles for the publication

of original research in the history of Afrikan peoples in the United States and elsewhere, including scholarly essays and monographs.

49. Clarke wrote: "W. E. B. Du Bois is considered the father of the Concept of Pan-Africanism among blacks in the United States. In his long life he probably made the best intellectual contribution of the African descendants born in the western world." Clarke, "African Heritage: Historiography and Sources," 12.

50. Clarke wrote: "In the last ten years the best known books on Africa have been written by an English writer Basil Davidson. Mr. Davidson is not a historian in the general sense, he is a journalist who brings to the study of Africa his astute research and new insights into an old subject, which has been universally distorted. He has, in popularizing African History, made the subject readable to a large number of people who have no prior knowledge of it, and to new students who are open minded sufficiently to disregard the many misconceptions relating to Africa." Clarke, "African Heritage: Historiography and Sources," 12.

51. Clarke, "African Heritage: Historiography and Sources."

52. What is interesting here is Clarke's use of the term *Afro-centric* long before it became popularized in the 1980s by Molefi Kete Asante and his seminal text, *Afrocentricity: The Theory of Social Change* (Buffalo, NY: Amulefi Publishing Company, 1980). Asante founded the first Ph.D. program in Africana Studies in the United States and the world during the fall semester of 1988 at Temple University in Philadelphia, Pennsylvania. By the time that Clarke developed this course, Asante had three years earlier completed his Ph.D. at the University of California, Los Angeles.

53. Clarke, "African Heritage: Historiography and Sources."

54. See in JHCP, SRBC the following by Clarke: "African Heritage: Historiography and Sources; A Study of the Historical Writings of Edward Wilmot Blyden, Sir Harry Hamilton Johnston, George Shepperson, Carter G. Woodson, W. E. B. Du Bois, and Basil Davidson," Africana Studies and Research Center, Cornell University, fall Semester 1971 and spring Semester 1972; "African History from the Origin of Man to 1600 A.D," Department of Black and Puerto Rican Studies, Hunter College of the City University of New York, fall Semester 1973; "African-American History I: From Slavery to Emancipation," Department of Black and Puerto Rican Studies, Hunter College of the City University of New York, fall 1983; "Dimensions of World History," Department of Black and Puerto Rican Studies, Hunter College of the City University of New York, fall 1985; "Dimensions of World History,"

Department of Black and Puerto Rican Studies, Hunter College of the City University of New York, spring 1986; "Nineteenth Century Resistance Movements: African and Afro-American," Africana Studies and Research Center, Cornell University, Seminar Course, fall Semester 1970.

55. As quoted by Herb Boyd and Sharon Fitzgerald, "The Powerful Legacies of Two Giants," *American Visions* 13, no. 5 (October–November 1998): 30–33.

56. Elliott P. Skinner, letter to Tilden J. LeMell, 24 April 1973, JHCP, SCRBC.

57. Clarke, "A Selected List"; ibid., "Contemporary Authors"; ibid., "RE: Curriculum Guide"; ibid., "An Account"; ibid., "Who's Who"; ibid., Curriculum Vitae; ibid., Hunter College Staff; JHCP, SCRBC.

58. Ibid., "African-American History I: From Slavery to Emancipation," Department of Black and Puerto Rican Studies, Hunter College of the City University of New York, fall 1983, JHCP, SCRBC.

59. Ibid.

60. Clarke launched his syndicated book review column, "African World Bookshelf," in 1961 with the Chicago-based Associated Negro Press. See Claude A. Barnett, letter to John Henrik Clarke, 24 February 1961, JHCP, SCRBC. According to the report in *The Columbus Times*, the column was distributed to more than fifty newspapers in the United States and internationally. Before that, from 1947 to 1949, he had been book review editor for the *Negro History Bulletin*. See John Henrik Clarke, letter to Claude A. Barnett, 23 January 1961, JHCP, SCRBC; and Clarke, "Who's Who".

61. Jose Manuel Torres Santiago, letter to John Henrik Clarke, December 1987, JHCP, SCRBC. In a letter under Hunter College letterhead, the department chair, Torres Santiago, wrote to Clarke the following: "Dear Professor Clarke: I am writing to advise you that the department P & B has voted not to recommend you for reappointment. Accordingly, your appointment at Hunter College will expire January 31, 1988." Clarke would be 73. Perhaps it was not without significance that the chair referred to the department as "P & B," that is, Puerto Rican and Black, as opposed to its actual name, Black and Puerto Rican.

62. John Henrik Clarke, "Dimensions of World History," Department of Black and Puerto Rican Studies, Hunter College of the City University of New York, fall 1985, JHCP, SCRBC.

63. Ibid.

64. Ibid., "Dimensions of World History," Department of Black and Puerto Rican Studies, Hunter College of the City University of New York, spring 1986, JHCP, SCRBC.

65. Ibid., "Dimensions," fall 1985.

66. Ibid., "Dimensions," spring 1986.

67. Ibid., "Dimensions," fall 1985.

Chapter Four

AFRICANA HISTORY: A WEAPON OF LIBERATION

There is nothing in my life that takes precedence over my commitment to African people, teaching their history, the fight for
their total liberation and restoration of their place among the
nations of the world.

—John Henrik Clarke, 1982[1]

The final interpretation of African History is the responsibility
of scholars of African descent.

—John Henrik Clarke, 1967[2]

One of Clarke's early efforts to teach Afrikan world history was
a lecture he gave to a mass meeting of the Brooklyn Unit of
the late Marcus Garvey's Universal Negro Improvement Association (UNIA) in February 1954 titled "The Conflict in South Africa
and What's Behind It." The flyer announcing the event noted "Mr.
Clarke has written many short stories, poems and articles that
have appeared in magazines in America, Europe, and Africa. He
has been a student of African history for nearly twenty years and
studied under Dr. Willis N. Huggins, Prof. Charles C. Seifert and
Dr. Leo Handsberry [sic] of Howard University."[3] Only two years
later, he would join the staff of lecturers at the New School for Social
Research, where from 1956 to 1958 he would occasionally teach
various topics in Africana history.

Four years later, his teaching career would gather momentum. From 1962 to 1963, he taught continental and U.S. Afrikan history at the Adult Education Division of Malverne High School, called the People's College, in Malverne, Long Island, where he was "the first teacher to be given a special license by the State of New York to teach this subject." From there, he accepted an appointment to the directorship of the Heritage Teaching Program of HARYOU-ACT's Community Action Institute. Solely responsible for its conception, development, and implementation, Clarke's position gave him both financial stability and an unprecedented opportunity to construct and control what was, in fact, a community-based and -oriented Africana Studies program that each week taught and trained several hundred Afrikan youths and adults.

It was, moreover, an Africana Studies program that directly sought to cultivate youth and adult leadership committed to effective social action. In other words, Clarke was training activists, and his program of education in Afrikan heritage was essential to their effectiveness and to the programmatic and ideological directions they would adopt. The literature explaining the larger project's purpose stated that the "core of the HARYOU-ACT programs is the persistent emphasis and insistence upon social action rather than dependence upon mere social service. HARYOU-ACT's goal is to develop in Central Harlem a community of excellence through the concern and initiative of the people of the community." Moreover, it read:

> Social action in its operational sense means and demands the stimulation of concern among individuals who share a common predicament, who are victims of long-standing community problems and injustices, who can be induced not only to identify these problems but to seek to determine the methods by which they can be resolved, and who are able to develop and sustain the initiative for the type of collective action which, in fact, does resolve or change these problems.[4]

Within one month of his start, Clarke noted, his program of study, teaching, and training was fully operational, the twelve Heritage classes held from Monday through Thursday serving "about 750 youth and from 25 to 50 adults per week." These classes were based on "Curriculum Guides to the Study and Teaching of African and Afro-American History" he had developed to inform and to support the teaching and training process.[5]

Clarke's "Curriculum Guides," reproduced in a text of speeches published twenty-six years later and updated to the mid 1970s, covered eighty-nine sessions in sixty-four pages and four basic lesson plans on continental and U.S. Afrikan history: "Africa's Place in World History from the Origin of Man to 1600 A.D.," which offered thirty sessions in twenty-four pages; "Africa's Place in World History from 1600 A.D. to the Present," which covered sixteen lessons in thirteen pages; "Africa's Place in African-American History from Slavery to Emancipation," which presented thirteen sessions in twelve pages; and "Africa's Place in African-American History from the Reconstruction to the Present," which introduced thirty sessions in eleven pages.[6] The reading guides covering the human experience on the Afrikan continent were "designed as an introduction to African world history" that would "stimulate a continuous study of the subject." Not only is Afrikan history a very old and very important element of world history, but, he added, "There is no way to understand world history without an understanding of African history."[7] As regards the experience of Afrikans in the Americas, Clarke wrote the reading guides were developed as a survey of "the historical experience of African people in the United States from the pre-Columbian presence" to the period of Reconstruction and beyond. Indeed, he observed, new information by both Afrikan and European researchers "proves beyond question that people of African descent have had a pre-Columbian presence in what is called the 'New World.'"[8] In addition, he noted, "Because early African-American history is inseparable from African history, it is important for students in this course to have at least a basic background knowledge of what happened in Africa before the slave trade."[9]

As was typical of Clarke's approach to the study, writing, research, and teaching of Africana history, his program was ambitious. A year after he had assumed the directorship, he recounted in August 1965 that "General Heritage activities"—indeed, he was describing his own activities—"consist of the compiling and cataloguing of a future Heritage Library, the writing of a weekly Heritage Bulletin that is distributed to the staff of HARYOU-ACT and all units in Community Action,[10] the preparation of original heritage teaching materials, and serving as consultant to all units within HARYOU-ACT with Heritage Teaching programs."[11] In the latter case, assisted by two teachers, Keith E. Baird and James E. Campbell, Clarke personally taught five of the courses, while Baird taught three and Campbell the remaining four. Clarke's week of teaching began with a Monday class from 5–6:30 p.m., during which—aided by a student assistant instructor—he led an estimated seventy-five to one hundred members of the Neighborhood Youth Corps in lecture and discussion "of the contributions of the people of African descent to the development of the Americas, North, South and the Caribbean area." Later that evening, from 8–9:30 p.m., he taught from forty to fifty adult members of Joint Organizations Mobilized for Action (JOMA) in "lectures and discussions of the historical background to current events as it effects [sic] the people of African descent, mainly those in the United States."[12]

On Tuesday, from 3–5 p.m., Clarke instructed from twenty to twenty-five members of the Group Work Heritage Leadership Class of Community Action. These youths were working in various community centers, where they taught heritage classes to other youths and young adults. Clarke led them in lectures and discussions concerning the problems of teaching the Heritage curriculum. At the same time on Thursday afternoons, Clarke lectured to from seventy-five to one hundred youths of the "Community Action advanced unit, concerned with political education and methods for community improvement." His lectures covered background information on the political history of Afrikans in the United States generally and in Harlem particularly. From 5–6:30 p.m., Clarke then taught the Heritage Leadership Class, also known as the Special Heritage Group. By August 1965, however, this class was being reorganized because most of its members "have been assigned to community centers where they are now teaching Heritage classes," or because they were promoted to other leadership positions.

Baird and Campbell taught classes for the remaining seven groups: about twenty children and teenagers, ages eleven to fifteen, of the Heritage Program for Youth in Group Work; about sixty to eighty youths in the Heritage Program for Beginners in Community Action; about 200 to 300 youths, ages ten to nineteen, divided in two separate groups of the Junior Guard Cadets; about 400 to 500 youths, ages ten to eighteen, of the Minisink Center Cadets; two respective sessions of fifty to sixty children, ages nine to twelve, and eighty to one hundred teenagers, ages thirteen to sixteen, of the St. Martin's Cadets; and about thirty to thirty-five youths, ages eleven to fourteen, who were from the church community.[13]

Clarke did not, however, limit himself or the teaching program to these activities. Rather, he utilized the program to make citywide community educational outreach a priority as well. The Queens-Nassau Branch of the Association for the Study of Negro Life and History, for example, announced its sponsorship of an eight-session workshop course in U.S. and continental Afrikan history taught by Clarke and his Heritage Program staff, Baird and Campbell. The ninety-minute sessions from 1 April–3 June, beginning at 8 p.m., took place at the Lutheran Church of the Resurrection in St. Albans, Queens. The schedule was as follows:

- 1 April, "Africa in Antiquity: Africa Before the Christian Era," Clarke
- 15 April, "The Glory of East Africa: Egypt, Kush, Ethiopia," Baird
- 22 April, "The Relevance of the African Past," Campbell
- 29 April, "The Kingdoms of the Western Sudan: The Rise and Fall, and the Diaspora," Clarke
- 13 May, "The African in the New World," Baird
- 20 May, "Africa in the Making of America," Campbell
- 27 May, "Emancipation and the Dream Deferred," Clarke
- 3 June, "Confrontation—Black and White: Diagnosis and Prognosis," Clarke, Baird, Campbell[14]

In addition to the Heritage program's community outreach efforts and its training initiatives for developing youth and adult activism and leadership, Clarke regularly lectured to the staff of other programs in HARYOU-ACT on various subjects in Africana history and culture. In October 1965, for example, he prepared a lecture titled "The Golden Age in Africa before the Christian Era" for the staff of the After School Study Centers, the first of what was to be a series of five lectures. In three main parts, Clarke's presentation offered: (1) a discussion of Afrika as the birthplace for humankind, citing the evidence from L. S. B. Leakey; (2) an exploration of the southern origins of North Afrikan civilizations, chiefly the Afrikan Nile Valley of ancient Egypt, with its cultural origins in Uganda and Somalia; and (3) a survey of chronological developments in Afrika before Christ, in which he traced its beginnings from the ancient Nile Valley, a 10,000-year old civilization that was born, reached its height, and was in decline "before Europe was born." Here Clarke surveyed major developments in Kemetic civilization from 6500–1350 B.C.E.[15]

Clarke's personal commitment to teaching and training others in Africana history and culture extended well beyond the classrooms, churches, and community centers of central Harlem and New York City. He also elected to volunteer his time, talents, curricula, and personal expenses to the community educational efforts launched by Afrikan activists, who were assisted in some instances by northern European volunteers, in the southern states. There he "spent long weekends in the South teaching in Freedom Schools. This has been very rewarding and because it has been at my own expense, very costly."[16]

When, after four years, he left HARYOU-ACT at the end of 1968, Clarke accepted an appointment in 1969 as teacher of Africana history at the Head Start Training Program at New York University. During the Spring semester of that year, he also taught a course at the New School for Social Research titled "A Survey of African History."[17] By this time, the series of televised lectures he had developed in conjunction with an eight-member advisory board of Afrikan scholars and intellectuals, including five from Columbia University (which coproduced the series with WCBS-TV), was airing daily.

Nevertheless, concerned as he was with advancing the teaching of Africana history by every conceivable means, Clarke saw "Black Heritage: A History of Afro-Americans" not only as an opportunity to promote a new understanding of Africana history through the medium of television to a metropolitan New York City-wide audience. By 1970, he was working with advisory board chairman and historian Vincent Harding to edit a series of twenty or more illustrated books to be published by Holt, Rinehart and Winston, Inc., that were to be used in high schools and universities. The books were to be based on the lectures from the television series and were to include three or more lectures per book. Clarke and Harding solicited contracts with the participants, more than thirty Afrikan poets, writers, playwrights, artists, historians, political scientists, sociologists, anthropologists, and other scholars, educators, journalists, and political activists from the Afrikan diaspora and continent. Clarke's concern for pedagogy and creating new curricular materials for the teaching of this history was ever paramount.[18]

Thus, it is understandable that he would later lament that, despite his best efforts, he and Harding failed to get very many of the proposed books published because they were unable to get clearance to use the material from all the lecturers in the series. In the end, he complained in 1972, "one book in the series called 'The Slave Trade and Slavery' was published about two years ago. There might be two or three more."[19]

Still, Clarke made the promotion of the teaching of Africana history one of his central missions. This included his efforts at in-service trainings for teachers, supervisors, and administrators in the public schools. Among his many efforts during the two years between 1967 and 1969 alone were:

- 27 September and 11 October 1967, in-service course called "The Negro in America" for teachers in the Great Neck Public Schools on Long Island, New York. In two sessions, "The African Background" and "The Colonial Experience," the director of the Heritage Teaching Program surveyed seventeen major themes in continental Afrikan history from the dawn of humankind to the twentieth century. They included a survey of some of the great personalities of ancient Afrika, a history of the interaction of ancient Afrika and ancient Rome, an examination of major civilizations of ancient East Afrika and the Sudan, a discussion of West Afrikan empires and kingdoms during and after the middle ages, and explorations of the European slave trade, European colonialism in Afrika, nation-formation in South Africa in the seventeenth through nineteenth centuries, nationalism in nineteenth century West Afrika, and continental Afrikan independence movements of the twentieth century. His bibliography listed forty-two books and a special Afrika issue of *Freedomways*, which Clarke had edited, titled "The New Image of Africa," Fall 1962.[20]

- 12 March 1968, in-service course in Afrikan history titled "Great African Rulers," sponsored by the New York City Board of Education and programmed by the African-American Institute of New York City, for teachers in the New York City Public Schools. Clarke surveyed four major themes in continental Afrikan history: Afrika at the dawn of history and the beginning of organized societies, leadership in the early empires of the Western Sudan, the fall of the Western Sudan, and leadership and resistance to colonial rule in South Africa. His bibliography listed forty-two books and a special Afrika issue of *Freedomways*, which Clarke had edited, titled "The New Image of Africa," Fall 1962.[21]

- 23 April 1968, in-service course in Afrikan history titled "Africa's Oral Tradition," sponsored by the New York City Board of Education and programmed by the African-American Institute of New York City, for teachers in the New York City Public Schools. Clarke surveyed four major themes: traditions of origins and lost grandeur in East Afrika and among the Zulu of South Africa, oral tradition among southern Afrikans from Botswana and Namibia, legends of ancient East Afrika of the Sudan and Ethiopia, and oral tradition in West Afrika. He provided a bibliography of twenty-nine books.[22]

- 18 March 1969, in-service course in Afrikan history titled "Africa: The Colonial Period," sponsored by the New York City Board of Education and programmed by the African-American Institute of New York City, for teachers, supervisors, and administrators in the New York City Public Schools. The special consultant to the WCBS TV series, "Black Heritage: A History of Afro-Americans," surveyed two major themes: Afrika on the eve of the colonial period, and the golden age of inner West

Afrika and the rise of Askia Muhammad Toure. He provided a bibliography of eighteen books.[23]

- 16 and 29 April 1969, in-service course in Afrikan history titled "Societies and Cultures of West Africa," sponsored by the New York City Board of Education and programmed by the African-American Institute of New York City, for teachers, supervisors, and administrators in the New York City Public Schools. Clarke explored two major themes: the peopling of the Western Sudan and the emergence of nation states. He provided a bibliography of twenty-two books.[24]

- 20 September 1969, lecture titled "Africa: The Last Age of Grandeur, 1076–1591 A.D." to the Institute on Special Educational Problems Occasioned by Desegregation, State University of New York at Albany. Clarke, now an adjunct professor at Hunter College, discussed two major themes he had explored earlier: the peopling of the Western Sudan and the emergence of nation-states. He provided a suggested reading list of eleven books.[25]

- 24 September 1969, in-service program on Negro literature, history and culture sponsored by the Board of Cooperative Educational Services First Supervisory District, Westchester County, in Yorktown Heights, New York. Clarke's lecture, "History and the New Age of Man," covered several themes in Afrikan history of the continent and the diaspora. They included discussion of the ancient Afrikan Nile Valley, the rise of ancient Mediterranean Europe, Afrikans and the rise of Christianity and Islam, Afrikans in the conquest of Spain, the rise and fall of the Western Sudan, Afrikans in the making of the Americas, Afrikan armed struggle in the Americas during the enslavement era, armed anticolonial struggle in Afrika, the nineteenth-century origins of twentieth-century struggle, Black power and Black history in the twentieth-century United States, and Afrikan personalities in the twentieth-century United States: Booker T. Washington, W. E. B. Du Bois, A. Philip Randolph, Marcus Garvey, Martin Luther King, Jr., and Malcolm X.[26]

Eighteen years later, his commitment to the transformation of primary and secondary public education was as keen as ever. Participating in a movement to Afrikanize education in the public schools, the seventy-two-year-old professor emeritus in 1987 authored and edited baseline essays in social studies and Africana history for integration into the curriculum of the Portland (Oregon) Unified School District.[27]

Clarke's in-service trainings in Africana history were not limited to teachers, supervisors, and administrators in the public schools, but extended to personnel in higher education as well. He lectured widely at university campuses—at both graduate and undergraduate programs—before and after he joined the faculties at Hunter College and Cornell University. In July 1968, for example, the fifty-three-year-old director of the Heritage Teaching Program lectured on the subject of "The Origin of the Black Urban Ghetto" at Columbia University's School of Library Sciences. Clarke discussed the multiple causes of Afrikan migration from the South and urbanization in the northern cities beginning in the late nineteenth century; the historical origins and development of the Afrikan community in Harlem, what he called "the most famous ethnic ghetto in the world"; and the structure of the Harlem community, including its ethnical, political, economic, cultural, and sociological aspects, as well as its national and international importance. Clarke also provided a suggested reading list of nineteen books and essays.[28] Two months later, he lectured on Africana history at New York University's Graduate School of Social Work and its "Concentrated Course on History and Lifestyles of Negro and Puerto Rican People." His two ninety-minute lectures, "African Culture History: Impact of Colonialism and the Slave Trade" and "The Impact of African Culture and the Slave System in the United States on the Pre-Civil War Culture of Afro-Americans," ran consecutively between 9:30 a.m. and 12:30 p.m.[29]

Shortly before he joined the faculty at Hunter College's Department of Black and Puerto Rican Studies, Clarke's efforts also focused on developing and strengthening the emerging discipline of Africana Studies. One of his earliest major efforts was his development of a series of eight two-hour lectures, from 7 July–1 August 1969, called "Dimensions of the Black Experience" for a colloquium on Black history hosted by Columbia University's Afro-American

Studies Program. Clarke's colleague James P. Shenton, a professor of history, was the program's coordinator. Shenton had served, along with Clarke, on the Black Heritage television series' advisory board and had been one of its lecturers.[30] The colloquium schedule of lectures, which included Richard B. Moore[31] and William Strickland, both of whom had also participated in the television series, were as follows:

- 8 July, "Africa, The Last Age of Grandeur, 1076 A.D.–1591 A.D.," Clarke
- 10 July, "The Significance of the Year 1492," Clarke
- 15 July, "The Slave Trade and the Making of the New World," Clarke
- 17 July, "The Anatomy of Slavery as an American Institution," Moore
- 22 July, "The Dilemma of the 'Free' Black American (Black Abolitionists and Others)," Clarke
- 24 July, "Reconstruction and Aftermath," Strickland
- 29 July, "The Making of the Urban Black Ghetto, 1876–1945," Clarke
- 31 July, "Men and Movements in the Black Urban Ghetto: The Search for Leadership," Clarke.

As usual, Clarke's outline for the colloquium lectures included a bibliography for each of them, totaling 153 books in all.[32] In addition, he provided a special, fifteen-page, three-part bibliography for the lecture series consisting of 206 books, novels, government and private agency reports, essays in newspapers and in academic, literary, intellectual, and popular journals that covered issues in continental Afrikan history, U.S. Afrikan history and culture, and the community of Harlem. "For this bibliography," he noted, "I have selected what, in my opinion, are some of the best new books on African and Afro-American History."[33]

What was also usual was the scholar's concern for the bibliography's usefulness as a tool in teaching Africana history. His selection of twenty-seven "books on African History" were intended as those "not difficult to use as basic texts in teaching this subject."[34]

Further, he provided a suggested reading list for a general survey course in U.S. Afrikan history that ranged "from informative books for young readers (that are also suitable for adults) to exciting works or original scholarship." Clarke added significantly: "The books have been arranged in order to create a self-teaching course in Afro-American History."[35] He arranged and divided the five-page reading list of eighty-four books, novels, and government reports as follows: General History; 1619–1861: a general history, "Slavery as an Institution," "Resistance and Struggle Against Slavery"; 1861–1900: "The Negro and the Civil War," "Reconstruction," "The Era of Re-Oppression"; 1900–1941: "The New Resistance," "From South to North"; 1947–1967: "Yesterday, Today, Tomorrow."[36] Moreover, Clarke's four-page bibliography on "the world's most famous ethnic community" consisted of ninety-one books, government reports, and articles.[37]

Clarke's momentum continued. On 6 June 1970, after a year of teaching in the Department of Black and Puerto Rican Studies, the University of Denver during its commencement ceremonies awarded him an honorary doctorate. He shared the honor that day with United States Senator Eugene McCarthy, D-Minnesota, and Ian MacGregor, chairman and chief executive officer of American Metal Climax, Inc., a major company in the metals and mining industry.[38] Clarke's friend, Lerone Bennett, Jr., the historian and senior editor at *Ebony* magazine, offered his congratulations. "This is a long overdue recognition of your enormous contributions in the field of African history."[39] University of Denver officials were even more specific. "As a poet, historian of the Black heritage and editor," they extolled, "he has been in the forefront of writers and educators concerned with the development of Black studies programs and in the development of a cohesive history of the world's Blacks."[40]

Bolstered by this important recognition of his accomplishments and contributions to the emerging field of research, teaching, and outreach, Clarke continued his efforts to guide and promote the discipline's development. One month after his honor at the University of Denver, Clarke, now an associate professor at Hunter, was participating in the second Colloquium on Black History at Columbia University's Afro-American Studies Program, this time lecturing on the subject of "Problems in Teaching and Understanding African History." His talk explored the distortion and excision of Afrikan history from the main currents of human history; new evidence that contradicted the old white supremacist arguments about Afrikan history and Afrikan people; an examination of some of the old assumptions that justified Afrikan subordination in European society and culture and Africans' historiographical defamation; the need for new definitions and new approaches to the study, research, writing, and teaching of Africana history and the evidence that supports them; and a discussion of the pioneering Afrikan scholars in the fields of U.S. and continental Afrikan history who contributed mightily to the new evidence that warranted the new approaches and interpretations for which Clarke called.[41]

Clarke's contributions to the development of Columbia University's Afro-American Studies Program were apparently of such significance that he was honored for them five years later. Columbia's president named him associate in the University Seminar on African-American Studies, a nonsalaried three-year appointment effective 1 July 1974–30 June 1977.[42]

The associate professor was in demand not only in New York City but also at Africana Studies departments and programs across the United States. As an example, from 7–8 May 1971, he delivered four three-hour lecture sessions in the Afro-American Studies Lecture Series of the Department of Ethnic Studies at the University of California, Berkeley: "African History and Its Relation to World History," "African Culture, the Basis of World Culture," "Afro-American History: Main Currents, 1600–Present," and "Afro-American Culture and Its Impact on the Making of the 'New World.'"[43]

Of particular interest were the two lectures on the role of Afrikans in the history of the Americas during several different eras. "The objective of this lecture is to give students of black history and students in general who are interested in beginning a serious study of the role of African people in history, a concise course that will also be an analysis of the most useful source materials in this rapidly developing field of study," Clarke wrote of his first three-hour lecture on Afrikan history in the Americas. "In dealing with the main themes of Afro-American history, the total impact of the Africans on the so-called 'New World' will be examined in detail."

Among the issues that underscore that impact is the observation that "the phrase 'New World' is highly questionable in light of the old and new evidence that tends to prove that people of African descent were in large parts of North and South America and the Caribbean Islands long before Christopher Columbus opened up this part of the world for European settlement." Clarke concluded that the "course will be taught from *an Afro-centric point of view*, using mainly the books and documents by writers of African descent in all cases where this material is available"[44] (added emphasis).

Aside from lecturing at universities, Clarke also promoted the teaching of Africana history in his various personal and professional associations. In addition to collaborating with the African-American Institute in in-service training sessions for teachers, supervisors, and administrators of the New York City public school system, Clarke served as a pedagogical consultant to the organization. His task was to evaluate the institute's existing materials on Afrika and to offer assessments as to how they might be used in the construction of teaching curricula for various levels of students, from children through adults.[45] This concern for pedagogy and the development of Africana Studies curricula was also one of his major interests at the Atlanta, Georgia-based Institute of the Black World (IBW). Clarke served as one of the founding members of the Governing Council of the IBW, which was formed in 1970 and remained briefly a part of the Martin Luther King, Jr., Memorial Center before it severed its affiliation to become an independent research institution.[46] Clarke's colleague and friend, the historian Vincent Harding, served as the institute's director. In a May 1970 document that outlined the IBW's mission titled "Towards a Black Agenda," Harding noted that "we have a collective commitment to work as fully as we can towards Black control over the definition of the Black experience."[47]

As with the African-American Institute, Clarke believed an important aspect of fulfilling that agenda lay in the development of Africana Studies curricula and pedagogy. In September 1970 he told Harding he was collecting various copies of his syllabi and curricula so that "the Institute [can] have on file some of the more meaningful work that I have developed over the past ten years." Clarke envisioned the Institute of the Black World as "a depository for reference data of this nature pertaining to the teaching of Black History. I think it would be a good idea for you to send out a general letter to black teachers in this field asking that copies of their lesson plans and reference data be deposited at the Institute." Clarke felt that "If the response were what it should be, the Institute would be one place where you could go to study the development of teaching techniques relating to African and Afro-American Studies."[48]

Indeed, in the most perfect of worlds, Clarke confided to a friend five years later, traveling to and teaching in Afrika, devoting time to research and writing while there, and examining the teaching about Afrika in Afrika, would constitute his ideal sabbatical experience.

> I intend to take a sabbatical beginning in the fall of 1977. Right now my plans are not concrete. I know that I would like to spend a good part of the year in Africa, maybe as a visiting professor at one of the African universities conducting seminars on the Africans outside of Africa (mainly in North and South America and in the Caribbean Islands). I would want to have the kind of schedule that would permit me enough time to do some sustained and indepth [sic] writing.
>
> My other preference, which is somewhat ideal, is spending four months travelling in Africa visiting various schools and collecting basic history texts while preparing a book on the image of Africans in Africa. I think there is a need for an indepth [sic] overview of how African history is being taught by African teachers in African schools. To take on the whole continent may be too ambitious. A more practical approach may be to concentrate on West Africa using two English-speaking countries, such as Nigeria and Sierra Leone, and two French-speaking countries, such as Senegal and Guinea.[49]

Clearly, Clarke approached the issue of the teaching of Africana history with a missionary's zeal. He repeatedly expressed his willingness to share what he knew and had developed in the field after decades of research, writing, and teaching, even if it cost him the loss of deserved recognition for his enormous contributions. Thus, three years earlier, in October 1972, he wrote to a friend and colleague at Boston University's African Studies Center:

I have enclosed the basic syllabus for the courses that I am presently teaching at Hunter and Cornell and some other data on African and Afro-American History taken hurriedly from my files. This is the kind of material that I used to send you about once a year. If there is anything here that would be of any benefit to any member of your staff please feel free to let them see it or have a copy made, though the main purpose for me sending it is for whatever use you can personally make of it. This is where I differ with our good friend Elliot Skinner [chair of the Department of Anthropology at Columbia University], I am not worried about people stealing from me. In fact, so much has been stolen from me for so long that when something new comes out on African or Afro-American history I feel a little offended if someone has not paid me that compliment. Seriously though, I think it is time that Black teachers especially those who have taught long enough to know how to develop creative approaches to teaching should send copies of their syllabus out to as many people as they have time for. The ideas in this field are not sacred and we who can develop them should be a little more generous.[50]

Clarke's view of the significance of Africana history to Afrikans in the United States inspired the selfless and collegial attitude with which he approached this subject. In short, his philosophy of teaching was decidedly and unapologetically political. To Clarke, the teaching of Africana history was an essential aspect of the Afrikan revolutionary liberation struggle in the United States and throughout the Afrikan world. "Politically I have been anti-capitalist for all of my adult life. I have and still do oppose every form of colonialism, and my teaching about history is a not-too-subtle attack on colonialism and all forms of oppression," Clarke told students in Hunter College's Department of Black and Puerto Rican Studies in 1970. "My fundamental belief is that history is a tool of liberation, and anybody who has listened to my lectures with their ears and their senses and not their prejudices would know the nature of my political commitment: It is toward the liberation of all oppressed people the world over." The fifty-five-year-old professor also disclosed that in his youth he, too, had been active in advocating for the establishment of the field of study in which he was now teaching. "[A]long with other young radicals of the 1930s and 1940s in Harlem," he informed students, "I participated in the fight for the first black studies programs in New York City."[51]

It must be underscored that the political dimensions of the commitment of Afrikan scholars and intellectuals to history had different implications than those for European supremacists. Unlike them, academicians who had no qualms in compromising historical truthfulness and accuracy for ideological and myth-making purposes—that is, the fabrication of a European supremacist mystique[52]—Afrikan scholars in general, and Clarke specifically, held that political commitment in no way compromised adherence to the quest for historical truthfulness. As Clarke's mentor William Leo Hansberry would assert, "The African, like the rest of mankind, has nothing to gain in the long run by suppressing the truth and suggesting the false for chauvinistic reasons."[53] To the contrary, they aimed to rescue, restore, and affirm historical truthfulness. In their view, the commitment to historical truthfulness, and the rendering of that truthfulness in the writing and teaching of history, constituted an unavoidably political act because they were striving to overthrow the ideological infrastructure of a hegemonic system of domination and oppression that had falsified the historical experience. In the end, the unfolding of truthfulness about the Afrikan world experience constituted a strategic discrediting of white supremacist mythology, which masqueraded as history, and which fabrications, falsifications, and distortions helped to consolidate Afrikan subordination and rendered all but impossible an accurate awareness of both the global Afrikan and European human experience.

As early as 1841, the Afrikan human rights activist James W. C. Pennington addressed the question in *A Text Book of the Origin and History of the Colored People*. Pennington, who enjoyed considerable national and international stature in the nineteenth century, maintained that exploring the true dimensions of Africana history was imperative to discern "the relative position of the colored people in the different periods among the different nations" and to answer the question of "who and whence are the colored people" in light of the fact that "we suffer much from the want of a collocation of historical facts so arranged as to present a just view of our origin."[54] Nearly 100 years later, in the last chapter ("The Propaganda of History") of his classic *Black Reconstruction in America,* William Edward Burghardt Du Bois, Harvard University's first Afrikan Ph.D., similarly rebuked European supremacist propaganda in the academy by admonishing: "If history is going to be scientific, if the record of human action is going to be set down with that accuracy and faithfulness of detail which will allow its use as a measuring rod and guide-post for the future of nations, *there must be some standards of ethics in research and interpretation.*" The problem, Du Bois maintained, is "more than mere omission and difference of emphasis"[55] (added emphasis).

Clarke—in the company of innumerable Afrikan scholars who preceded him and who were his contemporaries—maintained that Europeans, not Afrikans, were the perpetrators of the obscene fabrication, falsification, and distortion of the historical record, and it is they who directly and materially (even politically) benefited from its mutilation. Thus, if Afrikan historical achievements could be perceived as exaggerated or fantastic, it was a tribute to the phenomenal success of European supremacist monopolization of information about the world, which had rendered the notion of Afrikan humanity and Afrikan agency a conceptual impossibility. The Afrikan historian Maghan Keita, concurring in *Race and the Writing of History,* notes "the question of the 'black' in global historical development is so crucial 'that it has become a problem of epistemology.' It has become central to our definition of knowledge in the modern age." Significantly, Keita further explains, "In the modern period it has been read in such a manner as to indicate that the presence of the black is ahistorical and characteristic of the absence of knowledge, whereas the absence of the black constitutes a bona fide historical event and is therefore worthy of being classified as knowledge. That is, the event, civilization, person, or peoples become *worth* knowing if there is *no* black presence"[56] (original emphasis).

Nearly three decades earlier, Clarke had made similar observations. "Europeans and white people in general, who have benefited from the distortion of World History, know more about History than they are prepared to admit," he explained. "They had to know this in order to distort history so effectively and use this distortion as an element of world control. *They knew that history is a two edged sword that can be used both as an instrument of liberation and enslavement, depending on how it is manipulated*"[57] (added emphasis).

This conclusion informed the inestimable value he saw in the teaching of Africana history and its power to transform the consciousness of Afrikans suffering the demoralizing after-effects of cultural imperialism and colonization. For in his view, and in the view of innumerable others, European supremacist propaganda in history represented a systematic campaign of psychological warfare designed to disrupt and to compromise the integrity of the Afrikan personality. In 1933, the Harvard University-trained Afrikan historian and educator Carter Godwin Woodson, in *The Miseducation of the Negro*, addressed the pedagogical problems and the psychological consequences of a Eurocentric education for Afrikan people. "[T]aught the same economics, history, philosophy, literature and religion which have established the present code of morals, the Negro's mind has been brought under the control of his oppressor," he observed. "The same educational process which inspires and stimulates the oppressor with the thought that he is everything and has accomplished everything worth while, depresses and crushes at the same time the spark of genius in the Negro by making him feel that his race does not amount to much and never will measure up to the standards of other peoples." The nature of American educational propaganda is such, Woodson added, that "Negroes are taught to admire the Hebrew, the Greek, the Latin and the Teuton and to despise the African." He concluded: "The thought of the inferiority of the Negro is drilled into him in almost every class he enters and in almost every book he studies."[58] Hence, the responsible Afrikan scholar was obliged to respond. Ronald E. Butchart, commenting on Du Bois's philosophy of education, maintained "W. E. B. Du Bois once argued that the proper education for oppressed groups ... had a special, critical purpose. He knew, as have all serious educators since Socrates accepted his cup, that education was always and everywhere political." Indeed, the scholar-activist held that for "the oppressed, the political role of schooling had to be aimed precisely at finding the means to end the oppression."[59]

Clarke well understood, as the Afrikan psychologist Amos N. Wilson stated so cogently, that "To manipulate history is to manipulate consciousness; to manipulate consciousness is to manipulate possibilities; and to manipulate possibilities is to manipulate power."[60] Hence, in February 1966 Clarke spelled out in a letter to his friend,—the writer, actor, and political activist Julian Mayfield—the true aim of his teaching at the Heritage Teaching Program.

> Now as for me, I have been engaged in some kind of struggle for the people of African descent all my life. My unorthodox teaching methods here at HARYOU-ACT have gotten so much results in teaching black children to believe in themselves again and to see the grandeur of their history, and many times I have gone into New York high schools to lay the facts on the line in open defiance of the bigots now teaching black children that they have never been anything in black history but drawers of water and hewers of wood. The fact is that I have made a lot of physically [sic] crippled children straighten up and believe in themselves again, and I have taught many of them to wear their blackness with pride without having the rash arrogance that is so typical of nearly every white person that walks this earth. So far as I am concerned, that, too, is a revolution. It is one that I am capable of instigating and carrying out, while as a soldier on the field of battle I might be a complete failure. But as a teacher of history of my people, particularly to young, black teen-agers, I am as much a revolutionist as any soldier who has took to the field. I think ... a whole lot of people will be truer revolutionists when they understand that in a revolution there are places for all types – from a sharpshooter with a rifle to an unorthodox, but very effective teacher of African history.[61]

This theme of the development of a pedagogy integral to the Afrikan liberation struggle was an ever-present one in Clarke's discussion of Africana Studies teaching. Eight years later, he noted the emerging discipline had aggressively inserted itself into the European academy and, consequently, the impact of that insertion was engendering the eruption of an epistemological contest with profound political and even psychocultural implications. The Afrika-centered point of view—informed by new evidence and new interpretations of Africana history that were seriously challenging and eroding Eurocentric perspectives regarding various dimensions of the world experience—was generating increasing paranoia and hostile reaction within both the European academy and American society. In a lecture titled "Black Studies: A Dilemma at the Crossroads" delivered in February 1974 to the Afro-American Studies Program at Northeastern University in Boston, Massachusetts, Clarke explained the discipline's link to broader dimensions of Afrikan struggle. "When a people redefine themselves, they seek new directions and they are not satisfied until they become their own masters." Noting the irony of the fact that some of the most strident attacks on Africana Studies departments and programs emanated from reactionary Afrikan academics and civil rights figures, Clarke speculated a psychological dynamic—fear of the implications of self-determination—may possibly motivate their opposition. "Could part of this dilemma be," he asked, "that some of us have been slaves so long that we are now afraid to become our own masters?"

Clearly, the scholar-activist explained, the discipline "is a threat to those who have written world history glorifying themselves at our expense," while simultaneously "it is a challenge to those of us who intend to shape 'Black Studies' into an instrument of our liberation." For Europeans, their fear was obvious. "Now that the victims of this expansion of Europe are freeing themselves, the dilemma with European people everywhere is 'how will we walk the earth in safety when we are no longer its masters?'" For Afrikans, questions of personal and collective courage and inner resolve were at the heart of the issue. "The dilemma with African people is how do we conquer the doubts within ourselves and claim all of the earth's geography that rightfully belongs to us? Our problems are more internal than external." In the final analysis, Clarke concluded, those Afrikan scholars committed to Africana Studies "are involved in a restoration project. We are trying to restore what slavery and colonialism took away. We are also involved in a search for an ideology—the political meaning of our existence as a people."[62]

Notes

1. John Henrik Clarke, "Response to James E. Jackson's Article in the November 12, 1982 Issue of the Daily World," 2 December 1982, JHCP, SCRBC.

2. Ibid., "A New Approach to African History," Speech delivered at the Regional Conference on Afro-American history, sponsored by Detroit

Federation of Teachers and Michigan Federation of Teachers, University of Detroit, Detroit, Michigan, 11–13 May 1967, JHCP, SCRBC.

3. JHCP, SCRBC.

4. See "History of HARYOU-ACT," JHCP, SCRBC.

5. Schedule of the Heritage Program, Community Action Institute, HARYOU-ACT, Inc., 9 August 1965, JHCP, SCRBC.

6. John Henrik Clarke, ed., *New Dimensions in African History: The London Lectures of Dr. Yosef ben-Jochannan and Dr. John Henrik Clarke* (Trenton, NJ: Africa World Press, 1991), 141–204.

7. Ibid., 141–142.

8. Ibid., 180, 181.

9. Ibid., 194.

10. An example is the *Heritage Bulletin*, nos. 9 and 10 (Weeks March 18 and March 25, 1965), JHCP, SCRBC, in which the main lesson was an essay titled "The Search for Timbuctoo." Eight typewritten pages in all, six of its pages were dedicated to a history of the ancient city in what is now in the Republic of Mali, which figured so prominently in the medieval period of the Western Sudan, its trans-Saharan trade and its period of empire building, and in the European imagination and history of exploration into the interior of West Afrika. The final two pages were devoted to a listing of sixteen important dates in Africana history during the month of March from the years 1539 to 1959, and to a suggested reading list of eleven books on continental Afrikan history.

11. Schedule, JHCP, SCRBC.

12. Ibid. James E. Campbell was founder and director of the Liberation School of Malcolm X's Organization of Afro-American Unity. He had had extensive experience in the citizenship rights movement, having worked with Martin Luther King, Jr.'s Southern Christian Leadership Movement and the Student Nonviolent Coordinating Committee. He also had experience with freedom schools organized in the South. He brought this expertise to the OAAU Liberation School. The Pan Afrikanist orientation to his curriculum was designed for youth and adults. Both Baird and Clarke lectured on occasion to these classes. Campbell also structured Sunday evening political education sessions for the OAAU leadership during a time when Malcolm was traveling to Afrika. These classes focused on discussion and analysis of the speeches and documents Malcolm was sending back to the United States. See William W. Sales, Jr., *From Civil Rights to Black Libera-*

tion: Malcolm X and the Organization of Afro-American Unity (Boston: South End Press, 1994), 22, 112, 120–122.

13. Schedule, JHCP, SCRBC.

14. JHCP, SCRBC.

15. John Henrik Clarke, "The Golden Age in Africa before the Christian Era," Lecture Notes, 1 October 1965, JHCP, SCRBC.

16. Ibid., letter to Adelaide Cromwell Hill, 30 September 1966, JHCP, SCRBC. One notes that while Clarke was doing all of these things, he was also working as associate editor at *Freedomways* magazine, where he served as the chief creator of its special issues, including those that focused separately on Afrika, Harlem, and the civil rights movement.

17. See Clarke, Curriculum Vitae, and an undated memorandum to the class of "A Survey of African History," New School for Social Research, JHCP, SCRBC.

18. Letter of Agreement between the Black Heritage Committee, Inc. and Vincent Harding, 31 August 1970, JHCP, SCRBC.

19. John Henrik Clarke, letter to E. U. Essien-Udom, 31 October 1972, JHCP, SCRBC.

20. Ibid., in-service course, "The Negro in America: The African Background and the Colonial Experience," sponsored by the Public Schools of Great Neck, New York, 27 September and 11 October 1967, JHCP, SCRBC.

21. Ibid., in-service course in African History, "Great African Rulers," sponsored by the New York City Board of Education and programmed by the African-American Institute of New York City, 12 March 1968, JHCP, SCRBC.

22. Ibid., in-service course in African History, "Africa's Oral Tradition," sponsored by the New York City Board of Education and programmed by the African-American Institute of New York City, 23 April 1968, JHCP, SCRBC.

23. Ibid., in-service course in African History, "Africa: The Colonial Period," sponsored by the New York City Board of Education and programmed by the African-American Institute of New York City, 18 March 1969, JHCP, SCRBC.

24. Ibid., in-service course in African History, "Societies and Cultures of West Africa," sponsored by the New York City Board of Education and programmed by the African-American Institute of New York City, 16 and 29 April 1969, JHCP, SCRBC.

25. Ibid., "Africa: The Last Age of Grandeur, 1076–1591 A.D.," Institute on Special Educational Problems Occasioned by Desegregation, State University of New York at Albany, 20 September 1969, JHCP, SCRBC.

26. Ibid., in-service program on Negro Literature, History and Culture, lecture titled "History and the New Age of Man," sponsored by the Board of Educational Services First Supervisory District, Westchester County, New York, 24 September 1969, JHCP, SCRBC.

27. Ibid., ed., *Social Studies: African American Baseline Essays* (Portland, OR: Portland Unified School District, 1987).

28. Ibid., "The Origin of the Black Urban Ghetto," Social Sciences-Unit Studies, School of Library Sciences, Columbia University, 24 July 1968, JHCP, SCRBC.

29. Ibid., "African Culture History: Impact of Colonialism and the Slave Trade" and "The Impact of African Culture and the Slave System in the United States on the Pre-Civil War Culture of Afro-Americans," Concentrated Course on History and Lifestyles of Negro and Puerto Rican People, Graduate School of Social Work, New York University, 18 September 1968, JHCP, SCRBC.

30. See "Syllabus of Black Heritage: A History of Afro-Americans," Office of Radio and Television, Columbia University, no date, JHCP, SCRBC.

31. Born in Barbados, W.I., on 9 August 1893, Moore emigrated to the United States in 1909. An intellectual without university portfolio, Moore was a political and labor activist, and one of the founding members of the 21st A.D. Socialist Club around 1915, a Harlem political club formed by Pan-Caribbean and U.S. Afrikans that served as a study group and educational forum. In March 1920 he co-founded *The Emancipator*, a Marxist magazine. He was an important member of the African Blood Brotherhood, a secret organization with ties to the Communist Party founded in 1918 or 1919 and disbanded around 1923 or 1924. The ABB was a paramilitary organization committed to the defense and liberation of Afrikans throughout the Americas, as well as to the liberation and redemption of Afrika. By 1921, Moore had broken with the Socialist Party, joining the Communist Party in the following year. By 1942, the CPUSA expelled him for his Pan Afrikanist and nationalist views. A powerful orator, writer, and thinker, Moore is perhaps best known for his book *The Name Negro: Its Origin and Evil Use* (New York: Afroamerican Publishers, 1960). He died on 18 August 1978 in Washington, DC. According to Sinnette, Moore was for 25 years owner of the Frederick Douglass Bookstore on West 125th Street and an avid book

collector who began collecting in 1918. See Sinette, *Schomburg*, 86; Linden Lewis, "Richard B. Moore: The Making of a Caribbean Organic Intellectual," *Journal of Black Studies* 25, no. 5 (May 1995): 589–609.

32. John Henrik Clarke, "Dimensions of the Black Experience: Outline of Eight Lectures for the Colloquium on Black History," Afro-American Studies Program, Columbia University, 7 July–1 August 1969, JHCP, SCRBC.

33. Ibid., "Dimensions of the Black Experience-Bibliography," Colloquium on Black History, Afro-Americans Studies Program, Columbia University, 7 July–1 August 1969, 2, JHCP, SCRBC.

34. Ibid., 2.

35. Ibid., 6.

36. Ibid., 6–11.

37. Ibid., 11–15.

38. Note MacGregor's association with the CIA, according to Ken Laurence, "Academics: An Overview," in *Dirty Work 2: The CIA in Africa*, ed. Ellen Ray, William Schaep, Karl Van Meter, and Louis Wolf (Secaucus, NJ: Lyle Stuart, 1979), 80–85.

39. Lerone Bennett, Jr., letter to John Henrik Clarke, 3 June 1970, JHCP, SCRBC.

40. News Release, Public Relations Office, University of Denver, 6 June 1970, JHCP, SCRBC. Twenty-two years later, Clarke received an honorary doctorate from the University of the District of Columbia on 9 May 1992. Although the idea of earning a Ph.D. was something he had considered, he also felt that he had more than an earned the doctorate through the body of his work.

41. John Henrik Clarke, "Problems in Teaching and Understanding African History," Second Colloquium on Black History, Afro-Americans Studies Program, Columbia University, 13 July 1970, JHCP, SCRBC.

42. Marion E. Jemmott, letter to John Henrik Clarke, 12 February 1975, JHCP, SCRBC. Jemmott, at this time, was acting secretary of Columbia University.

43. John Henrik Clarke, "African History and Its Relation to World History," Afro-American Studies Lecture Series, Department of Ethnic Studies, University of California-Berkeley, 7 May 1971; ibid., "African Culture, The Basis of World Culture," Afro-American Studies Lecture Series, Department of Ethnic Studies, University of California-Berkeley, 7 May 1971; ibid., "Afro-American History: Main Currents, 1600–Present," Afro-American Studies

Lecture Series, Department of Ethnic Studies, University of California-Berkeley, 8 May 1971; ibid., "Afro-American Culture and Its Impact on the Making of the 'New World,'" Afro-American Studies Lecture Series, Department of Ethnic Studies, University of California-Berkeley, 8 May 1971, JHCP, SCRBC.

44. Ibid., "Afro-American History," 8 May 1971. A sample of Clarke's range of discussion for the years 1968–1972 include some of the following lectures he delivered at various forums across the United States: "The Harlem Renaissance," "The Aftermath of Reconstruction, 1876–1915," "The Impact of the African Personality on the Ancient World," "Relations of the Past" (examining Afrikan peoples' relations with other peoples in ancient times), "Arts, Culture, and Survival," "The Destabilization of the African World" (looking at Afrika, the Caribbean, and the United States), "South Africa: From the Last Zulu Uprising in Natal in 1906 to the Tragedy at Sharpeville," "The Three Main Phases of the Life of Malcolm X," "Africa, The Last Phase of Liberation," "Civilizations and City States in Ancient East Africa," "Education for a New Reality," "Ethiopia from Ancient Times to 1900," "The Paul Robeson Era," "The Search for Africa in the New World," "Politics in the 1970s," "Black History: A Tool for Black Liberation," "The Black Politician," "The Myth of Black Anti-Semitism," and "Political Linkages Between Africa and the Caribbean." JHCP, SCRBC.

45. Ibid., memorandum to Elizabeth Gardner, 27 November 1967, JHCP, SCRBC. Gardner was a research assistant at the African-American Institute in New York City and the subject of the memorandum was his first report on the "Evaluation of Teaching Materials Relating to Africa."

46. Vincent Harding, letter to John Henrik Clarke, 9 September 1970, JHCP, SCRBC. Harding was writing as IBW director.

47. Ibid., "Towards a Black Agenda," Institute of the Black World, Atlanta, Georgia, 1 May 1970, JHCP, SCRBC.

48. John Henrik Clarke, letter to Vincent Harding, 23 September 1970, JHCP, SCRBC.

49. Ibid., letter to Elliot Skinner, 23 September 1975, JHCP, SCRBC. Eighteen years later at an Africana Studies conference in Accra, Ghana, Clarke commented during a question-and-answer session on the pedagogical needs for effective national development in continental Afrikan states, stating: "Another thing you're going to have to do, if you want to free your nation, then you're going to have to put your writers and your historians to work creating text books that reflect your point of view in history. The textbooks

in most African schools still reflect the colonial point of view because they're still using the old colonial text. That should have been the first thing they did." Ibid., "Reflections and Observations: Ghana Remembered, 'Then and Now,'" 17th Annual Conference, National Council for Black Studies, Accra, Ghana, 26 July 1993, Transcript of Remarks, 23–24, JHCP, SCRBC.

50. Ibid., letter to Adelaide Hill, 31 October 1972, JHCP, SCRBC.

51. Ibid., memorandum to De Hostos and Toussaint L'Ouverture Student Organizations and their Representatives, 18 March 1970, JHCP, SCRBC. In the heady days of the late 1960s and early 1970s, Clarke addressed his memorandum to students at Hunter College who objected to the content of his lectures, arguing, apparently, that he was not sufficiently revolutionary in his views. The tenor of his remarks suggests he was responding to the charge that he was biased toward Afrikans from the United States and against Puerto Rican and Caribbean Afrikan students. The students called for his resignation from the Department of Black and Puerto Rican Studies.

52. For example, W. E. B. Du Bois in his 1935 examination of the historiography on Afrikans and the American Reconstruction noted the white supremacist consensus among historians, political scientists, and other academicians at Columbia University. See W. E. Burghardt Du Bois, *Black Reconstruction in America: An Essay toward a History of the Part Which Black Folk Played in the Attempt to Reconstruct Democracy in America, 1860–1880* (New York: Russell and Russell, 1962; originally 1935), 718–719. On this issue of white supremacist fabrications, falsifications, and distortions of the Afrikan character, which necessarily translate themselves into European white supremacist historiography, see also, among numerous examinations, Ronald Takaki, *Iron Cages: Race and Culture in 19ᵗʰ Century America* (New York: Oxford University Press, 1990); Winthrop Jordan, *The White Man's Burden: Historical Origins of Racism in the United States* (New York: Oxford University Press, 1974); George M. Frederickson, *The Black Image in the White Mind: The Debate on Afro-American Character and Destiny, 1817–1914* (New York: Harper Torchbooks, 1971).

53. Joseph E. Harris, ed., *Africa and Africans As Seen by Classical Writers: The William Leo Hansberry African History Notebook*, vol. 2 (Washington, DC: Howard University Press, 1977), xxi.

54. James W. C. Pennington, *A Text Book of the Origin and History, etc., etc. of the Colored People* (Hartford, CT: L. Skinner, Printer, 1841; reprint Detroit: Negro History Press, n.d.).

55. Du Bois, *Black Reconstruction*, 714, 713.

56. Maghan Keita, *Race and the Writing of History: Riddling the Sphinx* (New York: Oxford University Press, 2000), 17.

57. John Henrik Clarke, "History As an Instrument of Liberation," Prepared for Teachers Corps, Session in Black History, Providence, Rhode Island, 2 November 1972, JHCP, SCRBC.

58. Carter Godwin Woodson, *The Miseducation of the Negro* (New York: AMS Press, 1977; originally Washington, DC: The Associated Publishers, 1933), xiii, 1, 2.

59. Ronald E. Butchart, "'Outthinking and Outflanking the Owners of the World': A Historiography of the African American Struggle for Education," *History of Education Quarterly* 28, no. 3 (Fall 1988): 333. Butchart himself asserted: "If history is to have value beyond a literary form of collecting antiques, it must provide a guide to action. For those struggling against oppression and for justice, history must appraise the past to suggest political, social, and economic strategies for the present and the future. Like schooling, history, too, is inescapably political."

60. Amos Wilson, *The Falsification of Afrikan Consciousness: Eurocentric History, Psychiatry and the Politics of White Supremacy* (Brooklyn, NY: Afrikan World InfoSystems, 1993), 2.

61. John Henrik Clarke, letter to Julian Mayfield, 21 February 1966, JHCP, SCRBC.

62. Ibid., "Black Studies: A Dilemma at the Crossroads," Afro-American Studies Program, Northeastern University, 8 February 1974, JHCP, SCRBC.

Chapter Five

THE FORCE AND IMPLICATIONS OF AFRIKAN AGENCY AND HUMANITY

The air everywhere around is poisoned with truncated tales of our origins. That is also part of the wreckage of our people. What has been cast abroad is not a thousandth of our history, even if its quality were truth. ... From the unending stream of our remembrance the harbingers of death break off meaningless fractions. Their carriers bring us this news of shards. Their message: behold this paltriness; this is all your history.
—Ayi Kwei Armah, *Two Thousand* Seasons[1]

Concurrent with the Black man's search for an identity in America has been his search for an identity in the world, which means, in essence, his identity as a human being with a history, before and after slavery, that can command respect.
—John Henrik Clarke, 1974[2]

Despite the pervasiveness of the notions of white supremacy and Afrikan inferiority that have undergirded the culture of American society, there were always cohorts of Afrikan intellectuals in successive generations who resisted in varying capacities the stultifying and pernicious mythology. In the writing of history, James W. C. Pennington (1807–1870) offered a refutation as early as 1841 in *A Text Book of the Origin and History of the Colored People*. Not only did Pennington, a graduate of Yale College's (now Yale

University) school of divinity and an ordained Christian minister, refute the charge of Afrikan inferiority on biblical grounds, but he also employed classical Roman, Greek, and contemporary European scholarship to establish the antiquity of Afrikan civilization in the Nile Valley.[3]

Three years later, Robert Benjamin Lewis (b. 1802) published a history titled *Light and Truth: Containing the Universal History of the Colored and Indian Race, from the Creation of the World to the Present Time* in which he argued that all of human history began in Afrika with Afrikans, and that Afrikans were a powerful and centrally important presence in the ancient world.[4] William Wells Brown (1814–1884), in *The Black Man: His Antecedents, His Genius, and His Achievements* (1863) and in *The Rising Sun; or, The Antecedents and Advancement of the Colored Race* (1874), also expounded upon Afrikan global achievements in antiquity, noting, among other things, that the ancient Egyptian civilization was an Afrikan heritage.[5] Likewise, George Washington Williams (1849–1891) presented in the first volume of *History of the Negro Race in America from 1619 to 1880* (1883) a powerful image of Afrikans in the ancient world, observing that their presence and influence extended well beyond Afrika into southern and far east Asia.[6] The work of these and numerous other researchers and intellectuals of the nineteenth century addressed not only questions of the Afrikan role in human antiquity but also the more contemporary conditions, challenges, and achievements of Afrikans on the continent and in the Caribbean and in the larger North, Central, and South American diaspora.[7]

In addition to establishing the parameters of Afrikan accomplishment and influence in antiquity, Afrikan scholars in the nineteenth century also sought to demolish Anglo-European supremacist claims by establishing their true historical condition in relation to the Mediterranean Europeans of classical antiquity. In this capacity, Brown, famed as a human rights activist and novelist, in *The Black Man* assailed Anglo-American culture as falling far short of its chauvinistic claims. "From whence sprang the Anglo-Saxon? For, mark you, it is he that denies the equality of the negro. ... [David] Hume says they were a rude and barbarous people, divided into numerous tribes, dressed in the skins of wild beasts," he explained. "Druidism was their religion, and they were very superstitious. Such is the first account we have of the Britons. When the Romans invaded that country, they reduced the people to a state of vassalage as degrading as that of slavery in the Southern States." Brown concluded: "Caesar, in writing home, said of the Britons, 'They are the most ignorant people I ever conquered. They cannot be taught music.' Cicero, writing to his friend Atticus, advised him not to buy slaves from England, 'because,' said he, 'they cannot be taught to read, and are the ugliest and most stupid race I ever saw.'"[8]

Sixteen years later, the Afrikan physician and explorer Martin R. Delany (1812–1885), in a social scientific discussion of contemporary theoretical explanations of race, complexion, humanity, and human achievement, pronounced: "The African branch of this [human] family [of races] is that which was the earliest developed, taking the first strides in the progress of the highest civilization known to the world, and for this cause, if for no other, it may be regarded as the oldest race of man, having doubtless centuries prior to the others, reared imperishable monuments of their superior attainments."[9] Bishop Henry McNeal Turner of the African Methodist Episcopal Church praised the work, declaring "I have read this book with ecstasy, not only of the information it has afforded me, but because it is a full, complete and unanswerable refutation of all the abominable theories and false statements set afloat about the colored race." Turner admonished the new book's would-be readers: "Now is the time for our elders, young ministers, orators, school teachers, and people generally, to post themselves upon the all-absorbing subject of their race so as to be prepared to silence the batteries of all the Negro haters and condemners of the land."[10]

Not only were such perspectives not uncommon among certain intellectuals of the nineteenth century, but apparently Afrika-centered research and publication were yielding, among some literate in the English language at least, their desired results. "History says we are Africans," remarked J. H. Scott of Duffield, West Virginia, in a December 1880 letter published in *The Christian Recorder*. "O yes; we are Africans. Read Dr. William Wells Brown and Martin Delany's works."[11] Indeed, as early as 1828, *Freedom's Journal* published a letter to the editor by "A Constant Reader," who stated, "I enclose you [sic] for publication in your very useful paper some observations upon the history of our colour, which I have extracted from the 'African

Repository and Colonial Journal' for March 1825." The significance of the research lay in its conclusions concerning Afrikan people. "You will find that our origin is such, that no one, however exalted his station in life, need be ashamed of having descended from black parentage. ... that our origin is reproach to us, I most positively deny." The extracted article, titled "Observations on the Early History of the Negro Race," explored the Afrikan origins of Nile Valley civilization and its importance in world history and culture.[12]

Table 5.1

Selected List of Nineteenth Century Afrikan Intellectuals in the United States Exploring Afrikan History and Agency in Antiquity[13]

Author	Text	Year of Publication
James W. C. Pennington	*A Text Book of the Origin and History of the Colored People*	1841
Robert Benjamin Lewis	*Light and Truth: Containing the Universal History of the Colored and Indian Race, from the Creation of the World to the Present Time*	1844
William Wells Brown	*The Black Man: His Antecedents, His Genius, and His Achievements*	1863
William Wells Brown	*The Rising Sun; or, The Antecedents and Advancement of the Colored Race*	1874
Martin R. Delany	*Principia of Ethnology: The Origin of Races and Color, with an Archeological Compendium of Ethiopian and Egyptian Civilization, from Years of Careful Examination and Enquiry*	1879
George Washington Williams	*History of the Negro Race in America from 1619 to 1880*	1883

Of course, as already discussed in chapter 1, this Afrikan- and Afrika-centered historiography assumed a more systematic and organized character by the late nineteenth century, when Afrikan intellectuals and scholars focused their efforts upon the formation of scholarly associations that carried on the work of lone pioneer researchers and writers earlier in the century. Certainly, the most successful of these was the Association for the Study of Negro Life and History, founded in 1915. The organization continues to function as the Association for the Study of African American Life and History. Its *Journal of Negro History*, established in the following year, 1916, remains today, as the *Journal of African American History*, the chief vehicle for the serial, peer-reviewed publication of research on U.S. Afrikan history by professional academic historians.

This Afrika-centered historiography was, nonetheless, apposed to the full weight, prestige, and formidable power of the orthodoxy of the European academic world. The fundamental significance in the respective influence of the contrasting views inhered in the relative power of the Afrikan and European peoples in the world at that time. Consequently, while Afrikan intellectuals who had gained literacy in European culture challenged the juggernaut of European supremacist discourse—not insignificantly employing the research of dissident and heterodox European scholarship and intellectualism as well as their own original research and interpretations of the historical evidence—they lacked the power to control the discourse about Afrikans or Europeans in the European world. At the same time, however, they enjoyed greater success within the relative suzerainty of the Afrikan sphere, which, nevertheless, remained fundamentally subject to external European control. Hence, as would be expected, white supremacy as an interpretative framework for the research and writing of history proved an entrenched, normative epistemology in virtually all, including the most reputable, European academic institutions. It, thus, defined the debate regarding the history, agency, and humanity of Afrikan people within the context of global European culture.

Europeans of such stature as Georg Wilhelm Friedrich Hegel (1770–1831), the noted German philosopher and one of the most influential intellectuals in European culture, pronounced "The Negro, as already observed, exhibits the natural man in his wild and untamed state. We must lay aside all thought of reverence and morality—all that we call feeling—if we would rightly comprehend him; there is nothing harmonious with humanity to be found in this type of character."[14] Louis Agassiz of Harvard University, the Swiss naturalist and major European theorist who is reputed to have done more to establish and enhance the prestige of American biology than anyone else during the nineteenth century, in 1863 dismissed the prospect of social equality for Afrikans with Europeans in the United States with the assertion it was "impracticable," the "natural impossibility" of such a thing "flowing from the very character of the negro race."[15] Decades later, Columbia University historian John W. Burgess contended in *Reconstruction and the Constitution* (1902) that "A black skin means membership in a race of men which has never of itself succeeded in subjecting passion to reason, has never, therefore, created any civilization of any kind."[16] Two generations later, Arnold J. Toynbee of the University of London similarly claimed in *A Study of History* (1947) the "Black races alone have not contributed positively to any civilization—as yet. The white races hold the lead."[17]

In keeping with this orthodoxy, Hugh Trevor-Roper of Oxford University derisively mocked in *The Rise of Christian Europe* (1965): "Undergraduates, seduced, as always, by the changing breath of journalistic fashion, demand that they should be taught the history of black Africa. Perhaps, in the future, there will be some African history to teach. But at present there is none, or very little: there is only the history of Europeans in Africa. The rest is darkness ... And darkness is not a subject for history." Attempting to dignify Afrikan "darkness" as history would be "to amuse ourselves with the unrewarding gyrations of barbarous tribes in picturesque but irrelevant corners of the globe: tribes whose chief function in history, in my opinion, is to show to the present an image of the past from which, by history, it has escaped."[18] Such views by individual scholars underscored a larger significance, a greater unanimity of perspective, a conformity to an epistemology of the inferiority of Afrikan peoples (and its corollary, the superiority of European peoples) that dominated academic discourse and that ideologically and structurally configured the social order.

As a consequence, what emerged was a battle between the Afrikan image in the European mind and the Afrikan image in the Afrikan mind.[19] While what passed for reality in European supremacist consciousness was sufficient—oftentimes even to alienated Afrikan intellectuals who had become literate in European culture and who had internalized its white supremacist claims[20]—it proved inadequate and incredible to many Afrikans. Hence, one of Clarke's major professors, African studies founder William Leo Hansberry of

Howard University, remarked that at the beginning of his studies in continental Afrikan history and anthropology as a youthful under-graduate he was "quite ignorant of the fact that under the combined influence of ethnocentrism and colonialism there were wide-spread tendencies in certain circles in the Western world to ignore or sup-press most types of *Africana* which presented Black peoples in a favorable light." Consequently, the singularity and ubiquity of these tendencies was of such effect that "I was tempted at times, I confess, to wonder if it were indeed true, as was then commonly believed, that Black Africa was altogether devoid of any history worthy of serious academic concern prior to the landing of Prince Henry the Navigator's hunters of men on 'Afric's coral strand' in 1442." Nonetheless, Hansberry concluded, "the scattered bits of informa-tion which I had picked up about Ancient Kush and Old Aethiopia, together with a kind of intuitive faith in the basic equality of all the major divisions of the human race, made it impossible for me to believe that Africa—the second largest of the continents—had remained throughout untold ages, a cultural wasteland until Chris-tian slave traders from 'enlightened' European lands 'sowed the seeds of civilization' for the first time on her 'culturally barren shores.'"[21]

Similarly, Clarke's friend and colleague, the Senegalese scien-tist, anthropologist, historian, and Egyptologist Cheikh Anta Diop, remarked upon the impact of this intellectual and psychological warfare on the consciousness of Afrikans whose minds, through European higher education, had become steeped in white suprema-cist convictions of the history and capabilities of Afrikan people, rejecting, sometimes vehemently, the possibility that the terms *civi-lization* and *Afrikan* were not oxymoronic. "In truth, many Africans find this vision too beautiful to be true; not so long ago some of them could not break with the idea that Blacks are non-existent culturally and historically," he maintained. For those so effectively indoctrinated it "was necessary to put up with the cliché that Afri-cans had no history and try to start from there to build something modestly!"[22]

Two of Clarke's mentors, Willis N. Huggins and John G. Jackson, in their 1937 work *Introduction to African Civilizations with Main Currents in Ethiopian History*, commented on these sentiments, such as Hegel's calumny that Afrika was "the Unhistorical, Undeveloped

Spirit," observing such "pronouncements were accepted at their face value in the great seats of learning in Europe and in America." But they would dismiss them as lacking in academic seriousness. Although, according to European orthodoxy, "No countenance, of course, could be given to any data that would show that the black race had developed any cultures, built any great empires or created organized civil life," rigorous and truthful investigation could only arrive at the opposite conclusion. "*Real* scientific investigators, men *zealous for truth* in their craft *and versed* in ancient and oriental history, are well aware of the fact that non-African Mediterranean cultures were long the borrowers of culture from alien folk, namely the African." In reality, they maintained, "Little is admitted, freely—though much is known—of the cultural contributions of the black races to civilization"[23] (added emphasis). This said, Afrikans had an obligation to examine their history from a historically truthful perspective, a perspective, they will discover, that is fraught with agency. "If black men are willing to look at all, they should look, and teach their children to look, at themselves when they were equal, dominant, and ruling forces in the world."[24]

While, then, there was a continuity of Afrikan scholarship on Afrikan antiquity and its role in human culture and civilization, the relatively weak hold it had on academic discourse in the European world meant that Afrikans held captive in that world had continually to rediscover the evidence in succeeding generations. This resulted, of course, from the European academy's impenetrability to Afrikans, rendering the Afrikan scholar's voice mute in this strategic domain of knowledge production and authentication. It also resulted from a relatively weak and undercapitalized educational infrastructure within the Afrikan nation that would have been the means by which to transmit intergenerationally the ongoing research of Afrikan scholars, a problem about which many of the late nineteenth and early twentieth century Pan Afrikan nationalist intellectuals—such as John Edward Bruce and Arturo Alfonso Schomburg—were concerned. As a consequence, often one of the initial responses to European supremacist propaganda was simply incredulity on the part of Afrikans whose educations had exposed them to little else. Indeed, for many intellectuals who would position themselves in the forefront of the academic resistance, the descriptions offered by white supremacist academicians were so jarringly at odds with their own experiences, so exaggerated in their assertions, that they constituted not only an affront to their humanity but to their intelligence, to their common sense, and to their actual knowledge of themselves. This was the case, for example, with the Jamaican independent historian and anthropologist Joel Augustus Rogers (1880–1966), who in 1946 reflected on the initial impetus of his search for a truthful understanding of Afrikan world history.

I have often been asked what led me to begin my researches on what for a better name I will call Negro history. As I look back on it now, I think it really began in my early childhood when it was firmly impressed upon me by the ruling classes that black people were inherently inferior and that their sole reason for being was to be servants to white people and the lighter-colored mulattoes. The blacks, I was told, had never accomplished anything in all of history ... and that such signs of civilization they now showed were due to the benevolence of Christian whites who had dragged them from Africa and cannibalism, thereby plucking them as "brands from the burning" of hell and eternal torment.

The Christian blacks themselves said amen to this and joined in spreading the doctrine. My Sunday school teacher, an almost unmixed Negro, told us that black people were cursed by God and doomed to eternal servitude to white people ... The slavemasters and kidnappers had indeed done their work well. They had so incorporated their iniquities with the Christian religion that when you doubted their racism you were contradicting the Bible and flying in the face of God Almighty.

... However, even at the risk of eternal torture I could not swallow what this sincere, but gullible, tool of the master class was telling me. There was a streak of logic in me that prevented it. ...

I had ... noted that some of the brightest of my schoolmates were unmixed blacks and some of them were more brilliant than some of the white ones. ... I also saw around me black physicians and lawyers, all graduates of the best English and Scottish universities. If the Negro strain were inherently inferior, why had these black people been able to accomplish these things and be more advanced than some of the barefooted white adults I knew? ...

... As I grew older I revolted more and more at this asinin-
ity concocted by the "master race" but I had no books at hand to
contradict it, nor knowledge of any kind.[25]

Added to initial skepticism, one of the most significant sources of
intellectual resistance was the family lore, those stories told by family
members that recalled the struggles and deep inner feelings and
perspectives of Afrikans that were routinely hidden from European
outsiders; the stereotypes of a chauvinistic and alien people proved
wholly incompatible with the sense of themselves that Afrikans had
cultivated over generations.[26] Those persons so inoculated escaped
the insidious demoralization that had ravaged the psyche of so many
because, as Clarke reminisced in the 1970s, "In spite of growing up
in such abject poverty, I grew up in *a very rich cultural environment
that had its oral history* and with people who not only cared for me
but pampered me in many ways." He added, "I know that this kind
of upbringing negates all the modern sociological explanations of
black people that assume that everybody who was poor was without
love"[27] (added emphasis).

Hence, in the absence of witnessing middle class Afrikan
achievement, the humanity inherent in the family and the community fostered in Clarke a profound skepticism of white supremacist
propaganda. Indeed, the power of his family narrative was that it
constituted excursions into historical memory based on the stories
of his great grandmother, born under the regime of enslaver dictatorship, who related to him accounts of the indomitable inner spirit,
valor, and honor of Afrikan people in her memory and the memories
of those who preceded her. In short, the impression of humanness
and agency was so powerful upon his imagination and the strength of
his sense of himself that when told in kindly fashion by a European
lawyer for whom as a youth he worked after school that Afrikan
people had no history, Clarke recalled the assertion "insulted every
part of me to the very depth of my being."[28]

My first teacher was my great grandmother whom we called
"Mom Mary." She had been a slave first in Georgia and later
in Alabama where I was born in Union Springs. It was she
who told us *stories about our family and about how it had resisted*

slavery. ... Mom Mary was the historian of the family. ... This great grandmother was so dear to me that *I deified her* in almost the same way that many Africans deify their old people. I think that my search for identity, my search for what the world was about, and my relationship to the world began when I listened to the stories of that old woman. ... *She thought that the human being should not permit himself to be dehumanized,* and her concept of God was so pure and so practical that she could see that *resistance to slavery was a form of obedience to God. She did not think that any of us children should be enslaved,* and she thought that anyone who had enslaved any one of God's children had violated the very will of God[29] (added emphasis).

At bottom, then, it was clear that the white supremacist charge that Afrikans had no history was a declaration that Afrikans were not human, and this assertion, to intellectuals like Clarke, was simply impossible. Further, they well understood that the fact of Afrikan humanity meant that Afrikan agency had to be evident in history. Hence, the assertion that Afrikans had no history meant Afrikans lacked agency and, therefore, humanity. These two claims on the part of the whole of European settler society were impossible to reconcile with the reality of one who lived the experience of being human, who saw it in his and her daily life, and who intuitively sensed, despite the pervasiveness of propaganda to the contrary, that a greater evidence of this humanity beyond the family and the local community to the whole of a people awaited formal discovery.

Thus, it was at this juncture of the conflict between direct awareness and ideological pronouncement and ascription that an epistemological confrontation erupted, one that sparked for Afrikans the systematic individual and group investigation of the evidence of the Afrikan role as human in the broader context of the global human experience. It was simply inconceivable that Afrikans alone among the world's peoples would have had no role on the stage of human history. Was it reasonable or even logical to assume that Afrikan achievements (and, therefore, humanity) in reality could be so dismal?[30]

The response that emerged, then, was the historical examination of the humanity of Afrikan people through evidence of their agency in the history of the world. These investigations inaugurated by individuals and associations of individuals then led to enormously important and fundamental research questions, among those listed in the table below.

Table 5.2
Fundamental Research Questions Concerning Afrikan Agency and Humanity

- What was the role of Afrikans in the origins of humanity?
- What was the role of Afrikans in the origins of human society?
- What were the exemplar accomplishments of Afrikan people in various ages and in various places on the Afrikan continent from antiquity to the present?
- What role or influence in history did Afrikan people exercise on other peoples who were not Afrikan?
- How could Afrikans explain their present subordination to European peoples historically without reverting to white supremacist propagandistic explanations?
- What is the destiny of Afrikan people based upon their past experiences and human achievements?

It was in pursuit of answers to these questions that the Afrikan intellectual and scholar became enormously, but pleasantly, surprised. For far from the modesty of accomplishment one might have expected in the epistemological ecology of white supremacy, one discovered that the enormity of the evidence of Afrikan agency explained the intense and fanatical character of the white supremacist myth. Its unrelenting severity and the absolutist posture of its claims were merely symptoms of the profound contradictions it was attempting to conceal.

In other words, this discovery had wider implications. It both confirmed and underscored the conclusion that the denigration of Afrikan agency emerged from political and ideological motives and did not result from the rigors of systematic academic inquiry. "When people move you out of history, they're trying to oppress you and to make you think that you need to be oppressed," Clarke explained in a lecture to a community audience less than a decade before his death. "[Y]ou cannot consciously oppress a consciously historical people because a consciously historical people would not let it happen." In an era of postsovereignty, when Afrikans across the globe were conquered and subordinated to foreign rulers, the psychological dimensions of this new historical realization were potentially revolutionary because—of central importance—it would lead to a new sense of agency and humanness. "If you realized how much you meant to the world, and how much has been extracted from you in order to make the world, you would walk out of oppression. You wouldn't even have to fight to walk out of it; you'd just walk out of it. … You would realize your own definition of yourself."[31]

Integral to this new sense of agency and humanness, which derived from this discovery of the history of Afrikan agency, is the presumption that Afrikans in the United States were Afrikan; there was, therefore, no disjuncture between Afrikan history and culture in the continent and Afrikan history and culture in the United States. The entire cultural heritage of Afrika belonged organically, as a matter of birthright, to Afrikans who had, and whose ancestors had, been relocated to Anglo-American dictatorship. The logic of this heritage, according to Clarke and others like him, was that it supplied a cultural vision that did not—and, indeed, could not—rest upon Europe because it predated Europe. It, therefore, provided a superlative source of Afrikan agency, for it engendered an epistemology that superseded the white supremacist worldview, rendering it not only specious but, ultimately, irrelevant.

This historical understanding obviated the psychological paralysis that typified assimilationist thought, which, burdened by an inferiority complex, embraced the validity of a white supremacist epistemology, finding it impossible to contemplate an existence in which the connection to Europeans and their society could ever be severed. The nineteenth-century lecturer and activist Maria W. Stewart (1803–1879) expressed characteristic assimilationist sentiments when she stated in a lecture in Boston in 1832: "If we say we will go to a foreign land, the famine and pestilence are there, and there we shall die. … Come let us plead our cause before the whites: if they save us alive, we shall live—and if they kill us, we shall but die." For Stewart, as for other assimilationists over the centuries, the psychological paralysis extended not only to the inability to envision a destiny that did not contemplate dependency upon European overlordship, but that also engaged a perpetual quest for European validation. Were nonenslaved Afrikans, she continued, "to turn their attention more assiduously to moral worth and intellectual improvement, this would be the result: prejudice would gradually diminish, and the whites would be compelled to say, unloose those fetters!"

> Though black their skins as shades of night,
> Their hearts are pure, their souls are white.[32]

As enslavement was the principal rationale upon which the claim of the absence of Afrikan agency and humanity was advanced, Clarke located agency in the context of the history and varied nature of Afrikan resistance to foreign enslavement. This agency included the struggle for the inter-Afrikan solidarity and cultural continuity (by which is meant the determination to replicate Afrikan patterns of living, social organization, and values in the new environment) that had its genesis in the resistance to capture in and deportation from Afrika; and the resistance to enslavement and exile that occurred in the Americas. This resistance was initiated along the coastlines of West and West Central Afrika and continued in the Americas, where "the struggle to maintain an African cultural continuity" inspired armed resistance in South America and the Caribbean islands. Indeed, the nature of Afrikan agency in the United States was influenced by Afrikan agency in other parts of the Americas. Especially important in Afrikan armed struggle in the United States during the era of enslaver domination was the Haitian Revolution. Concurrently, Afrikans also "began to produce, especially in the East and in the New England states, a reading, writing, and newspaper publishing class."[33] This was chiefly tied to the abolitionist activism of Afrikan intellectuals, their launching of newspapers in the nineteenth century, and their development of a literature of resistance as seen in David Walker's *Appeal to the Colored Citizens of the World* (1829).[34]

Agency is also demonstrated in Martin Robison Delany's emergence as a major proponent of Afrikan nationalism prior to the Civil War; continuing Afrikan nationalist movements in the postbellum period; the impact of such figures as Booker T. Washington, William Monroe Trotter, and W. E. B. Du Bois on the concept of

Afrikan solidarity; the revolutionary impact of the early twentieth-century Pan Afrikanist movement led by Marcus Garvey; the Pan Afrikanist movement led by Du Bois; and the resurgence of Pan Afrikan nationalism attendant upon the Italian invasion of Ethiopia in 1935. In addition, Clarke pointed to a history of agency in the Montgomery, Alabama, bus boycott movement of the late 1950s and the emergence of the Afrikan citizenship rights movement; the Afrikan nationalist alternative seen in the rising popularity of the Nation of Islam, the emergence of Malcolm X as a public figure and Pan Afrikan nationalist leader; and the synergism inherent in the independence movement in Afrika and its impact on conceptions of Pan Afrikanism in the mid twentieth century.[35]

The significance of Pan Afrikanism is that it expressed an autonomous Afrikan response to oppression by Europeans. Undergirded by sociological transformations in the United States and the larger Americas leading toward multiethnic consolidation, it represented a posture that sought to coordinate the actions and sentiments of Afrikans dispersed in Afrika and the Americas to create a unified front of resistance. In the United States it was respectfully discussed and debated in various Afrikan-led fora. Significantly, it represented an important expression of Afrikan agency *par excellence*.

Clarke also noted that there was an ineradicable interrelationship between agency, images, the human imagination, and human possibilities: Images could exercise either an empowering or an immobilizing effect on human agency. "Most human behavior is controlled by images. Image is a factor in how people look at themselves and what they use to reflect themselves. The control of images is a major factor in world power."[36] Hence, it was important to underscore that Afrikans gave the world its first images and its first symbols, as in hieroglyphics, which were images that reflected the meaning of words and ideas.

In considering the significance of images and concepts, he offered both concepts that need to be abandoned and those that need to be adopted. Among the latter was the concept of Afrikan history as the basis of world history, an overturning and repudiation of the white supremacist epistemology of "whiteness" as the advent and as the driving force of all human agency. Among the former, and as a corollary, were notions that those who are Afrikans and indigenous to Afrika were any people other than black, e.g., Europeans and Arabs. Thus, he rejected the notion of "Black Afrika" because it presupposed the existence of a legitimate "White Afrika." Likewise, the notion of "Arab Afrika" is equally pernicious, because it fails to take cognizance of the negative role Arabs played in Afrika as conquerors and enslavers. In his view, any people in Afrika "who cannot be classified as African is either an invader or a descendant of an invader."[37]

In examining Afrikan world history, Clarke offered a periodization that outlined the broad scope of Afrikan agency into two golden ages—from the time of Imhotep, the great multigenius of the Third Egyptian Dynasty, to the first invasion from Western Asia in 1675 B.C.E. The recovery from that invasion until the first rise of Europe with the Greeks and later the Romans constituted the second golden age. The significance of this history is that it unfolded "before Europe was born."[38] Indeed, he added, the collapse of the second golden age occurred because invasions from western Asia and finally Europe destroyed Afrikan sovereignty in the lower portion of the extended Nile Valley. The challenge of the contemporary understanding of history is to correct the distortion and mutilation of the human experience that emerged subsequent to the second rise of Europe in the fifteenth and sixteenth centuries of the common era. The significant development in this period is not only the burst of European expansion that led ultimately to global colonization and the enslavement of Afrikans and their dispersal from Afrika to the Americas in the millions. It also involved the European "colonization of history and information about history."[39]

This colonization includes erasure of the awareness of the fact that Afrikans came to the Americas before Columbus, and, thus, before they were made captives by European enslavers or served as facilitators and collaborators in European conquest. They came, to the contrary, of their own initiative and by means of their own exploration.[40] Hence, the key theme that underlay Clarke's view— contrary to that declared by Trevor-Roper—is that the history of Afrikans does not depend on Europe. It was, rather, interrupted and held hostage by Europe.

In lectures titled "The Impact of the African on the 'New World': A Reappraisal" (1970) at the American Historical Association meeting in Boston and "The African Impact on Latin America and the Caribbean Islands" (1975) at the Black Child Development Institute of Columbia, Maryland,[41] Clarke outlined Afrikan agency in exploring and settling in the Americas millennia before Columbus and Spaniard invasion. "We can say now positively that Africans were in the Caribbean Islands and in North and South America long before the European age of exploration." Citing research from European scholars Leo Wiener, Harvard University professor of Slavic languages and literatures; Alexander Von Wutheneau, University of the Americas (Mexico City, Mexico) professor of art history; and independent English scholar James Bailey,[42] Clarke noted the sum of their research demonstrated Afrikans exerted tremendous cultural influence on indigenous civilization of the Americas, including in the area of religion, where, among other things, "to an extraordinary extent, ... the Indian medicine-man owes his evolution to the African medicine-man."[43]

Wiener's contribution disclosed, noted Clarke, that "American archaeology on the subject is built on 'sand and suppositions' and ... the chronology of cultural development for both of these peoples is totally out of order." Wiener also called attention to Christopher Columbus's diaries, saying Columbus admitted "he found a dark-skinned people in the Caribbean Islands trading with Indians. Columbus infers that they were people from the coast of Guinea (West Africa)."[44] The Harvard University-trained Afrikan historian Carter G. Woodson in *The African Back Ground Outlined* (1936)[45] also found, Clarke related, "that Africans discovered America long before the Europeans had any such dreams, for the Occident was all but in a state of savagery until awakened by contact with the more enlightened Orient during the Crusades." Skeletal and ethnological research documents Afrikan presence and cultural influence on the indigenous people in both religion and language. As well, the evidence makes clear that West Afrikans possessed the maritime skill to cross the ocean from the West Afrikan to the American coast.

Further, work by the independent Afrikan researcher Harold G. Lawrence indicated Afrikans from the Mali and Songhai empires (thirteenth through the sixteenth centuries) crossed the Atlantic Ocean and established trade relations with the indigenous people of the Americas. "'Proof of this,'" Clarke quotes Lawrence, "'is evidenced by the fact that Columbus was informed by some men, when he stopped at one of the Cape Verde Islands off the coast of Africa, that Negroes had been known to set out into the Atlantic from the Guinea coast in canoes loaded with merchandise and steering towards the west.'" He continued: "'The same Christopher Columbus was further informed by the Indians of Hispaniola when he arrived in the West Indies that they had been able to obtain gold from black men who had come across the sea from the south and southeast. ... It must be added that Amerigo Vespucci on his voyage to the Americas witnessed these same black men out in the Atlantic returning to Africa.'" Not only Vespucci, but other European explorers, including Balboa, encountered small settlements of Afrikans in various parts of the areas they invaded. Early art, legends, and burial grounds in the Americas yield abundant evidence of Afrikan presence predating Spaniard invasion. According to indigenous sources, Afrikans could be found throughout Mexico, Central America, and in South America as far south as Peru and the Andes Mountains.[46]

This evidence, Clarke asserted, must also be juxtaposed to the fact that Afrikans accompanied the Spaniard invasion of the Americas, in which project they came "as explorers, adventurers, craftsmen, and freebooters long before slavery was the main reason for their presence." An Afrikan piloted one of Columbus's ships, thirty Afrikans accompanied Balboa's encounter with the Pacific Ocean in 1513, Afrikans participated in Cortez's conquest of Mexico, while others proved integrally important to the success of Spaniard exploration and conquest in Mexico, Central America, South America, and what is now the southwestern United States.[47]

Indispensable to a proper understanding of this Afrikan history and Afrikan agency is also the role of Afrikan women. First, Clarke argued, her role in the development of early societies in Afrika was central, including, of course, in the development of home and family, as well as in the domestication of animals and the development of agriculture. In the more sophisticated societies of the Nile Valley, women were even recognized as powerful deities in the established cosmological order.

Second, Clarke maintained, there are the histories of dominant personalities who made major contributions in statecraft, diplomacy, and international relations, in human and social rights, in war, and in resistance to imperialism in Afrikan history. These lessons transcend the fact that the actors were female and serve to illustrate their contribution to the forward flow of Afrikan and of human history in the broadest sense. Among such personalities was the ancient Egyptian monarch Hapshetsut, "the first of the great women in history" who, challenging male domination in the Egyptian kingship, "asserts herself as the first of the great female pharaohs." Under her rule, she "unites Egypt with Kush and makes peace with nations in south and east African coast as far as Punt, present day Somalia" and who "sends emissaries to Asia to make peace with the kingdom of Camay, present day India."[48] Indeed, Clarke continues, Hapshetsut is "the first statesman in history to embark on such international peace missions."[49] Other female state rulers in Kush millennia later stopped the southward expansion of European military invasion into Afrika under the Greeks and the Romans, or, in the modern period of enslaver disruption, stood at the forefront of diplomatic and military resistance to European invasion and colonization in West Central Afrika and in West Afrika.[50]

Not only does history provide evidence of Afrikan agency and, therefore, that Afrikans are human, but Clarke also advanced that the exploration of this history provides the basis for Afrikan agency in the face of foreign oppression in the present time. "Because our memories are short and we have not, creatively, connected history into an instrument of our Liberation," he asserted in a 1975 lecture at the Center for African and African-American Studies at Atlanta University, "most of us do not know that there was no ideology in the world until we created one. Therefore our search for an ideology is a search for our lost values, culturally, politically and socially."[51]

In short, Afrikan historical investigation, which is engaged within the context of a countervailing white supremacist epistemology created by European settlers, serves simultaneously to explain the nature of the Afrikan past and, following that, to provide the framework for formulating an explanation, or an epistemology, of the meaning of the Afrikan present and the possibilities and imperatives of the Afrikan future. Indeed, Afrikan historical investigation has created the necessity for a new explanation and new meaning within this context. Further, the content of this new meaning is necessarily premised upon Afrikan sovereignty as a fundamental posture and lens through which to examine the present and the future. This necessity arises from the realization that Afrikan sovereignty constitutes both the history and the implications of the history of Afrikan agency that has been uncovered. Hence, the explanations of white supremacy, which posited that the destiny of Afrikans was to serve European interests and to subordinate themselves to those interests, had now become obsolete. Clarke, therefore, advanced that the driving logic of Afrikans casting about for a framework in which to understand the meaning of their existence in these changed epistemological circumstances—their struggle in the present, their past as a guide, and their future as an inevitability—is based in the fact that all people need an ideology, a framework in which to understand the meaning of their existence. At a very basic level, the need for an ideology is to explain how and why a people will continue their existence on the planet, which has the effect of aiding and deepening human agency.

One of the most critical problems, however, is that the absence of historical memory vitiates Afrikan drive and initiative, confuses the people as to the proper direction they should take as a people, and drives them to borrow ideologies that (while unknown to them) derived from their own culture in antiquity, were reconceived and redesigned to address the problems and challenges to meaningful existence for other people. These reformulations were adapted to circumstances that had no direct relevance to Afrikan experiences, needs, or interests. Hence, the "tragedy of our present position is that we are searching for an ideology among second and third rate people who got their ideology, their religion, and the basis of what they call culture, originally from us."[52] In this category Clarke cited European socialism, inspired by the German philosopher Karl Marx and the Russian Bolshevik Vladimir Lenin. By contrast, an Afrikan form of socialism "was old among us before Europe was born." In fact, he added, before "the second rise of Europe in the fifteenth and sixteenth centuries, most of the people in the non-European world lived in communal socialist societies."[53]

Africana Studies philosopher Reiland Rabaka notes an earlier critique offered by W. E. B. Du Bois, first articulated in 1907, that discussed "deficiencies in the Marxist tradition which included, among other things, a silence on and an inattention to: race, racism, and anti-racist struggle; colonialism and anti-colonial struggle; and the ways in which *both* capitalism and colonialism exacerbate not simply the economic exploitation of non-European peoples, but continue colonization and violation (both physical and psychological) beyond the realm of political economy"[54] (original emphasis). While Du Bois, like Clarke, agreed that the future for Afrikans lay in socialism, he was, also like Clarke, "extremely adamant in stating that continental and diasporan Africans should not graft Eurocentric (Marxist-Leninist) and or Asio-centric (Maoist) communism or socialism onto African life-worlds." He urged, instead, critical study of its relevance and suitability to Afrikan needs. Du Bois contended the question of its applicability had to be worked out by Afrikan reason and experimentation and not by imposed dogma.[55]

Clarke, himself a socialist, and going further than Du Bois, maintained Afrikan socialists must begin to appreciate the enormous possibilities for Afrikan agency, or its paralysis, by either expanding their understanding to one that is self-oriented or Afrika-centered; or by restricting it to one that is alien-oriented or Europe-centered. If Afrikan socialists were to accept themselves as Afrikan, and were to accept that within their culture were answers to problems, they could creatively approach and effectively solve contemporary challenges to Afrikan freedom, rather than futilely insisting upon rigidly applying approaches that were never intended to address, let alone solve, Afrikan social problems. "The ideas that went into the making of what we are now calling Socialist or Communist are as old as thinking man. There is no question about these ideas being older than Europe. When the ideas began among early men and societies, Europe did not exist."[56]

This could be clearly seen in early Afrikan socialistic societies, including in the communalism of the smaller, less complex food-gathering societies. But this held true for more developed and technologically advanced Afrikan states in later eras. Akhenaton, the king of the eighteenth Egyptian dynasty, expounded a philosophy of nonviolence that had strong socialist elements. This socialistic ethos can also be seen in the fact that the structure of Afrikan economies in precolonial times offered a land tenure system that was free of feudalism. It can also be witnessed in the nature of social welfare built into the structure and ideological functioning of Afrikan societies that undergirded the social security of children, widows, and elders. In the modern colonial period, some of the earliest articulations of this socialistic ethos could be seen in an examination of some of the nineteenth-century intellectuals such as the Gold Coast activist Casely Hayford's examination of the land question and the Liberian scholar Edward Wilmot Blyden's discussion of socialist concepts in Afrikan societies before conquest by Europe. Consequently, the failing of alienated Afrikan intellectuals is their incapacity to comprehend that the relevance of the European approach to socialism is limited, that it lacked universal application; its articulations of problems and solutions relate solely to the peculiarities of the European historical and social experience, which, in large measure, are inapplicable to the Afrikan historical and social experience.[57]

Hence, this ahistoricism, this profound ignorance of Afrikan history and culture among alienated Afrikan intellectuals, highlights an epistemological crisis in Afrikan consciousness. The problem of Afrikan intellectuals engaging rather passionately and fruitlessly in debates about the merits of socialism and capitalism, as defined in European terms, is, ultimately, unproductive, Clarke argued, because it vitiates agency by assuming and proposing that Afrikans cannot provide answers for themselves. This is not to say, of course, that there is no need to move toward some form of socialism for optimal benefit to human society. "Men of vision and intelligence, with a knowledge of history, no longer debate this point," he asserted. The central problem, rather, is that the depth of cultural and historical amnesia that exists among the Afrikan advocates of European-conceived socialism undermines Afrikan agency; such advocacy arises from a consciousness that has been colonized. "These new self-proclaimed, 'Theoreticians,' act as though Black people have no ideological contribution to make to their own salvation," Clarke complained. "If the matter was left to them, they would lead us—like whores and hungry dogs, in search of the political and ideological leavings of a dying people." To the contrary, he proposed, "For our salvation we should draw on the intellectual heritage of the whole world, starting with our own intellectual heritage." To act successfully with a clear sense of independence and a firm sense of purpose—in other words, with agency—depends upon Afrikans first and foremost knowing and accepting themselves.[58]

Further, what should also be of concern to Afrikan intellectuals is the fact that Marx's ideas regarding socialism were being advanced at the same time that European states were systematically destroying "the pure socialist structures of African societies." Instead of slavishly adhering to foreign ideological doctrines, Clarke admonished, Afrikan intellectuals should, first, as Du Bois had also counseled, insist that concepts of socialism and communism be flexible and responsive to differing conditions and needs throughout the Afrikan world. More importantly, he asserted, it is imperative in the quest for the restructuring of Afrikan life that Afrikans shape all ideologies as instruments that serve their own interests. This is at the heart of Afrikan agency in the current time. "If we are going to be masters of our destiny, we must be masters of the ideas that influence that destiny." Hence, he reminded, the historic and preeminent ideological response of Afrikans to the challenge of human existence in the modern or postsovereign era, in which the question of socialism has been subsumed, has been Pan Afrikanism.[59]

Afrikan world history unquestionably demonstrates humanity and agency, Clarke continued. Afrika is the home of the origination of human beings, making Afrikans the mothers and fathers of humankind; Afrika is the incubator for the beginnings of human society; the growth of Afrikan societies and the peopling of Afrika were indigenous, coming from within Afrika, not from outside of it; and the most magnificent of human civilizations, ancient Egypt, originated from the southern interior of Afrika. These basic realities contradict deliberate fabrications that declared Afrikans had no culture prior to European conquest, that ancient Egypt was a "white" nation and that its culture was European or Asian but not Afrikan, that Afrika made no contribution to the development of Europe, that the enslavement of Afrikans was for them a blessing in disguise, and that Afrikans had no civilizations and made no contribution to the progress of humankind prior to European contact.[60]

To this last assertion, Clarke observed that humanity and agency were inseparable, because to be human is to be an agent and to be an agent is a consequence of being human. Hence, he dismissed the notion that there could ever be a people without a history, because, he declared, "There is no such thing as a people without a history or a culture. People make history and create culture simply by living."[61]

On the basis of great personalities alone, such as the Egyptian legends and monarchs Imhotep (2980 B.C.E.), Hatshepsut (1500 B.C.E.), Akhenaton (1350 B.C.E.), Makeda of Ethiopia (970 B.C.E.), Piankhi of Meroitic Sudan and Egypt (720 B.C.E.), agency and power are evidently an integral part of the Afrikan historical experience. But even beyond great Afrikan personalities, one can trace the influence of the ancient civilizations they represent. "There were, in this ancestry, rulers who expanded their kingdoms into empires with great and magnificent armies whose dimensions dwarfed entire nations into submission, generals who advanced the technique of military science, scholars whose vision of life showed foresight and wisdom, and priests who told of gods that were strong and kind."[62] This examination extends into the western Sudan with the massive medieval empires such as Ghana (300–1076 C.E.), Mali (1076–1332 C.E.), and Songhai (1335–1590 C.E.), and the smaller but still impressive West Afrikan states that include those formed by the peoples in or of Kanem-Bornu, Mossi, Yoruba, Benin, and Hausa. While all of these states came to an end as a consequence of invasion and conquest, "I want to make it clear that the Black Race did not come to the United States culturally empty-handed." Among other things, "the forefathers of the Africans who eventually became slaves in the United States lived in a society where university life was fairly common and scholars were beheld with reverence."[63]

Indeed, he noted, the experience of West Afrika is not without its grand achievements. From the early part of the fourteenth century until the Moorish invasion and destruction of the Songhai empire in 1591, the intellectual center of West Afrika lay in the Songhai city of Timbuktu at the University of Sankore. "Black scholars were enjoying a renaissance that was known and respected throughout most of Africa and in parts of Europe." While West Afrikan scholars of the Islamic complex could from Sankore hold their own with the Arab scholars at the prestigious universities in Morocco, Tunis, and Egypt, the Arabs were not always equal to the rigorous academic requirements at Sankore. Ahmed Baba, the last chancellor of the University of Sankore, represents "a brilliant example of the range of and depth of West African intellectual activity before the colonial era." He was the author of more than forty books, most of them treating different themes. His personal library contained 1,600 volumes, one of the richest of his day.[64]

The Afrikans' absence of memory of the foregoing achievements resulted from European conquest, which—with its concomitant developments in the production of knowledge in areas of science, history, religion, economics, among other fields—displaced and suppressed in the consciousness of all the peoples Europeans conquered the awareness of their centeredness in all fields of human knowledge and human study of and solutions to the challenges of human living. Hence, Clarke proposed, there is the need for a renewed understanding of Afrikan history that conforms to the way in which it was perceived and developed by Afrikans prior to European conquest. This renewed sense of history must be framed in terms of the history of the world and not narrowly defined in terms of enslavement. In short, what is contemplated is an "Afro-centric view of history," dispensing with a "Euro-centric view of history." Central to this matter of interpretation is the fact that there is a "relationship of history to power" even as there is a "relationship of a people's history to their humanity." In a postsovereign era, when Afrikans have been subjected to psychological warfare to damage the psyche so as to better effectuate their subordination by conquerors, there is the necessity of "a new way of looking at a people's history and memories, in order to stimulate pride in themselves and a love of themselves."[65]

An example of Clarke's argument can be seen in an aspect of indigenous Yoruba culture. Afrikan agency and Afrikan humanity as a central framework through which to understand the human experience is clearly seen in the Yoruba spiritual system called Ifa and its teaching concerning the significance of Ile-Ife, the holy city of beginnings, for understanding the origins of human beings and human society. In an interview with Ifa elders in Ile-Ife, Osun State, in Yorubaland, Nigeria, published in 1985, the Ifa scholar and priest S. Solagbade Popoola explored this understanding with one of the high priests of Ifa, Chief Fasuyi Kekere-Awo, the representative of Ijo Orunmila Adulawe at Ile-Ife.

> Chief Fasuyi maintained that the world started from Ile-Ife.
> ... He went further to say that even people from Saudi Arabia
> emigrated to their present place of abode from Ile-Ife and not

the other way around. The Europeans, Asians, Australians, Americans all have a common origin in Ile-Ife.

Chief Fasuyi was then asked to explain why it is that those people from across the Ocean are "white" or light in colour while Africans are black. He referred us to a portion of Eji-Ogbe in Odu Ifa where the origin of "whites" was explained and narrated. The "whites" generation was classified into three groups: those moulded by Obatala (Orisa Nla), those moulded by Oluorogbo and those moulded by Olokun. Because they were moulded by three different sources, that was the reason why they had differences in complexion and intelligence. But one thing certain is that Obatala moulded the European groups. Up till today, we still have "Igbo Oyinbo" (whiteman's jungle) in Ile-Ife here, *even before the advent* [of Europeans] *to Africa* (original emphasis).[66]

Chief Fasuyi further explained, writes Popoola, that Obatala sought divination and offered sacrifices in the creation of the white-skinned groups. Odu Ifa (or the Ifa scriptures) indicate that before the Europeans emigrated from Ile-Ife they informed Obatala of their intent to leave, and he blessed them and gave them a greeting specific to them.

Greeting: *Alo* (Hello)
Response: *Alo* (Hello)
Greeting: *Ewo maanio* (It is taboo to forget this greeting style.)
Response: *Ewo danindanin* (It is a serious taboo.)[67]

The clear import of this epistemology of human origins is that the consciousness that created it cannot feel threatened by white supremacy because white supremacy is conceptually incomprehensible. Further, the notion of Afrikan agency is both implicitly and explicitly expressed. This incomprehension of both white supremacy and the absence of Afrikan agency and humanity, which is white supremacy's corollary, prevails because Europeans exercise no real or *felt* power in Ile-Ife. Thus, European claims to superiority, and to Afrikan inferiority, only gain relevance in a context of power in which its configurations entail the conquest and cultural absorption or assimilation of Afrikan consciousness into a European conceptual and historiographical universe. Another way of seeing this is that only those Afrikans who through conquest acquired literacy in European culture were compelled to confront or to submit to the ideas that were current within that culture, and to offer either capitulation or challenge and refutation to its chauvinistic or supremacist articulations. In short, the contest of the historiographical struggle by Afrikans in the European world engages the effort by Afrikans to rescue and to restore consciousness to an understanding of Afrikan humanity and Afrikan agency that existed unencumbered and unaffected by the depredations of European supremacist conquest and propaganda. Clarke, then, was stating that this contest ultimately required a shift in the balance of power away from European hegemony to Afrikan sovereignty. This interconnection between power and consciousness explains his grasp of the strategic relevance of Afrikan anticolonialism (Afrikan agency) to an authentic and autochthonous understanding of Africana history and humanity.

It follows, then, that Clarke would note that epochal changes of global proportions were rendered not only upon Afrikan realities but in the world by what he called "the second rise of Europe," which began in the fifteenth and sixteenth centuries, providing a key dividing line in the development of human consciousness and human society. "This was a period when entire peoples and societies were displaced from their cultural moorings." This global disruption by European states had profound meaning for human civilization because the process of European expansion "destroyed nations and civilizations that were old before Europe itself was born. We have not recovered from this event and neither has the world. This was a pivotal time in the history of the world. The origins of most of our present day problems can be traced to this period in history." Hence, Afrikans are faced in the modern period with an assessment of their own collective worth as a people. "How important are we as a people? Who do we need and who needs us?"[68]

Perhaps one of the most interesting aspects about the second rise of Europe is the fact that the Portuguese, who were the first to break out of the stranglehold of Muslim domination in the western Mediterranean, were not initially looking for slaves in Afrika. In addition to their search for direct access to the famed gold wealth of the western Sudan, the Portuguese were in search of a powerful Christian state with which to establish a strategic military alliance against Arab and Muslim power. The devastation of enslavement arose later from European intrigue in Afrika, and the nature of that devastation evolved to the point that Afrikans, after more than 400 years in the United States, still remain aliens among the people who established the state and who forced Afrikans to contribute their labor to the enrichment of the state.[69]

Clarke also argued the concept of race was part of the epistemological arsenal of European world conquest that militated against a true understanding of the humanity of human beings. "There is no such thing as a race. Nature created no races; man created races and racial classifications. ... Who benefited from this artificial creation at first and who benefits from it now?" Clarke asked.[70] The notion of race had to fit within an explanatory scheme that abetted an intended crime against human beings. "Racism was created to justify the slave trade, to justify the colonial system, to justify the utter ruthlessness that had to go into the makings of modern capitalism."[71]

Still, Clarke maintained, racism as an antihuman epistemological weapon extends back into antiquity and owes its pernicious origins to the Hebrew scriptures, which advanced the mythological notions of a chosen people and a people allegedly cursed by God.[72] The notion of a people cursed by God arises from the story of a drunken Noah cursing his grandson Canaan, his son Ham's son, to be a slave of slaves because of Ham's purported indiscretion in seeing, mocking, and reporting his father's condition of being naked and in a drunken stupor.[73] Citing particularly lurid accounts of the alleged curse of Canaan in Robert Graves and Raphael Patai's *Hebrew Myths: The Book of Genesis*,[74] Clarke notes that certain accounts were virulently and grotesquely racist. According to one version of the myth, woolly hair, black skin and ugliness, red eyes, elongated genitals, sexual obsession, enslavement, and lying to and hatred of their enslavers were features of the curse Noah cast upon Afrikan people.[75] An analysis of the language and concepts used indicates that the interpretation could not have emerged from antiquity, when the word *Negro* did not exist (until its introduction by Spanish and Portuguese enslavers of the fifteenth and sixteenth centuries), and when the association of blackness with ugliness and shame was inconceivable.[76]

Although the original point of the myth was to serve as the Hebrew ideological justification for the enslavement and oppression of the Canaanite people in ancient times, later its utility was "gratefully borrowed by Christians in the Middle Ages," who saw it as useful rationale for the implementation of enslavement as a means of replenishing a labor supply ravaged by plague. Drawing from the association of Ham with "blackness" and Afrikan heritage, Europeans developed a color-based notion of caste that gave legitimacy to the idea that Afrikans should be enslaved to Europeans.[77] In addition to Jewish racism, however, one cannot but acknowledge that similar color-based mythologies justifying enslavement can be found in ancient Greek, Hittite, and later Byzantine culture, he observed.[78]

The epistemological dimension to white supremacy is not only found in the Judaeo-Christian religious tradition but also in the European historical tradition. The eruption of Europe in its imperialist thrust into the world in the fifteenth and sixteenth centuries led not only to the colonization "of the bulk of the world's people." In addition, and in concert with this imperialist thrust, Europeans also—as Clarke would often remark—"colonized the interpretation of history itself. Human history was rewritten to favor them at the expense of other people. The roots of modern racism can be traced to this conquest and colonization."[79] In short, racism involved a critically important epistemological conquest.

Hence, it was necessary during this period to formalize the concept of race and to make it a category of knowledge that could sustain the change in the power arrangements of Europeans to the rest of the world. While drawing from concepts in classical Greek culture, intellectuals of the European enlightenment period began the systematic development of the idea, under the rubric of scientific inquiry, as a human classificatory scheme.[80]

Aside from religion, history, and developing notions of science, there is, of course, the economic motive. In addition to the riches accrued by the criminal enterprise, there is the relation of the extraction of raw materials of Afrika, Asia, South America, and the Caribbean to the supply of labor, which financed the European industrial revolution.[81] Sanctioned by both the Catholic and Protestant forms of Christianity, "the ghastly traffic in human misery was given the cloak of respectability."[82] Clearly, in Clarke's view, these various epistemological and materialist factors—religion, history, science, economics—were useful in the conspiracy to strangle the notion among Europeans that Afrikans were human beings and to justify the notion that Afrikans had no history and agency. The act of oppression, which dehumanized Afrikans, had to be supported by the ideological dehumanization of Afrikan people, which, Clarke argued, manifest in textbooks, in geographies, in travel books, and in the intentional and systematic destruction of indigenous Afrikan culture in the Americanization/enslavement process.[83] Changes in the form of oppression—enslavement, colonialism, neocolonialism, segregation—share the common ideological foundation of white supremacy. This explains the contemporary struggle for Africana Studies, Clarke concluded. "On university campuses and in international conferences they [Afrikans] are demanding that their history be looked at from a black perspective or from an Afrocentric point of view."[84]

The extent of the epistemological alternative, which Clarke called the "Afro-Centric view" of Afrikan history, was total. "The tragedy of African History, and World History in general, is that in most cases, it is told from a European point of view, in an attempt to justify European domination over most of the world." In re-viewing history from an Afrika-centered analysis, Clarke noted that even Europe, resplendent in its omnipotence in recent times, had to be reconceptualized. In the broad scope of human history Europe represents the last of several cultural complexes to emerge as a powerful and dominant force in world history. Prior to the modern or postsovereign era, however, "there was no Europe, as such, in ancient times. What we call early Europe was really the northern sphere of the Afro-Mediterranean world."[85]

The ramifications of this reconceptualization is that it demythologized Europe of its omniscience, omnipotence, and its centeredness in the understanding of global human history, placing it instead within a context of Afrikan agency and sovereignty. Most significantly, it summons new manifestations of Afrikan agency by breaking the notion that the nature of the Afrikan encounter with Europe and the European encounter with Afrika has always been an asymmetrical power arrangement in which Europeans were always the superiors. By implication, current arrangements in intellectual, cultural, political, social, economic, and, ultimately, military terms are called into question, have to be seen as of an ephemeral character, and are subject, with sustained Afrikan initiative, to revolutionary, systemic reversal. "My opinion is that we will have to make a basic decision fundamental to our survival as a people," Clarke stated in a lecture delivered in 1977 at the First Annual Black Unity and Futurism Conference in Minneapolis, Minnesota. "We will have to decide whether we will be the rear guard in building a social order that is ruled by others or the vanguard in building a social order that we will control. I do not believe that genuine Black solidarity will come until we unite in making this decision."[86]

Notes

1. Ayi Kwei Armah, *Two Thousand Seasons* (Popenguine, Senegal: Per Ankh, 2000; originally Nairobi, Kenya: EAPH, 1973), 21–22.

2. John Henrik Clarke and Amy Jacques Garvey, ed., *Marcus Garvey and the Vision of Africa* (New York: Vintage Books, 1974), xvi.

3. James W. C. Pennington, *A Text Book of the Origin and History, etc. etc. of the Colored People* (Hartford, CT: L. Skinner, Printer, 1841; reprint Detroit: Negro History Press, n.d.), 22–23.

4. R. B. Lewis, *Light and Truth: Containing the Universal History of the Colored and Indian Race, from the Creation of the World to the Present Time* (Boston: Published by a Committee of Colored Gentlemen, Benjamin F. Roberts, Printer, 1844), 10, 13, 15, 19.

5. William Wells Brown, *The Black Man: His Antecedents, His Genius, and His Achievements* (New York: Thomas Hamilton, and Boston: R. F. Wallcut, 1863); ibid., *The Rising Sun; or, The Antecedents and Advancement of the Colored Race* (Boston: A.G. Brown and Company, Publishers, 1874).

6. George Washington Williams, *History of the Negro Race in America From 1619 to 1880. Negroes as Slaves, as Soldiers, and as Citizens; together with a Preliminary Consideration of the Unity of the Human Family, an Historical Sketch of Africa, and an Account of the Negro Governments of Sierra Leone and Liberia; 1619 to 1800*, 2 vols., vol. 1 (New York: G.P. Putnam's Sons, 1883), 18–19.

7. For a more extended discussion, see Ahati N. N. Toure, "Nineteenth Century African Historians in the United States: Explorations of Cultural Location

and National Destiny," in *Black Cultures and Race Relations*, ed. James L. Conyers, Jr. (Chicago: Burnham, 2002), 16–50.

8. Brown, *The Black Man*, 33–34.

9. Martin R. Delany, *The Origin of Races and Color* (Baltimore, MD: Black Classic Press, 1991; originally *Principia of Ethnology: The Origin of Races and Color, with an Archeological Compendium of Ethiopian and Egyptian Civilization, from Years of Careful Examination and Enquiry*, Philadelphia: Harper & Brother, Publishers, 1879), 38.

10. Henry McNeal Turner, "A Great Book. Ought to be Read by Everybody – Only Those Blind to Their Interests Will Fail to Get It," *The Christian Recorder*, 30 September 1880. Turner's endorsement was part of advertisement for Delany's book featured in the newspaper throughout 1880. Published weekly by the African Methodist Episcopal Church, which was headquartered in Philadelphia, the newspaper ran from 1861 to 1902, although it enjoyed a brief and abortive run in 1854.

11. J. H. Scott, "Who Are We?" *The Christian Recorder*, 30 December 1880.

12. A Constant Reader, "For Freedom's Journal," *Freedom's Journal*, 5 December 1828. The contributor neglected to cite the essay's author. The newspaper, published in New York City from 1827 to 1829, was the first published by Afrikans in the United States.

13. Pennington, *A Text Book*; Lewis, *Light and Truth*; Brown, *The Black Man*; ibid., *The Rising Sun*; Williams, *History of the Negro Race*; Delany, *The Origin of Races*.

14. Georg Wilhelm Friedrich Hegel, *Philosophy of History*, trans. J. Sibree (New York: P. F. Collier and Son; London: The Colonial Press, 1900), 93.

15. As quoted by Stephen Jay Gould, *The Mismeasure of Man* (New York: W. W. Norton, 1981), 43, 48.

16. As quoted by W. E. B. Du Bois, *Black Reconstruction in America: An Essay toward a History of the Part Which Black Folk Played in the Attempt to Reconstruct Democracy in America, 1860–1880* (New York: Russell and Russell, 1962; originally 1935), 718–719. See John W. Burgess, *Reconstruction and the Constitution, 1866–1876* (New York: C. Scribner's Sons, 1902).

17. Arnold J. Toynbee, *A Study of History*, vols. 1–6 abridged (New York: Oxford University Press, 1947), 54.

18. Hugh Trevor-Roper, *The Rise of Christian Europe* (New York: Harcourt, Brace & World; London: Thames and Hudson, 1965), 9.

19. See George M. Frederickson, *The Black Image in the White Mind: The Debate on Afro-American Character and Destiny, 1817–1914* (New York: Harper Torchbooks, 1971); Winthrop D. Jordan, *White Over Black: American Attitudes toward the Negro, 1550–1812* (New York: W. W. Norton and Company, 1977; originally Chapel Hill: The University of North Carolina Press, 1968); Winthrop D. Jordan, *The White Man's Burden: Historical Origins of Racism in the United States* (New York: Oxford University Press, 1974). The texts present discussions of the Afrikan image in the white supremacist European mind.

20. The fiery abolitionist Frederick Douglass provides an apt example, when in 1846 he declared: "The black man (unlike the Indian) loves civilization. He does not make very great progress in civilization himself, but he likes to be in the midst of it, and prefers to share its most galling evils, to encountering barbarism." See Frederick Douglass, "The Negro's Right to Remain in America," a speech in the 27 March 1846 issue of the *Liberator*, in Philip S. Foner, ed., *Frederick Douglass: Selections From His Writings* (New York: International Publishers, 1945), 53–54, and "Proceedings of the Colored National Convention Held in Rochester July 6th, 7th and 8th, 1853" in Howard Holman Bell, ed., *Minutes of the Proceedings of the National Negro Conventions, 1830–1864* (New York: Arno Press and The New York Times, 1969), 36.

21. William Leo Hansberry, "W. E. B. Du Bois: His Influence on African History," unpublished remarks, JHCP, SCRBC. The foregoing were remarks intended for a memorial program for Du Bois hosted by *Freedomways* magazine. As Hansberry was ill, he was unable to attend or to read the remarks himself and asked that they be read in his absence. Phaon Goldman, letter to John Henrik Clarke, 15 March 1965, JHCP, SCRBC.

22. Cheikh Anta Diop, *African Origin of Civilization: Myth or Reality*, ed. and trans. Mercer Cook (New York: Lawrence Hill Books, 1974), xiv.

23. Willis N. Huggins and John G. Jackson, *Introduction to African Civilizations with Main Currents in Ethiopian History* (Baltimore: Inprint Editions, 1999; originally New York: Avon House 1937), 23, 44, 40, 48.

24. Ibid., 22.

25. J. A. Rogers, *World's Great Men of Color*, vol. 1, ed. John Henrik Clarke (New York: Touchstone, 1996; originally New York: J. A. Rogers, 1946), 1–4.

26. An example of this is seen in James D. Anderson, *The Education of Blacks in the South, 1860–1935* (Chapel Hill: The University of North Carolina Press, 1988), 4–32. He notes that northern European missionaries who came to the

South to teach literacy to Afrikans newly freed from enslavement after the Civil War were astounded and offended to discover Afrikans were not at all deferential to Europeans, nor uncertain of their group purpose when it came to their education. "Many missionaries were astonished, and later chagrined, however, to discover that many ex-slaves had established their own educational collectives and associations, staffed schools entirely with black teachers, and were unwilling to allow their educational movement to be controlled by the 'civilized' Yankees." Although Afrikans appreciated northern support, the missionaries soon discovered "they resisted infringements that threatened to undermine their own initiative and self-reliance." Indeed, writes Anderson, the missionaries were thoroughly unprepared for Afrikans' sense of strength and independence. On this point, see also John W. Blassingame, *The Slave Community: Plantation Life in the Antebellum South* (New York: Oxford University Press, 1972, 1979); Sterling Stuckey, *Slave Culture: Nationalist Theory and Foundations of Black America* (New York: Oxford University Press, 1987); and Michael A. Gomez, *Exchanging Our Country Marks: The Transformation of African Identities in the Colonial and Antebellum South* (Chapel Hill: The University of North Carolina Press, 1998).

27. John Henrik Clarke, "A Search for Identity," *Social Casework* 51, no. 5 (May 1970): 262.

28. Ibid., 262.

29. Ibid., 260.

30. Robert W. July, *A History of the African People*, 5th ed. (Prospect Heights, IL: Waveland Press, 1998), 165. Interestingly, in 1998, July, like Clarke, was professor emeritus at Hunter College.

31. John Henrik Clarke, "The Preservers of Afrikan World History," address to New York community audience, circa 1990s, DVD, available from the Nubian Network, http://www.blackconsciousness.com.

32. Maria W. Stewart, "Lecture, Delivered at the Franklin Hall, Boston, Sept. 21, 1832," in *Spiritual Narratives*, ed. Henry Louis Gates, Jr. (New York: Oxford University Press, 1998), 51, 52.

33. John Henrik Clarke, "The Black American's Search for an Ideology," Eighth Conference of the Center for African and African-American Studies, Atlanta University, Atlanta, Georgia, 4–6 December 1975, 5, JHCP, SCRBC.

34. Ibid., "Beyond Black Survival A World of Challenge," First Annual Black Unity and Futurism Conference, Minnesota Springhill Conference Center, Minneapolis, Minnesota, 18–20 November 1977, 3–5, JHCP, SCRBC.

35. Ibid., 3–5.

36. Ibid., "African People: Their Image in Early World History," Black History Week Commemoration, Ethnic Studies Program, Illinois State University, Normal-Bloomington, Illinois, 3 February 1978, 1, JHCP, SCRBC.

37. Ibid., 1–2. Note Jared Diamond, *Guns, Germs, and Steel: The Fates of Human Societies* (New York: W. W. Norton, 1999), 378. He argued for a "white" Afrika as a legitimate and historical reality that happens also to claim the geography and civilization of the ancient Nile Valley.

38. Ibid., 2.

39. Ibid., 3.

40. Ibid., 3.

41. Ibid., "The Impact of the African on the 'New World': A Reappraisal," American Historical Association, Boston, Massachusetts, 28–30 December 1970; ibid., "The African Impact on Latin America and the Caribbean Islands," Black Child Development Institute, Inc., Conference at the Urban Life Center, Columbia, Maryland, 3–6 December 1975, JHCP, SCRBC.

42. Leo Wiener, *Africa and the Discovery of America* (Philadelphia: Innes and Sons, 1920–1922); Alexander Von Wuthenau, *The Art of Terracotta Pottery in Pre-Columbian Central and South America* (New York: Crown Publishers, 1970, ©1969); and James Bailey, *God-Kings and Titans: The New World Ascendancy in Ancient Times* (New York: St. Martin's Press, 1973).

43. Clarke, "The Impact of the African," 1–2.

44. Ibid., "The African Impact on Latin America and the Caribbean Islands," Black Child Development Institute, Inc., Conference at the Urban Life Center, Columbia, Maryland, 3–6 December 1975, 1–2, JHCP, SCRBC.

45. Carter Godwin Woodson, *The African Background Outlined; or, Handbook for the Study of the Negro* (Washington, DC: Association for the Study of Negro Life and History, 1936).

46. Clarke, "The Impact of the African," 2–4. Clarke was citing "African Explorers of the New World," *Crisis* magazine (June–July 1962).

47. Ibid., "The African Impact," 2–3.

48. Ibid., "The African Woman as a Figure in World History," Lecture at Livingston College, 22, July 1970, 1, JHCP, SCRBC.

49. Ibid., 2.

50. Ibid., 2–3.

51. Ibid., "The Black American's Search for an Ideology," Eighth Conference of the Center for African and African-American Studies, Atlanta University, Atlanta, Georgia, 4–6 December 1975, 1, JHCP, SCRBC.

52. Ibid., 1.

53. Ibid., 1–2.

54. Reiland Rabaka, "W. E. B. Du Bois and/as Africana Critical Theory: Pan-Africanism, Critical Marxism, and Male Feminism," in *Afrocentricity and the Academy: Essays on Theory and Practice*, ed. James L. Conyers, Jr. (Jefferson, NC: McFarland, 2003), 76.

55. Ibid., 77.

56. Clarke, "The Black American's Search," 3.

57. Ibid., 4.

58. Ibid., 2.

59. Ibid., 4.

60. Ibid., "African History as the Basis of World History," Black Child Development Institute, Inc., Conference at the Urban Life Center, Columbia, Maryland, 3–6 December 1975; First lecture, Thursday, 4 December 1975, 1–2, JHCP, SCRBC.

61. Ibid., "Myths and Misconceptions About African History," Lecture at De Hostos College, Grand Concourse, Bronx, New York, 25 September 1981, 3, JHCP, SCRBC.

62. Ibid., "African History as the Basis," 5.

63. Ibid., 3–5.

64. Ibid., 6–7.

65. Ibid., "Myths and Misconceptions," 2–4.

66. S. Solagbade Popoola, "Pilgrimage to Ile-Ife," *Orunmila* 1 (July 1985): 13.

67. Ibid., 13.

68. John Henrik Clarke, "The Politics of Black Survival," Lecture at Black Studies Department, Rutgers, The State University of New Jersey, Newark, New Jersey, 27 October 1976, 2–3, JHCP, SCRBC.

69. Ibid., 4–5.

70. Ibid., "Race: The Historical Development of A Myth," Forum on Strategies to Defeat Mounting Racism, Black Liberation Press, New York City, held at Columbia University, October 1978, 1, JHCP, SCRBC.

71. Ibid., 2.

72. Ibid., 3.

73. Ibid., 5.

74. Robert Graves and Raphael Patai, *Hebrew Myths: The Book of Genesis* (New York: McGraw-Hill, 1964).

75. Clarke, "Race: The Historical Development," 7–8.

76. Ibid., 8.

77. Ibid., 10.

78. Ibid., 10.

79. Ibid., 13. See also ibid., "Race: An Evolving Issue in Western Social Thought," Extension of paper prepared for the International Conference on Race Relations, sponsored by the Graduate School of International Studies, University of Denver, Denver, Colorado; presented at Aspen, Colorado, 7–9 June 1970, 6–9, JHCP, SCRBC.

80. Ibid., "Race: The Historical Development," 14.

81. Ibid., 14.

82. Ibid., 15.

83. Ibid., 17.

84. Ibid., 20.

85. Ibid., "The Historical Roots of Terrorism Against African People," The Conference on Terrorism in the Contemporary World: An International Symposium, Glassboro State College, Glassboro, New Jersey, 26–28 April 1976, 1, JHCP, SCRBC.

86. Ibid., "Beyond Black Survival," 6.

Chapter Six

THE IMPERATIVE OF PAN AFRIKANISM AND THE QUEST FOR NATIONAL SOVEREIGNTY

I am a strange child,
In a strange land;
The West is neither my
Home nor my haven.
...
You may root me here
In this alien soil,
But I will not grow.
I may never go back to
The East, where I belong;
But I will forever nurse the desire. ...

   —John Henrik Clarke, Sad Child, 1948[1]

Having "found Africa" my life has become wholly absorbed!
  —Shirley Graham Du Bois, letter to John Henrik Clarke,
               1964[2]

A careful reading of the thought and writings of Afrikan national-ists in the United States discloses that the source of their sense of nationality is based fundamentally on culture and not race. Despite the frequency with which the word and concept of race may be commonly employed in American discourse, and its epistemological dominance in European culture with regard to conceptualizing critical differences among human groups, a more insightful exploration of Afrikan reasoning on the question of what is at the core of the distinction between Afrikans and Europeans in the United States rests in ideas and arguments that transcend mere physical appearance or notions of biological and genetic distinctiveness.[3] This fact informs Clarke's analysis of the basis of the struggle for Afrikan nationalism and Afrikan internationalism. Indeed, a fundamental disagreement over cultural identity is at the heart of the age-old dispute between Afrikan nationalist and Afrikan assimilationist intellectuals concerning assessments as to the correct direction of political and social struggle and destiny. Assimilationist or integrationist intellectuals argued the inextricability of Afrikan and European national destinies in the United States because they saw (or desired to see) themselves basically as European, despite acknowledged differences in physical appearance, genetic descent, and geographical, cultural, and historical origin. On the other hand, Afrikan nationalists and Pan Afrikanists saw the inextricability of the destinies of Afrikans of various nationalities in the diaspora and the continent because they saw themselves as Afrikan, not European. The imperative of this vision of globalism was based in the commonality of geographical origin, historical and cultural heritage, and genetic descent. "Because our origin is Africa, our political heartbeat should be in tune with Africa," Clarke asserted. "No matter where we live on the face of the earth, we should proclaim ourselves an African people. *That is our nationality*, no matter what nation we were born in and what nation we choose to live in"[4] (added emphasis). Therefore, he admonished, "We must stop killing ourselves about belonging to mother countries not of our making."[5]

Table 6.1

Cultural Propositions of Afrikan Assimilationism/Americo-European Nationalism vs. Pan Afrikan Nationalism

Weak Cultural Bond		Strong Cultural Bond		Cultural Nationality
with Europe/ Europeans	+	with Afrika/ Afrikans	=	Pan Afrikan Nationalism
with Afrika/ Afrikans	+	with Europe/ Europeans	=	Americo-European Nationalism

The obverse of these positions underscores this reality. Afrikan integrationists saw, at best, a tenuous relationship between themselves and continental Afrika and Afrikans in the face of their undisputed Afrikan origins, the weakness of that relationship based essentially in the contention that indigenous Afrikan culture was irreversibly alien to them.[6] In an essay published posthumously in 1969, Martin Luther King, Jr., one of the foremost twentieth-century advocates of Afrikan assimilationism, argued that the link to Afrika was only partially genetic and not at all cultural; it was, rather, and at best, "an identification that is rooted largely in our color."[7] By contrast, so integral and irrevocable was the cultural connection to Europe and European nationality, he contended two years earlier, "that the black man needs the white man and the white man needs the black man."[8] The redoubtable Frederick Douglass, who anticipated King by more than a century, denounced Afrikan nationality as the "narrow, bitter and persecuting idea that Africa, not America, is the Negro's true home."[9] Afrikan nationalists and Pan Afrikanists affirmed independence from Europeans on precisely the same grounds; they argued the relationship remained as it was from the beginning of their encounter in the modern period, the cultural connection between the two peoples seen, at best, as imperialistic and, therefore, coerced, contrived, alien, and alienating.

This debate between these two Afrikan groups—inconceivable before their departure from the Afrikan homeland—was initiated upon their advent to the United States and their subjection to the totalitarian nature of white supremacist European dictatorship.[10] Afrika historian Michael A. Gomez notes that for assimilationists from "the beginning of the nineteenth century into the final decade of the twentieth, their primary objective would be admission into the [European] club. They would seek nothing less than equal status and privilege in the land of their birth. They would want nothing less than full acceptance [by Europeans]." By contrast, "the majority of the African-based community, beginning as early as 1830, defined the problem very differently," he explained. "The problem, as they saw it and experienced it and knew it intuitively, was the fundamental and unequivocal rejection of Africa as equal."[11]

In short, in a nihilistic effort to escape the pain of inferiorization as Afrikans within European culture, assimilationists defected from Afrika and the quest for the restoration of Afrikan nationality (indeed, they declared war upon it) and, instead, became staunch European nationalists. This could be seen, for example, in the resolutions of the Fifth Annual National Convention of the Free Peoples of Color, held 1–5 June 1835 in Philadelphia, Pennsylvania. The thirty-five delegates from six states and Washington, D.C., resolved, among other things, to petition for citizenship in the United States; to seek the abolition of the American Colonization Society, which aimed to repatriate nonenslaved Afrikans to Afrika; and to "recommend as far as possible, to our people to *abandon the use of the word 'colored,' when either speaking or writing concerning themselves; and especially to remove the title of African from their institutions, the marbles of churches, and etc.*"[12] (added emphasis). The significance of the latter resolution is that the delegates hoped to eliminate the distinction between themselves and Europeans by abolishing through language the idea that they had any connection to Afrika at all.

Assimilationist Afrikan historiography, following a century later, also championed this position. Carter G. Woodson, in his otherwise seminal classic *The Mis-Education of the Negro* (1933), took a similar stance nearly a century later when arguing against Afrikan nationality, positing "We are not all Africans ... because many of us were not born in Africa; and we are not all Afro-Americans because few of us are natives of Africa transplanted to America."[13] The noted historian Nathan I. Huggins continued to uphold this assimilationist tradition of declaring the abolition of Afrikan nationality when he asserted fifty-three years later: "Afro-Americans ... are ... a new people for whom after several generations in America *it was impossible to trace back to any tradition beyond the American experience itself*"[14] (added emphasis). Concurring, fellow historian Benjamin Quarles observed: "If, strictly speaking, *there is no such thing as Negro history*, it is because his past has become so interwoven into the whole fabric of our [Americo-European] civilization"[15] (added emphasis). The eminent historian John Hope Franklin also agreed, contending in 1947 "it must be admitted that the effect of acculturation on the Negro in the United States has been so marked that today he is as truly American as any member of other ethnic groups that make up the American population." Franklin's historiographical objective in his survey history, significantly titled *From Slavery to Freedom: A*

History of American Negroes, was to "tell the story of the process by which the Negro has sought to cast his lot with an evolving American civilization."[16] Further underscoring this defection to European nationality was Earl E. Thorpe in *Black Historians: A Critique*. In his examination of the work of Charles H. Wesley, he noted, quoting Wesley: "History should be reconstructed *so that Negroes shall be regarded as Americans* and not simply as slaves *or as an alien part of the* [American] *population*"[17] (added emphasis).

Indeed, these historiographical claims were hardly original. Several decades earlier, fellow historian Joseph T. Wilson, in *The Black Phalanx: A History of the Negro Soldiers of the United States in the Wars of 1775–1812, 1861–'65* (1888), argued, in effect, that Afrikans had culturally and genetically disappeared from the United States. "In spite of his surrounding and state of public opinion the African lived, and gave birth, largely through amalgamation with the representatives of the different races that inhabited the United States, to a new race,—the *American Negro*"[18] (original emphasis). This new people, sprung up in the Afrikans' stead, provided the ideal "materials to build into the citizenship framework of the Republic," Wilson petitioned the Americo-European rulers in his history, published six years earlier, *Emancipation: Its Course and Progress, from 1481 B.C. to A.D. 1875* (1882). Unlike European immigrants, he proposed, these assimilationist Afrikans required no "violent change of ideas and customs, nor purging out of socialistic or monarchical notions." As they are not "aliens in religion nor social customs, there is no danger to be feared from *them* to *our* peculiar form of government." In fact, the Americans can be assured of their unstinting commitment to the preservation of the status quo, of "a Samson's strength that may be relied upon for the defense of, *but will never be exerted in the pulling down* of the educational and religious pillars that support *our* republican form of government"[19] (added emphasis).

Wilson's advocacy of European nationality was replicated in the works of other nineteenth-century assimilationist historians who championed European nationalism by highlighting Afrikan allegiance in American military conflicts. They include William Cooper Nell in *The Colored Patriots of the American Revolution* (1855), William Wells Brown in *The Negro in the American Rebellion: His Heroism and His Fidelity* (1867), and George Washington Williams in *A History of the Negro Troops in the War of the Rebellion* (1888).[20] As Brown declared in 1863: "if true patriotism and devotion to the cause of freedom be the test of loyalty, and should establish one's claim to all privileges that the government can confer, then surely the black man can demand his rights with good grace." He concluded: "Whenever the rights of the [European] nation have been assailed, *the negro has always responded to his country's call*, at once, and with every pulsation of his heart beating for freedom"[21] (added emphasis).

Cultural and political defection from Afrika and Afrikan nationality, however, was by no means unique to assimilationism in the United States. By 1912, six years after the defeat of the last Zulu effort to preserve Afrikan sovereignty from the juggernaut of British and Boer imperialism in South Africa, an emerging Afrikan petit-bourgeois elite, with the creation of the African National Congress, switched the Afrikan project from independent rule to European assimilationism. Perhaps persuaded by the European invaders' decisive military defeat of the independence struggle of the various indigenous nations of the region, these new leaders emerged with a project to redirect Afrikan efforts *into* the Anglo-Boer political and social structure. Their project was the product of a profound cultural transformation resulting from European missionary education that led them to think of themselves as belonging to the European polity called South Africa, alienating them from the nationalist aspirations of the Afrikan mainstream, which had fought for continued Afrikan rule. This new elite saw themselves no longer simply as Afrikan but also as European. "Leadership of the Congress came very pre-dominantly from members of the Western-educated elite. They were respectable middle-class men *strongly attached to the life style and values of white society*," maintains J. D. Omer-Cooper, a historian of southern Afrika. "*They had no desire or intention to overthrow white society or white supremacy in South Africa. They simply wished to be accepted by white society*"[22] (added emphasis).

As in the United States and South Africa, this defection from Afrika and Afrikan nationality also obtained in the late nineteenth century among assimilationists colonized and formerly enslaved by the French in the Caribbean islands of Martinique and Guadeloupe and in Guyane, South America. They, too, shared a similar devotion to European nationality. Many "people in Cayenne [Guyane's capital] feared complete conquest by their neighbors or even by the

English-speaking North Americans. *They fought to remain French,*" explained Brian Weinstein in his 1972 biography of the African-Guyanese Felix Eboue, who served as France's colonial administrator in Central Afrika. "*Becoming more French* was what the progressives of the time wanted; their conservative enemies in France were trying to deprive black men in the colonies of the possibility of *integration into the French nation. No one talked of independence.*" Moreover, Weinstein added, "few Guyanese and Antilleans associated their destiny with that of Africa. ... *More important was the fact they were not African in culture. They loved France, wanted French culture to be theirs, and believed that being French was the only way* to have a successful career and lead a satisfactory life"[23] (added emphasis).

Table 6.2
Afrikan Assimilationist/Americo-European Nationalist Historiography

Historiographical Concern:	Successful assimilation of Afrikans as equals and as Americo-Europeans
Cultural Process:	Complete genetic and cultural absorption by Europeans or cultural hybridism as ethnic Europeans
Political Struggle:	Successful struggle for American citizenship rights as the central and exclusive goal
Cultural Destiny:	Europeanization
National History:	Americo-European
Power Posture:	Success depends upon European initiative

Likewise, in the matter of the writing and interpretation of history, assimilationist historians were principally concerned with the process by which Afrikans struggled to succeed in the quest of integrating or assimilating as equals and as Europeans within the mainstream of European culture in the United States. On the cultural level, this process ideally entails either complete absorption into the European genetic and/or cultural mainstream, or a form of hybrid European ethnic identity (Americans or Europeans of Afrikan ethnic descent), comparable to the ethno-European American identities of Irish-Americans, Italian-Americans, Polish-Americans,

German-Americans, Jewish-Americans, and other European immigrants assimilating into Anglo-American culture.[24] On the political level, this process inheres in the struggle for American citizenship rights as the central and only legitimate teleology of the Afrikan experience.[25] Such a historiography championed that the struggle for unproscribed Europeanization—even if with the preservation of some elements of a distinctive Afrikan cultural identity—was the only credible interpretation of the nature and purpose of Afrikan struggle in the United States. Concomitant with that is the notion that Afrikan history in the United States is primarily an *American*, not Afrikan, phenomenon.

Those Afrikans concerned with the perpetuation and progression of Afrikan nationality and Afrikan internationalism vigorously objected to this culturally genocidal proposition. W. E. B. Du Bois in 1960 (one year before he emigrated to Ghana, and three years before he discarded American citizenship and adopted Ghanaian nationality) addressed the issue in a speech titled "Whither Now and Why." In his address, Du Bois admonished:

> … what we must now ask ourselves is when we become equal American citizens *what will be our aims and ideals and what will we have to do with selecting these aims and ideals.* Are we to assume that we will simply adopt the ideals of Americans and become what they are or want to be and that we will have in this process no ideals of our own?
>
> *That would mean that we would cease to be Negroes* as such and become white in action if not completely in color. *We would take on the culture of white Americans doing as they do and thinking as they think.*
>
> Manifestly this would not be satisfactory. Physically *it would mean that we would be integrated with Americans* losing first of all, the physical evidence of color and hair and racial type. *We would lose our memory of Negro history* and of those racial peculiarities which have been long associated with the Negro. *We would cease to acknowledge any greater tie with Africa than with England or Germany.* …
>
> … As I have said before and I repeat I am not fighting to settle the question of racial equality in America by the process

of getting rid of the Negro race; getting rid of black folk, not producing black children, forgetting the slave trade and slavery, and the struggle for emancipation; of forgetting abolition and especially of ignoring *the whole cultural history of Africans in the world.*

... The deficiency of knowledge of Negro history and culture, however, will remain and this danger must be met or else American Negroes will disappear. Their history and culture will be lost. Their connection with the rising African world will be impossible[26] (added emphasis).

Like Du Bois, Afrikans examining the question of European assimilationism from the vantage of Afrikan nationality saw that far from ensuring equality with Europeans, assimilation accompanied enslavement, subordination, colonialism, oppression, and caste. Hence, they reasoned, liberation from caste, subordination, oppression, and colonialism can be achieved through independence (or nationalism) from assimilating or integrating forces, groups, nations, and agendas. Further, assimilation of this character signified the loss or surrender of original identity (nationality) to the identity (nationality) of the force, group, or nation that holds power. In this context the identity (nationality) of the assimilated or integrated group is structured, framed, and defined according to, in relation to, and in the interests of, the oppressing or colonizing force, group, or nation and the social order it constructed, maintains, and controls. Consequently, they observed, assimilation or integration is always central to the agenda of a conquering, colonizing, and oppressive force, group, or nation. Amilcar Cabral, the late West Afrikan revolutionary leader of Guinea-Bissau, aptly outlined this when he remarked that foreign domination and conquest (assimilation) could "be maintained only by the permanent, organized repression of the cultural life of the people concerned. ... In fact, to take up arms to dominate a people is, above all, to take up arms to destroy, or at least to neutralize, to paralyze, its cultural life. For, with a strong indigenous cultural life, foreign domination cannot be sure of its perpetuation."[27] Clarke, agreeing, also chastised: "As a people, each time we forget that our Blackness (or Africanity) is our rallying cry, our window on the world, and the basis of our first allegiance, we have found ourselves in serious trouble."[28]

Table 6.3
Theoretical Implications of European Assimilationism for Pan Afrikan Nationalism

Theorizing Power

- Instead of equality, assimilation accompanies enslavement, subordination, colonialism, oppression, and caste and is necessary for their effectiveness.
- Independence yields liberation from caste, subordination, oppression, and colonialism.
- The quest for assimilation promotes dependency and subordination to European rule.

Theorizing Nationality

- Assimilation signifies the loss or surrender of Afrikan nationality and its supplantation by European nationality.
- The supplanted European nationality is structured, framed, and defined according to, in relation to, and in the interests of, European rule.

In the end, Afrikan nationalists reasoned the quest for assimilation and for European acceptance represented, in reality, a quest for deeper subordination to European rule and underscored that the group seeking that acceptance had ceded to the ruling group the right to rule and to control the social order. Such a cession of power makes the status of the questing group perpetually tenuous or insecure, because the subordinated and assimilated group must depend upon the extent to which the ruling group accords or withholds participation in the social order over which the ruling group has exclusive control. In other words, the quest for acceptance is a decision to remain perpetually powerless within the social order of another group's design and creation. It is for this reason Clarke warned in 1992 that "no people can survive as a people living under a culture and a religion and a political theory that they, in fact, did not in part create. In short, no people can borrow a destiny from another people."[29]

This explains Clarke's cultural position; it illuminates the focus of his writing and his interpretation of history. As with other Afrikan nationalists and Afrikan internationalists, the historiography of Afrikans who asserted Afrikan nationality concerned itself with the struggle for the end of white supremacist colonial rule by cultural, political, economic, military, and territorial independence from the European people of the United States. Unlike its counter notion, it recognized the existence and motive of an integrationist or assimilationist dynamic in the course of the history of Afrikan struggle in the United States, but it did not credit it as the singular, principal, or legitimate struggle of Afrikan people. Further, whereas an assimilationist historiography was principally concerned with explicating the Afrikan experience in the United States as an *American* experience, a Pan Afrikan nationalist historiography views the Afrikan experience in the United States as an *Afrikan* experience, centered in and flowing from the history of the Afrikan continent itself.

Pan Afrikan nationalism is distinct from Afrikan nationalism in that the former may be defined as the movement toward national independence from Europe (including the United States, a European settler state) that embraces the notion of a unified Afrikan world family or Afrikan world community, and that affirms solidarity with the struggles of other peoples in the world against colonialism, cultural subordination, and human oppression and exploitation. Adhering to Malcolm X's definition, Afrikan nationalism, strictly speaking, simply means the struggle of Afrikans in the United States to realize national independence, state sovereignty, and authentic nationality apart from the American/European economic, political, and cultural complex.[30] Yet both Afrikan nationalism and Pan Afrikanism are expressions of Afrikan nationality, for Afrikans conceptualized it as a means of preserving their cultural integrity in response to the loss of sovereignty (and the enduring quest for its reclamation) under European dictatorship in the Americas.

Table 6.4
Pan Afrikan Nationalist Historiography

Historiographical Concern:	Successful struggle to end European rule and to recapture Afrikan sovereign rule
Cultural Process:	Cultural disengagement from Europe/Europeans or de-Europeanization; Re-assimilation into the indigenous Afrikan cultural community through the development of Afrika-centered national consciousness
Political Struggle:	Afrikan rule or national/state sovereignty; Cultural, political, economic, military, and territorial independence from Europe/Americo-Europe
Cultural Destiny:	Re-Afrikanization
National History:	Continental and diasporan Afrikan
Power Posture:	Success depends upon Afrikan initiative

Clearly, then, an informed examination of the implications of Clarke's definition of the struggle of Afrikans in the United States for nationality independent of Europe and of Europeans, and for a form of Afrikan internationalism that would have the effect of overthrowing global European hegemony and reestablishing Afrikan world sovereignty, underscores the central role of culture. Among other things, the rationale of the nationalist thrust as he articulated it is based in at least four propositions (see Table 6.5): (1) that Europeans are a foreign people (which is to say, they are not Afrikan); (2) that these foreign people are enemies and have acted as enemies to Afrikans (enslavement, colonialism, and imperialism serving as proofs); (3) that Afrikans did not choose their current association with Europeans (again, evidenced by enslavement, colonialism, and imperialism); and (4) that the subordination of Afrikans in and to Europeans and their society is not a fait accompli for all time because, among other reasons, Afrikan historical and cultural memory posits a consciousness of nationality (sovereignty) that undermines the notion that Europeanization could ever become either legitimate or permanent.

Table 6.5
John Henrik Clarke's Four Historical Propositions of Pan Afrikan Nationalism

- Europeans are a foreign people.
- Europeans are and have acted as enemies to Afrikans.
- Afrikans did not choose their current association with Europeans.
- Subordination of Afrikans to Europeans is a temporary condition.

Interestingly, this last point is not without significance. An important corollary for exponents of Afrikan nationality is an optimism regarding the capability of Afrikans to chart their own destiny. In other words, a core dynamic of Pan Afrikan nationalism is its insistence upon and confidence in Afrikan agency. "We have not studied our enemies well enough to know that they're weaker than anything we ever thought they were," Clarke reflected in an interview published posthumously, in 2001. "Victory over them is not so difficult if we came together and really believed it."[31]

Assimilationists, by contrast, tend toward pessimism concerning the prospects of Afrikan agency, particularly efforts not engaged in soliciting active European support, and typically admit little possibility of an Afrikan destiny divorced from Europeans. As King, one of the chief exponents of this view, argued so vigorously regarding Pan Afrikanism, "I don't think the nonwhites in other parts of the world can really be of any concrete help to us … We don't *need* to look for help from some power outside the boundaries of our country"[32] (original emphasis). Further, he maintained, "behind Black Power's legitimate concern for group unity and black identity lies the belief that there can be a separate [from Europeans] black road to power and fulfillment. *Few ideas are more unrealistic.*"[33] In short, the defection from Afrika and Afrikan nationality, and the corresponding adoption and promulgation of European nationality, observed Amos N. Wilson, the late Afrikan psychologist and revolutionary theorist, correlates with "the subject's misperception and underestimation of his own capacity to successfully thwart the coercive and punitive actions of the dominant agent." Their experience of white supremacy has persuaded them "that Whites are invincible," undermining their self-confidence, narrowing "their vision of their possibilities and power," and restricting "their aspirations to the narrow confines of racial accommodation and assimilation, ... rather than expanding their aspirations to include the overcoming of White power and achieving full, unfettered self-liberation."[34] In Wilson's diagnosis, the "assimilationist often accepts, consciously or unconsciously, the idea that the white man will continue to rule the world. He bases his ideology and political action on the concept that somehow our destiny is not to overthrow the white man, ... but ... to ... become a part of them."[35]

This conclusion is brilliantly illustrated in the vehement opposition directed by Roy Wilkins, executive director of the National Association for the Advancement of Colored People, against Clarke's eighteen-week, 108-episode television history lecture series, which aired on New York City's WCBS TV, "Black Heritage: A History of Afro-Americans," beginning in January 1969. In a five-page draft letter to the editor, Wilkins outlined his objections to the lecture series by underscoring what he perceived to be its Afrikan nationalist and Pan Afrikanist interpretation of Afrikan history in the United States, an interpretation that violated a binding commitment to European nationality and, consequently, could not be accepted as genuine history. When the series began, Wilkins wrote, "we contended that those episodes and the outlines of the syllabus indicated clearly that the series was not to be a history of the Negro but rather was designed to impress one viewpoint—that of the so-called Black Revolution—upon viewers and the nation."[36] By the series' conclusion, it was clear to him that the content and emphasis devoted to various periods of history "were only incidental to Negro-American history."[37]

One especially egregious example, objected Wilkins, were four lectures devoted to the life and career of the early twentieth-century Pan Afrikan nationalist leader Marcus Garvey, who, through his Harlem-based (yet international) Universal Negro Improvement Association and African Communities League (UNIA and ACL), organized the largest Afrikan mass movement in the history of both the United States and the world. To the contrary, the NAACP executive director complained, Garvey could well have been marginalized in any discussion of Afrikans in the United States because "even a casual glance at the history of the black American makes it plain that emigration to Africa or to any other land has never figured importantly in his lamentations, struggles and plans for the future."[38] Rather than presenting legitimate history, the episodes discussing Garvey emphasized a "non-existent movement" that offered a theme that "suited the present-day propagandists for Black Separatism." Of course, Wilkins' denunciation—exactly like that of the assimilationist Afrikans of the French Antilles—was guided by the NAACP's ideological and programmatic goal: "to win citizenship equality for *the Negro minority* in a multiracial society." Consequently, "One would think, then, that any history of *the black minority*, at least from 1909 forward, would deal with the failures and successes of *the minority* in its progress toward the chosen goal"[39] (added emphasis).

Consistent with his cultural commitment to European nationality and his profound hostility to Afrikan nationality, Wilkins argued the role of the NAACP (an elitist organization founded in 1909 by wealthy Europeans and supported by middle class Afrikans that, unlike the UNIA, never commanded a mass Afrikan following and was not, at the national level, Afrikan-led) was logically central to any authentic historiography of the Afrikan experience in the United States.[40] The explication of that role in the lecture series, he felt, was sorely lacking, with the result that its emphasis on Afrikan nationalism and Afrikan internationalism seriously endangered prospects for the success of the assimilationist quest for acceptance and unification with Europeans. Instead of a dialogue of attempted reconciliation with Europeans, the series' lectures were deliberately confrontational, inspired by "race-hate talk" and "violence" foreign to the Afrikan community's concern with racial integration. Fatal to the imperative of the Afrikan quest for European nationality, and to its implied concession to unquestioned European rule, "the talks on 'Black Heritage' strove, often grotesquely, to create the climate of confrontation, of a conscious struggle between racial groups, of judgments and actions predicated upon the manipulation of blacks by whites." Like King, and consistent with the strategic priority of Afrikan-European unification, Wilkins also opposed the notion that the Afrikan struggle in the United States could be linked to anticolonial struggles of Afrikan and other peoples throughout the world, a view he felt implicitly and explicitly expressed in the series.[41] Such a relationship, he contended, could only be tenuous at best.[42]

In the end, Wilkins viewed as catastrophic the idea that the series would become a vehicle for instruction in primary, secondary, and university classrooms or, as stated by its developers, that the lectures would also be published in book form to meet an anticipated educational demand. "This prospect is appalling," he lamented. For, among other things, it constituted the "crime of promulgating a distinct minority viewpoint as the history of a whole people." The only conceivable result, Wilkins prophesied, would be "the inevitable and highly destructive confusions and conflicts in our [Americo-European] future national life."[43]

Clarke's view of history, as has already been noted, posited a decidedly different national destiny for Afrikans in the United States. First, it was clear that an accurate reading of Afrikan history underscored that Afrikans and Europeans are a distinctly different people who do not belong to each other either culturally or historically, for, Clarke categorically stated, Europeans are "a people who do not share our cultural and historical background."[44] In a paper titled "Black Americans: Immigrants against Their Will," which he delivered in April 1974 at the Center for African and African-American Studies of Atlanta University, Clarke observed the "Africans and the Europeans have met many times on the crossroads of history."[45] Implicit in this statement is that they are not the same people; the American context does not alter their distinctive difference in cultural or historical terms. This is not a racial judgment, for, as Clarke noted, "There existed in Africa, prior to the beginning of the slave trade *a cultural way of life* that in many ways was equal, if not superior, to *many of the cultures* then existing in Europe"[46] (added emphasis). When examining them as a subject of historical research, and in defining the basis of their distinctiveness, "there is a need to locate Africans on the maps of human *geography, history and culture*"[47] (added emphasis). Indeed, the fact that Afrikans did not come to the Americas "culturally empty-handed"[48] highlights an implicit refutation of either the appropriateness or desirability of assimilation into European cultural identity and society. Consequently, the European assault against Afrikans, and in many instances, the destruction of Afrikan culture that served as a concomitant of white supremacist enslaver domination, has "created a dilemma that the African has not been able to extract himself from to this day."[49] For accompanying the European kidnapping of Afrikans to the Americas, "every effort was made to destroy his memory of ever having been a part of a free and intelligent people."[50]

There were logical implications that followed upon this. In an essay titled "Image and Mind Control in the African World: Its Impact on African People at Home and Abroad" published nearly twenty years later, Clarke observed that Afrikans—"the oldest of the world's people"—were "an independent people" for "thousands of years before Europe itself existed."[51] Naturally, then, because enslavement to Europeans constitutes "a short period in our history," Afrikans in the European world, as a consequence of enslavement and colonialism, find themselves "in an alien cultural incubator, do not feel comfortable with it, and are rebelling against it. We are like a body rejecting an alien organ."[52]

Further, one of the important issues in Afrikan nationalist analysis deals with European motives and the prospects for peaceful coexistence. As a foreign people, Clarke noted, Europeans initiated a series of actions during what he called the second rise of Europe in the fifteenth century, which eventually disclosed to Afrikans the true nature of their aims, demonstrating they are and have acted as enemies of Afrikan freedom, sovereignty, independence, and inter-cultural cooperation. Highlighting European cultural alienness and hostility to Afrikans, Clarke remarked: "The main problem with the African, in dealing with the European during this early period, was the African's tragic lack of information about the intentions of the Europeans. *He had never dealt extensively with these kind of people*"[53] (added emphasis). While the bounty and pleasantness of the natural environment in Afrika engendered kinder and more expansive societies and social personalities, the relative harshness and poverty of the European natural environment engendered an ethos of competition and combativeness that was incomprehensible in Afrika. As a consequence, Afrikans were ill prepared to implement adequate security measures to anticipate and to defend themselves against foreign aggression.[54]

Even the nature of European enslavement highlighted these differences, for it was a practice radically different from anything Afrikans had previously known. Contrary to the "form of domestic slavery [that] existed in West Africa prior to contact with Europeans," the "tragic and distinguishing feature of the slave trade that was introduced by the Europeans was that it totally dehumanized the slave, and denied his basic personality."[55] This policy of dehumanization continued throughout both the periods of enslaver domination and colonialism as a continuing feature of European oppression. Indeed, rationales for this dehumanization were elaborated into religious and pseudoscientific explanations that included, most significantly, the development of the "myth of a people with no history."[56] This myth, aimed ultimately at justifying inhuman criminality, "nearly always read the African out of human history, beginning with the classification of the African as a lesser being." Europeans even mobilized their religious faith to persuade themselves that their conquest was both beneficent and beneficial, and further, that Afrikans would appreciate the goodness and correctness of conquest.[57] In essence, according to Clarke, Afrikans had come upon a people whose sociopathology, as evidenced by their behavior and attitudes toward Afrikans, represented an amplification of behaviors and attitudes that had long been in evidence among themselves within Europe.[58]

As enemies, therefore, Europeans attempted "to destroy every element of the culture" of the Afrikans, to deny and demean the individual and collective personality of their captives, and to "ruthlessly sell family members away from each other."[59] This explains why, as a routinized policy, the "family, the most meaningful entity in African life, was systematically and deliberately destroyed."[60] The roots of this dehumanizing and genocidal assault aimed to keep Afrikan captives in a state of total disorientation, psychological breakdown, and enduring trauma. Integral to this process, therefore, was the institution of a reign of terror. "The Africans, upon entering into the slave system of the Americas, became exposed to the most diabolical and consistent application of mental and physical torture the world has ever known."[61] Afrikans resisted, however, which frightened their enslavers. To counter their resistance, the enslavers developed a program to immobilize them that sought to destroy their psychological integrity. "They decided that a full course of action, spiritual and physical, as well as psychological, must be implemented if Africans were to be transformed from proud rebellious men to docile servants."[62] Not only did their plans include "the most extreme forms of torture," Clarke observed, but a critical component of these plans was psychological subversion. "The Christian Church came up with a design to bring about complete subversion of the Africans to the desired slave code of conduct demanded by *the feudal society of the Americans*"[63] (added emphasis).

Moreover, there was never an intention—contrary to the illusions sedulously cultivated by the assimilationists—to extend the promises of European democracy to Afrikans, for, in essence, European inimicality to Afrikans never ceased in the United States. "When the American dream was dreamed it was not dreamed for us. When the American promise was made it was not made for us. When white America announced 'Liberty and Justice for all,' we were not a part of that 'all' then and we are not a part of it now," Clarke would remark in a speech titled "The Status of African People: A World View," delivered at the First Annual Conference of the State of the Race in Los Angeles in October 1977.[64] Instead of signifying a move toward genuine democratization, or a cessation of hostilities, purported progressive adjustments in the United States represented modifications or updates in systemic modes of abuse and subordination consistent with, and dictated by, European interests. In other words, the demise of legalized enslavement "was not the end of racism as it affected Africans and other non-white people throughout the world; it was only a radical change in how it would be manifested." Thus, "the system of chattel slavery gave way to the colonial system. ... The Europeans would now change the system of capturing Africans and other non-white people and enslaving them thousands of miles from their homes," he explained of the new enslavement modality. "They would now enslave them on the spot, within their own countries, and use them as markets for the new goods coming out of the developing European industrial revolution and out of their countries and their labors to produce grist for new European mills."[65] In other words, Europeans benefited economically from their crimes against Afrikans, and maximizing those benefits required modal changes.[66] Consequently, Clarke concluded, "The slave trade was not abolished. It was transformed. Our problem today is that we cannot acknowledge this and deal with slavery in its present form."[67]

Clearly, then, the fact that Afrikans did not choose their historical and ongoing association with Europeans can be seen in all that is mentioned above and can be inferred by Afrikan resistance to the nature of the association. In fact, he observed, "the whole of the nineteenth century for us can justifiably be called 'The Century of Resistance.'"[68] Among Afrikans, the scope of this resistance was global, occurring both in the continent and in the Americas, in the United States and in the Caribbean islands to which they were taken. Moreover, Clarke maintained there were two distinct freedom movements in the United States in the first part of the nineteenth century. One involved armed struggle. The second engaged political activism.[69]

From this it followed, in Clarke's view, that Afrikan subordination to Europeans in the United States and in the world could only remain a temporary condition in Afrikan life; based on culture and history, Afrikans are not Europeans and, furthermore, predate the existence of Europeans as a human grouping in the history of the world. Afrikans in the United States were, thus, "an African people a long way from home." Indeed, Clarke expressed optimism in the late 1970s in the ephemeral nature of European global hegemony, asserting the "leadership of the world is changing hands. Some of the hands reaching out to take over world leadership must be our hands." It was imperative, therefore, for Afrikans to recognize that, having been so long out of power, they were misguidedly looking for leadership from a people whose power was in decline.[70] Although for the past 500 years Europeans had decided that they would exert exclusive control over the peoples and regions of the world, Clarke observed two decades later, the "period when Africans and non-European people nullify that decision is at hand." There is "an awakening in the world, a desire among non-Europeans to be the masters of themselves." Indeed, he added, there "are forces in the universe, including forces among Europeans, who are willing to recognize that the period of European dominance of the world is over."[71]

Consistent with this view, Clarke's vision of Afrikan nationalism and Pan Afrikanism also encompassed a vision of Afrikans in the role of world leadership as exemplar and inspiration rather than in rule and domination. Not only should Afrikans completely control their own movement, he argued, but they should also serve a vanguard role in the global movement for political change, displacing both the Russians and the Chinese in leadership of the socialist movement. Clarke held that socialism was not in debate, but the nature of the socialism was in question. "We should take over the world's socialist move-ment and make it more relevant to all people," he proposed. "We should study and use the best socialist values of African societies that existed, not only before Karl Marx was born, but before Europe itself was born."[72] In addition, he urged that Afrikans "draw heavily on the legacy of oppression in order to end oppression, everywhere."[73]

The logic of this view inheres in the assumption that the nature of Afrikan destiny ultimately defies the vagaries of European world power, resting instead, and more securely, in Afrikan historical consciousness and initiative. This was a strategic realization, Clarke contended. "No one can oppress a consciously historical people. A consciously historical people know that they are part of the world's humanity," he explained. "To know that you are part of this human-ity leads you to understand that you are an extension of every man, and no one can oppress you unless you oppress yourselves, directly or indirectly."[74]

Significantly, then, the importance of Pan Afrikan nationalism lies precisely in its relationship to historical consciousness, which Clarke held to be the foundation of the possibility and realization of human liberation. For him, Pan Afrikan nationalism proceeded from an Afrika-based historical consciousness, manifesting an implicit and explicit quest for the restoration of Afrikan sovereignty and world power that obtained prior to the period of European world hegemony, which began in the fifteenth and sixteenth centuries of the common era. It was, therefore, this historical consciousness that informed Clarke's "profound commitment to African Nationalism and Pan-Africanism."[75]

> I am an African world nationalist, a pan-Africanist and a social-ist, and I see no contradiction in being all three simultaneously. There is nothing in my life that takes precedence over my com-mitment to African people, teaching their history, the fight for their total liberation and restoration of their place among the nations of the world. This has been the all consuming passion of my existence.[76]

Hence, the struggle for Afrikan nationality, in Clarke's view, was not a call for mere celebration of cultural distinctiveness or for recognition of the same by other nations. It was, rather, a genuine quest for state sovereignty. "We can learn again what we lost, namely, how to structure and manage the state, which is the cultural and political container for the people, the infrastructure that holds a people together. The people's allegiance is always to the state." In the United States, however, Afrikans are a stateless people, aliens to the American state. They are not Americans, but a people colonized by the Americans whose destiny and urgent task is to achieve national independence. "When you have no state, you become, as we are in the United States, a large nation within a nation, searching for a nationality."[77]

Hence, Clarke argued, while Pan Afrikan nationalism is the product of the recollection of historical power, and while it also, therefore, calls for Afrikan initiative in the restoration of that remembered power, it is also made effective by the acquisition, maintenance, and protection of Afrikan power. In short, Pan Afrikan nationalism, he maintained, was both a call to power and a necessity to regain power, for a "powerless people is a fragmented people." Pan Afrikanism, which constitutes a form of Afrikan nationalism, involved the collective action of Afrikan people to restore or preserve their nationhood, culture, and sovereignty, he explained, whether the threat to their sovereignty arises from internal or external forces.[78] Consequently, the pursuit of power requires that Afrikans in the United States develop the intellectual, technical, and scientific capability to rule themselves; it entails the "need to restore our confidence and sharpen our skills ... until we understand every component that goes into the making and maintenance of a nation."[79] In other words, Clarke's vision was that there is an urgent quest for power, for the management of the state, and challenging Europeans for the right to rule a state, for a "people's great show is about power—taking it and keeping it by any means necessary."[80]

This definition of Pan Afrikanism underscored one of his severest criticisms of Pan Afrikan movement in the twentieth century. In a 1976 lecture to the Department of Afro-American Studies at Amherst College titled "Pan Africanism as an Ideology in Movement," Clarke criticized the contemporary Pan Afrikanist movement as effete and immature, primarily intellectual in practice, and unconnected to movement that either seizes power or that is intent upon seizing it. This was strikingly unlike Pan Afrikanist movement in the nineteenth century, or during the eras of Afrikan antiquity and precoloniality that preceded it. In the twentieth century, however, in marked contrast to what obtains in the Afrikan world, the most effective movements have emerged from Europe and Asia, where the strategic importance of military, commercial, and cultural dimensions to "pan" movements are well understood and implemented.[81]

In addition to the need for power, without which effective unification cannot take place, the importance of being culturally Afrikan is absolutely necessary for the uncompromised pursuit of such power and the realization of Afrikan unification. European assimilationist cultural defection is at once the culprit behind Afrikans' inability to effectively mobilize against anti-Afrikan forces in the world.[82] These forces have mobilized to control Afrikan resources; Afrikans' collective poverty globally is reflected in the fact that the wealth-producing resources are not under their control—despite in some instances political appearances to the contrary—but in the hands of foreigners. The greatest tragedy of Afrikan people, and the reason their considerable global resources are not in their own hands, is due to their cultural defection and obeisance to Europe. The result is that Afrikans declare war against their own interests in vehement defense of European interests; the culture of Europe, as it is internalized, infecting Afrikan consciousness, is fatal to Afrikan power, initiative, self-determination, and strategic vision. Indeed, he elaborated:

> political, religious and ideological leadership of the Afrikan world, in most cases, is not coming from African people. We are at war with ourselves over other people's interpretation of politics, religion and ideology. We display an ignorance of our early history, in Africa, when our thinkers conceptualized the future basis for mankind's political, religious and ideological existence. … why do so many of the philosophical gifts of our thinkers fall into the hands of other people who later claim our ideals as their own, after misinterpreting them, then use our ideals that we no longer recognize as ours, to enslave and control us? What is the basis for this naïveté, this weakness, that runs throughout our history as a people?[83]

... We have not fully realized that the political ideology of the slave master can never save us. And when the slave master, or his descendants, change their political ideology from right to left, the new ideology won't save us either—unless we control it. To be more precise, a people must be the instrument of their own liberation and the instrument must be under their control.[84]

The problem of cultural alienation, defection, and subversion is complicated by irresolution, Clarke added, a consequence of a people being long out of power. The result is that they panic when they get within proximity of its actual realization. This panic also explains such immobilizing behaviors as fruitless debates over other peoples' ideologies and Afrikan failure to seize power and to mobilize to maintain and extend it.[85]

This problem of cultural alienation, subversion, and defection is central to all other problems in the Afrikan quest for national power. This includes the problem of having historically chosen poor alliances that have not served Afrikan interests.[86] An illustration of this was postrevolutionary Haiti's support for Simon Bolivar's European settler revolution in South America. Despite Haiti's contribution to the pan-Spaniard settler struggle for independence from continental Spaniard imperialism in Venezuela, Colombia (including what later became Panama), Ecuador, Peru, and Bolivia, these same settlers aided their fellow European settlers, the Americo-Europeans in the United States, in undermining Afrikan sovereignty in Haiti. "The important thing here is that after Haiti had helped those white revolutionists and they had succeeded in overthrowing most of the Spanish and Portuguese dominating government in South America they joined the United States in boycotting and attempting to destroy Haiti, the same as the United States is now doing to Cuba," Clarke recalled. "The Haitian Revolution frightened all the white people in this hemisphere and in Europe. They joined with Americans in crippling Haiti that is crippled today."[87]

The lesson of Haiti is that there are no allies for Afrikans other than Afrikans. "I think if we are astute in choosing the first ally, the second could be chosen with a greater degree of assurance and safety," Clarke advised. "In order to choose the first ally, all we have to do is look in the mirror. The first ally is yourself. All other allies should be chosen based on how well you [collectively, as a people] are served. On this basis you choose allies or discard them."[88]

This professor of Afrikan World history remained, nonetheless, optimistic. "In spite of all these negative factors we can point to," he would state some two decades later, two years before his death, "I think, in the main, including those blacks who are confused, that we Africans are ready to begin to think out our own destiny on our own terms."[89]

Notes

1. John Henrik Clarke, *Rebellion in Rhyme: The Early Poetry of John Henrik Clarke* (Trenton, NJ: Africa World Press, 1991; originally *Rebellion in Rhyme*, Prairie City, IL: Decker Press, 1948), 43.

2. Shirley Graham Du Bois, letter to John Henrik Clarke, 13 October 1964, JHCP, SCRBC. Du Bois, the widow of William Edward Burghardt Du Bois, who had died slightly more than a year earlier, was writing from Accra, Ghana, West Afrika.

3. See, for example, John Henrik Clarke, *Notes for an African World Revolution: Africans at the Crossroads* (Trenton, NJ: Africa World Press, 1991); ibid., *New Dimensions in African History: The London Lectures of Dr. Yosef ben-Jochannan and Dr. John Henrik Clarke* (Trenton, NJ: Africa World Press, 1991); ibid., *Christopher Columbus and the Afrikan Holocaust: Slavery and the Rise of European Capitalism* (Brooklyn, NY: A&B Publishers Group, 1992); ibid., *Who Betrayed the African World Revolution? And Other Speeches* (Chicago: Third World Press, 1994); ibid., *My Life in Search of Africa* (Chicago: Third World Press, 1999); Asa G. Hilliard, *The Maroon Within Us: Selected Essays on African American Community Socialization* (Baltimore, MD: Black Classic Press, 1995); ibid., *African Power: Affirming African Indigenous Socialization in the Face of the Culture Wars* (Gainesville, FL: Makare Publishing, 2002); Marimba Ani, *Yurugu: An African-Centered Critique of European Cultural Thought and Behavior* (Trenton, NJ: Africa World Press, 1994); Molefi Kete Asante, *Afrocentricity: The Theory of Social Change* (Chicago: African American Images, 2003; originally Buffalo, NY: Amulefi, 1980); ibid., *The Afrocentric Idea* (Philadelphia, PA: Temple University Press, 1987); ibid., *Kemet, Afrocentricity and Knowledge* (Trenton, NJ: Africa World Press, 1990); Chancellor Williams, *The Destruction of Black Civilization: Great Issues of a Race From 4500 B.C. to 2000 A.D.* (Chicago: Third World Press,

1987); John G. Jackson, *Introduction to African Civilizations* (New York: Kensington Publishing, 1970); Yosef A. A. ben Jochannan, *Africa: Mother of Western Civilization* (Baltimore, MD: Black Classic Press, 1988; originally New York: Alkebu-lan Book Associates, 1971); ibid., *Black Man of the Nile and His Family* (Baltimore, MD: Black Classic Press, 1989; originally New York: Alkebu-lan Associates, 1970, 1972); ibid., *Our Black Seminarians and Black Clergy Without a Black Theology: The Tragedy of Black People/Africans in Religion Today* (Baltimore, MD: Black Classic Press, 1998; originally New York: Alkebu-lan Book Associates, 1978); ibid., *African Origins of the Major "Western Religions"*, vol. 1, *The Black Man's Religion* (Baltimore, MD: Black Classic Press, 1991; originally New York: Alkebu-lan Books Associates, 1970); Amos N. Wilson, *The Falsification of Afrikan Consciousness: Eurocentric History, Psychiatry and the Politics of White Supremacy* (Brooklyn, NY: Afrikan World InfoSystems, 1993); James L. Conyers, Jr., ed., *Afrocentricity and the Academy: Essays on Theory and Practice* (Jefferson, NC: McFarland, 2003); ibid., *Black Cultures and Race Relations* (Chicago: Burnham, 2002); Maulana Karenga, *Odu Ifa: The Ethical Teachings* (Los Angeles: University of Sankore Press, 1999); ibid., *Maat, The Moral Ideal in Ancient Egypt: A Study in Classical African Ethics* (New York: Routledge, 2004); Maulana Karenga and Jacob H. Carruthers, ed., *Kemet and the African Worldview: Research, Rescue and Restoration* (Los Angeles: University of Sankore Press, 1986).

4. Clarke, *Who Betrayed?*, 54. See also ibid., *New Dimensions*, 31, where he states: "No matter where you are and no matter what religion you might belong to, and no matter what kind of schooling you have gone through, you are distinctly an African person. You are a supporter of some loyal feelings for every African person that walks this earth, and if you have confusion about that, you have confusion that is detrimental to the freedom of your own people."

5. Kwaku Person-Lynn, ed., "On My Journey Now: The Narrative and Works of Dr. John Henrik Clarke, The Knowledge Revolutionary," *The Journal of Pan African Studies: A Journal of Africentric Theory, Methodology and Analysis* Special Issue, 1, no. 2 (Winter–Fall 2000) and 2, no. 1 (Spring–Summer 2001): 219–220.

6. See also John Henrik Clarke, "African Studies in the United States, An Afro-American View," *Africa Today* 16, no. 2 (April–May 1969): 11–12.

7. Martin Luther King, Jr., "A Testament of Hope," in *A Testament of Hope: The Essential Writings and Speeches of Martin Luther King, Jr.*, ed. James M.

Washington (New York: HarperSanFrancisco, 1986), 318. This essay was published posthumously, in 1969.

8. Ibid., *Where Do We Go from Here: Chaos or Community?* (Boston: Beacon Press, 1967), 52, 54.

9. As quoted by Cyril E. Griffith, *The African Dream: Martin R. Delany and the Emergence of Pan African Thought* (University Park: The Pennsylvania State University Press, 1975), 67.

10. See Julius Gould and William L. Kolb, ed., *A Dictionary of the Social Sciences* (New York: UNESCO and The Free Press, 1964), 719.

11. Michael A. Gomez, *Exchanging Our Country Marks: The Transformation of African Identities in the Colonial and Antebellum South* (Chapel Hill: The University of North Carolina Press, 1998), 292.

12. "Fifth Annual National Negro Convention, 1835," in *A Documentary History of the Negro People in the United States*, vol. 1, *From Colonial Times through the Civil War*, ed. Herbert Aptheker (New York: Citadel Press, 1979), 159.

13. Carter Godwin Woodson, *The Mis-Education of the Negro* (Washington, DC: The Associated Publishers, Inc., 1969; originally 1933), 200.

14. Nathan I. Huggins, "Integrating Afro-American History," in *The State of Afro-American History: Past, Present, and Future*, ed. Darlene Clark Hine (Baton Rouge: Louisiana State University Press, 1986), 160–161.

15. Benjamin Quarles, *The Negro in the Making of America* (New York: Macmillan, 1969), 7.

16. John Hope Franklin and Albert A. Moss, Jr., *From Slavery to Freedom: A History of African Americans* 7th ed. (New York: Alfred A. Knopf, 1994), xxxii.

17. Earl Thorpe, *Black Historians: A Critique* (New York: William Morrow, 1971), 136–137.

18. Joseph T. Wilson, *The Black Phalanx: A History of the Negro Soldiers of the United States in the Wars of 1775–1812, 1861–'65* (Hartford, CT: American Publishing Company, 1888; reprint New York: Arno Press and The New York Times, 1968), 25–26.

19. Ibid., *Emancipation: Its Course and Progress, from 1481 B.C. to A.D. 1875, with a Review of President Lincoln's Proclamation, the XIII Amendment, and the Progress of the Emancipation Monument* (Hampton, VA: Normal School Steam Press Print, 1882; reprint New York: Negro Universities Press, 1969), 155.

20. William C. Nell, *The Colored Patriots of the American Revolution: With Sketches of Several Distinguished Colored Persons: To Which Is Added a Brief Survey of the Condition and Prospects of Colored Americans* (Boston: Robert F. Wallcut, 1855); William Wells Brown, *The Negro in the American Rebellion: His Heroism and His Fidelity* (Boston: Lee Shepard, 1867); and George Washington Williams, *A History of the Negro Troops in the War of the Rebellion, 1861–1865, Preceded by a Review of the Military Services of Negroes in Ancient and Modern Times* (New York: Harper Brothers, 1888). For more on this discussion, see Ahati N. N. Toure, "Nineteenth Century African Historians in the United States: Explorations of Cultural Location and National Destiny," in *Black Cultures and Race Relations*, ed. James L. Conyers, Jr. (Chicago: Burnham, 2002), 16–50.

21. William Wells Brown, *The Black Man: His Antecedents, His Genius, and His Achievements* (New York: Thomas Hamilton, and Boston: R. F. Wallcut, 1863), 49.

22. J. D. Omer-Cooper, *History of Southern Africa*, 2nd ed. (Portsmouth, NH: Heinemann, 1994), 162.

23. Brian Weinstein, *Eboue* (New York: Oxford University Press, 1972), 7–8, 22–23. For a discussion of the impact of French cultural imperialism on the assimilationism of Afrikans in Senegal from the eighteenth through the twentieth centuries, see also Janet G. Vaillant, *Black, French, and African: A Life of Leopold Sedar Senghor* (Cambridge, MA: Harvard University Press, 1990), 34–63.

24. King argued this position. In opposing both Afrikan nationalism and Pan Afrikanism in the United States, he offered what he called a Hegelian synthesis that held Afrikans were no longer Afrikan but "Afro-American, a true hybrid, a combination of two cultures." Despite this proposed hybridity, and even because of it, King argued Afrikans had been rendered indigenous to Europe; he centered Afrikan cultural and historical identity in the United States exclusively in the United States, beginning with enslavement to Europeans. See his cultural arguments against black power in *Where Do We Go*, 52–54.

25. See Julian Mayfield, "Into the Mainstream and Oblivion," in *The American Negro Writer and His Roots* (New York: American Society of African Culture, 1960), 30. Mayfield made a distinction between political citizenship rights (the enjoyment of human rights in the country of residence or citizenship) and cultural assimilationism, a view Clarke appears also to have held in the 1970s. Mayfield defined an acceptable form of "integration" as "the attain-

ment of full citizenship rights in such areas as voting, housing, education, employment, and the like. But if ... integration means completely identifying the Negro with the American image—that great-power face that the world knows and the Negro knows better—then the writer must not be judged too harshly at balking at the prospect."

26. W. E. B. Du Bois, "Whither Now and Why" (1960) in W. E. B. Du Bois, *The Education of Black People: Ten Critiques, 1906–1960*, ed. Herbert Aptheker (New York: Monthly Review Press, 2001), 193–194, 195, 196–197. See also Mayfield, "Into the Mainstream," 29. "Recently an African student, long resident in this country, confessed to a group of his intimates that he did not trust the American Negro. 'What will you do,' he asked them, 'in the unlikely event that the United States becomes involved in a colonial war in Africa?' The immediate answer was: 'Man, we will shoot you down like dogs.' The remark prompted general laughter, but, on reflection, it is not amusing.

"The visiting student had sensed what his friends already took for granted: that the contemporary American Negro is faced with a most perplexing dilemma. He does not know who he is or where his loyalties belong."

27. Amilcar Cabral, "National Liberation and Culture," in Amilcar Cabral, *Return to the Source: Selected Speeches of Amilcar Cabral*, ed. Africa Information Service (New York: Monthly Review Press, 1973), 39–40.

28. John Henrik Clarke, "The Status of African People: A World View," extracted from the keynote speech, delivered at the First Annual Conference of the State of the Race, Los Angeles, California, 28–30 October 1977, 5, JHCP, SCRBC.

29. Ibid., "The Influence of Arthur A. Schomburg on My Concept of Africana Studies," *Phylon* 49, nos. 1, 2 (1st and 2nd Quarters, Spring and Summer, 1992): 4–5.

30. "A revolutionary wants land so he can set up his own nation, an independent nation. ... When you want a nation, that's called nationalism. ... If you're afraid of black nationalism, you're afraid of revolution. If you love revolution, you love black nationalism." See Malcolm X, "Definition of a Revolution," in *Malcolm X: The Man and His Times*, ed., John Henrik Clarke (Trenton, NJ: Africa World Press, 1990; originally New York: Collier Books, 1969), 273–276.

31. Person-Lynn, "On My Journey Now," 209.

32. King, "A Testament of Hope," 318–319.

33. Ibid., *Where Do We Go*, 48.

34. Amos N. Wilson, *Blueprint for Black Power: A Moral, Political and Economic Imperative for the Twenty-First Century* (Brooklyn, NY: Afrikan World Info-Systems, 1998), 13.

35. Ibid., *Afrikan-Centered Consciousness versus the New World Order: Garveyism in the Age of Globalism* (Brooklyn, NY: Afrikan World InfoSystems, 1999), 61.

36. Although the series aired only in the New York metropolitan area, Wilkins apparently attempted to mobilize a national campaign against it. The NAACP executive director was quoted in a letter dated 3 June 1969 from Russell W. Nash, president of the Iowa Human Rights Coalition in Dubuque, to Douglas Grant, vice president of WMT-TV of Cedar Rapids, JHCP, SCRBC. In the letter Nash quotes Wilkins as follows: "It is quite clear that the program will not be a history of Afro-Americans but an interpretation of history from a single point of view: the contemporary left-of-center black militant minority view, liberally garnished with the thrust of a new apartheid."

37. Roy Wilkins, 5-page draft letter to the editor, n.d., JHCP, SCRBC. Wilkins's accusation is a curious one. The project's eight-member advisory board included five university academics from Columbia University and Spelman College. Two of them were listed as historians, one as a sociologist, another as an associate professor of social work, and another as lacking an indication of academic discipline. Of the forty-five participants listed in the series syllabus, there were twenty-three lecturers, professors, and administrators representing nineteen university affiliations: Atlanta University, College of the City of New York, College at New Paltz of the State University of New York, Columbia University, Fairleigh Dickinson University, Federal City College, Howard University, Morehouse College, Morgan State College, New York University, North Carolina College, Northwestern University, Roosevelt University, Spelman College, Union Theological Seminary, University of Ibadan, University of Michigan, University of the West Indies, and Virginia State College. Among them were ten historians, three sociologists, two political scientists, one a professor in English and another in Creative Writing. Among the more prominent names were Lerone Bennett, Jr., Horace Mann Bond, Harold Cruse, St. Clair Drake, E. U. Essien-Udom, Charles V. Hamilton, Vincent Harding, C. Eric Lincoln, Benjamin Quarles, Sterling Stuckey, and Earl Thorpe. The participants also included writers, editors, poets, essayists, journalists, music critics, playwrights, actors, clerics, human rights activists, and students. Among the better known names were Rev. Albert Cleage, founder of the Shrine of the Black Madonna of the Pan African Orthodox

Church; James Farmer, at one time executive director of the Congress for Racial Equality (CORE); James Forman, director of International Affairs of the Student Non-violent Coordinating Committee (SNCC); journalist and SNCC activist Joanne Grant, editor of *Black Protest: History, Documents, and Analyses, 1619 to the Present* (New York: Fawcett, 1968); famed poet and writer Leroi Jones (Amiri Baraka); music critic Julius Lester; actor and writer Julian Mayfield; famed poet Larry Neal; writer, editor, and activist Jack O'Dell; and Harlem-based National Black Theatre director Barbara Ann Teer. Further, the 108, thirty-minute lectures were grouped under twenty-seven general headings that included lectures on Afrikan origins, enslavement, abolitionism, segregation, Civil War, Reconstruction, and twentieth-century social, political, and cultural developments. See "Syllabus, Black Heritage: A History of Afro-Americans," Office of Radio and Television, Columbia University, n.d., JHCP, SCRBC. See also John Henrik Clarke, "We See Ourselves in New Ways," *New York Times*, 15 June 1969, D19–20. Clarke said there were thirty-one lecturers in the series, although one notes that some sessions involved panelists, not lecturers per se.

38. Globally, Garvey's movement garnered a membership estimated at several million in the Americas, Afrika, and Europe, with his headquarters and strongest support base in the United States. Contrary to Wilkins' assertion, his movement could scarcely be characterized as "non-existent." Nor was his movement unique in Afrikan history in the United States. See Griffith, *The African Dream*, 67–69, 107–120; Nell Irvin Painter, *Exodusters: Black Migration to Kansas after Reconstruction* (New York: W. W. Norton, 1976, 1986).

39. Wilkins, 5-page draft letter.

40. Interestingly, notes Herbert Aptheker, *Afro-American History: The Modern Era* (New York: Carol Publishing Group, 1971), 133–134, the founding officers of the NAACP were European progressive era reformers: Moorfield Storey of Boston, Massachusetts, national president, long-time president of the Anti-Imperialist League, former secretary to Republican U.S. senator Charles Sumner, and noted Boston attorney; William English Walling of New York, chairman of the executive committee, a socialist leader; John E. Milholland of New York, treasurer, an industrialist and leader in the Constitution League; Oswald Garrison Villard, disbursing treasurer, owner of the *New York Post* and *The Nation*, born into abolitionist and railroad-building families, grandson of the famed abolitionist William Lloyd Garrison; and Frances Blascoer of New York, executive secretary. W. E. B. Du Bois, as director of publicity and research, was the only Afrikan in the executive

national leadership of the organization. In addition, the NAACP's general committee consisted of sixty-five persons, thirty-nine of whom were European and twenty-six of whom were Afrikan. See also Herbert Aptheker, ed., *A Documentary History of the Negro People in the United States, 1910–1932,* vol. 3, *From the N.A.A.C.P. to the New Deal* (Secaucus, NJ: The Citadel Press, 1973), 27, 29. In reality, the NAACP was a European-led and controlled organization into which a certain cohort of middle class Afrikans were recruited. This further explains Wilkins's hostility to Afrikan nationalism and Afrikan internationalism.

41. Under the syllabus's section 26, "What Is the Future of Black America?", there are three panel discussions led by Vincent Harding. The third and final of them, titled "Our Future with the Third World," featured panelists Leroi Jones and James Forman. Likewise section 20, titled "The Freedom Movement: America and Beyond," also featured two lectures by Essien-Udom titled "The Freedom Movement in Africa" and "The Freedom Movement in the Third World."

42. Wilkins, 5-page draft letter.

43. Ibid. Wilkins's attitude may well have been informed by the FBI's regard for him. William C. Sullivan, FBI assistant director and head of the agency's counterintelligence program (COINTELPRO), directed a covert operation designed to compel Martin Luther King, Jr., to commit suicide before accepting the Nobel Peace Prize in 1964. Under his direction, the FBI produced a composite tape recording of some of King's sexual liaisons with other women and an anonymous letter urging him to commit suicide or have the evidence of his marital infidelity publicly disclosed, sending them both to King. In part, the letter praised Wilkins, in contrast to King, as "a man of character." David J. Garrow, Ward Churchill, and Jim Vander Wall cite evidence that Wilkins was an FBI ally and informant. See Ward Churchill and Jim Vander Wall, *The COINTELPRO Papers: Documents from the FBI's Secret Wars against Dissent in the United States,* 2nd ed. (Boston: South End Press, 2002), 97, 351n19; David J. Garrow, *Bearing the Cross: Martin Luther King, Jr., and the Southern Christian Leadership Conference* (New York: William Morrow, 1986), 373, 686–687n6. Wilkins's close and collaborative relationship with the FBI would further explain his repudiation of Afrikan nationality and the subservient position he held for the Afrikan "minority" within the Americo-European order.

44. Clarke, *Notes for an African,* 333.

45. Ibid., "Black Americans: Immigrants against Their Will," CAAS Occasional Paper No. 15, Center for African and African-American Studies, Atlanta University, Atlanta, Georgia, April 1974, 1, JHCP, SCRBC. An essay of the same title was later published in an edited volume treating the immigrant experience in the United States. See John Henrik Clarke, "Black Americans: Immigrants Against Their Will," in *The Immigrant Experience in America*, ed. Frank J. Coppa and Thomas J. Curran (Boston: Twayne Publishers, 1976), 172–191.

46. Ibid., 12.

47. Ibid., 1.

48. Ibid., 12.

49. Ibid., 13.

50. Ibid.

51. Ibid., *Notes for an African*, 329.

52. Ibid., 329, 362.

53. Ibid., "Black Americans," 5.

54. Ibid.

55. See Joseph E. Inikori, "Slavery in Africa and the Transatlantic Slave Trade," in *The African Diaspora*, ed. Alusine Jalloh and Stephen E. Maizlish (College Station: Texas A & M University Press, 1996), 39-72. Inikori argues that the practice of involuntary servitude in precolonial Afrika more closely resembles serfdom in medieval Europe than the enslavement system Europeans developed later.

56. Clarke, "Black Americans," 10.

57. Ibid., 13.

58. Ibid., 16–19.

59. Ibid., 14.

60. Ibid., 14, 16.

61. Ibid., 20.

62. Ibid.

63. Ibid., 21.

64. Ibid., "The Status of African People: A World View," extracted from the keynote speech, delivered at the First Annual Conference of the State of the Race, Los Angeles, California, October 28–30, 1977, 2, JHCP, SCRBC.

65. Ibid., "Black Americans," 19–20.

66. Ibid., 20.

67. Ibid., "The Status," 3.

68. Ibid., "Black Americans," 23.

69. Ibid., 24.

70. Ibid., "The Status," 1.

71. Kwaku Person-Lynn, ed., *First Word: Black Scholars, Thinkers, Warriors, Knowledge, Wisdom, Mental Liberation* (New York: Harlem River Press, 1996), 15.

72. Clarke, "The Status," 7.

73. Ibid., 8.

74. Ibid., *Notes for an African*, 338.

75. Ibid., "The Status," 5.

76. Ibid., "Response to James E. Jackson's Article in the November 12, 1982 issue of the Daily World," 2 December 1982, JHCP, SCRBC.

77. Person-Lynn, *First Word*, 22.

78. John Henrik Clarke, "Pan Africanism as an Ideology in Movement," bicentennial lecture delivered to the Department of Afro-American Studies, Amherst College, 17 April 1976, 1, 5, JHCP, SCRBC.

79. Ibid., "The Status," 1.

80. Ibid.

81. Ibid., "Pan Africanism," 2–3. Decades later, European intellectuals would elaborate upon Clarke's arguments in works that highlight the relationship of culture and ethnicity to global economic and political power. Notable among them are Joel Kotkin, *Tribes: How Race, Religion, and Identity Determine Success in the New Global Economy* (New York: Random House, 1992) and Samuel P. Huntington, *The Clash of Civilizations and the Remaking of the World Order* (New York: Touchstone, 1996). Others, more negatively framed, in that they sounded alarms concerning the decline of Anglo-European cultural hegemony and its implications for Anglo-European political and economic dominance in the United States, include Arthur M. Schlesinger, Jr., *The Disuniting of America: Reflections on a Multicultural Society* (New York: W. W. Norton, 1991, 1998); Samuel P. Huntington, *Who Are We?: The Challenges to America's National Identity* (New York: Simon & Schuster, 2004); John J. Miller, *The Unmaking of Americans: How Multiculturalism Has Undermined the Assimilation Ethic* (New York: Free Press, 1998); Allan David Bloom, *The Closing of the American Mind: How Higher Education Has Failed Democracy and Impoverished the Souls of Today's Students* (New York: Simon & Schuster, 1987); Clarence E. Walker, *We Can't Go Home Again: An Argument about*

Afrocentrism (New York: Oxford University Press, 2001); and John J. Miller, *Alternatives to Afrocentrism* (Washington, DC: Center for the New American Community, Manhattan Institute, 1994) and in its second edition *Alternatives to Afrocentrism* (Washington, DC: Center for Equal Opportunity, 1996).

82. Ibid., "The Status," 3–4.

83. Ibid., 4.

84. Ibid., 6.

85. Ibid., 7–8.

86. Ibid., 5–6.

87. Ibid., letter to William Marshall, 5 March 1974, JHCP, SCRBC. In the letter, Clarke stated support for the Spaniard settler Simon Bolivar's Latin American revolution came under the rule of Henri Christophe, when, in fact, it was under Alexandre Petion. After the 17 October 1806 assassination of Jean-Jacques Dessalines, who stewarded the revolution to victory on 1 January 1804 and who assumed leadership of Haiti, the country was divided between a republic dominated by half-castes under the leadership of Petion in the southern and western portions of the country, and Christophe's Afrikan-dominated monarchy in the northern section of the country. In 1820, the country was restored to rule under a single state with Petion successor Jean Pierre Boyer after the deaths of Petion in 1818 and Christophe in 1820. The half-castes, also called people of color, were a social group of both European and Afrikan descent who saw themselves as distinct from and superior to Afrikans by virtue of their European ancestry. This group's identification was principally with the European world, especially on the level of culture, despite their rejection by Europeans as an inferior caste. It was Petion who, in exchange for his considerable support of Bolivar's struggle, persuaded the Latin American to abolish the enslavement of Afrikans in the territories Bolivar liberated from Spain. See Laurent Dubois and John D. Garrigus, ed., *Slave Revolution in the Caribbean 1789–1804: A Brief History with Documents* (Boston/New York: Bedford/St. Martin's, 2006), 191; ibid., *Avengers of the New World: The Story of the Haitian Revolution* (Cambridge, MA: The Belknap Press of Harvard University Press, 2004), 303; C. L. R. James, *The Black Jacobins: Toussaint L'Ouverture and the San Domingo Revolution*, 2nd ed. (New York: Vintage Books, 1963), 411; Dantes Bellegarde, "President Alexandre Petion," *Phylon* 2, no. 3 (3rd Quarter 1941): 205–213; John Edward Baur, "Mulatto Machiavelli, Jean Pierre Boyer, and The Haiti of His Day," *Journal of Negro History* 32, no. 3 (July 1947): 307–353; Vincent

Bakpetu Thompson, "Leadership in the African Diaspora in the Americas Prior to 1860," *Journal of Black Studies* 24, no. 1 (September 1993): 45–46; Tekla Ali Johnson, "Colonial Caste Paradigms and the African Diaspora," *The Black Scholar* 34, no. 1 (Spring 2004): 23–33; ibid., "The Enduring Function of Caste: Colonial and Modern Haiti, Jamaica, and Brazil," *Comparative American Studies* 2, no. 1 (March 2004): 61–73.

88. Ibid., "The Status," 6–7.

89. Person-Lynn, *First Word*, 16.

Chapter Seven

PAN AFRIKAN NATIONALISM IN ACTION: THE ORGANIZATION OF AFRO-AMERICAN UNITY AND THE AFRICAN HERITAGE STUDIES ASSOCIATION

I knew then that I came from an old people and that I was older than my oppressor, that I was older than Europe and that my people dated back to the very dawn of history and that we were the senior people of the whole world. I knew then what my pursuit in life would be and that would be to define history as it relates to my people, and to convert history into an instrument of liberation. That is the mission of my life and that is the only legacy I care to leave.

—John Henrik Clarke, 1970[1]

Clarke's critique of Afrikan consciousness can be understood in the context of his own commitment to Afrikan nationality, his belief that the role of the intellectual and scholar was to materially serve, through the use of his and her expertise, the struggle of the Afrikan nation to sovereignty. Two examples of this are his work with Malcolm X in founding the Organization of Afro-American Unity (OAAU) in 1964, and his activism and leadership in the struggle to wrest Afrikan control of the organizational and research agenda of the African Studies Association (ASA) in 1968–1969 and the subsequent founding of the African Heritage Studies Association (AHSA).

William W. Sales, Jr., in his study of Malcolm X and the founding of the OAAU, notes that Clarke was among several who played major roles in its creation, which resulted from a number of confluent factors. They included the impact of Malcolm's first trip to Afrika from 13 April to 21 May 1964, the influence of Julian Mayfield and other Pan Afrikanists who had left the United States and repatriated to Ghana, the vision of Pan Afrikanism as practiced and articulated by the more revolutionary-oriented states of Ghana, Guinea, Egypt, Algeria, and Mali; and "the influence of Harlem-based intelligentsia, most notably John Henrik Clarke, and others like Sylvester Leaks and the Harlem Writers Guild of John Oliver Killens."[2]

While the OAAU was formally established on 28 June 1964, a mere thirteen months and three days after the OAU's founding on 25 May 1963,[3] Malcolm conceived of the idea in the beginning of the year, between his first and second trips to Afrika. Its conception resulted from discussions and planning in both Afrika and the United States and, according to Sales, preceded Malcolm's formal departure from the Nation of Islam in March 1964. To begin work on its development, Malcolm recruited Lynn Shifflet, an NBC producer, to assist him in secretly pulling together a core group of Afrikan intellectuals and activists who would help him create a new Pan Afrikan nationalist organization. Shifflet chaired the meetings, whose participants included Clarke, Killens, A. Peter Bailey,[4] Muriel Gray, and several members of Malcolm's Muslim Mosque, Inc. Sales notes the "contributions of Dr. Clarke and the author John O. Killens were important, even crucial, but they were performed in an advisory capacity, which was largely the stance of these people throughout the life of the OAAU." The meetings focused on programmatic and ideological questions and positions but neglected work on the organization's structure. Clarke proposed what was to become the organization's name, secured the OAU's charter from its United Nations mission in New York City, and drafted the OAAU's Aims and Objectives, finalizing the text in collaboration with Malcolm and Shifflet.[5] Clarke recalled that certain portions of the document were drafted in his living room, while the OAAU charter, in the main, was modeled after the OAU charter "almost word-for-word."[6] In a public lecture in Harlem decades later, Clarke commented on his memories of this process.

> Of the Muslim Mosque Incorporated I will say very little because in detail I know very little. Of the Organization of

Afro-American Unity modeled after the Organization of African Unity I can talk with greater degree of clarity because I was a part of the mechanics of putting it together. And I secured the constitution of the Organization of African Unity in order to model one after the other, and the shaping and the writing of the constitution happened to take place and happened to have taken place in my living room. ... I still have the draft notes. No one's ever seen Malcolm working over something, trying to mold a plan for the salvation of a people. He was as happy as a child molding this and this I will never forget.[7]

The OAAU was founded to achieve several strategic aims. Among them was to serve as an umbrella organization for the different factions of the Afrikan struggle in the United States, especially to effect collaboration between integrationists and nationalists, so as to be recognized by Afrikan, Asian, and Muslim governments as the official representative of the Afrikan movement in the country.[8] Such recognition would yield a major strategic victory. For one thing, it would render the Afrikan struggle in the United States an integral part of the nationalist, anticolonial movement in Afrika and Asia. It would, further, give the Afrikan and Muslim states the ability to actively and officially support the movement in such international fora as the OAU and the UN. Simultaneously, it would also give weight to OAAU support of Afrikan and Asian struggles against colonialism and neocolonialism, as well as greater leverage in its power contest with the American government. Much of this had been conceptually worked out in numerous discussions Malcolm had had in the United States, Afrika, and Asia, including discussions with Afrikan and Asian state leaders with whom he met during his first trip abroad. As part of the planning, insiders report discussions were ongoing between Malcolm X and Martin Luther King and their representatives to coordinate their efforts and arrive at a modus vivendi for this new initiative.[9]

During his second visit to Afrika (from 9 July to 24 November 1964),[10] OAAU activists were tremendously encouraged by Malcolm's success at the OAU's Second African Summit held in Cairo, Egypt, from 17 to 21 July 1964. A month later, the OAAU chairman publicly announced the organization was making progress with the leaders of

Afrikan states and its intent to integrate the Afrikan human rights struggle in the United States with the continental Afrikan struggle against colonialism and neocolonialism. Malcolm and the OAAU achieved a political and diplomatic coup when invited to address the heads of the thirty-three independent Afrikan states at the OAU conference, presenting a formal memorandum on the oppression of Afrikans in the United States. The memorandum inspired the heads of state to pass a resolution condemning U.S. oppression of Afrikans in the country.

The OAAU memorandum charged the Americans with a form of oppression worse than that which obtained in South Africa and with skillfully manipulating the Afrikan struggle by deploying sympathetic liberal Europeans to persuade human rights activists to confine the struggle to a domestic citizenship rights effort. Such an approach served to block the support and intervention of continental Afrikan states within the context of international human rights standards and influence. Malcolm observed the Americans, through their state department, recognized the strategic potential of the OAAU's initiative to "internationalize America's race problem by lifting it from the level of civil rights to a struggle for the universally recognized HUMAN RIGHTS." It is "on these grounds we could then bring America before the United Nations and charge her with violating the UN Declaration of Human Rights and thereby of also violating the UN Charter itself."[11] Of significance, too, is the fact that Malcolm described the OAAU as representing an Afrikan independence movement. "[F]or we awakening Afro-Americans are well aware today that a United Africa is a strong Africa, and it is only in the STRENGTH of our African brothers that we in America will ever realize *a true solution to our own struggle for independence* and the recognition and respect of our own human rights"[12] (added emphasis). Days later, the OAAU intensified its momentum in Cairo on 28 July 1964, when, as OAAU chairman, Malcolm called upon OAU secretary general Diallo Telli "to demand that the United Nations Commission on Human Rights launch an immediate investigation into the inhuman destruction of Afro-American life and property."[13]

Four months later, in Paris, France, Malcolm elaborated upon his view of the importance of the OAAU's work at that point. "'If you hate the roots you will hate the tree; if you love the roots, you will love the tree,'" he told an audience in November. "This idea was the basis of the Black Nationalist Movement and until now has constituted the essence of the new awareness of the Black Men on the American Continent. ... Our task is to be a link between the people of Africa and the people of African origin in America."[14] In pursuing the establishment of concrete relations between the struggle in Afrika and in the United States, Malcolm, as the OAAU's representative, met with consistently positive receptions from government officials, heads of state and government, and leaders of armed nationalist movements against European colonialism in various capitals in Afrika, including Cairo, Egypt; Khartoum, Sudan; Addis Ababa, Ethiopia; Nairobi, Kenya; Dar-es-Salaam, Tanzania; Lagos, Nigeria; Accra, Ghana; Monrovia, Liberia; Conakry, Guinea; and Algiers, Algeria. In western Asia he traveled to Mecca, Saudi Arabia; Beirut, Lebanon; and to Kuwait.[15] The OAAU chairman reported that among the heads of state with whom he met were President Kwame Nkrumah of Ghana, President Sekou Toure of Guinea, President Abdel Nasser of Egypt, and President Julius Nyerere of Tanzania.[16] Sales writes that the OAAU's diplomatic mission in 1964 was a stellar success, as the OAAU chairman visited or passed through thirty countries and met with Afrikan heads of state who also included Kenya's Jomo Kenyatta, Uganda's Milton Obote, and Nigeria's Nnamdi Azikiwe.[17]

When asked if an independent Afrikan state within the United States were a solution, Malcolm responded he would not foreclose consideration of any proposed solution. "Other independent states have been set up. They set up Israel and they weren't called separationists," he retorted. "But when they start talking about setting up something wherein we can rule ourselves, we're labelled separationists. But we are not separationists, nor are we integrationists. We're human beings."[18]

The OAAU chairman further asserted that cultural oppression also informed American political oppression. "As far back as 1959 some of these racists in the American Government outright expressed the fear that if the African image became positive on the African continent that it would have a tendency to make the Afro-American begin to identify with Africa—sympathize with Africa—" he charged, "and the fear was that the Afro-American allegiance might become stronger for Africa than it is now for America."[19] To prevent this possibility, the Americans cynically initiated superficial reforms. In truth, however, they have "only been maneuvering to keep the Afro-American from developing a tendency to want to identify with Africa, that will outstrip his tendency to want to identify with America," he continued. "They want to try and Americanize us for fear that now we might become Africanized."[20]

The OAAU's pursuit of this struggle for increasing Afrikanization included the recruitment of soldiers to armed revolutionary movements to end colonial occupation in Afrika. In an undated news release from the OAAU's Information Bureau in Accra, Ghana, titled "Afro-American Troops for Congo-Malcolm X," the chairman announced that thousands of Afrikans from the United States were willing to join the military struggle to expel foreign invaders from the Congo to safeguard its independence. "We want the O. A. U. to know that there are thousands of Afro-Americans who are ready to place ourselves at your service to help drive those South African murderers from the Congo," he declared. "Many Afro-Americans are unemployed ex-servicemen who are experienced in every form of modern warfare and guerilla fighting." The news release indicated this was part of a letter the OAAU chairman had sent to OAU secretary general Diallo Telli. "We of this generation are fed up with colonialism, imperialism … and all other forms of racism," Malcolm declared, "and we are ready to strike whatever blow is necessary to sweep the racists from this earth, at once and forever."[21]

Table 7.1
Organization of Afro-American Unity's Strategic Aims and Objectives

- To unify the different factions of the Afrikan struggle in the United States under an international human rights agenda

- To secure active and official support from Afrikan, Asian, and Muslim states in the OAU and the UN

- To become the internationally recognized official representative of the Afrikan movement in the United States, especially in Afrika and Asia

- To integrate the Afrikan struggle in the United States into the nationalist, anticolonial movement in Afrika and Asia
- To culturally re-Afrikanize Afrikans in the United States
- To nurture an independence movement among Afrikans in the United States
- To facilitate effective Afrikan globalization to counter and neutralize European global power
- To end European colonial domination of Afrikans in the United States

In an assessment published four years after Malcolm's assassination, Clarke called the "formation of the Organization of Afro-American Unity and the establishment of the official connection with Africa ... one of the most important acts of the twentieth century." The OAAU briefly served as "an official link with the new emerging power emanating from both Africa and Asia" and, consequently, "projected the cause of Afro-American freedom into the international arena of power."[22]

This achievement, however, thrust the OAAU chairman into the immediate danger of the imperialist response that effected his assassination, Clarke concluded, for by internationalizing the Afrikan human rights struggle in the United States, moving it beyond an internal contestation with Europeans for citizenship rights, and by forging alliances with revolutionary, anticolonial forces in Afrika, Malcolm propelled himself "into the cross fire of that invisible, international cartel of power and finance which deposes presidents and prime ministers, dissolves parliaments, if they refuse to do their bidding." Clarke maintained that in his view Malcolm, Democratic Republic of the Congo prime minister Patrice Lumumba, who was assassinated in 1960, and the Swedish economist and second United Nations secretary general Dag Hammarskjold, who died in a 1961 plane crash in the Congo while trying to secure a cease fire, were all eliminated by the same interests. Adding to the reasons for Malcolm's assassination was the OAAU's stated intention to charge the United States before the United Nations and international tribunals with genocide against Afrikans in the country.[23]

Clarke also underscored the significance of the cultural component of the OAAU's program. A key OAAU objective was to "revamp our entire thinking and redirect our learning so that we can put forth a confident identity and wipe out the false image built up by an oppressive society." Critical to this transformation was a focus on means by which to effect epistemological transformations. Hence, the OAAU argued for a foundational approach to mental liberation through the systematic study of "the different philosophies and psychologies." Particularly striking is its advocacy for training in Afrikan and other languages and the rationale that informed that approach, for an essential aspect of this effort would be systematic mastery of languages other than English, a European language. In particular, Clarke noted, the OAAU's cultural program stated that plans were being developed "for the study of languages of eastern origin such as Swahili, Hausa, and Arabic. *Such studies will give us, as Afro-Americans, a direct access to ideas and history of our ancestors, as well as histories of mankind at large"* (added emphasis). Indeed, Clarke remarked in 1969, this cultural program highlights the perceptiveness of Malcolm's political vision. "More so than any other Afro-American leader, Malcolm X realized that there must be a concomitant cultural and educational revolution if the physical revolution is to be successful."[24]

Two years earlier, in 1967, Clarke had published in the Paris-based, international journal *Présence Africaine* a joint assessment of Malcolm's and the OAAU's significance with Sylvester Leaks, a journalist Malcolm had hired in 1959 to edit the New York edition of the *Muhammad Speaks* newspaper, the official organ of the Nation of Islam. The OAAU's strategic mission was captured in Malcolm's recognition "that the struggle for black freedom was neither social nor moral. It was, and is, a power struggle; a struggle between the white haves and the black have-nots. A struggle of the oppressor and the oppressed," they commented. "And if the oppressed is to breach the power of the oppressor he must either acquire power or align himself with power."[25] It is this strategic understanding that explains why the OAAU, patterned deliberately after the OAU, urged the unification of the Afrikan world in the Americas and Afrika. Malcolm's and the OAAU's global, internationalist vision sought the coordination of some 200 million Afrikans in the Americas—North, South, Central, and Caribbean—with 300 millions on the Afrikan continent. This urgency of unification would have made Afrikans, the second largest people on the earth, a global, unified power.[26]

What Malcolm X and the OAAU had achieved in less than a year of international diplomacy was phenomenal and must have presented an alarming, even terrifying, specter to the American rulers. Consequently, Sales concluded, the removal of Malcolm and the OAAU became an imperative of American state policy.

> Malcolm X attempted in the OAAU to implement the beginnings of a revolutionary option within the Civil Rights movement. Through internationalization of the Civil Rights movement into a human rights movement and the serious consideration of all options including self-defense and urban guerilla warfare, Malcolm hoped to negotiate successfully the dilemma of cooptation and repression. ... Malcolm's strategy precipitated a united elite stance committed to repressing his leadership and the OAAU. This coalescence of elite opposition occurred before the OAAU had consolidated any advantages which might have accrued from the new approach. As a result, the OAAU was destroyed as an effective organization and Malcolm X was physically removed from the African American freedom movement.[27]

In summary, the American reaction to Malcolm X and the OAAU was informed by the U.S. state's appreciation of the implications of the organization's strategic goals and objectives: (1) to unify the different factions of the Afrikan struggle in the United States under an international human rights agenda; (2) to secure active and official support from Afrikan, Asian, and Muslim states in international fora and organizations, such as the OAU and the UN; (3) to become the internationally recognized official representative of the Afrikan movement in the United States, especially in Afrika and Asia; (4) to seamlessly integrate the Afrikan struggle in the United States into the nationalist, anticolonial movement in Afrika and Asia; (5) to culturally re-Afrikanize Afrikans as part of a larger aim to mature an independence movement in the United States; and (6) to facilitate global Afrikan unification to neutralize global European power and end European colonial domination of Afrikans in the United States.

In a letter to Mayfield in June 1965, five months after Malcolm's assassination, Clarke hinted at his knowledge of the American awareness of the import of the OAAU's initiatives. "Quite a lot has been done to break up the OAAU. The organization is now in shambles," he revealed. "There is much more to this than I have time to tell you. Some pressures from the highest level in Washington and elsewhere were brought to bear in the destruction of what could have been the greatest force to emerge among black people in this century."[28]

Three years later, in 1968, Clarke would find himself at the center of an effort to wrest from Europeans scholarly control of the information generated concerning Afrikan people and the Afrikan continent in the eleven-year old African Studies Association (ASA). That effort would in the following year (1969) lead to the founding of the African Heritage Studies Association (AHSA), an organization to which Clarke would be elected president. It would also demonstrate continuity with the Pan Afrikan nationalist objectives of his work with the OAAU and the larger cultural and political movement among Afrikans in the United States that "unleashed the desire for an indigenous scholarship of Black peoples, scholarship initiated in the colleges and universities as 'Black Studies.'" This movement, observed the noted Afrikan political scientist Ronald W. Walters, "challenged the hegemony of white scholarship in all of the social sciences, and Black caucuses were created inside the major white scholarly organizations during this period."[29] Indeed, the challenge offered by Afrikan scholars to the European-dominated African Studies Association was replicated in other efforts in academia, leading also to the establishment of independent Afrikan scholarly associations in disciplines that included sociology, political science, and political economy.[30]

With respect to the systematic study of Afrika, the struggle was engaged at the ASA's eleventh annual meeting in Los Angeles, which was held on 16–19 October 1968. An Afrikan caucus—called by P. Chike Onwuachi, director of the African-Caribbean Studies Center at Fisk University—formed in opposition to European control of the organization, issuing a statement on 19 October that set out the concerns and aims of Afrikan scholars regarding the ASA. Among other things, the caucus called upon the ASA to render "itself more relevant and competent" to deal with the challenges of Afrikan people globally, and to facilitate this objective by broadening Afrikan participation "in all phases of the Association's operations." The caucus noted the irony of the fact that in an organization "dealing with predominately Black countries and societies," only one Afrikan held a policy-deciding position and too few of the conference's program chairs and participants were drawn from Afrikan scholars engaged in the study of Afrika. In general, it assessed, "the Association reflects the white caste and is identified with a white posture."[31]

Of further significance, the caucus called upon the association to broaden its research interest beyond its singular focus on the Afrikan continent to the systematic study of Afrikans globally. As well, it called for broadening the association's membership beyond academicians to include "those engaged in fields closely related to African and Afro-American studies, with particular emphasis on Black youth, inside and outside the universities." Hence, the caucus asserted, the viability and relevance of the association is directly related to whether it decides to significantly strengthen "its ties with Black Africanists." This would include recruiting U.S. and continental Afrikan scholars to direct the "rapidly developing" Africana Studies programs in the United States and working to change "American public opinion based on deep racism and ignorance of the Black people whom the African Studies Association takes as its subject."[32] An ASA ad hoc committee, having met with representatives of the Afrikan caucus, agreed to concern itself with implementing the caucus's demands.[33]

In their private meetings, however, the Afrikan scholars were engaged in exploring a two-pronged agenda. Not only did they aim to "project black scholarship into decision-making positions" in the ASA, they also intended "to form a separate organization of black scholars who will interest themselves in all things that bear the name African, especially African history."[34] Its reach would be global, acting as "a clearing house and liaison among Black scholars all around the world, listing research topics and experts with their fields, in order to correct the present monopoly of information about Black cultures and histories in white hands."[35] They agreed to hold an organizing meeting in Harlem, New York City, on 28 December that would set about determining a permanent name for the organization, an agreement as to who could become members, and its relationship to African studies programs in predominantly Afrikan and European universities in the United States. The scholars also agreed that whenever possible, "all meetings of this organization will be held in the black community or at a predominantly black school." Clarke, as director of the Heritage Program of HARYOU-ACT, was to be one of the hosts of the Harlem meeting.[36]

A second meeting, held at the Federal City University in Washington, D.C., on 27–29 June 1969 at the official invitation of the university's president, consummated their organizational efforts by creating the African Heritage Studies Association. This second meeting addressed several issues related to Afrikan concerns with the ASA that had been raised in Los Angeles, prefiguring the eruption that was to occur in the upcoming October ASA meeting in Montreal, Canada. It also addressed the newly created AHSA's organizational agenda. The matter of consolidating Afrikan organizational and research control of the ASA was discussed, including a planned (but never held) meeting of the executives of the AHSA with those of the ASA in the upcoming Montreal conference. As for the AHSA, the scholars agreed that the new organization should, among other things, work not only to strengthen Afrikan participation and control of African studies, but also the newly-emerging, Afrikan-created discipline of Africana Studies. This initiative to promote and to control the systematic study, research, and teaching of continental and global Afrika would be directed, including on the primary and secondary school level, through the institutional engagement of predominantly Afrikan colleges and universities. AHSA founders also discussed organizing work by committees and subcommittees, and publishing a newsletter and launching an academic journal.[37]

Table 7.2
Aims and Objectives of the African Heritage Studies Association[38]

Education

1. (a) Reconstruction of African history and cultural studies along Afro-centric lines while effecting an intellectual union among black scholars the world over.

    (b) Acting as a clearing house of information in the establishment and evaluation of a more realistic African Program.

    (c) Presenting papers at seminars and symposia where any aspect of the life and culture of the African peoples are discussed.

    (d) Relating, interpreting and disseminating African materials for Black education at all levels and the community at large.

International

2. (a) To reach African countries in order to facilitate greater communication and interaction between Africans and Africans in the Americas.

    (b) To assume leadership in the orientation of African students in the U.S. and orientation of Afro-Americans in Africa (establish contacts).

    (c) To establish an Information Committee on African and American relations whose function it will be to research and disseminate to the membership information on all aspects of American relations with respect to African peoples.

Domestic

3. (a) To relate to those organizations that are predominately involved in and influence the education of Black people.

    (b) To solicit their influence and affluence in the promotion of Black Studies and in the execution of AHSA programs and projects.

    (c) To arouse social consciousness and awareness of these groups.

    (d) To encourage their financial contribution to Black schools with programs involving the study of African peoples.

Black Students and Scholars

4. (a) To encourage and support students who wish to major in the study of African peoples.

    (b) To encourage Black students to relate to the study of the heritage of African people, and to acquire the range of skills for the production and development of African peoples.

(c) To encourage attendance and participation including the reading of papers at meetings dealing with the study of African life and history so that the African perspective is represented.

(d) To ask all Black students and scholars to rally around AHSA to build it up as a sturdy organization for the reconstruction of our history and culture.

Black Communities

5. (a) To seek to aid Black scholars who need financial support for their community projects or academic research.

(b) To edit a newsletter or journal through which AHSA activities will be known.

Notably, although Clarke was a central figure in the October 1968 initiative in Los Angeles and the subsequent events that followed from it, he had not yet been offered a faculty appointment at a university. That offer would come less than a year later when he would accept a position as adjunct professor and architect of the Africana Studies curriculum of the newly created Department of Black and Puerto Rican Studies at Hunter College of the City University of New York. Without academic portfolio, Clarke was, nonetheless, one of fourteen members of the Black Caucus's ad hoc committee. They included Harold Weaver of the Center for African Studies at St. John's University; Shelby Lewis of the Department of Political Science at Southern University-Baton Rouge; P. Chike Onwuachi, director of the African-Caribbean Studies Center at Fisk University; Nell Painter of San Jose City College; and Andrea Crease of African Studies and Research at Howard University. Others were identified as Len Jeffries and Maina D. Kogombe of New York City; J. K. Obatala of Monrovia, California; Joseph O. Kofa and Samuel T. Massaquoc of San Francisco, California; Ihieukwumere A. Anozie and Ronald Taylor of Los Angeles, California; and Mike Searles of Washington, D.C.[39]

The permanent break between Afrikan and European scholars would, however, be dramatically concluded in the following year, 1969, when the ASA held its twelfth annual meeting in Montreal. Clarke was, once again, a central figure in the Afrikan initiative.[40] Afrikan scholars and students, charging that the European-controlled organization and its work were "fundamentally invalid and illegitimate," held "a plenary session of the African peoples," where they raised these concerns as an unscheduled part of the conference's proceedings, "having long disapproved of the complexion, activities, direction and selection of participants of this organization and its conference."[41] They also disrupted the four-day conference through a series of demonstrations that underscored their rejection of an arrangement that precluded Afrikan control of an association committed to the systematic study of the Afrikan continent. Afrikan scholars declared the ASA's "present relationship to Africa is damaging and injurious to the welfare of African peoples."[42] In short, they launched a putsch and took control of the conference proceedings. Led primarily by Afrikans from the United States, with support from Afrikans of the Caribbean and Afrikan continent, they forced the cancellation of thirty of the fifty-five scheduled sessions.[43]

The Afrikan conferees (in reality, under the leadership of the AHSA[44]) aimed to compel European acceptance of an initiative that would restructure the association. Such restructuring, they said, would include redefining the association's ideological orientation and purpose. In what appears to be a draft statement, they demanded that "the study of African life be undertaken from a Pan-Africanist perspective," rejecting the association's Eurocentric approach, which promoted "the tribalization of African peoples by geographical demarcation on the basis of colonialist spheres of influence." They further enumerated several necessary ideological and structural changes to an "organization which purports to study, research and teach authoritatively about African peoples and culture." First, they demanded that the ASA immediately change its ideological framework, "which perpetuates colonialism and neocolonialism," and adopt a posture that deals "truthfully and realistically with African peoples." Second, as concerns the association's structure, Afrikan scholars insisted upon a change in constitutional procedures that enabled Europeans to elect a predominantly European board of directors, which controlled the association's agenda for scholarship on Afrikan life. Third, they also held that the twelve-member board of directors must be evenly divided between Afrikans and Europeans. Fourth, Afrikan scholars also called for a change in the association's membership rules, which they charged restricted their

participation. Fifth, they demanded that Afrikans enjoy equal representation with Europeans in determining the allocation of research
funds. The scholars had resolved that "African peoples will no longer
permit our people to be raped culturally, economically, politically and
intellectually merely to provide European scholars with intellectual
status symbols of African artifacts hanging in their living rooms and
irrelevant and injurious lectures for their classrooms."[45]

ASA vice president L. Gray Cowan, who would ascend to the
ASA's presidency a year later, announced to *The New York Times* that
the association had agreed to form a thirty-member ad hoc committee of fifteen Afrikans and fifteen Europeans to consider the restructuring of the board of directors and the executive offices.[46] This offer
came in response to categorical Afrikan rejection of an ASA proposal
that only three Afrikans be specially elected to its twelve-member
board of directors, leaving the other nine to be elected according to
current rules.[47] The caucus countered it would provide a list of fifteen
names provided six Afrikans be placed on the twelve-member board
of directors on a provisional basis. It was a "conditional acceptance,"
reflecting the suspicion that the Europeans had no serious intentions
of negotiating in good faith.[48] Eventually, by a 103 to 97 vote, the
ASA's predominantly European membership rejected the Afrikan
demands for equal Afrikan-European representation on the board
of directors.[49] In his retrospective examination, Clarke, as AHSA
president, would remark upon the irony of such an official rejection
of "minimal demands" by "an organization of scholars whose prestige
and output depends upon maintaining good relations with Africans
both in terms of gaining entry into African countries and obtaining
reliable information for [sic] them."[50]

Contributing to this rejection, Clarke wrote in his retrospective
analysis of events, was the fact that Afrikans defined Afrikans as
including "all black people." This Afrikan repudiation of artificial,
European-created divisions based on geography and informed by
colonialist interests "offended a large number of the white 'scholars'
attending the conference. They resented the projection of African
people as a world people with a common cause and a common
destiny." Moreover, he observed, they resented, more than anything
else, the solidarity and association of Afrikans in the United States
with those of Afrika. "The demands of the blacks attending this

conference had exposed the neo-colonialism that a large number of these so-called scholars had been practicing for years. Africa to them was a kind of ethnic plantation over which they reigned and explained to the world. Most of them even resented Africans being considered authorities on Africa."[51] In an address to the AHSA's second annual conference at Howard University in May 1970, at which some 2,000 attended, some traveling from as far as Ethiopia and Cote d'Ivoire, Onwuachi, chairman of the AHSA's executive board, elaborated upon the European reaction. "For insisting that the African Studies Association make some organizational changes in conformity with the realities of the present struggles of Black peoples all over the world with their Pan-African perspectives, the white and 'Negro' bigots of the Association dubbed the Black Caucus racists and militants."[52]

Having lost control of the conference, ASA officials were compelled to give some attention to Afrikan demands. Afrikan scholars' stinging condemnation of the proceedings in their official 15 October 1969 "Statement of the Black Caucus," later published in Clarke's first presidential report to the African Heritage Studies Association, characterized the ASA as an "organization which purports to study Africa [but] has never done so." They condemned "the intellectual arrogance of white people which has perpetuated and legitimized a kind of academic colonialism" in the social and cultural study of Afrikan peoples. They also categorically dismissed the association's work as "irrelevant to the interests and needs of Black people" and assessed its research as being "geared toward proposals which extend the old material interests of the European nations." Indeed, the Afrikan scholars added, "International research controlled, directed and financed by Western interests is a subtle, but potent, mechanism of social control and exploitation of African peoples and resources." The granting agencies that support the study of Afrika, the scholars contended, "are the same people and organizations which exploit African peoples throughout the world and undermine and retard our political development." Furthermore, they observed, representatives of these inimical interests were actually attending the conference.[53]

As far as the AHSA leadership and membership were concerned, the ASA was an organization that directly and indirectly affected the lives and livelihood of Afrikan scholars and students.

Its annual meetings brought together not simply academics but also government officials, journalists, business persons, representatives of foundations, and others. The meetings were, thus, of extraordinary consequence. The research generated by its scholars, they argued, not only controlled and influenced the image of Afrika in the world, but it also substantively influenced United States foreign policy decisions in Afrika.[54]

Based on this assessment, the Afrikan caucus announced its suspension of the conference proceedings, which would instead be dedicated to addressing their concerns. It also announced the existence of the alternative Afrikan-led and -founded organization that had been the subject of discussion and organizational meetings in the previous year.[55]

> The direction and content of African Studies must come from Black people through an international Pan African organization along the lines of the African Heritage Studies Association. Therefore the offices of the African Studies Association are declared vacated and this Ad Hoc Committee assumes control so that Black people can determine future definition and content of African Studies.[56]

In his presidential report to the AHSA, Clarke noted that the Afrikan initiative at the Montreal meeting enjoyed strong support among many highly placed individuals and luminaries of the Afrikan world. Among other things, Afrikan concern regarding European control of the research on Afrika was not new; it had been raised in two earlier conferences of the International Congress of Africanists that had met in Accra, Ghana, and Dakar, Senegal.[57] Clarke was well aware of this because, as an active member of the congress since its founding in 1962, he had also attended and presented a paper at its 1967 conference in Dakar.[58] At Montreal, the Senegalese ambassador to Germany, Gabriel d'Arboussier, who had been scheduled to deliver the keynote address for the conference's opening session, voiced support for the Afrikan action. As well, Clarke reported, Robert Gardiner, director of the United Nations Economic Commission for Africa, actively participated in the Afrikan caucus's meetings and supported its demands. Further, many of the Afrikan guests invited by the ASA and the Canadian African Studies Committee also agreed with the action taken against the ASA and signed a written statement of support, which the legendary negritude poet Léon Damas of French Guiana, South America, publicly read.[59] The declaration of solidarity reiterated the caucus's charge that "African Studies as conceived within the context of colonialism and imperialist domination of the African continent have served exclusively to reinforce an ideology which serves their domination in the interest of foreign capital and to exploit the African continent."[60]

Nearly three decades later, the conflict between Afrikans and Europeans over the control of the systematic study of Afrika and its peoples was still engaged. Lisa Brock, associate professor of African History and Diasporan Studies at the School of the Art Institute of Chicago, and chair of the Department of Liberal Arts, remarked upon this in an essay titled "Questioning the Diaspora: Hegemony, Black Intellectuals and Doing International History from Below." She observed: "Realities that African-American intellectuals know quite well—that there was a Black tradition of scholarship on Africa in the Americas long before 1948 and that peoples of African descent have been marginalized within the African Studies establishment—are finally getting a much needed airing." Indeed, she added, "Scholars of African descent have often felt like round pegs in the 'official' square holes of African Studies." This has been effected on the part of European Africanists "by a malignant neglect and/or diminishing of their/our angle(s) of vision, their/our positionality(ies) and their/our ability(ies) to construct paradigms and set agendas for the study of Africa." In Brock's view, the conflict between Afrikans and Europeans in the study of Afrika in the United States lies principally in the fact of the divergent and conflicting interests that drive their respective motives in studying Afrika. On the one hand, the partnership between European scholarship, U.S. private foundations, and U.S. governmental agencies was directed by priorities of U.S. national security as well as development and related issues. For Afrikans of the Americas, by contrast, the Afrikan continent was homeland and heritage and seen as integral to the struggle for liberation from global foreign domination.[61] Clarke himself would remark that African studies was more than "an academic discipline and nothing more." It was, instead, an enterprise of strategic significance to Afrikans "that extends far beyond the academic community and is a part of an international struggle to control image and information. When you control what a people knows about themselves, you can also control what they think about themselves and what they do about themselves."[62]

Formal negotiations and discussions continued between the two organizations in 1970, but by this time there were few grounds for collaboration. An indication of the irreconcilability of the two groups could be seen in efforts made by Afrikan ASA board members Willard Johnson and Johnetta Cole to redirect the ASA's mission to conform with global Afrikan interests. Their "Resolution on the African Studies Association's Commitment to the Liberation and Dignified Survival of African People" called on the ASA to actively commit itself to work for global Afrikan liberation and to set aside a portion of the membership dues to create a fund for this purpose that would be governed by a board of directors whose members would be selected by the ASA, the AHSA, and by the continental Afrikan members of the ASA, if the latter two groups wished to participate. The Johnson-Cole resolution also called for the control by AHSA, if it so wished, of a plenary session at the ASA's annual meetings, and the control of another plenary session by Afrikan scholars, if Afrikan ASA members so chose. Finally, Cole and Johnson also reiterated the AHSA's call to restructure the ASA's board of directors so that Afrikans and Europeans would be equally represented.[63] Although the ASA conferees narrowly approved the Johnson-Cole resolution at their annual meeting on 23 October 1970, board member Ruth Morgenthau mobilized a mail vote campaign that resoundingly overturned it by a margin of 607 to 272 by late January 1971.[64] For Afrikan scholars who had attempted to work within the ASA, and for those who had joined the AHSA, the resolution's defeat signaled that the ASA was irrevocably hostile to Afrikan liberation from European colonialist and neocolonialist domination. Indeed, it was now abundantly clear that the AHSA's commitment to the "[r]econstruction of African history and cultural studies along Afro-centric lines while effecting an intellectual union among black scholars the world over" was antithetical to the ASA's principal goals and objectives.[65] As the Afrikan historian Sterling Stuckey was to observe shortly after the resolution's defeat, "American intellectuals and American oppressors of blacks have often been closely, sometimes indistinguishably linked."[66]

While Afrikan efforts to reshape the ASA in an Afrikan image and according to Afrikan interests were repulsed, the AHSA's battles with the ASA spilled over into other fronts within the field of African studies. One such front was the third congress of the International Congress of Africanists held in Addis Ababa, Ethiopia, in December 1973. There Afrikan scholars scored victories against the ASA that they had been unable to secure within the ASA itself. Among them was a speech, delivered by Ethiopia's monarch, the Emperor Haile Selassie, which set the tone for the Afrikan offensive.

> It cannot be denied that in the past the conduct of study and research on Africa was in the hands of non-Africans. The nature and content of such study and research was therefore primarily determined by non-African needs and interests. The time has now come when Africa, having abandoned the subservient status, is guiding her own destiny in the political and economic spheres. In the academic sphere, as well, the time seems to have come when Africans can abandon the role of subservience and embrace that of full and equal participation. ... it cannot ... be denied that Africans need to carry a greater share of the study and research on their continent than they do at present. Their greater participation can no doubt help to re-direct Africanist research into areas of greater relevance to Africa's needs and interests.[67]

Consistent with the emperor's observations, a Pan Afrikanist delegation from the United States aggressively pushed for and succeeded in asserting Afrikan control of the meeting—something Clarke maintained had been absent in the first two meetings in 1963 and 1967, which had been controlled and dominated by the ASA. So total had European control been in the previous two meetings that no U.S. Afrikan had delivered a paper in 1963, and only one U.S. Afrikan (Clarke) had done so four years later. In 1973, by contrast, "The Africans took over, and the Afro-Americans played a major role and presented papers in a number of sessions; and one Afro-American [Clarke] was elected to the Permanent Council that will

cover the Congress for the next five years and plan future meetings."
In other words, Clarke's election to the council, for the first time
gave U.S. Afrikans a decision-making position in the Congress. This
achievement, secured in Afrika four years after the confrontation in
Montreal, was for AHSA members a cause for celebration.[68]

Ultimately, the AHSA was simply a vehicle for Clarke's vision
of global Afrikan unity that was the necessary precondition for
Afrikan world sovereignty. The AHSA's role, like that of the OAAU
that preceded it, was, therefore, a means by which to ideologically
and culturally structure global relationships among Afrikans that
would enable them to develop the capacity to resist and, ultimately,
to destroy European domination. This explains why the basic aims
of the AHSA accorded with what had also been pursued and articulated in the OAAU, and why the first level of struggle involved the
quest to wrest intellectual control from Europeans of the systematic
study of Afrika and its peoples. Indeed, Clarke maintained, this
political, revolutionary, liberational aim of Afrikan scholarship by
means of the AHSA presents to "the closely connected group of
white 'authorities' on Africa" a specter that

> frightens them because this means that they will lose their
> control over information about Africa. They resent the idea
> of any Black person taking it upon himself to question their
> authority and examine their credentials. That is precisely what
> the members of the African Heritage Studies Association intend
> to do. First, they intend to ask for an entirely new approach
> to African History. This new approach must begin with a new
> frame of reference.[69]

This new frame of reference, Clarke stated in his articulation
of the AHSA's ideological framework, entailed a commitment to
"the preservation, interpretation, and creative presentation of the
historical and cultural heritage" of Afrikans in its global diaspora
and on the continent, interpreting Afrikan history "from a Pan-
Africanist perspective that defines all black people as an African
people."[70] Indeed, this orientation to Afrikan nationality was of
strategic significance, for it was the key to the struggle to restore
Afrikan global power. "What and who are the African people? *We*

make no sharp distinction between the Africans in Africa and the people of African descent in other parts of the world. This at once projects the possibility of a world union of African people"[71] (added emphasis). Significantly, while the concept of world union expressed the logical implications of the powerfully unifying notion of Afrikan nationality, it also implied the evolution of some formulation of Afrikan state power, as yet undefined, to create, to sustain, and to elaborate this called for Afrikan world union.

Further, Clarke's vision of Afrikan world union embraced the idea that Afrikans, after having regained their sovereignty, would play a vanguard role in the liberation of humankind. From the position of Afrikan world union Afrikans would also launch "a broader program of internationalism that will embrace all people." The nature of their power position entailed a moral obligation to complete the liberation process for the world. "We must use our radicalism to build the kind of world where all people can walk in peace, justice, and without fear. This may be our mission and the finest legacy that we can leave to the people of the world."[72]

The critical, indeed central, role of the intellectual and scholar was, thus, to contribute to the success of this enterprise by means of the AHSA, which was to serve as a strategic resource in its realization. The organization was constituted of "scholar-activists" committed to the global restoration of Afrikan power and self-determination by means of achieving "the cultural unity of the black peoples of the world."[73] The primary role of its members "is to define the historical currents relating to this action in such a manner that when this inevitable action occurs it can proceed with a maximum of involvement of the people and a minimum of confusion."[74] In other words, the AHSA is tasked to define the method and to underscore the importance of effecting this process of global Afrikan union. In addition, it must also discover the means by which to "heal the deep psychological wounds that are the legacy of the slave trade and the colonial system."[75]

For Clarke, Pan Afrikan nationalism was an imperative, a necessary precondition for the actualization of national sovereignty. "Our original place of origin was Africa and no matter where we live on earth, we are an African people. Our approach to African History and culture everywhere will be in keeping with this definition," he declared. "We intend to use history as a force for our liberation and as a basis of African world unity. We depend on an honest and creative approach to history to tell what we have been, what we are and what we still must be."[76]

Notes

1. John Henrik Clarke, "New Perspectives on the History of African Peoples," Louisiana Educational Association, 1 May 1970, 3, JHCP, SCRBC.

2. William W. Sales, Jr., *From Civil Rights to Black Liberation: Malcolm X and the Organization of Afro-American Unity* (Boston: South End Press, 1994), 60, 100, 118. Sylvester Leaks was a journalist Malcolm hired in 1959 to edit the New York edition of the *Muhammad Speaks* newspaper, the official organ of the Nation of Islam.

3. Colin Legum, "The Organization of African Unity—Success or Failure?" *International Affairs* 51, no. 2 (April 1975): 208; Sales, *From Civil Rights*, 106.

4. Bailey was an OAAU founding member and editor of the organization's newsletter *Backlash*. At the time of the publication of Clarke's edited volume on Malcolm, Bailey was associate editor of *Ebony* magazine. See John Henrik Clarke, ed., *Malcolm X: The Man and His Times* (Trenton, NJ: Africa World Press, 1990; originally New York: Collier Books, 1969).

5. Sales, *From Civil Rights*, 105. Clarke recalled that one of the capacities in which he served Malcolm was as a supplier of information, one of those he called "Malcolm's history cabinet" or "Malcolm's 'shadow cabinet' of non-Muslims who fed him information behind the scenes." The information he provided Malcolm would then use quite successfully in speeches and public debates. See Kwaku Person-Lynn, ed., *First Word: Black Scholars, Thinkers, Warriors, Knowledge, Wisdom, Mental Liberation* (New York: Harlem River Press, 1996), 17.

6. Person-Lynn, *First Word*, 17.

7. John Henrik Clarke, "The Meaning of Malcolm X," video recording of a speech delivered in Harlem, New York City, unknown date. Clarke remarked he decided after Malcolm's assassination to say little about his relationship with him and his involvement in the OAAU because of the frequency with which many persons who had avoided Malcolm when he was alive pretended to be a friend and staunch supporter after his death. He did not want to be

perceived as such a person. See also Sales, *From Civil Rights*, 105. Clarke also discussed his relationship with Malcolm X and the founding of the OAAU in Person-Lynn, *First Word*, 16–20.

8. Malcolm's adherence to the Islamic faith, and his having founded the Muslim Mosque, Inc., put him in the strategic position of being the representative of Afrikan Muslims in the United States. See Abdullah Abdur-Raazaq, Oral Histories, The Malcolm X Project at Columbia University, http://www.columbia.edu/cu/mxp/araazaq.html.

9. Herman Ferguson, telephone interview with Spartacus R, Global African Peoples' Radio, London, England, 2 August 2006; ibid., "The Price of Freedom," *Souls* 7, no. 1 (2005): 96–97; ibid., Oral Histories, The Malcolm X Project at Columbia University, http://www.columbia.edu/cu/mxp/hferguson.html; Karl Evanzz, *The Judas Factor: The Plot to Kill Malcolm X* (New York: Thunder's Mouth Press, 1992); Max Stanford, Oral Histories, The Malcolm X Project at Columbia University, http://www.columbia.edu/cu/mxp/mstanford.html; Ossie Davis, Oral Histories, The Malcolm X Project at Columbia University, http://www.columbia.edu/cu/mxp/odavis.html; Abdullah Abdur-Raazaq, Oral Histories, The Malcolm X Project at Columbia University, http://www.columbia.edu/cu/mxp/araazaq.html; Sales, *From Civil Rights*.

10. Sales, *From Civil Rights*, 100.

11. Malcolm X, "The 2nd African Summit Conference," 21 August 1964, JHCP, SCRBC. This was a statement Malcolm, as head of the Organization of Afro-American Unity (OAAU), made to the news media in Cairo, Egypt, on 21 August 1964. The OAAU released it to the news media on 1 September 1964 in New York City from its Harlem headquarters at the Hotel Theresa.

12. Ibid.

13. Ibid., letter to Diallo Telli, 28 July 1964, JHCP, SCRBC. Malcolm addressed the letter as OAAU chairman to Telli as OAU Secretary General.

14. Ibid., "The Black Struggle in the United States," *Présence Africaine* 26, no. 54 (Second Quarterly 1965): 8.

15. Ibid., 22.

16. Ibid., 8.

17. Sales, *From Civil Rights*, 100.

18. Malcolm X, "The Black Struggle," 15.

19. Ibid., 9.

20. Ibid.

21. "Afro-American Troops for Congo-Malcolm X," news release from the OAAU Information Bureau, Accra, Ghana, n.d., JHCP, SCRBC.

22. Clarke, *Malcolm X*, xxiii.

23. Ibid., xxiv.

24. Ibid., xxii.

25. John Henrik Clarke and Sylvester Leaks, "Malcolm X: His Grandeur and Significance," *Présence Africaine* no. 62 (2nd Quarterly 1967): 79.

26. Ibid., "Malcolm X," 80.

27. Sales, *From Civil Rights*, 212.

28. John Henrik Clarke, letter to Julian Mayfield, 1 June 1965, JHCP, SCRBC. Clarke had also written to Mayfield, who was in Accra, Ghana, as editor of *The African Review*, immediately upon Malcolm's assassination on 21 February 1965. In a letter dated 24 February 1965, Clarke captured some of the emotion and turmoil generated by Malcolm's murder. "In the meantime, you know by now that Malcolm has been slain and there is stark confusion here." He added: "We are in a bad way for leadership and for quite a few other things because Brother Malcolm was one of the strongest and clearest voices to emerge from our group in this century. He was a man with a lot to learn and he was learning it – and learning it fast!" Ibid., letter to Julian Mayfield, 24 February 1965, JHCP, SCRBC.

29. Ronald W. Walters, *Pan Africanism in the African Diaspora: An Analysis of Modern Afrocentric Political Movements* (Detroit: Wayne State University Press, 1993), 365.

30. Ibid.

31. Statement of the Black Caucus to the African Studies Association, 19 October 1968, JHCP, SCRBC; John Henrik Clarke, "Confrontation at Montreal: The Fight to Reclaim African History," First Report to the African Heritage Studies Association, n.d., 2, JHCP, SCRBC; ibid., "The Fight to Reclaim African History," *Negro Digest* 19, no. 4 (February 1970): 12; Walters, *Pan Africanism*, 366.

32. Statement of the Black Caucus, 19 October 1968.

33. Nell Painter, "Summary of the Meeting of the African Studies Association Board and the Black Caucus, Los Angeles, 19 October 1968," JHCP, SCRBC.

34. Organizing Meeting of the Association of Black Scholars, n.d., JHCP, SCRBC.

35. Nell Painter, "Abridged Minutes of the Black Caucus Meeting of 18 October 1968," JHCP, SCRBC.

36. Organizing Meeting; Painter, "Abridged Minutes"; Walters, *Pan Africanism*, 367. Walters reports the meeting was held in Clarke's home.

37. Clarke, "Confrontation at Montreal," 3–5; ibid., "The Fight," 12–14. Walters, *Pan Africanism*, 367.

38. Taken verbatim from the Brochure of the AHSA, JHCP, SCRBC.

39. Ad Hoc Committee – Black Caucus, 18 October 1968, JHCP, SCRBC; Clarke, "Confrontation at Montreal," 2.

40. Walters, *Pan Africanism*, 367.

41. Statement, n.d., JHCP, SCRBC; Thomas A. Johnson, "Blacks Interrupt Parley on Africa," *The New York Times*, 19 October 1969; "Statement of the Black Caucus" in John Henrik Clarke, "Confrontation at Montreal: The Fight to Reclaim African History," First Report to the African Heritage Studies Association, n.d., JHCP, SCRBC.

42. "Statement of the Black Caucus."

43. Johnson, "Blacks Interrupt"; Walters, *Pan Africanism*, 367. See also Clarke, "Confrontation at Montreal," 5. In a retrospective he published as AHSA president, Clarke remarked that the Afrikan initiative could have met with greater success had more of the Afrikan conferees been aware of the organizational initiatives that had developed since the previous year's meeting in Los Angeles. "Part of the confusion at Montreal was due to the fact that the main aims and objectives of the A.H.S.A. had not been known to any appreciable number of the attending black intellectuals, who could have explained these objectives to the students. Had these objectives been known, the revolt against the domination of the conference by white 'scholars' might still have occurred; but it is my opinion that this revolt would have been more orderly and constructive."

44. In addition to Clarke, the negotiating team included AHSA members Dr. P. Chike Onwuachi and Dr. Nicholas Onyewu, both from Nigeria; Kenneth McIntyre, a jazz musician and music professor at SUNY Old Westbury; and Dr. Acklyn Lynch of Federal City College. See Walters, *Pan Africanism*, 368; Clarke, "The Fight," 60.

45. Statement, n.d. A sixth demand addressed a problem with Afrikan students attending Sir George Williams University in Montreal, calling on the ASA to provide financial support to them and to issue a public statement regarding their situation. Clarke, "The Fight," 60–61.

46. Johnson, "Blacks Interrupt Parley." The brief article was to be included in the February–March 1970 issue of the *African Heritage Newsletter*. It summarizes the substance of a 3 January meeting held in New York City and is apparently written by Cowan, who is identified as ASA president. See also the list of ASA presidents on the organization's official website, http://www. africanstudies.org/ASA%20Pres.htm.

47. Statement, n.d.

48. Clarke, "Confrontation at Montreal," 10; ibid., "The Fight," 62–63.

49. Ibid., 8. See also Walters, *Pan Africanism*, 368; Clarke, "The Fight," 61. Walters says the vote was 104 to 93.

50. Ibid. See also Walters, *Pan Africanism*, 369. Walters notes that Clarke was elected first president of the AHSA in a June 1969 Washington, D.C., meeting. At the time, in terms of academic portfolio, he was an adjunct professor of Africana Studies at Hunter College. Yet "his intellectual leadership and challenge to the ultra-academistic approach and Eurocentric interpretation of African scholarship by whites was an important source of direction for the new organization and an entire generation of younger Black scholars."

51. Ibid.; ibid., "The Fight," 60.

52. P. Chike Onwuachi, "Ideological Perspectives of the African Heritage Studies Association," *African Heritage Newsletter* 2, no. 1–2 (January–February 1971): 1, JHCP, SCRBC; Rudy Johnson, "Parley Stresses African Heritage," *New York Times*, 10 May 1970, 59.

53. "Statement of the Black Caucus."

54. Clarke, "Confrontation at Montreal," 7. Sterling Stuckey would amplify this charge by Afrikan scholars in an essay published in 1971 in the *New York Times*. See Sterling Stuckey, "Black Studies and White Myths," *New York Times*, 13 February 1971, 27.

55. Ibid., "Confrontation at Montreal," 3. Clarke noted the Afrikan scholars who had formed the caucus during the eleventh annual African Studies Association conference in Los Angeles in October 1968 created the African Heritage Studies Association at a 27–29 June 1969 meeting at the Federal City College in Washington, D.C. This meeting followed an organizing meeting hosted by Clarke and held in Harlem in late December 1968.

56. "Statement of the Black Caucus."

57. John Henrik Clarke, "Towards Pan-Africanism: Report from Addis Ababa, Ethiopia, December 1973, the Third International Congress of Africanists,"

Black World (March 1974): 71–72. "In spite of the fact that the first two Congresses were held in Africa," he wrote, "they were dominated by white scholars, mainly from the U.S. based organization, the African Studies Association. No papers by Black American scholars were presented at the First Congress and only one at the Second Congress. Behind the scene, white scholars manipulated both the First and Second Congresses." See Clarke, "The Fight," 61.

58. *The Columbus Times*, Vol. IX, no. 16, Fifth week of January 1980, JHCP, SCRBC. See also John Henrik Clarke, Curriculum Vitae, JHCP, SCRBC.

59. French Guiana, established by the French in 1604, the site of notorious penal colonies until 1951, remains an overseas department of France. See CIA World Factbook, https://www.cia.gov/cia/publications/factbook/geos/fg.html. See also Walters, *Pan Africanism,* 368. Walters says Damas was living in Paris at the time. He adds he was to have been a plenary speaker and was initially confused by the Afrikan action.

60. Clarke, "Confrontation at Montreal," 9; Walters, *Pan Africanism,* 367; Clarke, "The Fight," 61–62.

61. Lisa Brock, "Questioning the Diaspora: Hegemony, Black Intellectuals and Doing International History from Below," *Issue: A Journal of Opinion* 24, no. 2 (1996): 9. Brock was not alone. In remarks published in the Winter 1996 edition of the *Bulletin of the Association of Concerned Africa Scholars,* U.S. Afrikan scholars registered complaints about the field and of the ASA that were consistent with charges made nearly 30 years earlier. See *Bulletin of the Association of Concerned Africa Scholars,* no. 46 (Winter 1996).

62. John Henrik Clarke, "International Aspects of African Studies 1968–1978: A Decade of Change, Challenge and Conflict," 21st Annual Meeting of the African Studies Association, Baltimore, Maryland, 1–4 November 1978, 1–2, JHCP, SCRBC.

63. "African Studies Association and African Liberation," *African Heritage Newsletter* 1, nos. 1–2 (November–December 1970): 9, JHCP, SCRBC.

64. "African Studies Association," 9; "African Liberation Fund Rejected by African Studies Association," *African Heritage Newsletter* 2, nos. 1–2 (January–February 1971): 8, JHCP, SCRBC.

65. "Africanism: Toward a New Definition," brochure for the second annual conference of the African Heritage Studies Association, JHCP, SCRBC. The conference was held at Howard University, 1–3 May 1970. See also "African Liberation Fund Rejected," 8. The newsletter reported Johnson and Cole left the ASA board of directors in response to the ASA's rejection of

their resolution. Other Afrikans, it reported, also left leadership positions in the organization in response to the resolution's defeat.

66. Stuckey, "Black Studies and White Myths," 27.

67. Clarke, "Towards Pan-Africanism," 74–75.

68. Ibid., 72–73, 76. The delegation included James Turner, director of the Africana Studies and Research Center at Cornell University (Turner led the delegation), and Patricia Karouma, Milfred Fierce, Mae King, Shelby Smith, Steven McGanns (graduate student), Clarke, Asa Davis, Rukudzo Murapa, Leonard Jeffries, Rosalind Jeffries, Isaac Akinyobin, Joseph Harris, Walter Rodney (who was then based in Tanzania), Ahmed Mohiddin (of Makerere University), and Elliot Skinner.

    Further, the issue of getting a U.S. Afrikan on the Permanent Council was the subject of behind-the-scenes debate and maneuvering throughout the length of the conference. Turner, who led the U.S. Afrikan delegation, and who was AHSA president, insisted that a member of the AHSA be placed on the Permanent Council because the ASA had for a decade had one of its members on the council.

69. Ibid., "The Image of Africa in the Mind of the Afro-American: African Identity in the Literature of Struggle," Phelps-Stokes Seminars on African-American Relations, *The Afro-American Connection*, Moton Conference Center, Capahosic, Gloucester, Virginia, 5–7 October 1973, 29, JHCP, SCRBC.

70. Ibid., "The Ideological Framework of AHSA," Draft version, 12 October 1970, 1, JHCP, SCRBC; ibid., "The Ideological Framework of AHSA," *African Heritage Newsletter* 1, no. 1–2 (November–December 1970): 2, JHCP, SCRBC.

71. Ibid., "The Image of Africa," 30.

72. Ibid., "The Black Radical Tradition," Seton Hall University, South Orange, New Jersey, 1 March 1974, JHCP, SCRBC.

73. Ibid., "The Ideological Framework, Draft version," 1; ibid., "The Ideological Framework," 2.

74. Ibid., "The Ideological Framework, Draft version," 1–2; ibid., "The Ideological Framework," 2.

75. Ibid., "The Ideological Framework, Draft version," 2; ibid., "The Ideological Framework," 2.

76. Ibid., "The Image of Africa," 30.

Chapter Eight

THE DYNAMICS OF AFRIKAN CULTURE

... you have received the white man' Baor. His spirit lives in you. In a way you are not here yet. It's as if the real you is somewhere else, still trying to find the route home. ... You carry something in you, something very subtle, something that comes from your contact with the whites—and now you want to be here where you once belonged. You cannot live here as you are now without turning this place into what you are. This is what the white man did throughout the land of the Black man. ... You are not white, and because you were born here, you must be made to fit into this place. You must be able to come home completely before your white nature changes your village by forcing it to come to you.
—from Malidoma Patrice Some, *Of Water and the Spirit*[1]

Right now I would like nothing better than to leave the U.S.A. and take up residence in Africa for at least three years. There are so many things happening in Africa that I need to be close to.
—John Henrik Clarke, early 1960s[2]

Despite the fact that Afrikans were brought, beginning in the early seventeenth century, to the English settlements that would evolve into the United States, not all succumbed to the psychological and cultural decentering and derangement that was the objective of totalitarian dictatorship. This preference for Afrika and

Afrikan nationality was transmitted intergenerationally, nurtured undetected by European society in large part because that society did not respect Afrikans enough to take them seriously as cultural, intellectual, or human beings. "Clearly," wrote the late Afrikan historian John W. Blassingame in his classic text *The Slave Community* (1972), "one of the general means by which Africans resisted bondage was by retaining their link with their past. Rather than accept the slaveholder's view of his place in society, the African tried to hold onto the African cultural determinants of his status."[3] Blassingame explores the varied ways in which cultural continuity was preserved, including in the area of Afrikan languages and Afrikan religions and religious practices.

While certain Afrikans who became literate in European culture and language acceded to structuring their thoughts and aspirations within the confines of acceptable European conceptual frameworks—what the formerly enslaved Charles Ball called in 1837 "the American negro, who knows nothing of Africa, her religion, or customs, and who has borrowed all his ideas of present and future happiness, from the opinions and intercourse of white people, and of Christians"[4]—others remained defiant. There were among the captives, according to Ball, those Afrikans whose memories of Afrika and of freedom rendered them contemptuous of their enslavers and of subordination to them, and their chief desire was to return to their respective homelands. "Throughout their sojourn in America, Africans were quite unimpressed with the culture and achievements of the slaveholder," observes Afrika historian Michael A. Gomez. "Although there were surely those who acquiesced to their enslavement to the point of obsequity, it is important to note that the overwhelming characterization of the African-born was consistently one of defiance."[5]

This orientation would, of course, be passed on with varying success to their progeny. Hence, it is no surprise that Clarke, born fifty years after the demise of a form of legal enslavement that followed the conclusion of the Civil War, credited his formerly enslaved great grandmother with inspiring and nurturing his developing Afrikan consciousness. The oral historian of the family, she "introduced me to my African heritage," he would recall decades later. "So, very early in life I knew that I had an African heritage to reclaim."[6]

Indeed, cultural resistance, which often merged seamlessly with political and military resistance, was common throughout the Americas. The Africalogist Tolagbe Ogunleye notes that Afrikans in Spaniard-held Florida, who had liberated themselves by escaping from plantations in Georgia, South Carolina, Tennessee, Alabama, and Louisiana, established for more than 150 years "autonomous African settlements" and "were involved in a formalized Pan-African nationalist movement."[7] From the mid seventeenth through the mid nineteenth centuries, self-emancipated Afrikans "who fled enslavement on Southern plantations lived autonomously in Florida, ostensibly using discrete African art forms, traditions, and sensibilities in their modes of communications, rituals, subsistence strategies, and battle plans to attain and sustain freedom and autonomy."[8] She adds: "Some of the residents of these settlements had never been enslaved. They were born, reared, and died at a ripe old age within these communities."[9]

Moreover, these communities successfully engaged American military forces in their quest to remain independent. "For more than a century," Ogunleye notes, "southern militiamen, mercenaries, and military forces from the United States routinely invaded the sovereign nation of Florida and completely destroyed the self-emancipated Africans' homes, plundered their livestock, and waged war against these Africans and their offspring in an attempt to conquer and reenslave them."[10] Although the Americans never succeeded in reenslaving them, they did manage to treat with them for their removal to the U.S.-controlled Oklahoma territory. This American achievement came, however, at great cost, both in terms of military expenditures and humiliating defeats. Afrikans had established a formidable military presence in Florida in the late eighteenth and early nineteenth centuries, and had prosecuted a relentless guerrilla war of liberation against American forces that, in its final phases, lasted for more than four decades.

Before its capture by an American military incursion, Fort Ashila,[11] about sixty miles from the American border, stood as a symbol of Afrikan military defiance of the enslaver dictatorship. The British, to spite the Americans after their withdrawal at the conclusion of the War of 1812, had handed the fort over to Afrikan freedom fighters. When American forces bombed and captured the fort on 27 July 1816, they sent some $200,000 in seized armaments and other materials to New Orleans, including 2,500 stand of musketry, 500 carbines, 500 steel scabbard swords, 4 cases containing 200 pairs of pistols, 300 quarter casks of rifle powder, 162 barrels of cannon powder, and other military clothing and supplies.[12] Ogunleye relates revolutionary feeling was at such strength that many Afrikans enslaved in the United States escaped to Florida to join the war of liberation.[13] In addition, she writes, the self-emancipated Afrikans enlisted enslaved Afrikans in the United States as double-agents who led American military forces into fatal ambushes, supplied American weapons to the Afrikan liberation army, and provided critical intelligence on American movements and intentions.[14]

Afrikan captives launched similar revolutionary struggles in other regions in the Americas, including Brazil and Suriname in South America, Jamaica and Haiti in the Caribbean islands, and Mexico, bordering what was to become the United States to the South.[15] In 1537 Afrikans enslaved in Mexico City sought to overthrow the Spaniard government by killing the Spanish crown's representative in Mexico, freeing themselves, and replacing the colonial regime "with an African king of their own." Although this revolutionary effort was discovered and repressed by Spaniard counterintelligence, numerous other movements between 1540 and 1580 succeeded, sometimes involving "substantial cooperation between black and indigenous populations."[16] Perhaps the most successful revolutionary campaign was led by the redoubtable Yangi, who from 1570 to 1609 governed an independent Afrikan settlement that directly and devastatingly engaged Spaniard military forces from his stronghold in the Orizaba Mountains, eventually defeating them and forcing the Spaniards to sue for peace. Although formerly enslaved in Mexico, Yangi held he had been a state ruler in Afrika.[17]

Cultural resistance, of course, took many forms, its strength inspired and sustained by the force of Afrikan cultural and historical memory. Although born in the enslaver dictatorship of the United States, Ball is extraordinarily conscious of Afrika-born Afrikans. Among other reasons, including the ubiquity of their presence during the period of his enslavement, his grandfather was born there, was proud of his heritage, and was a person of pronounced independence of mind. His grandfather, thus, played a profound role in Ball's emotional and family life during his childhood years.[18] Indeed, Ball in his autobiography offers accounts of this cultural and intellectual resistance precisely among Afrikans who endured white supremacist enslaver dictatorship, and who are generally assumed in American historiography not to have been capable of cultural or intellectual resistance. Harriet Jacobs in her autobiography, published in 1861, likewise recounted that she and her fellow captives would secretly mock the European preachers who espoused the enslavers' teachings that Afrikans were sinful if disobedient and faced deserved divine retribution. Jacobs cites a song regularly sung by enslaved Afrikans: "Ole Satan's church is here below; Up to God's free church I hope to go."[19]

The formerly enslaved Frederick Douglass is perhaps the most scathing of all the Afrikans who recorded their experiences of the totalitarian nature of enslaver dictatorship. His repudiation of "the religion of the south" was absolute. In 1845 he characterized it as "a mere covering for the most horrid crimes,—a justifier of the most appalling barbarity,—and a dark shelter under, which the darkest, foulest, grossest, and most infernal deeds of slaveholders find the strongest protection." Devoutly Christian enslavers "are the worst," he asserted. "I have ever found them the meanest and basest, the most cruel and cowardly, of all others."[20]

Gomez captured this Afrikan skepticism in his assessment of the dynamics of Afrikan culture in the first quarter of the nineteenth-century United States when he wrote that "at least two distinct and divergent visions of the African presence in America had achieved sufficient articulation and were in competition. One, drawing from the promise of the American liberal ideal and nurtured by faith in an expansive understanding of Christianity's potential, would engage in any number of strategies to become a partner in the American venture." On the other hand, Afrikans whose assessment of the American experience led them to question the possibility "of ever becoming full participants in the American political experiment, placed their trust in that which transcended temporal powers and in ways which were familiar and reassuring, bringing them as close to the bosom of Africa as they could get."[21] These latter, Gomez underscores, constituted the majority of the Afrikan group.

One of the icons in American historiography about the early republic, the French aristocrat Alexis de Tocqueville, writing two years before Ball, made insightful note of the assimilationist tendency within Afrikan thought (but, in error, universalized it) when he observed:

> In one blow oppression has deprived the descendants of the Africans of almost all the privileges of humanity. The United States Negro has lost even the memory of his homeland; he no longer understands the language his fathers spoke; he has abjured their religion and forgotten their mores. Ceasing to belong to Africa, he has acquired no right to the blessings of Europe; he is left in suspense between two societies and isolated between two peoples, sold by one and repudiated by the other; in the whole world there is nothing but his master's hearth to provide him with some semblance of a homeland. ...
>
> Plunged in this abyss of wretchedness, the Negro hardly notices his ill fortune; he was reduced to slavery by violence, and the habit of servitude has given him the thoughts and ambitions of a slave; he admires his tyrants even more than he hates them and finds his joy and pride in a servile imitation of his oppressors. ...
>
> The Negro makes a thousand fruitless efforts to insinuate himself into a society that repulses him; he adapts himself to his oppressors' tastes, adopting their opinions and hoping by imitation to join their community. From birth he has been told that his race is naturally inferior to the white man and almost believing that, he holds himself in contempt. He sees a trace of slavery in his every feature, and if he could he would gladly repudiate himself entirely.[22]

Typical of white supremacists, de Tocqueville underestimated the intelligence and awareness of enslaved Afrikans, as has already been seen. However accurate he may have been about the dilemma and psychological torment of the assimilationist consciousness, he could not have known he grossly erred in his assertion that Afrika had lost all meaning for Afrikans in the United States. For scholars like Clarke, whose mainstream Afrikan social origins were reflected in his historiography of the Afrikan presence on American soil, Afrika was never forgotten.[23] Instead, it provided a beacon of hope and a vision of freedom to which many Afrikans would return or seek to return psychologically, culturally, and physically over the generations. One of the ways in which this is seen is in the successive Afrikan-led repatriation movements in the United States that included efforts to resettle in Sierra Leone, Liberia, Nigeria, Ghana, and other parts of the Afrikan continent from at least the eighteenth through to the twenty-first centuries.[24] Another way in which it is seen is in the overriding importance that Afrikans placed upon their history in Afrika before the coming of the European enslavers.[25]

Table 8.1
Forms of Afrikan Cultural Resistance in the Americas, 16ᵗʰ –19ᵗʰ Centuries

- Armed struggle to achieve and maintain independence
- Successful and attempted independent settlement and/or state creation
- Intellectual skepticism of European rationales for Afrikan enslavement
- Skepticism of Eurocentric religion
- Indigenous Afrikan spiritual practices
- Language resistance
- Indigenous conceptual and definitional framing of the Afrikan experience in the Americas
- Repatriation to Afrika
- Afrikan history movement

Not surprisingly, the move toward Afrika and Afrikan consciousness was normative and understandably so. Anthropological and linguistic research by Joseph E. Holloway and Winifred K. Vass has uncovered that enslaved Afrikans in the United States expressed themselves quite eloquently on the question of their assessment of the American experience in their own indigenous languages.[26] This is aptly illustrated, for example, in the 270 Bantu language names they gave to many of the localities in which they were held captive in Alabama, Georgia, Florida, Mississippi, North Carolina, South Carolina, Virginia, Texas, and Louisiana. A small sampling of such names include Abita Springs, Louisiana, from *a bita*, meaning "of handcuffs, manacles"; Ambato, Alabama, from *ambata*, meaning "lie on top of each other, be piled up, packed on top of the other, bodies crowded together (as in the hold of a slave ship)"; Benaja, North Carolina, from *benzaja*, meaning "made to work, forced to labor"; Kiowa, Alabama, from *kuyowa*, meaning "to be famished, weakened with hunger, exhausted"; Lula, Mississippi, from *lula*, meaning "be bitter, refuse to obey, be refractory"; Tahoka, Texas, from *tauka*, meaning "be cast off, shed, as leaves off a tree"; and Wataccoo, South Carolina, from *wataku*, meaning "be naked, without clothing."[27] These names are trenchant commentary, powerfully demonstrating the content of indigenous Afrikan thinking in the context of the encounter with the totalitarian dictatorship. They explicate their self-consciousness of their humanity, their irrepressible sense of their right to be free and independent.

Decades earlier, Lorenzo Dow Turner's seminal and pioneering research had uncovered the cultural basis for this resistance. Turner's study of the continuity of Afrikan cultural practice and expression culminated in his 1949 *Africanisms in the Gullah Dialect*. From 1932 to 1947 Turner conducted a fifteen-year investigation of the dialect of the Gullah people of coastal and island South Carolina and Georgia. His research included intensive studies of five West Afrikan languages at the School of Oriental and African Studies at the University of London during the academic year 1936 to 1937.[28] He found that "Gullah is a creolized form of English revealing survivals from many of the African languages spoken by the slaves who were brought to South Carolina and Georgia during the eighteenth century and the first half of the nineteenth."[29] Among the subjects Turner also investigated was the origin and practice of personal names among the Gullah. He identified these names coming from a vast array of groups and languages from West, Central, and Southern Afrika, including the Bambara, Edo, Ewe, Efik, Fante, Fon, Ibibio, Gbari, Hausa, Igbo, Kongo, Mbundu, Kpelle, Mande, Malinke, Mandinka, Mandingo, Nupe, Susu, Twi, Temne, Tshiluba, Wolof, Vai, and Yoruba.[30]

Table 8.2
Percentages of Afrika-Born Afrikans Among Afrikans in the United States, 1680 –1810[31]

Period	Percentage
1680 to 1720	66
1720 to 1760	33
1790 to 1810	22

Gomez's research also points out the cultural source of what would later evolve into twentieth-century Afrikan cultural and intellectual movement and resistance. His work identified specific regions in Afrika from which Afrikans were kidnapped to the United States as well as the regions of the United States to which they were confined and in what ethnical concentrations.[32] Further, he writes, demographic research reveals that from 1680 to 1720, two of every three Afrikans, or 66 percent, were born in Afrika. The percentage decreased to 33 percent, or one of every three, from 1720 to 1760, although by then the greatest percentage of Afrikans in the United States were persons born in Afrika or born to and reared by those born in Afrika. From 1790 to 1810, 22 percent were born in Afrika, declining precipitously after 1810. Yet, much of the Afrikan population was only two generations removed from Afrika.[33] This fact would, of course, exercise a profound influence upon the Afrikan attitude toward both Afrika and the United States and the Afrikan cultural approach to these two regions of the world.

Moreover, Gomez establishes that Afrikans kidnapped and exiled to the United States came from seven major areas of Afrika: 14.5 percent from Senegambia (modern Gambia and Senegal), 15.8 percent from the area of Sierra Leone (modern Guinea-Bissau, Guinea, Sierra Leone, Liberia, and Cote d'Ivoire), 13.1 percent from the Gold Coast region (Ghana), 4.3 percent from the Bight of Benin (modern Togo, Benin, and southwestern Nigeria), 24.4 percent from the Bight of Biafra (southeastern Nigeria, Cameroon, and Gabon), 26.1 percent from West Central Afrika (including the Democratic Republic of the Congo and Angola), and 1.8 percent from the Mozambique-Madagascar region (including Mozambique, parts of Tanzania, and Madagascar).[34]

Inside the United States, Bambara (from Senegambia), Fon, Ewe, and Yoruba (from the Bight of Benin) were taken in significant numbers to New Orleans and Louisiana. In Virginia and Maryland, the Igbo (from the Bight of Biafra) and secondarily the Akan (from the Gold Coast) predominated, with, also, significant numbers of Senegambians. In South Carolina and Georgia, by contrast, Senegambians, Angolans, and Congolese (from West Central Afrika) predominated, with high numbers also of Sierra Leoneans in South Carolina and coastal Georgia.[35] Under such circumstances, contrary to de Tocqueville's contention, it was impossible for the memory of Afrika to have been expunged. Only an ideological conclusion, not an empirical one, could have overlooked this reality.

Table 8.3
Seven Regions of Afrika Contributing to the U.S. Afrikan Population, 17th –19th Centuries[36]

Region	Countries	Percentages
Senegambia	Gambia, Senegal	14.5
Sierra Leone	Guinea-Bissau, Guinea, Sierra Leone, Liberia, Cote d'Ivoire	15.8
Gold Coast	Ghana	13.1
Bight of Benin	Togo, Benin, southwestern Nigeria	4.3
Bight of Biafra	southeastern Nigeria, Cameroon, Gabon	24.4
West Central Afrika	Democratic Republic of the Congo, Angola	26.1
Mozambique-Madagascar	Mozambique, parts of Tanzania, Madagascar	1.8

Thus, in 1958, when Clarke made the first of many journeys to the Afrikan continent, his reconnection to the culture there proved surprisingly immediate in many ways. In one instance, he related an incident that occurred when he was traveling in Ghana on a bus that had "broken down." A passing Ewe truck driver delivering bread to a local market stopped and beckoned to Clarke to join him, saying he would be willing to take Clarke to his destination. The Ewe man's willingness to assist Clarke was motivated by his perception that

Clarke was a fellow Ewe. So adamant was the driver that Clarke was Ewe that he took Clarke to meet his "headsman," remarking, "This man don't know he's Ewe, poor fellow. How can we help him?" The "headsman," after lining Clarke alongside ten Ewe men to demonstrate their shared ethnic physical characteristics, declared "He is our son. He is home. He is welcome."[37]

Reflecting on the incident years later, Clarke remarked, "something happens inside of you when you feel that you have found your homeland. It's a spiritual happening to know that there is some place in this world where, by physical identity, you are accepted as part of a people. And no matter what doubt you might have, they have no doubt in their minds that, physically, you belong to them." For Clarke this was an inimitable experience, one that "never happened any other place in my travels."[38]

Table 8.4
Regional Ethnical Concentrations of Afrikans in the United States to 19th Century[39]

Ethnicity/Region	U.S. Region	Afrikan Regional Origin
Bambara	Louisiana	Senegambia
Fon	Louisiana	Bight of Benin
Ewe	Louisiana	Bight of Benin
Yoruba	Louisiana	Bight of Benin
Igbo	Virginia/Maryland	Bight of Biafra
Akan	Virginia/Maryland	Gold Coast
Senegambians	Virginia/Maryland	Senegambia
Angolans	South Carolina/Georgia	West Central Afrika
Congolese	South Carolina/Georgia	West Central Afrika
Sierra Leoneans	South Carolina/Georgia	Sierra Leone

More profound, however, was the impact of Afrikan culture and spirituality on him during that first stay in Ghana. It is noteworthy that Clarke's Harlem studies in the 1930s of Afrikan history and culture had apparently well prepared him for his personal discovery and embrace of an indigenous Afrikan spiritual system that in his estimation surpassed in quality anything that arose from Europe or

Arabia. Equally significant, it also demonstrates the continuity of Afrikan cultural resistance manifest centuries before. Decades later, in the mid 1990s, he would discuss the lifelong impact of his experience in a speech to an Afrikan community audience in the Newark, New Jersey, area. Although his rearing had been Baptist, "Once I went to Ghana and studied indigenous African belief systems—I am a part of one of their belief systems. I don't think that Christianity, Islam, or any of them is better than African belief systems, once you understand them," he said. "And I have no apologies about it," he added categorically. "I belong to the belief system of the Ga people of Ghana."[40]

In another speech delivered five years before his death, Clarke elaborated upon his practice of a faith that eschewed proselytizing, embodied tolerance, and expressed a quality of humaneness he held was unparalleled, markedly absent in the monotheistic traditions.

> No matter what you think of religions, man has not reached the point of strength and security where he can live without it. One of the main reasons I can live without all of them is the fact that I have found something for myself that I think is better than all of them. In the finalizing of that search, with my first visit to Ghana, 1958, my introduction to Akan belief systems and Ga belief systems—belief systems that the Afrikan fashioned for himself that had more humanity in it than anything I have ever seen in organized religions, and more binding loyalty—I said this is for me.[41]

A hint of his sensitivity to indigenous Afrikan spirituality can be seen in an essay published in 1961 titled "The New Afro-American Nationalism," three years after his first sojourn in Afrika. Clarke noted a movement among Afrikans in the United States—what he called a new and "vital manifestation" of nationalism—included an increasing trend of "turning away from both Christianity and Islam. There is a growing tendency to study and adhere to religions and customs that originated and developed in Africa." This included devotion to traditions originating from the Fon of Dahomey and the Yoruba of southwestern Nigeria. The irony of this development in the United States, he observed, lay in a counter trend among Afrikans on the

Continent who were turning away from "old African religions and ways of life," accepting them only "selectively and with some reservations." A further distinction was evident in the observation that this nationalist movement in the United States was primarily proletarian-sponsored and led, independent of and unsupported by the "Negro leadership class." By contrast, "a more articulate educated elite" led nationalist developments in Afrika.[42]

Despite these contradictions, Clarke assessed Europeanized and Christianized continental Afrikans as "beginning to feel spiritually unfulfilled" and as a consequence were, "with new insight, ... looking back and reevaluating the worth of old African ways of life, while concurrently looking forward to the building of modern and industrialized states."[43] Although there were significant differences in the approaches of the two groups in the United States and Afrika, they were, he rather optimistically asserted, headed fundamentally to the same goal of full, unfettered freedom, reclaiming Afrikan culture and history and rejecting the notion that Europe and North America represented "the only accomplishment that can be called civilization."[44]

To be sure, Clarke's vision of Afrikan liberation was the central inspiration underlying his articulation of the critical importance of culture in the struggle against foreign domination and for Afrikan sovereignty. The "cultural heritage of a people," he held, "is directly related to their history." It followed that Afrikans in the United States could not be an authentic people, nor truly understand themselves, by neglecting or casting aside their continental Afrikan origins and culture. "The culture of a people is the fuel that feeds the fires of their ambition, pride and self-esteem. A people must take pride in their history and love their own memories in order to fulfill themselves."[45] In short, Clarke asserted there was an inextricable interrelationship between history and culture. The fact that Afrikans in the United States had a continental Afrikan history necessitated that they also embrace a cultural way of life that was continentally Afrikan if they were to become a whole, strong, and free people. History, therefore, entailed more than cognitive awareness. History, Clarke proposed, compelled cultural transformation and commanded cultural practice.

This conception of the interconnection between history, culture, liberation, and life practice explains his critique of global Afrikan adherence to foreign religions such as the monotheistic traditions of Judaeo-Christianity and Islam. While Christianity had no shortage of critics because of its instrumentality as a weapon of European white supremacist oppression, Islam, because of the Nation of Islam's success in positioning it as an authentically "Black" oppositional cultural response to European hegemony, was less critically scrutinized. Yet it engaged, according to Clarke, an equally baneful manipulation of Afrikan consciousness. Perhaps ironically, Malcolm X's immense popularity also contributed to the positive and uncritical way in which Islam was viewed in Afrikan culture in the United States.

Nonetheless, Clarke contended, the strategic importance of religious adherences could not be overstated, for both Christianity and Islam were historically religions of imperial conquest detrimental to Afrikan culture and sovereign consciousness. The dangers lie in the perverse way in which foreign cultural influences informed religious interpretation and practice, engendering in Afrikans untoward deference and subordination by establishing the false contention that Afrikan culture was inferior, sinful, and illegitimate in contrast with the foreigner's culture, which is sanctified by the foreigner's religion. Hence, he warned in a speech titled "The Search for the African State of Mind and Being through African Liberation," which he delivered to a community audience in 1993, a "conquered people, so beaten down, accept the conqueror's way of life and glorify the conqueror's way of life and forget that he ever had a way of life of his own distinction that was more functional than the way of life he has right now." The religions "brought in by conquerors not only impose a spiritual way of life on people, but impose a custom on people that the conqueror imposed on the religion so that the religion could fit with his custom. Then he imposes it on you and destroys your custom."[46] When a people are conquered "culturally or spiritually by other people," he continued, the conquerors "impose their way of life on the people to the extent of suppressing the way of life that is indigenous. And when you develop a habit of bending and twisting your soul to accommodate an alien way of life, you live in a crouch."[47]

In another speech to a community audience in New York City titled "Black People Need to Listen," delivered sometime in the early 1990s, Clarke again underscored the cultural implications of foreign religions on Afrikan freedom, admonishing his listeners that the "imprisonment of your mind around concepts that you have not properly examined has made you a pawn in somebody else's game because you have not examined the game. And the game was to control you."[48] The problem, then, with foreign religions is that they command loyalty to the people who created and who control them; Afrikans who embrace them abandon their allegiance to Afrikans and realign their loyalties to the people who created or control the religions they embrace. There is, consequently, an unavoidable political and colonialist dimension to religious faith. With Christianity this allegiance is directed toward serving European interests, whereas with Islam it is directed toward serving Arab interests.[49]

Table 8.5
John Henrik Clarke's Theorizing about the Relationship between Religion and Culture

- There is a political and colonialist dimension to religious faith.
- Culture is embedded and inseparable from religious interpretation and practice.
- A conqueror's religion glorifies the conqueror's culture and suppresses the culture of the conquered people.
- A conqueror's religion facilitates the replacement of the indigenous culture with a foreign culture.
- A conqueror's religion serves to deepen and maintain conquest.
- Conquered people under the influence of a conqueror's religion switch their allegiance from their people to the conquering people.
- The culture and interests of a people seeking liberation and independence must determine religious practice and interpretation.

Clarke's caution to Afrikans regarding Islam inhered in his awareness that Arabs, no less than Europeans, were historically supremacist enslavers of Afrikan people. They continued to be supremacist enslavers in the closing years of the twentieth century in such countries as Mauritania and Sudan. This was a matter about which he was unrelentingly critical of Afrikan Muslims who ignored these ongoing realities in deference to solidarity with their Arab co-religionists. In addition, in contemporary Arab societies, the Arabic word referring to Afrikans underscores their inferiorization in that culture, he observed. "You go live in a neighborhood in Cairo or any other Moslem country. The children come out to you and address you in a name that means slave," he chastised. "Now, what happened to these misguided African Moslems who think they are different when the Arab was in the slave trade before Islam and he is still in the slave trade?"[50]

> The Arab wants Africa just as much as the European because there are Arabs who wish to depopulate Africa and take it. There are Africans being killed in the Sudan right now solely because they are not Moslems. There are Africans who are being driven out of Mauritania who are Moslems, being driven out solely because they are not Arabs.
>
> There are black Moslems who have not lifted their voice against this one iota. There are black Moslems who are teachers of African history and who come to the part of the invasion of the western Sudan, inner West Africa, from Morocco by the Moslems—they leave that part out. There's a whole literature on this destruction. This invasion facilitated the spread of the slave trade inland and wrote doom for all the independent states in inner West Africa and coastal West Africa. The Arab slave trade had already destroyed the independent states in eastern Africa.
>
> We will not deal with the invader who came to stay. We will rationalize this and say "It's just evil Arabs and not Islam." Every organized religion that was brought into Africa was the handmaiden of a conqueror—Christianity, Islam, and the Hebrew faith.[51]

Another area of fundamental cultural conflict involves the status of women in Islamic culture, which, Clarke maintained, is inimical to their status in Afrikan culture and tradition. Drawing, however, in part upon cultural analysis advanced by the nineteenth-century Pan Afrikan nationalist intellectual Edward Wilmot Blyden in work that included the classic *Christianity, Islam and the Negro Race* (1888),[52] he noted that Islam tempered and modified by West Afrikans produced different social consequences for women's power. "Not a single woman ever rose to state power in Arab Islam. But in African Islam, which is revolutionary Islam, women not only came to state power, but headed the state of Zaria in Nigeria and did two things that the Arab would never let happen: the woman as head of a state and head of an army."[53] This occurred because the notion that women lacked the intellectual and ontological capacity to handle power was alien to Afrikan culture.[54] As well, he maintained, in indigenous Afrikan culture men did not fear women as they did in European and Arabian cultures.[55] He, therefore, chastised Afrikan women who sought in Islam the protection of womanhood from men, noting that in Arab Islam the woman becomes a vassal just "as the woman in Europe was a vassal to the Catholic church and enslavement by men in all of the years before the Protestant Reformation."[56]

In short, Clarke's central thesis was that differences in the cultures of West Afrikans and Arabs accounted for differences in women's status in these respective societies even when they both practiced Islam, an Arab cultural creation. Therefore, it is a people's culture and interests—especially those questing for liberation from oppression and for national sovereignty—that should determine religious practice and interpretation. Empirically, he argued, culture is embedded and inseparable from religious interpretation and practice. Thus, it was as a result of cultural dynamics that women's right to engage in economic production, including their control of the local markets, continued in Muslim areas of West Afrika, a phenomenon unknown in Arab culture. In those areas of East Afrika Islamized by Arabs, by contrast, there were fewer freedoms for Afrikan women, he argued, including their relative absence from the economic activity of the local markets. Because patriarchy informed Arab culture and defined the women's place within it, Islam practiced by them "declared war on the matrilineal system." The significance of the Afrikan matrilineal system is that descent through the woman institutionalized women's power such that "when it comes down to the female's time to come to power, she doesn't come to power just because she is a female. She comes to power because it is her time. And when it comes her turn, nobody can prevent her from coming to power." Further, women in matrilineal societies generally had the option of being "the king maker or the king. ... There are some countries, especially in southern Africa, where the woman can either be the maker of the king or be the candidate to be king." This was also in striking contrast to

European practice under feudalism, during which period "the white woman had no basic rights in Europe."[57]

In the end, Clarke concluded, there is nothing particularly compelling or sacred about the culturally foreign monotheistic religions. "It's so difficult to get people to recognize that certain things were imposed on you that were alien to your society that were out of other societies. And you accept these things and are willing to kill each other over them, and there isn't a word of truth in them."[58] He added:

> What you do not understand is that what you call Christianity existed in Africa in another form 3,000 years before the birth of Christ. And because you will not read books like John Jackson's *Christianity Before Christ*, or *The Pagan Origins of the Christ Myth*, or Percy Greaves' *Sixteen Crucified Saviors*, or James Fraser's *The Folklore of the Old Testament*, you will not recognize the fact that the bible is mainly folklore and fable. And you accept it as truth without examining any of it. And if you examined it, you would find out not only that it is not true, but some of it doesn't make sense. I question the intelligence of anyone who thinks the bible is true or is supposed to be true.[59]

If, however, certain Afrikans feel they must remain committed to these traditions, Clarke acceded, it is imperative that they be reformulated and subordinated to Afrikan culture and interests. Afrikans must be in complete control of their interpretation and practice; the religions must serve the interests of their liberation. "I'm saying reconceptualize them and keep them on your terms instead of their terms," he urged. "I'm not saying don't be a Moslem. There are more Moslems in Africa who are Moslem than there are Arabs in the world. ... I didn't say leave the religion. I say take it over."[60]

In critiquing foreign religions, Clarke made no exceptions for the Hebrew tradition; the insidious cultural and colonialist implications of the conquerors' religions remained constant whether they were Christian, Muslim, or Hebrew. In a speech to a community conference held in Brooklyn, New York, in 1992 on the subject of global white supremacy, he rejected the notion of Jerusalem as a holy city for Afrikans, declaring "I have no holy land outside of the physical property of Afrika, though what you are calling Jerusalem, and what you are calling the Middle East or western Asia was once an Afrikan colony or an extension of Afrika." Afrikans following the Hebrew and Christian traditions need to be cognizant of the fact that "the first holy city that Afrikans declared, or any other people declared in the whole world, is Abydos [a city of religious pilgrimage in ancient Egypt]. And that city is still there intact. Jerusalem has been destroyed several times." This notion of a holy land or a holy city outside of Afrika is insidious for Afrikans because it represents the sacralization of another people's culture and geography, while simultaneously dismissing Afrikan geography and culture as profane. "Jerusalem was given to us out of someone else's folklore," he explained, "while we ignored the city we built with our own hands, still standing, not holy to us because someone else told us another city was holy."[61]

At the base of all of Clarke's theorizing about Afrikan culture and human freedom is the question of the Afrikan state and its relevance to Afrikan liberation in both the Americas and in Afrika. Clarke did not exclude from this the necessity for Afrikans in the United States to form their own state. No genuine human freedom, no genuine human culture, no genuine practice of self-determination and self-actualization can exist or be nurtured, Clarke argued, without the ability of Afrikan people to regain the exercise of governance through the control of the state as they uniquely conceive it and construct it. "A greater tragedy," he would often lament, "is that not a single country in Africa today bases its law and religion on traditional culture and religions of the African people. Every state in Africa is an imitation of a European state." These states, he held, are alien to the indigenous Afrikan state structures (at least of the larger, more centralized states), which were multiethnic territorial states with loose borders and that facilitated in their original design "a cross fertilization of people, cultures, and institutions." The nation-state design evolved by Europeans crippled Afrikan development and progress, he held, because it "divides African cultures between national borders and prevents consolidations that formerly led to African multiethnic empires."[62]

This matter of the control and the management of the state, and the imperative that indigenous Afrikan culture inform the structure, philosophy, and functioning of that state, is Clarke's unique contribution to the discourse on Afrikan human freedom within Pan Afrikan nationalist intellectualism and within global Afrikan intellectualism in general. Indeed, Clarke held the nature of the Afrikan state, if it is to be authentic, cannot spring from a replication of the European state and its political systems, philosophies, and structures, but must be derived from state formations grounded in the philosophies, structures, and practices evolved in the Afrikan historical and cultural experience. Thus, in reflections on his first visit to Afrika and to Ghana at the seventeenth annual meeting of the National Council for Black Studies held in the summer of 1993 in Accra, the capital city of the West Afrikan nation, Clarke commented that he had "always believed," like other continental Afrikan traditionalists who theorized about the challenges of modernity, "that Africa had some solutions to African problems and that Africans had something to offer toward the structure of a state that would be distinctly African."[63] This is the only foundation that will undergird Afrikan cultural authenticity and facilitate the optimum human development for Afrikans, he asserted, whether they reside in the United States or in any other part of the Afrikan world.

Hence, in his lecture titled "The Search for the African State of Mind and Being through African Liberation," which he had delivered to a community audience earlier that year, he remarked upon the relationship between human culture, human freedom, human spirituality, and the Afrikan state.

> Now, my mental notes for this evening are a continuation of the last lecture, "The Search for the Afrikan State." Not only the search for the geographical Afrikan state, but the search for the cultural Afrikan state, the search for the spiritual Afrikan state, the search for that cultural container that gives people that assurance of their wholeness. I'm trying to explain to you that all Afrikan people in the world—no exception—live in artificial states designed by conquerors that are alien to their culture, alien to their needs, alien to their political development. And once they get rid of these states, they're going to have to fashion a state that will hold and contain the Afrikan soul. ...

Now, people are born and people develop within the context of a piece of geography of their own choosing, a spiritual way of life of their own choosing, and a cultural way of life of their own choosing. ... And when you live in a cultural container—that I call a state—of your own design, of your own development, your soul can walk upright and your body can walk upright.[64]

Clarke's analysis accorded with that of the West Afrikan revolutionary Amilcar Cabral of Guinea-Bissau, who held that a people's struggle to control their history has enormous economic and political implications. For when a people are seizing their right to have their own history, they are also seizing their right to control all productive forces in their lives. If a people are not doing this, Cabral held, they are not creating and are not in control of their own history, and they are, consequently, not in control of their own culture. Thus, both he and Clarke were clear: To have cultural development, a people must have the means and ability to create progress for themselves, and it is that which permits them to realize themselves. Demonstrably, this means that a people who are returning to the upward paths of their own culture are simultaneously regaining control of all productive forces.[65] In other words, as Clarke would say, a historically conscious and culturally grounded people are in control of a state that they have devised to serve themselves. If they do not enjoy such control, or if they are not striving to gain such control, they are neither, and can be neither, historically conscious nor culturally grounded.

Notes

1. Malidoma Patrice Some, *Of Water and the Spirit: Ritual, Magic, and Initiation in the Life of an African Shaman* (New York: Arkana, 1995), 176–177.

2. John Henrik Clarke, letter to Earl Sweeting, n.d., JHCP, SCRBC. The letter is judged to have been written in the early 1960s. Sweeting, a painter who studied with one of Clarke's professors, Charles C. Seifert, was living in Accra, Ghana.

3. John W. Blassingame, *The Slave Community: Plantation Life in the Antebellum South* (New York: Oxford University Press, 1972), 25.

4. Charles Ball, *Slavery in the United States: A Narrative of the Life and Adventures of Charles Ball, A Black Man, Who Lived Forty Years in Maryland, South*

Carolina, and Georgia as a Slave (Mineola, NY: Dover Publications, 1970; originally New York: John S. Taylor, 1837), 135.

5. Michael A. Gomez, *Exchanging Our Country Marks: The Transformation of African Identities in the Colonial and Antebellum South* (Chapel Hill: The University of North Carolina Press, 1998), 186, 187.

6. John Henrik Clarke, "Reclaiming the Lost African Heritage," Africa Conference, sponsored by the Social Sciences and Humanities Center, Teachers College, Columbia University, and presented at the International Center, International Studies in World Affairs, State University of New York, Oyster Bay, Long Island, 15 September 1966, 2, JHCP, SCRBC.

7. Tolagbe Ogunleye, "The Self-Emancipated Africans of Florida: Pan-African Nationalists in the 'New World,'" *Journal of Black Studies* 27, no. 1 (September 1996): 24, 25, 26.

8. Ibid., *"Aroko, Mmomomme Twe, Nsibidi, Ogede, and Tusona*: Africanisms in Florida's Self-Emancipated Africans' Resistance to Enslavement and War Stratagems," *Journal of Black Studies* 36, no. 3 (January 2006): 397.

9. Ibid., "Self-Emancipated Africans," 26.

10. Ibid., 32.

11. While the Americans called it Fort Negro, Afrikans called it Fort Ashila. Ogunleye indicates the word *ashila* is a Bantu verb that means to build or construct a house for some one else. See Yvonne Tolagbe Ogunleye, "An African Centered Historical Analysis of the Self-Emancipated Africans of Florida, 1738 to 1838" (Ph.D. diss., Temple University, 1995), 278.

12. Ogunleye, "African Centered Historical Analysis," 285. For more extensive discussion of the Afrikan war of liberation, see her discussion on pages 260–352.

13. Ibid., 314.

14. Ibid., 333–335.

15. See, among others, John Henrik Clarke, "African Cultural Response to Slavery and Oppression in the Americas and the Caribbean," in *African Presence in the Americas*, ed. Tanya R. Saunders and Shawna Moore (Trenton, NJ: Africa World Press, 1995), 73–95; ibid., "Pan-Africanism: A Brief History of an Idea in the African World," *Présence Africaine* no. 145 (1st Quarterly 1988): 26–56; Laurent Dubois and John D. Garrigus, ed., *Slave Revolution in the Caribbean 1789–1804: A Brief History with Documents* (Boston/New York: Bedford/St. Martin's, 2006); Laurent Dubois, *Avengers of the New World: The Story of the Haitian Revolution* (Cambridge, MA: The Belknap Press of

Harvard University Press, 2004); N. A. T. Hall, "Maritime Maroons: 'Grand Marronage' from the Danish West Indies," *William and Mary Quarterly* 42, no. 4 (October 1985): 476–498; Barbara Klamon Kopytoff, "Colonial Treaty as Sacred Charter of the Jamaican Maroons," *Ethnohistory* 26, no. 1 (Winter 1979): 45–64; Kenneth Bilby, "Swearing by the Past, Swearing to the Future: Sacred Oaths, Alliances, and Treaties among the Guianese and Jamaican Maroons," *Ethnohistory* 44, no. 4 (Autumn 1997): 655–689; Jacqueline Cogdell DjeDje, "Remembering Kojo: History, Music, and Gender in the January Sixth Celebration of the Jamaican Accompong Maroons," *Black Music Research Journal* 18, no. 1/2 (Spring 1998): 67–120; James D. Lockett, "The Deportation of the Maroons of Trelawny Town to Nova Scotia, Then Back to Africa," *Journal of Black Studies* 30, no. 1 (September 1999): 5–14; R. K. Kent, "Palmares: An African State in Brazil," *Journal of African History* 6, no. 2 (1965): 161–175; Irene Diggs, "Zumbi and the Republic of Os Palmares," *Phylon* 14, no. 1 (1st Quarter 1953): 62–70; Ernesto Ennes, "The Palmares "Republic" of Pernambuco Its Final Destruction, 1697," *The Americas* 5, no. 2 (October 1948): 200–216; Leonard Goines, "Africanisms among the Bush Negroes of Surinam," *The Black Perspective in Music* 3, no. 1 (Spring 1975): 40–44; Robert Nelson Anderson, "The Quilombo of Palmares: A New Overview of a Maroon State in Seventeenth-Century Brazil," *Journal of Latin American Studies* 28, no. 3 (October 1996): 545–566; Berta E. Pérez, "The Journey to Freedom: Maroon Forebears in Southern Venezuela," *Ethnohistory* 47, no. 3–4 (Summer 2000): 611–634; Barbara Klamon Kopytoff, "The Early Political Development of Jamaican Maroon Societies," *William and Mary Quarterly* 35, no. 2 (April 1978): 287–307; Richard Price, ed., *Maroon Societies: Rebel Slave Communities in the Americas*, 3rd ed. (Baltimore: The Johns Hopkins University Press, 1996); Mavis Christine Campbell, *The Maroons of Jamaica, 1655–1796: A History of Resistance, Collaboration and Betrayal* (Granby, MA: Bergin & Garvey, 1988); Richard Price, The Guiana Maroons: A Historical and Bibliographical Introduction (Baltimore: Johns Hopkins University Press, 1976); Robert Charles Dallas, *The History of the Maroons, from Their Origin to the Establishment of Their Chief Tribe at Sierra Leone, Including the Expedition to Cuba for the Purpose of Procuring Spanish Chasseurs and the State of the Island of Jamaica for the Last Ten Years with a Succinct History of the Island Previous to that Period* (London: Cass, 1968); Silvia W. de. Groot, *From Isolation towards Integration: The Surinam Maroons and their Colonial Rulers: Official Documents Relating to the Djukas, 1845–1863* (The Hague, Netherlands: Nijhoff, 1977); Alvin O. Thompson, *Flight to*

Freedom: African Runaways and Maroons in the Americas (Kingston, Jamaica: University of West Indies Press, 2006).

16. Ben Vinson III, "Fading from Memory: Historiographical Reflections on the Afro-Mexican Presence," *Review of Black Political Economy* 33, no. 1 (Summer 2005): 59.

17. Ibid., 59–60. Sagrario Cruz-Carretero, "Yanga and the Black Origins of Mexico," *Review of Black Political Economy* 33, no. 1 (Summer 2005): 75. Vinson says the Spaniards discovered an effort in 1611 by Afrikans to again overthrow their dictatorship and establish their own sovereign political rule.

18. Ball, *Slavery in the United States*, 5–8. See also an interesting argument by J. Alfred Cannon, "Re-Africanization: The Last Alternative for Black America," *Phylon* 38, no. 2 (2nd Quarter 1977): 203–210.

19. Linda Brent, *Incidents in the Life of a Slave Girl, Written by Herself* in *The Classic Slave Narratives*, ed. Henry Louis Gates, Jr. (New York: Mentor, 1987), 347–48, 397–98, 403–404.

20. Frederick Douglass, *Narrative of the Life of Frederick Douglass, an American Slave, Written by Himself*, ed. Houston A. Baker, Jr. (New York: Penguin Books, 1982), 117.

21. Gomez, *Exchanging Our Country Marks*, 291–292.

22. Alexis de Tocqueville, *Democracy in America*, ed. J. P. Mayer and Max Lerner, trans. George Lawrence (New York: Harper & Row, 1966), 292, 294.

23. John Henrik Clarke, "The Afro-American Image of Africa," *Black World* 23, no. 4 (February 1974): 7.

24. See, among others, Kwando M. Kinshasa, *Emigration vs. Assimilation: The Debate in the African American Press, 1827–1861* (Jefferson, NC: McFarland, 1988); William E. Bittle and Gilbert L. Geis, "Alfred Charles Sam and an African Return: A Case Study in Negro Despair," *Phylon* 23, no. 2 (2nd Quarter 1962): 178–194; Gregory Mixon, "Henry McNeal Turner versus the Tuskegee Machine: Black Leadership in the Nineteenth Century," *Journal of Negro History* 79, no. 4 (Autumn 1994): 363–380; Thomas H. Henriksen, "African Intellectual Influences on Black Americans: The Role of Edward W. Blyden," *Phylon* 36, no. 3 (3rd Quarter 1975): 279–290; Rina L. Okonkwo, "Orishatukeh Faduma: A Man of Two Worlds," *Journal of Negro History* 68, no. 1 (Winter 1983): 24–36; M. B. Akpan, "Liberia and the Universal Negro Improvement Association: The Background to the Abortion of Garvey's Scheme for African Colonization," *Journal of African History* 14, no. 1 (1973): 105–127; John Henrik Clarke, "Marcus Garvey: The Harlem Years," *Transition* no. 46 (1974): 14–15, 17–19; R. L. Okonkwo,

"The Garvey Movement in British West Africa," *Journal of African History* 21, no. 1 (1980): 105–117; John Henrik Clarke and Amy Jacques Garvey, ed., *Marcus Garvey and the Vision of Africa* (New York: Vintage Books, 1974); John Henrik Clarke, ed., *Malcolm X: The Man and His Times* (Trenton, NJ: Africa World Press, 1990; originally New York: Collier Books, 1969); ibid., *My Life in Search of Africa* (Chicago: Third World Press, 1999); ibid., *Notes for an African World Revolution: Africans at the* Crossroads (Trenton, NJ: Africa World Press, 1991); Richard Blackett, "Martin R. Delany and Robert Campbell: Black Americans in Search of an African Colony," *Journal of Negro History* 62, no. 1 (January 1977): 1–25; Hollis R. Lynch, "Edward W. Blyden: Pioneer West African Nationalist," *Journal of African History* 6, no. 3 (1965): 373–388; George E. Brooks, Jr., "The Providence African Society's Sierra Leone Emigration Scheme, 1794–1795: Prologue to the African Colonization Movement," *International Journal of African Historical Studies* 7, no. 2 (1974):183–202; Cassandra R. Veney, "The Ties That Bind: The Historic African Diaspora and Africa," *African Issues* 30, no. 1 (2002): 3–8; J. Ayo Langley, "Chief Sam's African Movement and Race Consciousness in West Africa," *Phylon 32, no. 2* (2nd Quarter 1971): 164–178; Lamin Sanneh, "Prelude to African Christian Independency: The Afro-American Factor in African Christianity," *Harvard Theological Review 77, no. 1* (January 1984): 1–32; Edward O. Erhagbe, "African-Americans and the Defense of African States against European Imperial Conquest: Booker T. Washington's Diplomatic Efforts to Guarantee Liberia's Independence 1907–1911," *African Studies Review* 39, no. 1 (April 1996): 55–65; Howard H. Bell, "The Negro Emigration Movement, 1849–1854: A Phase of Negro Nationalism," *Phylon Quarterly* 20, no. 2 (2nd Quarter 1959): 132–142; R. J. M. Blackett, "Return to the Motherland: Robert Campbell, a Jamaican in Early Colonial Lagos," *Phylon* 40, no. 4 (4th Quarter 1979): 375–386; George Shepperson, "Notes on Negro American Influences on the Emergence of African Nationalism," *Journal of African History* 1, no. 2 (1960): 299–312; Ben F. Rogers, "William E. B. DuBois, Marcus Garvey, and Pan-Africa," *Journal of Negro History* 40, no. 2 (April 1955): 154–165; Lamin O. Sanneh, *Abolitionists Abroad: American Blacks and the Making of Modern West Africa* (Cambridge, MA: Harvard University Press, 1999); Cyril E. Griffith, *The African Dream: Martin R. Delany and the Emergence of Pan-African Thought* (University Park: Pennsylvania State University Press, 1975); Tony Martin, *Race First: The Ideological and Organizational Struggles of Marcus Garvey and the Universal Negro Improvement Association* (Westport, CT: Greenwood Press, 1976); ibid., *The*

Pan-African Connection: From Slavery to Garvey and Beyond (Dover, MA: Majority Press, 1984).

25. Clarke, "The Afro-American Image," 5–21; ibid., "African Studies in the United States, An Afro-American View," *Africa Today* 16, no. 2 (April–May 1969): 10 – 12; ibid., "African-American Historians and the Reclaiming of African History," *Présence Africaine* no. 110 (2ⁿᵈ Quarterly 1979): 29–48.

26. That Afrikans enslaved in the United States spoke their indigenous languages is well established by a number of scholars. Among them is Gomez, *Exchanging Our Country Marks*, 154–185. See also the pioneering work by Lorenzo Dow Turner, *Africanisms in the Gullah Dialect* (Chicago: University of Chicago Press, 1949) in addition to Winifred Kellersberger Vass, *The Bantu Speaking Heritage of the United States* (Los Angeles: Center for Afro-American Studies, University of California, 1979).

27. Joseph E. Holloway and Winifred K. Vass, *The African Heritage of American English* (Bloomington and Indianapolis: Indiana University Press, 1993), 107, 123–127, 131–132, 134–135.

28. Turner, *Africanisms*, v.

29. Ibid.

30. Ibid., 31, 43.

31. Gomez, *Exchanging Our Country Marks*, 19–20.

32. Ibid., 17–37.

33. Ibid., 19–20.

34. Ibid., 29.

35. Ibid., 17–37, 38–153.

36. Ibid., 29.

37. Anna Swanston, *Dr. John Henrik Clarke: His Life, His Words, His Works* (Atlanta, GA: I Am Unlimited Publishing, 2003), 124.

38. Ibid., 125.

39. Gomez, 17–37, 38–153.

40. John Henrik Clarke, "Can Afrikan People Save Themselves?" address to northern New Jersey community audience hosted by Afrikan Echoes, during or after 1995, DVD, available from the Nubian Network, http://www.black-consciousness.com.

41. Ibid., "The Search for the African State of Mind and Being through African Liberation," 16 January 1993, distributed by Men of Respect Historical Society, New York, New York, available from http://www.menofrespect.com.

42. Ibid., "The New Afro-American Nationalism," *Freedomways* 1, no. 3 (Fall 1961): 289–292.

43. See opposing arguments concerning modernization and Afrikan culture in Ali A. Mazrui, "Africa Between Nationalism and Nationhood: A Political Survey," *Journal of Black Studies* 13, no. 1 (September 1982): 23–44 and J. F. Ade Ajayi, "The Place of African History and Culture in the Process of Nation-Building in Africa South of the Sahara," *Journal of Negro Education* 30, no. 3 (Summer 1961): 206–213.

44. Clarke, "New Afro-American," 291.

45. Ibid., 292.

46. Ibid., "The Search for the African."

47. Ibid. See also Gibreel M. Kamara, "Regaining Our African Aesthetics and Essence through Our African Traditional Religion," *Journal of Black Studies* 30, no. 4 (March 2000): 502–514.

48. Ibid., "Black People Need to Listen," address to New York community audience around the early 1990s, DVD, available from the Nubian Network, http://www.blackconsciousness.com.

49. Ibid.

50. Ibid., "Can Afrikan People." See also Theola Labbe, "A Legacy Hidden in Plain Sight: Iraqis of African Descent Are a Largely Overlooked Link to Slavery," *Washington Post*, 11 January 2004; available from http://www.washingtonpost.com; Mohamed E Abdel-Rahman, "Interactions Between Africans North and South of the Sahara," *Journal of Black Studies* 3, no. 2 (December 1972): 131–147; Opoku Agyeman, "Pan-Africanism versus Pan-Arabism: A Dual Asymmetrical Model of Political Relations," in *The Middle East Reader*, ed. Michael Curtis (New Brunswick, NJ: Transaction, 1986), 21–46.

51. Ibid., "Black People Need."

52. Edward Wilmot Blyden, *Christianity, Islam and the Negro Race*, 2nd ed. (Baltimore, MD: Black Classic Press; originally London, W. B. Whittingham & Co., 1888).

53. Clarke, "Can Afrikan People." See also ibid., "The Cultural Unity of African River Valley Civilizations," 17 March 1989, available from Men of Respect Historical Society, CD, http://www.menofrespect.com.

54. Ibid. See also Clarke, "The Cultural Unity."

55. Ibid., "The Cultural Unity."

56. Ibid., "Can Afrikan People."

57. Ibid. See also ibid., "The Cultural Unity"; ibid., "The Black Family in Historical Perspective," *Journal of Afro-American Issues* 3, no. 3/4 (Summer/Fall 1975): 337–338; ibid., "On 'The Cultural Unity of Africa,'" *Black World* 26, no. 4 (February 1975): 12–26.

58. Ibid., "Global White Supremacy: From the End of the Nineteenth Century to the Middle of the Twentieth Century and the Afrikan Independence Explosion," Symposium on Global White Supremacy, hosted by the United Afrikan Movement, Slave Theatre, Brooklyn, New York, 22 January 1992, DVD, http://www.tapvideo.com.

59. Ibid., "Black People Need."

60. Ibid., "Can Afrikan People."

61. Ibid., "Global White Supremacy." See also ibid., "Our Black Seminarians: An Introduction," in Yosef A. A. ben Jochannan, *Our Black Seminarians and Black Clergy Without a Black Theology* (Baltimore, MD: Black Classic Press, 1998).

62. Ibid., "Our Black Seminarians," no page number.

63. Ibid., "Reflections & Observations ... Ghana Remembered 'Then and Now.'" Seventeenth Annual Conference, 25 July–1 August 1993, National Council for Black Studies, Accra, Ghana, 25 July 1993, 12, JHCP, SCRBC.

64. Ibid., "The Search for the African."

65. Amilcar Cabral, "National Liberation and Culture," in *Return to the Source: Speeches of Amilcar Cabral*, ed. Africa Information Service (New York: Monthly Review Press, 1973), 43.

Chapter 9

THE CLARKEAN LEGACY AND CONTRIBUTION TO THE AFROCENTRIC PARADIGM

There is now an international struggle on the part of people of African descent against racism and for a more honest look at their history. On university campuses and in international conferences, they are demanding that their history be looked at from a black perspective or from an Afrocentric point of view.

—John Henrik Clarke, 1970[1]

When the Europeans began to re-emerge on the world scene in the 15th and 16th centuries, they colonized most of the world. Then, in their new institutions, they colonized the interpretation of history. They began to interpret history as though the world waited in darkness for them to bring the light. Non-European scholars, and non-European people in general, are now engaged in a fight to decolonize history. This is what Black scholars mean when they demand consideration from an Afro-centric view of history.

—John Henrik Clarke, 1971[2]

The books of Dr. Diop upset white scholars the world over and started a rage against him that has not abated. He challenged their interpretation of African history and backed his challenge with scholarship that they could not dismiss. Among the African writers using the French language, he launched the Afrocentric approach to history.

—John Henrik Clarke, 1975[3]

What is needed is an Afrocentric view of the African women in power.

—John Henrik Clarke, 1975[4]

N ell Irvin Painter, the distinguished scholar of African American history at Princeton University, although a critic of Clarke's Pan Afrikan nationalist historiography, described him in a 1998 essay of reflection occasioned by the senior scholar's death earlier that year as "a respected scholar," one who was "a pivotal figure in our intellectual history," and a "pioneer scholar of African-American history."[5] Officials at Hunter College, where Clarke taught for nearly two decades, acknowledged him as "Founder and former chairman of the Hunter College Black and Puerto Rican Studies Department" who "revolutionized the field of African Studies with his brilliant and iconoclastic writings," and who incorporated "African history and culture into the context of world history."[6] More soberly, the *Journal of Blacks in Higher Education* called him a "pioneering Afrocentrist."[7]

The following year, Robin D. G. Kelley, professor of history and Africana Studies at New York University, recalled he first encountered Clarke at a lecture when he was a first-year student at California State University at Long Beach, marveling at the elder scholar's "astounding bibliographic reach [which] sent us scurrying back to the library."[8] Clarke, Kelley observed, "epitomized the 'public intellectual' long before that term became popular." Kelley further underscored an important aspect of the late sage's scholarship when he recognized that "Clarke wrote for the [Afrikan] community rather than a strictly academic audience. He never compromised his critical stances or scholarly sophistication, but he always kept his prose accessible and engaging." The Harlemite's considerable body of published work "revealed a wide-ranging mind and iconoclastic, independent thinker."[9] Commenting succinctly on Clarke's erudition at the resplendent, six-hour Harlem funeral ceremony held on 21 July 1998 at the famed Abyssinia Baptist Church, the prolific Africalogist Molefi Kete Asante of Temple University said of the late elder: "All the professors I ever had at UCLA, all of them combined, did not know as much as John Henrik Clarke had forgotten."[10]

Clarke's death occasioned other commentary on the import and caliber of his intellectual accomplishments. Herb Boyd—journalist, author, and for some three decades adjunct professor in Africana Studies—praised Clarke as "a peerless scholar of African and African American history." Boyd regarded the African Heritage Studies Association, which Clarke helped to found and lead, as "the cutting edge organization fostering and promoting Black Studies and African centered education in North America." As far as research was concerned, he added, "It is not possible to find a valuable book on pan-africanism or black nationalism that does not bear Dr. Clarke's imprint." The impact of Clarke's death was, he wrote, "as though a university was taken from us."[11]

New York City political activist the Rev. Al Sharpton, who officiated the 21 September 1997 wedding of Clarke and long time friend and companion Sybil Williams, similarly observed that Clarke "forced the recognition of Africa as the epicenter of all history" and "gave critical analysis of distortions of Eurocentric philosophy and history." The late scholar, Sharpton continued, "changed the framework of thought" in the European academy and "transformed the intellectual environment" in the United States.[12] Concurring, New York journalist and activist Bruce Karriem declared Clarke was—after the famed novelist Richard Wright—Afrikan America's "second great literary genius" and a "cosmopolite who could debate points of history with the best minds in the world."[13] The independent historian William Loren Katz rhapsodized Clarke was "a great teacher, a giant of our times and a scholar for all seasons,"[14] while former New York City mayor David N. Dinkins extolled Clarke as "a tireless and singularly eloquent spokesperson for historical study."[15] Robert McG. Thomas, Jr., noted in an article in the *New York Times* that Clarke had the singular distinction of achieving full professorship without the benefit of either a Ph.D. or a high school diploma. He was "an imposing figure in Black intellectual circles" and "was on a first-name basis with many African leaders."[16]

The outpouring of praise for Clarke's life was tremendous within New York City's Afrikan community. Some 2,000 mourners crowded into the historic Abyssinia Baptist Church on 138th

Street in central Harlem, while others waited outside for a chance to enter the sanctuary, to view Clarke's body, which lay in state, and to attend the six-hour funeral service held as his initiation into eternity. Although noticeably absent, according to one observer, were representatives of Columbia University, New York University, the mayor's office, the governor's office, the NAACP, and the Urban League, countless other locally, nationally, and internationally prominent Afrikans—actors, poets, journalists, writers, scholars, religious leaders, political and community activists, politicians, lawyers, business persons, educators, mayors, and representatives of Tanzania and the Democratic Republic of the Congo—took the podium or sent letters and telegrams to pay homage to the elder scholar.[17] The revolutionary Pan Afrikanist Kwame Ture, in a message from his home in Guinea, West Afrika, highlighted Clarke's activism when he remarked the late scholar was "one of Afrika's greatest and most noble sons" whose "impact on the Afrikan world and its ideas is immeasurable," and who "worked insatiably for the total liberation of his people."[18] Likewise, the redoubtable New York attorney Alton Maddox declared, "We have been in the midst of one of the great Afrikan warriors of our time."[19]

In New York City, ceremonies celebrating his life also marked the first anniversary of his death.[20] In the following year, organizers there held a two-week celebration in his honor.[21] A year later, some 500 persons attended a four-hour event at Medgar Evers College honoring the Harlem sage.[22] In 2000, New York City lawmakers renamed Harlem's 137th Street, between Adam Clayton Powell, Jr., Boulevard and Frederick Douglass Boulevard, Dr. John Henrik Clarke Place.[23]

Although celebrated locally, nationally, and internationally, Clarke was not without his critics. Among them were Marxists, whose ideological positions jarred with his rejection of European-conceived socialism in favor of socialism developed from indigenous Afrikan conceptual practice and formulation, which he maintained predated both Marx and Europe by millennia. Clarke's resignation in February 1983 from the associate editorship of *Freedomways* magazine, a leftist publication, was occasioned by an attack launched by a colleague, James E. Jackson, a member of the political bureau of the Communist Party USA, and published in the CPUSA's *Daily World*. In a 12 November 1982 report titled "John Henrik Clarke: Advises

CIA and Joins 'Beat the Russians' Band," Jackson accused him of being an advocate for U.S. neocolonialist penetration of Afrika, preferring the United States over the Soviet Union in their struggle for control in Afrika. Jackson alleged that Clarke made these comments in a talk at the Harlem YMCA on 12 October 1982 that featured a brunch hosting U.S. War College graduates and CIA counter intelligence agency staff members and officers from Japan, Venezuela, and Australia. In a response typed on Hunter College stationery, Clarke disputed the facts Jackson alleged in his article and declared his commitment to socialism, Pan Afrikan nationalism, and Afrikan liberation remained unchanged.[24]

Also highly critical is former protégé Nell Irvin Painter, who met Clarke when she was a graduate student at Harvard University during the historic events within the African Studies Association that led to the founding of the African Heritage Studies Association in 1969, and who disclosed her feelings in a reflection on his life shortly following his death. In the 1960s, she wrote, "Clarke posed a sharp contrast to scholars associated with black history up to that time," whose work tended to focus on Afrikans only as victims of European oppression. In an assessment that captured Molefi Kete Asante's definition of Afrocentricity, Painter recalled "Clarke embodied the very thing we sought: an account of black history that put black people at the center, as actors and on their own terms."[25]

Painter, nevertheless, hinted at growing cultural and intellectual tensions between herself and her mentor. Interestingly, she subtly suggested these tensions inhered in Clarke's lack of training in the European academy, remarking, for example, she always felt Clarke viewed her, and the cadre of younger university-trained scholars who were her cohorts, somewhat ambivalently, while, by contrast, they enthusiastically looked to him as "a keeper of the flame in the 1960s." Eventually, however, the ardor of their intellectual collaboration cooled as "his kind of history" began to significantly diverge from "ours, which emanated from the universities." This divergence in historiographical inquiry coincided, she maintained, with larger fissures in the evolution of Afrikan-led studies of Afrikans in the United States in the 1980s. Afrikan scholarship in the United States at this period began to display various tendencies, some of which departed from Afrikan nationalism and graduated into what she implied were more expansive explorations of class and gender "within and around race." In her view, Clarke's thinking remained sclerotically nationalistic and, as a result, "his hostility to new themes" in the study of Afrikans in the United States marginalized him "within the field he had inspired in the late 1960s."[26]

The most telling and tragic instance of what amounted to her growing alienation centered in what she characterized as Clarke's unqualified rejection of black feminism. Indeed, she writes, Clarke, "like other Afrocentrists, ... regarded black feminism as cancerous at worst, diversionary at best. For him and his Afrocentrist colleagues, Africana scholarship must focus on black/white conflict undistracted by gender and class."[27]

W. D. Wright, professor emeritus of history at Southern Connecticut State University, offered another critique of Clarke's Pan Afrikan nationalist historiography in a book he published four years after Clarke's death titled *Black History and Black Identity: A Call for a New Historiography* (2002). He opposed Clarke's "Africancentric Perspective," apposing it to what he called his "Blackcentric Perspective." Examining an essay Clarke published titled "African-American Historians and the Reclaiming of African History,"[28] Wright rejected Clarke's historiographical assumption that Afrikans in the American diaspora, what Wright called the "West African Extensia," remained Afrikans, contending that in Clarke's own writings this assumption was inconsistently held. In short, he contended Clarke contradicted himself by using such descriptive terms as *Africans, Afro-Americans, Black Americans*, and *black people*, highlighting "the limitations of his Africancentric Perspective," an error that speaks to the cogency of what Wright offered as the "Blackcentric Perspective."[29]

Continuing his examination of Clarke's historiography in *Christopher Columbus and the Afrikan Holocaust: Slavery and the Rise of European Capitalism* (1993),[30] Wright disputed the notion that Afrikans could ever have been self-consciously Afrikan. The forcible deportation to the Americas, he maintained, made Afrikan consciousness impossible because it involved "a lengthy and even permanent physical separation of black people in Africa from Black people in North America and the placing of Black people in another and very different historical context and a very different cultural and social context." This required, Wright continued, "Black people to make an imperative cultural, social, psychological (including cognitive), and spiritual adaptation and reconstruction." This adaptation and reconstruction, he proposed, "could have destroyed, or at least seriously undermined and weakened an Africa-consciousness among Black people if such thoughts had existed in their minds."[31] The central argument here is that Afrikans, once transplanted to the Americas, ceased altogether to remain Afrikan and became instead indigenous Americans—that is, in this instance, "Blacks." As has been explored extensively in this study, it is a consistent cultural contention in Afrikan assimilationist (which is European nationalist) historiography.

Perhaps the harshest and most scandalous criticism came from Harvard University's Henry Louis Gates, Jr., professor of English and chairman of the Department of Afro-American Studies, whose denunciations were captured in a 20 July 1992 *New York Times* editorial titled "Black Demagogues and Pseudo-Scholars." Gates decried what he charged was an increasing level of anti-Semitism that is "most pronounced" among younger and educated Afrikans, whom he said were "twice as likely as whites to hold anti-Semitic views," a trend he maintained that "has been deeply disquieting for many black intellectuals." This allegedly new anti-Semitism was "engineered and promoted by leaders who affect to be speaking for a larger resentment. This top-down anti-Semitism, in large part the province of the better educated classes," represents a new manifestation of bigotry among Afrikans in the United States. It "belongs as much to the repertory of campus lecturers as community activists." Among those Afrikans Gates denounced as "demagogues" and "apostles of hate" was "Dr. John Henrik Clarke, professor emeritus of Hunter College and the great paterfamilias of the Afrocentric movement."[32]

Gates listed Clarke among a number of Afrikans he charged strategically employed bigotry for political purposes, enumerating two offenses. The first was Clarke's endorsement of a book published in 1978 and written by European Canadian author and anthropologist Michael Bradley, who argued for a biological and genetic factor in European aggression, sexism, and racism originating in the ice age. Among other things, Bradley asserted that "racism itself is a predisposition of but one race of Mankind—the white race." He argued, further, that nuclear war, environmental pollution, and the plundering of natural resources were primary threats to human existence that were "the result of peculiarly Caucasoid behavior, Caucasoid values, Caucasoid psychology."[33] Gates charged the book expressed virulently anti-European Jewish views. In rebutting Gates's charges, Bradley has noted he is of Sephardic Jewish origin, that both his Canadian publisher and one of two academics who wrote introductions for his book were European Jews, and that no charges of anti-European Jewish sentiments were ever raised in the initial critical reception of the work.[34] Clarke's second offense, according to Gates, was his repudiation of European Jewish control of the agenda governing the education of Afrikan children in New York City. The Harvard professor also paired the Afrikan academic Leonard Jeffries's widely publicized remarks on European Jewish complicity in the denigration of the Afrikan image in Hollywood films with anti-European Jewish denunciations by representatives of the Nation of Islam, whom he called Jeffries's "intellectual cohorts."[35]

Significantly, Gates's charges highlight the recurring dialectical tensions in Afrikan culture and intellectualism examined in this study, the charge of anti-European Jewish hatred serving as the means in assimilationist or Afro-European nationalist discourse to discredit the Afrikan nationalist quest for liberation from European overlordship. In this sense, Gates's cultural contention, reflected in his use of language, is identical to the NAACP national executive director Roy Wilkins's complaint some two decades earlier (already noted in this study) against the implications of Afrikan nationalism upon the Afrikan assimilationist or Afro-European nationalist quest to effect unification with the European mainstream.

Gates clarifies the strategic political and cultural implications of this issue. The real, core issue, he declares, involves a power struggle between two groups of Afrikans, the outcome of which will determine which form of nationalism—one that is European-conceived or one that is Afrikan-conceived—will direct the destiny of Afrikans in the United States. Hence, he writes, "anti-Semitism [is] a weapon in *the raging battle of who will speak for black America—those who have sought common cause with others* [the Afrikans who are European nationalists] *or those who preach a barricaded withdrawal into racial authenticity* [the Afrikans who are Afrikan nationalists]" (added emphasis). Gates adds, revealingly, "*the new anti-Semitism* arises not in spite of *the black-Jewish alliance* but because of it. For precisely such *trans-racial cooperation*—epitomized by the *historical partnership between blacks and Jews*—is what poses the greatest threat to *the isolationist movement*"[36] (added emphasis).

It is useful to reiterate, by comparison, this study's examination of Wilkins's objection to Clarke's Afrikan heritage television lecture series in 1969. He charged it was "an interpretation of history from a single point of view: the contemporary *left-of-center black militant minority view*, liberally garnished with the thrust of *a new apartheid*"[37] (added emphasis). The programs' emphasis "suited the present-day propagandists for *Black Separatism*." Moreover, he asserted, the true destiny of the Afrikan people in the United States was "to win citizenship equality *for the Negro minority in a multiracial society*." Instead of a dialogue of attempted reconciliation with Europeans, however, the lecture series was inspired by *"race-hate talk"* and *"violence"* and "strove, often grotesquely, *to create the climate of confrontation, of a conscious struggle between racial groups*"[38] (added emphasis). Clearly, the assimilationist charges in both eras are the same, because the agendas regarding Afrikan nationality remain unchanged. Afrikan assimilationists consistently condemn the Afrikan nationalist quest for independence as hate mongering and isolationist—as opposed to their goal of seeking rapprochement and unification with some or another portion of the European mainstream—because they are committed European nationalists.

In an essay the title of which, "Self-Made Angry Man," most likely sprouted from the imaginations of the editors at the *New York Times*, Robin D. G. Kelley noted seven years following Gates's scurrilous accusations that "the [European] mainstream construction of Clarke—the emissary of hate, the anti-Semite, the mythologist," was a misrepresentation of the man and his work.[39] Clarke published a lengthy response to Gates's slander in the 26 August–1 September 1992 edition of the weekly Brooklyn-based Afrikan newspaper, *The City Sun*, which their editors titled "Black Pseudo-Scholars Are 'In' with White America, but They Deserve to Be 'Outed,' Says Historian," but which Clarke had titled simply "A Dissenting View." Among other things, he questioned Gates's competence to offer an informed assessment of the Afrikan scholars he criticized, or an accurate history of the relationship between Afrikans and Jews, and he proposed the conflict between Afrikans and European Jews in the United States was a power struggle and nothing more.[40]

To be sure, Clarke had made his views known publicly twenty years earlier in a paper titled "The Myth of Black Anti-Semitism," which he prepared for the eighty-seventh annual meeting of the American Historical Association held in December 1972 in New Orleans, Louisiana.[41] In his paper Clarke pointedly questioned why the charge of anti-Semitism should be lodged against Afrikans in the United States and not "against more powerful people who are in a position to really harm the Jewish People?" He argued that generally Afrikans' Judaeo-Christian orientation led them to conceive of peoples of the Hebrew faith in quite positive terms, and to sentimentally identify their experiences under American dictatorship with the Hebrew biblical narrative of alleged suffering in ancient Egypt. In marked contrast with the modern charge of hatred leveled against them by some European Jews, Clarke advanced that the historical relationship between Afrikans and peoples of the Hebrew faith from antiquity through to the period of Afrikan ascendancy in the Muslim invasion of western Mediterranean Europe in 711 C.E. established that Jews have lived longer, and at peace, among Afrikans than among any other people in their history. Indeed, he added, if the Christian bible were to be believed, the Hebrew people (originally only seventy in number), after four centuries in ancient Egypt, would have to have been genetically, culturally, and religiously Afrikan. Consequently, "the charge of anti-Semitism against African people" is tantamount to accusing Afrikans of being "against their own religious and cultural creations."[42]

In short, Clarke argued, the charge lacked both factual and historical foundation. The contemporary conflict between Afrikans and Europeans of the Hebrew faith arose from the fact that European Jews, as Europeans, exercised a level of power over Afrikan lives in the United States in political, economic, and educational terms that Afrikans were vigorously challenging in their quest to transfer complete control into their own hands. In addition, Clarke also noted there was no such thing as a Jewish race; Europeans who embraced the Hebrew faith, the Ashkenazim who emerged in the tenth-century Rhineland in what was now modern Germany, were the largest among an international plurality of cultural and ethnical groups who constituted the peoples adhering to the Hebrew faith.[43]

In line with this, Clarke offered a number of other propositions that refuted the anti-Semitic claim. First, he argued "that the Jews of European descent had their early religious and cultural development in Europe," not in ancient Palestine, such that one could infer from the historical evidence that "the European Jews have no relationship to the Jews of the ancient world of North Africa and the Middle East except through religion." In other words, he implied, they were not true Semites. Indeed, he added, the Hebrew religion was almost as widespread as Christianity and unquestionably "older than the existence of Europe" and, thus, by implication, older than the existence of the Ashkenazim. As they were not the same people as the biblical Hebrews—whoever they might have been—they had no legitimate claim to Palestine in the modern period. Further, he implied, the Ashkenazim themselves could be reasonably said to be anti-Semitic, as they (as European settlers) monopolized power in the modern state of Israel and exhibited no meaningful solidarity with the numerous other Jewish peoples of various complexions, cultures, languages, and religious practices who lived in the state.[44] In his response to Gates, Clarke had charged that European Jews owed their primary loyalty to Europe. The Afrikans' conflict with them inhered, therefore, in their being implicated (no more and no less than any other Europeans) in the European effort to maintain control over Afrikan lives.[45] In his essay examining the alliance between Israel and South Africa published in 1981, nine years after his paper to the AHA, Clarke assessed "Both Israel and white South Africa are artificial settler states, created by the political backwash of Europe. They are parts of Europe, mentally and culturally, while being removed from it geographically."[46]

A final issue in the assessment of Clarke's legacy and contribution to Afrikan world intellectualism and culture relates to the paucity of the recognition of his contribution to the development of the Afrocentric paradigm, which is at the heart of, and can actually be said to be the core of, the discipline of Africalogy/Africana Studies in the United States. Molefi Kete Asante, founder of the first Ph.D. program in Africalogy/Africana Studies in the United States and the world, is generally credited as the "founder, principal theorist, and authority" of Afrocentricity.[47] When asked in 2002 to describe "the intellectual and developmental process that brought [him] to construct the theory of Afrocentricity," Asante, who cited as principal influences Maulana Karenga and Cheikh Anta Diop, never mentioned Clarke.[48] He explained that through the influence of these scholars he came to understand that Afrikans in the United States had been culturally dislocated in the European imagination and began to direct his studies in communications, his disciplinary training, to the cultural issue, focusing on the fact that Afrikans had been removed from their own cultural center to the periphery of Europe. Sanity could be restored if Afrikans understood they were agents in the world and not spectators, that they were participants and actors in history.[49]

Other scholars, among them Ama Mazama, Ruth Reviere, Clyde Ahmad Winters, and Maulana Karenga, have acknowledged the singular role Asante has played in formulating the Afrocentric paradigm, which has revolutionized both academic and popular Afrikan intellectualism in the United States.[50] There is no doubt that Asante's prodigious scholarship—he has authored or edited some sixty books and published some three hundred articles in his career thus far—is an irrefutably ground-breaking contribution to Afrikan intellectualism and culture in the United States and globally. Indeed, Asante's stature as an academician is stellar. The historian Diane D. Turner identifies him as one of the ten most widely quoted U.S. Afrikan scholars and as "one of the 100 leading thinkers in America during the 20th century."[51] Certainly, as well, the three pillars of his theorizing on Afrocentricity—*Afrocentricity: The Theory of Social Change* (1980), *The Afrocentric Idea* (1987), and *Kemet, Afrocentricity, and Knowledge* (1990)—were pivotal in the watershed impact this concept has had on Afrikan world culture and intellectualism.[52]

Still, the matter of Clarke's prior and seminal influence cannot be ignored. Clovis E. Semmes addressed this concern in an essay he published in 2001 in the *Western Journal of Black Studies* titled "Foundations in Africana Studies: Revisiting *Negro Digest/Black World*, 1961–1976." The *Negro Digest*, renamed the *Black World* in 1970 and published by the late John H. Johnson (who also published *Ebony* and *Jet* magazines), became, under the editorship of Hoyt W. Fuller, the most influential and widely-read Afrikan literary magazine in the United States, gaining as well an international reputation in the Afrikan world.[53] In addition, Semmes explains that under Fuller's direction the publication played a pivotal role "in the early construction of Afrocentric discourse and method." One of the leading figures in this early construction, he maintains, was the "historian John Henrik Clarke [who] developed extended theorizing on the content and form of an Afrocentric frame of reference, which, of course, had its roots in the political struggle to decolonize African history, and to which many African-descent scholars would contribute."[54] Semmes points to a series of essays Clarke published in the *Black World* between 1970 and 1975 in which he used the term "Afrocentric" to define a new framework for the study and interpretation of Afrikan world history and culture.[55]

Semmes also points out that this call for an Afrocentric approach to Afrikan world history and culture was shared by Clarke's colleagues in the AHSA. Among them was the organization's executive board chairman P. Chike Onwuachi, who in an October 1971 essay on Negritude stated, "The essence of Negritude must be articulated in Afrocentrism, the perspective in which the Black man is objectively translated in his true essence of being a WHOLE MAN and not as a pathological adjunct of the white man, nor as the invisible man in the white dominated world."[56] This call for, or elaboration of, an Afrocentric perspective or an Afrikan worldview was replicated in essays published by other scholars in the magazine from 1972 through 1974, Semmes observes. Indeed, in 1973 the *Black World* published the announcement of a summer school initiative at Atlanta University that offered "'a group of advanced Afrocentric courses.'" Semmes is quick to add, however, that during this period "Afrocentric theorizing was not dependent on the use of the term Afrocentric."[57]

Asante's definition of Afrocentricity, then, adds nothing essentially new to this theorizing of the 1970s. Rather, his key (and, indeed, invaluable) contribution is that he built upon, advanced, and systematized this theorizing, making it the explicitly recognized core, the paradigm, that informs the academic discipline that also emerged in the late 1960s and early 1970s—Africana Studies, or what he came to call Africalogy (a term, also spelled *Africology*, credited to Winston Van Horne, professor and founding chair of the Department of Africology at the University of Wisconsin-Milwaukee),[58] which is by definition "the Afrocentric study of phenomena, events, ideas, and personalities related to Africa." Similar to the critique offered by Clarke and his AHSA colleagues decades earlier, Asante established that the "mere study of phenomena of Africa is not Africalogy but some other intellectual enterprise. The scholar who generates research questions based on the centrality of Africa is engaged in a very different research inquiry than the one who imposes Western criteria on the phenomena."[59] Afrocentric scholarship means placing "African ideals and values at the center of inquiry. If this does not happen then Afrocentricity does not exist."[60] In short, "Centrism, the groundedness of observation and behavior in one's own historical experiences, structures the concepts, paradigms, theories, and methods of Africalogy," he explains. "As a discipline, Africalogy is sustained by a commitment to centering the study of African phenomena and events in the particular cultural voice of the composite African people."[61]

At its core, Asante elaborates, "Afrocentricity is actually a paradigm which infuses all phenomena from the standpoint of African people as subjects in human history rather than on the fringes of someone else's culture." Within the paradigm, he continues, there is also "Afrocentric theory," which locates thought through an analysis of its relationship to an orientation or perspective regarding the examination of phenomena. "In that sense, it becomes a perspective on facts, not the data themselves but the orientation that you have towards the data is what makes something Afrocentric." This orientation is said to be Afrocentric in that it begins with Afrikans as subjects and Afrikan culture as the starting point. Thus, any discussion of philosophy begins with an examination of the Afrikan context as central in terms of intellectual heritage, definitions, salient themes, and the like. The same is true of history, architecture, sociology, governance, or science, to cite a few examples. All begin from the Afrikan starting point as the central framework for intellectual inquiry. The paradigm of Afrocentricity "reorients the thinking of African people from any perspective, any intellectual perspective, any social perspective."[62]

Mazama explains that "Afrocentricity contends that our main problem as African people is our usually unconscious adoption of the Western worldview and perspective and their attendant conceptual frameworks." The Afrikan failure to recognize this "had led us, willingly or unwillingly, to agree to footnote status in the White man's book. We thus find ourselves relegated to the periphery, the margin, of the European experience, to use Molefi Asante's terms—spectators of a show that defines us from without." The remedy is, therefore, "to systematically displace European ways of thinking, being, feeling, and so forth and consciously replace them with ways that are germane to our own African cultural experience."[63]

Mazama's discussion of the characteristics of a paradigm is also reflective of Clarke's pioneering contribution to the development of the Afrocentric paradigm. She notes a paradigm links a self-contained community of practitioners together in a typically rigid and elaborated framework of beliefs. That is, a paradigm presupposes an integrated community of practitioners and a set of presuppositions, a worldview, that shapes and guides their inquiry. In addition to these cognitive and structural functions, Mazama adds a functional aspect of the Afrocentric paradigm. The production of knowledge, she maintains, is "for the sake of our liberation." A paradigm "must activate our consciousness to be of any use to us."[64]

As this study has already shown, the first listed of the AHSA's aims and objectives was the "Reconstruction of African history and cultural studies along Afro-centric lines while effecting an intellectual union among black scholars the world over."[65] In other words, in founding the AHSA in 1969 Clarke and his colleagues were engaged as their chief concern in an effort to forge an Afrocentric paradigm manifesting the cognitive, structural, and functional aspects Mazama discusses. The AHSA was, consequently, the beginning not only of the terminological articulation of the Afrocentric idea, but also of the attempt to work out the Afrocentric paradigm that Asante began to systematically develop and advance a decade later. It is significant that the scope of their vision of the community of scholars was global. This developing paradigm emphasized, as executive chairman Onwuachi was to expound in 1971, that true liberation rests in the necessity of fully embracing the Afrikan cultural heritage; using Afrikan culture (including its spiritual and communalistic elements) as a philosophical base; developing a consciousness of a "universal community of African peoples"; rejecting the notion that Afrikans should any longer function or see themselves as "a pathological adjunct of the white man or any other man"; rejecting European religion and embracing Afrikan spirituality; rejecting suicidal assimilation into European culture; and progressing toward a commitment to power and self-determination in both political and academic terms.[66]

This study demonstrates, consequently, that the development of the Afrocentric paradigm was a collective and intergenerational project and not an individualized effort. It is useful to recall the theoretical assumptions of the Afrikan academy in which Clarke was trained in the 1930s: (1) Afrikan agency as the historiographical starting point for historical interpretation, (2) Afrikan nationalism and Pan Afrikanism, (3) skepticism of assimilationism, Europeanization, and Christianization, and (4) indigenous Afrikan culture as the basis for modern Afrikan human development and society.[67]

It comes as no surprise, therefore, that many of the salient elements Asante and Mazama identify as constituting Afrocentricity are reflected in Clarke's work. They include Mazama's articulation in her essay "Afrocentricity and Spirituality," published in 2002, that Afrocentricity's ultimate goal is liberation, her discussion of the importance of Afrikan spirituality in the history of Afrikan liberation struggle, and her insistence that the unqualified embrace of Afrocentricity "entails being fully and consciously in tune with African metaphysics."[68] This study has shown these themes featured prominently in Clarkean discourse.

Similarly, Asante in "The Ideological Significance of Afrocentricity in Intercultural Communication," published in 1983, and "The Afrocentric Idea in Education," published in 1991, identified important themes in Afrocentric discourse also reflected in Clarke's earlier work. They include the anteriority of Afrikan civilization in human civilization and history, the feasibility of constructing effective and viable modern economic development in Afrika through systematic derivation and modeling from indigenous Afrikan culture, an Afrocentric approach to research that prioritizes the research of Afrikan scholars on questions of inquiry such that Afrikan scholars arrive at a method "to prevent the invisibility of our own scholars and history," a commitment to "intellectual integrity" in Afrocentric research that pursues "an absolute commitment to the discovery of the truth," and an exploration of the implications of European intellectual hegemony by stating in a way reminiscent of Clarke's phrasing, "Concomitant with the European colonization of Africa was the European colonization of information about Africa."[69]

As well, Asante's cultural critique of Islam in his seminal work, *Afrocentricity* (2003), also harmonizes perfectly with Clarke's critique discussed in chapter 8.[70] In "Afrocentricity and the Quest for Method," published in 1997, Asante discusses the fact that Afrikan intellectuals have an intellectual tradition that is independent of Europe that permits Afrikan scholars and intellectuals the possibility of epistemological autonomy. He also defines the "geographical scope of the African world, and hence, the Africalogical enterprise," as being global and Pan Afrikanist.[71] This study demonstrates each of these themes and methodological approaches were evident in Clarke's teaching, theorizing, and research in Africana Studies dating back to the 1970s.

In the end, Clarke's contribution to Afrikan intellectualism and culture is both singular and part of a cultural continuum. His contributions to the Afrocentric paradigm that informs Africana Studies/Africalogy include his emphasis on Afrikan agency and the implications of the anteriority of Afrikan culture and civilization for agency in Afrikan modernity; his theorizing about culture includes its application to challenges to Afrikan self-determination, authenticity, and wholeness. All of this theorizing arises from his historiography of the global Afrikan experience and the centrality of this historiography in the Afrikan struggle for liberation from European hegemony. Indeed, while the current discourse on Afrocentricity rests upon the imperative of liberation, Clarke introduced an aspect of the definition of liberation not commonly raised in Afrocentric discourse—that is, the imperative of Afrikan state sovereignty for all Afrikans globally. For Clarke, the highest level of Afrocentric human possibility could not be realized without it.

Notes

1. John Henrik Clarke, "The Growth of Racism in the West," *Black World* 19, no. 12 (October 1970): 10.

2. Ibid., "The Meaning of Black History," *Black World* 20, no. 4 (February 1971): 17.

3. Ibid., "On 'The Cultural Unity of Africa'," *Black World* 26, no. 4 (February 1975): 13.

4. Ibid., 17.

5. Nell Painter, "John Henrik Clarke, 1915–1998," *Crisis*, September/October 1998, 40.

6. Obituary, *New York Times*, 22 July 1998, A17.

7. "In Memoriam: John Henrik Clarke 1915–1998," *Journal of Blacks in Higher Education* no. 21 (Autumn 1998): 14.

8. Robin D. G. Kelley, "Self-Made Angry Man," *New York Times Magazine*, 3 January 1999, SM17.

9. Ibid., "Dr. John Henrik Clarke, The Peoples' Scholar," *Black Issues Book Review* 1, no. 5 (September/October 1999): 15.

10. Nubian Network, "The Initiation into Eternity for Dr. John Henrik Clarke, View 4," 21 July 1998, http://www.blackconsciousness.com/sshop/clark.html.

11. Herb Boyd, "In Memoriam: Dr. John Henrik Clarke (1915–1998)," *Black Scholar* 28, no. 3/4 (2001): 50–52.

12. Al Sharpton, "Dr. John Henrik Clarke," *New York Amsterdam News*, 23 July 1998, 13; Herb Boyd, "Clarke and Williams Solidify Union in Marriage," *New York Amsterdam News*, 25 September 1997, 3.

13. Bruce Karriem, "John Henrik Clarke: A Man for All Seasons," *New York Amsterdam News*, 23 July 1998, 12.

14. William Loren Katz, "A Giant in Our Time," *New York Amsterdam News*, 23 July 1998, 12.

15. David N. Dinkins, "John Henrik Clarke's Legacy Will Continue to Enrich Us," *New York Amsterdam News*, 23 July 1998, 13.

16. Robert McG. Thomas, Jr., "John Henrik Clarke, Black Studies Advocate, Dies at 83," *New York Times*, 20 July 1998, A13.

17. Richard Newman, "John Henrik Clarke," *Transition* no. 77 (1998): 4–8; Herb Boyd, "Father History Passes," *New York Amsterdam News*, cover.

18. Nubian Network, "The Initiation into Eternity for Dr. John Henrik Clarke, View 2," 21 July 1998, http://www.blackconsciousness.com/sshop/clark. html.

19. Ibid., "The Initiation into Eternity for Dr. John Henrik Clarke, View 3," 21 July 1998, http://www.blackconsciousness.com/sshop/clark.html.

20. Herb Boyd, "Series of Special Programs Marks the Anniversary of Historian's Death," *New York Amsterdam News*, 15–21 July 1999, 9.

21. Ibid., "Dr. Clarke Remembered," *New York Amsterdam News*, 20–26 July 2000, 8.

22. Ibid., "Hundreds Pay Tribute to Clarke," *New York Amsterdam News*, 19–25 July 2001, 6, 30.

23. Ibid., "137th Street to Be Renamed for John Henrik Clarke," *New York Amsterdam News*, 19–25 October 2000, 5; ibid., "Harlem Scholar Remembered," *New York Amsterdam News*, 23–29 November 2000, 4.

24. John Henrik Clarke, letter to Mary Kaiser, 23 February 1983, JHCP, SCRBC; James E. Jackson, "John Henrik Clarke: Advises CIA and Joins 'Beat the Russians' Band," *Daily World*, 12 November 1982, JHCP, SCRBC; John Henrik Clarke, "Response to James Jackson's Article in the November 12, 1982 Issue of the Daily World," unpublished press release, 2 December 1982, JHCP, SCRBC.

25. Painter, "John Henrik Clarke," 40.

26. Ibid.

27. Ibid. For the Afrocentric discourse on the issue of women and power, see, among others, Nah Dove, "African Womanism: An Afrocentric Theory," *Journal of Black Studies* 28, no. 5 (May 1998): 515–539; ibid., "Defining a Mother-Centered Matrix to Analyze the Status of Women," *Journal of Black Studies* 33, no. 1 (September 2002): 3–24; Pamela Yaa Asantewaa Reed, "Africana Womanism and African Feminism: A Philosophical, Literary, and Cosmological Dialectic on Family," *Western Journal of Black Studies* 25, no. 3 (2001): 168–176; Delores P. Aldridge, "Womanist Issues in Black Studies: Towards Integrating Africana Womanism into Africana Studies," in *Africana Studies: A Disciplinary Quest for Both Theory and Method*, ed. James L. Conyers, Jr. (Jefferson, NC: McFarland, 1997), 143–154; Vivian Gordon, "Black Women, Feminism, and Black Liberation: Which Way?," in *Africana Studies: A Disciplinary Quest for Both Theory and Method*, ed. James L. Conyers, Jr. (Jefferson, NC: McFarland, 1997), 155–174; Shawn R. Donaldson, "'Feminist' or 'Womanist'? A Black Woman Defining Self," in *Africana Studies: A Disciplinary Quest for Both Theory and Method*, ed. James L.

Conyers, Jr. (Jefferson, NC: McFarland, 1997), 175–179; Ahati N. N. Toure, "On the Myth of Male Supremacy: Adam and Eve and the Imperative of a New Afrikan-Centered Epistemology of Gender," in *Africana Studies: A Disciplinary Quest for Both Theory and Method*, ed. James L. Conyers, Jr. (Jefferson, NC: McFarland, 1997), 180–192; Oba T'Shaka, *Return to the African Mother Principle of Male and Female Equality*, vol. 1 (Oakland, CA: Pan Afrikan Publishers, 1995); John Henrik Clarke, "The Black Family in Historical Perspective," *Journal of Afro-American Issues* 3, no. 3/4 (Summer/Fall 1975): 336–342; ibid., "On 'The Cultural Unity," 12–26; Ama Mazama, "The Afrocentric Paradigm: Contours and Definitions," *Journal of Black Studies* 31, no. 4 (March 2001): 400–401.

28. John Henrik Clarke, "African-American Historians and the Reclaiming of African History," in *African Culture: The Rhythms of Unity*, ed. Molefi Kete Asante and Kariamu Welsh Asante (Trenton, NJ: Africa World Press, 1990; originally Westport, CT: Greenwood Press, 1985), 157–171. The essay originally appeared as "African-American Historians and the Reclaiming of African History," *Présence Africaine* no. 110 (2nd Quarterly 1979): 29–48. Before that it was a conference paper, "African-American Historians and the Reclaiming of African History," prepared for the Fourth Congress Session, International Congress of African Studies, Kinshasa, Zaire, 12–16 December 1978, JHCP, SCRBC.

29. W. D. Wright, *Black History and Black Identity: A Call for a New Historiography* (Westport, CT: Praeger, 2002), 123–127.

30. John Henrik Clarke, *Christopher Columbus and the Afrikan Holocaust: Slavery and the Rise of European Capitalism* (Brooklyn, NY: A&B Publishers, 1993).

31. Wright, *Black History*, 123–127.

32. Henry Louis Gates, Jr., "Black Demagogues and Pseudo-Scholars," *New York Times*, 20 July 1992, A15.

33. Michael Bradley, *The Iceman Inheritance: Prehistoric Sources of Western Man's Racism, Sexism and Aggression* (New York: Warner Books, 1978; originally Toronto: Dorset, 1978), 3. Clarke's introduction to the text was in a 1991 edition published by Kayode Publications of New York City.

34. Michael Bradley, "The Iceman Inheritance: A Frightening Publication History of Jewish Media Suppression," http://www.michaelbradley.info/books/iceman/iceman_promo.html; ibid., email to the author, 8 January 2007.

35. Gates, "Black Demagogues," A15. The effect of Gates's slander of Clarke erupted eleven years later in a controversy over the renaming of a middle

school in Kansas City, Missouri, in honor of the late scholar. Certain European Jewish residents of the city vigorously opposed the move on the grounds that Clarke was allegedly anti-Semitic. See Herb Boyd, "A Revered Elder at the Center of Controversy," *New York Amsterdam News*, 30 January–5 February 2003, 4, 30.

36. Ibid.

37. Quoted in Russell W. Nash, letter to Douglas Grant, 3 June 1969, JHCP, SCRBC. Nash was president of the Iowa Human Rights Coalition based in Dubuque. Grant was vice president of WMT-TV of Cedar Rapids.

38. Roy Wilkins, 5-page draft letter to the editor, no date, JHCP, SCRBC.

39. Kelley, "Self-Made Angry Man," SM17.

40. John Henrik Clarke, "Black Pseudo-Scholars Are 'In' with White America, But They Deserve to Be 'Outed,' Says Historian," *The City Sun*, 26 August–1 September 1992, 8, 37–38, JHCP, SCRBC.

41. Ibid., "The Myth of Black Anti-Semitism," Eighty-seventh Annual Meeting of the American Historical Association, Watergate Conference Center, New Orleans, Louisiana, 30 December 1972, JHCP, SCRBC. Clarke had also commented on this question in an essay that appeared in a Queens College Afrikan and Latino newspaper titled "Israel and South Africa: The Unholy Alliance Against African People," *The Globe*, 18 March 1981, 3, 5–6, 11, JHCP, SCRBC.

42. Ibid.

43. Ibid.

44. Ibid.

45. Ibid., "Black Pseudo-Scholars," 8, 37–38.

46. Ibid., "Israel and South Africa," 3. Note also the skepticism expressed by the European Jewish American academic Norman G. Finkelstein, *Beyond Chutzpah: On the Misuse of Anti-Semitism and the Abuse of History* (Berkeley and Los Angeles: University of California Press, 2005).

47. Diane D. Turner, "An Oral History Interview: Molefi Kete Asante," *Journal of Black Studies* 32, no. 6 (July 2002): 712.

48. Ibid., 717. Asante did acknowledge Clarke in the preface of his book, *The Afrocentric Idea*, noting "The work of John Henrik Clarke, the unswerving genius whose encyclopedic knowledge and critical acumen are without peer in this age, has influenced my outlook on history." See Molefi Kete Asante, *The Afrocentric Idea* (Philadelphia: Temple University Press, 1987), viii.

49. Ibid., 717–718.

50. See Ama Mazama, "The Afrocentric Paradigm," in *The Afrocentric Paradigm*, ed. Ama Mazama (Trenton, NJ: Africa World Press, 2003), 3–34; ibid., "The Afrocentric Paradigm: Contours and Definitions," 387–405; Maulana Karenga, *Introduction to Black Studies*, 3rd ed. (Los Angeles: University of Sankore Press, 2002), 45–49; Clyde Ahmad Winters, "Afrocentrism: A Valid Frame of Reference," *Journal of Black Studies* 25, no. 2 (December 1994): 170–190; Ruth Reviere, "Toward an Afrocentric Research Methodology," *Journal of Black Studies* 31, no. 6 (July 2001): 709–728.

51. Turner, "An Oral History," 712, 713.

52. Molefi Kete Asante, *Afrocentricity: The Theory of Social Change* (Buffalo, NY: Amulefi Publishing, 1980); ibid., *The Afrocentric Idea*; ibid., *Kemet, Afrocentricity and Knowledge* (Trenton, NJ: Africa World Press, 1990).

53. Clovis E. Semmes, "Foundations in Africana Studies: Revisiting *Negro Digest/Black World*, 1961–1976," *Western Journal of Black Studies* 25, no. 4 (Winter 2001): 196.

54. Ibid., 197–198.

55. Ibid., 198.

56. As quoted by Semmes, 199.

57. Ibid., 199–200.

58. See, for example, Winston A. Van Horne, "Africology: Considerations Concerning a Discipline," in *Contemporary Africana Thought, Theory and Action: A Guide to Africana Studies*, ed. Clenora Hudson-Weems (Trenton, NJ: Africa World Press, 2007), 105-127.

59. Molefi K. Asante, "Afrocentricity and the Quest for Method," in *Africana Studies: A Disciplinary Quest for Both Theory and Method*, ed. James L. Conyers, Jr. (Jefferson, NC: McFarland, 1997), 78.

60. Ibid., 71.

61. Ibid., 76.

62. Turner, "An Oral History," 718.

63. Mazama, "The Afrocentric Paradigm: Contours and Definitions," 387–388.

64. Ibid., 391–392.

65. Brochure of the AHSA, JHCP, SCRBC.

66. P. Chike Onwuachi, "Ideological Perspectives of the African Heritage Studies Association," *African Heritage Newsletter* 2, no. 1-2 (January–February 1971): 2–3, JHCP, SCRBC.

67. See discussion in chapter 1.

68. Ama Mazama, "Afrocentricity and African Spirituality," *Journal of Black Studies* 33, no. 2 (November 2002): 218–219, 232.

69. Molefi Kete Asante, "The Ideological Significance of Afrocentricity in Intercultural Communication," *Journal of Black Studies* 14, no. 1 (September 1983): 7, 10, 12–13; ibid., "The Afrocentric Idea in Education," *Journal of Negro Education* 60, no. 2 (Spring 1991): 177–178. See also ibid., "A Discourse on Black Studies: Liberating the Study of African People in the Western Academy," *Journal of Black Studies* 36, no. 5 (May 2006): 646–662.

70. See ibid., *Afrocentricity: The Theory of Social Change*, rev. and expanded (Chicago: African American Images, 2003), 6.

71. Ibid., "Afrocentricity and the Quest for Method," 71, 78.

Bibliography

John Henrik Clarke Papers
Schomburg Center for Research in Black Culture

Academic Lectures and Speeches

Clarke, John Henrik. "Reclaiming the Lost African Heritage." Africa Conference, Social Sciences and Humanities Center, Teachers College, Columbia University, and presented at the International Center, International Studies in World Affairs, State University of New York, Oyster Bay, Long Island, 15 September 1966.

———, "A New Approach to African History." Regional Conference on Afro-American History. Detroit Federation of Teachers and Michigan Federation of Teachers, University of Detroit, Detroit, Michigan, 11–13 May 1967.

———, "The Origin of the Black Urban Ghetto." Social Sciences-Unit Studies, School of Library Sciences, Columbia University, 24 July 1968.

———, "Dimensions of the Black Experience: Outline of Eight Lectures for the Colloquium on Black History." Afro-Americans Studies Program, Columbia University, 7 July–1 August 1969.

———, "Dimensions of the Black Experience-Bibliography." Colloquium on Black History, Afro-Americans Studies Program, Columbia University, 7 July–1 August 1969.

———, "New Perspectives on the History of African Peoples." Louisiana Educational Association, 1 May 1970.

———, "Race: An Evolving Issue in Western Social Thought." Extension of paper prepared for the International Conference on Race Relations, Graduate School of International Studies, University of Denver, Denver, Colorado; presented at Aspen, Colorado, 7–9 June 1970.

———, "Problems in Teaching and Understanding African History." Second Colloquium on Black History, Afro-Americans Studies Program, Columbia University, 13 July 1970.

———, "The African Woman as a Figure in World History." Livingston College, 22 July 1970.

———, "The Impact of the African on the 'New World': A Reappraisal." American Historical Association, Boston, Massachusetts, 28–30 December 1970.

———, "African Culture, the Basis of World Culture." Afro-American Studies Lecture Series, Department of Ethnic Studies, University of California-Berkeley, 7 May 1971

———, "African History and Its Relation to World History." Afro-American Studies Lecture Series, Department of Ethnic Studies, University of California-Berkeley, 7 May 1971.

———, "Afro-American Culture and Its Impact on the Making of the 'New World.'" Afro-American Studies Lecture Series, Department of Ethnic Studies, University of California-Berkeley, 8 May 1971.

———, "Afro-American History: Main Currents, 1600–Present." Afro-American Studies Lecture Series, Department of Ethnic Studies, University of California-Berkeley, 8 May 1971.

———, "History as an Instrument of Liberation." Teachers Corps, Session in Black History, Providence, Rhode Island, 2 November 1972.

———, "The Myth of Black Anti-Semitism." Eighty-seventh Annual Meeting of the American Historical Association, Watergate Conference Center, New Orleans, Louisiana, 30 December 1972.

———, "The Image of Africa in the Mind of the Afro-American: African Identity in the Literature of Struggle." Phelps-Stokes Seminars on African-American Relations, *The Afro-American Connection*, Moton Conference Center, Capahosic, Gloucester, Virginia, 5–7 October 1973.

———, "Black Studies: A Dilemma at the Crossroads." Afro-American Studies Program, Northeastern University, 8 February 1974.

———, "The Black Radical Tradition." Seton Hall University, South Orange, New Jersey, 1 March 1974.

———, "Black Americans: Immigrants Against Their Will." CAAS Occasional Paper No. 15, Center for African and African-American Studies, Atlanta University, Atlanta, Georgia, April 1974.

———, "The Black American's Search for an Ideology." Eighth Conference of the Center for African and African-American Studies, Atlanta University, Atlanta, Georgia, 4–6 December 1975.

———, "Pan Africanism as an Ideology in Movement." Bicentennial Lecture, Department of Afro-American Studies, Amherst College, 17 April 1976.

———, "The Historical Roots of Terrorism against African People." The Conference on Terrorism in the Contemporary World: An International Symposium, Glassboro State College, Glassboro, New Jersey, 26–28 April 1976.

———, "The Politics of Black Survival." Lecture at Black Studies Department, Rutgers, The State University of New Jersey, Newark, New Jersey, 27 October 1976.

———, "African People: Their Image in Early World History." Black History Week Commemoration, Ethnic Studies Program, Illinois State University, Normal-Bloomington, Illinois, 3 February 1978.

———, "Race: The Historical Development of A Myth." Forum on Strategies to Defeat Mounting Racism, Black Liberation Press, New York City, held at Columbia University, October 1978.

———, "International Aspects of African Studies 1968–1978: A Decade of Change, Challenge and Conflict." Twenty-first Annual Meeting of the African Studies Association, Baltimore, Maryland, 1–4 November 1978.

———, "African-American Historians and the Reclaiming of African History." Fourth Congress Session, International Congress of African Studies, Kinshasa, Zaire, 12–16 December 1978.

———, "Africana Studies, A Decade of Change, Challenge and Conflict." *Consolidating Africana Studies: Bonding African Linkages.* The Tenth Anniversary of the Africana Studies and Research Center, Cornell University, 26–28 September 1980.

———, "Myths and Misconceptions About African History." De Hostos College, Bronx, New York, 25 September 1981.

———, "Reflections & Observations ... Ghana Remembered 'Then and Now.'" Seventeenth Annual Conference, National Council for Black Studies, Accra, Ghana, 25 July–1 August 1993 (25 July 1993).

———, "Reflections and Observations: Ghana Remembered, 'Then and Now.'" Seventeenth Annual Conference, National Council for Black Studies, Accra, Ghana, 25 July–1 August 1993 (Transcript of Remarks, 26 July 1993).

———, "African World Civilization: 19th Century to the Present." Seventeenth Annual Conference, National Council for Black Studies, Accra, Ghana, 25 July–1 August 1993 (27 July 1993).

Community Lectures and Speeches

Clarke, John Henrik. "African History as the Basis of World History." Black Child Development Institute, Inc., Conference at the Urban Life Center, Columbia, Maryland, 3–6 December 1975 (4 December 1975).

———, "The African Impact on Latin America and the Caribbean Islands." Black Child Development Institute, Inc., Conference at the Urban Life Center, Columbia, Maryland, 3–6 December 1975.

———, "The Status of African People: A World View." Extracted from the keynote speech, delivered at the First Annual Conference of the State of the Race, Los Angeles, California, 28–30 October 1977.

———, "Beyond Black Survival A World of Challenge." First Annual Black Unity and Futurism Conference, Minnesota Springhill Conference Center, Minneapolis, Minnesota, 18–20 November 1977.

Course Syllabi

Clarke, John Henrik. "Study Guides in the History, Civilization, and Culture of Africa, for students in courses 29-201 and 29-203 (African History from the Origin of Man to 1600 A.D. and African Civilization to 1900 A.D.)." Department of Black and Puerto Rican Studies, Hunter College, the City University of New York, 1969.

———, "Nineteenth Century Resistance Movements: African and Afro-American." Africana Studies and Research Center, Cornell University, Seminar Course, fall semester 1970.

———, "African Heritage: Historiography and Sources; A Study of the Historical Writings of Edward Wilmot Blyden, Sir Harry Hamilton Johnston, George Shepperson, Carter G. Woodson, W. E. B. Du Bois, and Basil Davidson." Africana Studies and Research Center, Cornell University, fall semester 1971 and spring semester 1972.

———, "African History from the Origin of Man to 1600 A.D." Department of Black and Puerto Rican Studies, Hunter College of the City University of New York, fall semester 1973.

———, "African-American History I: From Slavery to Emancipation." Department of Black and Puerto Rican Studies, Hunter College of the City University of New York, fall 1983.

———, "Dimensions of World History." Department of Black and Puerto Rican Studies, Hunter College of the City University of New York, fall 1985.

———, "Dimensions of World History." Department of Black and Puerto Rican Studies, Hunter College of the City University of New York, spring 1986.

In-service Lectures

Clarke, John Henrik. "The Golden Age in Africa Before the Christian Era." Lecture Notes, 1 October 1965.

———, "The Negro in America: The African Background and The Colonial Experience." In-service course sponsored by the Public Schools of Great Neck, New York, 27 September and 11 October 1967.

———, "Great African Rulers." In-service course in African History sponsored by the New York City Board of Education and programmed by the African-American Institute of New York City, 12 March 1968.

———, "Africa's Oral Tradition." In-service course in African History sponsored by the New York City Board of Education and programmed by the African-American Institute of New York City, 23 April 1968.

———, "Africa: The Colonial Period." In-service course in African History sponsored by the New York City Board of Education and programmed by the African-American Institute of New York City, 18 March 1969.

———, "Societies and Cultures of West Africa." In-service course in African History sponsored by the New York City Board of Education and programmed by the African-American Institute of New York City, 16 and 29 April 1969.

———, "Africa: The Last Age of Grandeur, 1076–1591 A.D." Institute on Special Educational Problems Occasioned by Desegregation, State University of New York at Albany, 20 September 1969.

———, "History and the New Age of Man." In-service program on Negro Literature, History and Culture, lecture sponsored by the Board of Educational Services First Supervisory District, Westchester County, New York, 24 September 1969.

Concentrated Courses

Clarke, John Henrik. "African Culture History: Impact of Colonialism and the Slave Trade" and "The Impact of African Culture and the Slave System in the United States on the Pre-Civil War Culture of Afro-Americans." Concentrated Course on History and Lifestyles of Negro and Puerto Rican People, Graduate School of Social Work, New York University, 18 September 1968.

Teaching Documents

Clarke, John Henrik. "RE: Curriculum Guide to the Study and Teaching of African and Afro-American History; An Account of Applicant's Career as a Writer and a Teacher," 1966.

Letters

Barnett, Claude A. Letter to John Henrik Clarke, 24 February 1961.

Bennett, Lerone, Jr. Letter to John Henrik Clarke, 3 June 1970.

Brooks, Gwendolyn. Letter to John Henrik Clarke, 21 June 1967.

Clarke, John Henrik. Letter to Henry Allen Moe, 30 October 1951.

———, Letter to Julian Mayfield, 9 May 1958.

———, Letter to Henry Allen Moe, 13 October 1958.

———, Letter to Claude A. Barnett, 23 January 1961.

———, Letter to Julian Mayfield, 24 February 1965.

———, Letter to Julian Mayfield, 1 June 1965.

———, Letter to Julian Mayfield, 25 August 1965.

———, Letter to Julian Mayfield, 21 February 1966.

———, Letter to Adelaide Cromwell Hill, 30 September 1966.

———, Letter to Calvin H. Sinnette, 8 February 1969.

———, Letter to Robert D. Cross, 20 May 1969.

———, Letter to Adelaide Cromwell Hill, 11 June 1969.

———, Letter to Hoyt W. Fuller, 5 October 1969.

———, Letter to Ezekiel Mphahlele, 20 January 1970.

———, Letter to Lawrence Hill and Arthur Wang, 13 May 1970.

———, Letter to Lawrence Hill and Arthur Wang, 28 June 1970.

————, Letter to Vincent Harding, 23 September 1970.

————, Letter to E. U. Essien-Udom, 29 February 1972.

————, Letter to Adelaide Hill, 31 October 1972.

————, Letter to E. U. Essien-Udom, 31 October 1972.

————, Letter to William Marshall, 5 March 1974.

————, Letter to Hoyt W. Fuller, 11 March 1974.

————, Letter to Elliot Skinner, 23 September 1975.

————, Letter to Julian Mayfield, 26 October 1976.

————, Letter to Helga R. Andrews, 1 February 1982.

————, Letter to Mary Kaiser, 23 February 1983.

————, Letter to Earl Sweeting, n.d.

Cosby, Camille O. Letter to Trustees of the Phelps-Stokes Foundation, 14 November 1994.

Cross, Robert D. Letter to John Henrik Clarke, 14 May 1969.

Diggs, Mary H. Letter to John Henrik Clarke, 17 April 1969.

Du Bois, Shirley Graham. Letter to John Henrik Clarke, 27 February 1965.

————, Letter to John Henrik Clarke, 13 October 1964.

Goldman, Phaon. Letter to John Henrik Clarke, 15 March 1965.

Haley, Alex. Letter to Peter Schwed, 28 August 1978.

Hansberry, William Leo. Letter to John Henrik Clarke, 2 February 1965.

————, Letter to E. Jefferson Murphy, 27 June 1958.

Hantula, James N. Letter to John Henrik Clarke, 16 February 1966.

Harding, Vincent. Letter to John Henrik Clarke, 9 September 1970.

Jemmot, Marion E. Letter to John Henrik Clarke, 12 February 1975.

Letter of Agreement between the Black Heritage Committee, Inc. and Vincent Harding, 31 August 1970.

Nash, Russell W. Letter to Douglas Grant, 3 June 1969.

Santiago, Jose Manuel Torres. Letter to John Henrik Clarke, 1 December 1987.

Sinnette, Calvin H. Letter to Cyril D. Tyson, 20 August 1964.

Skinner, Elliot P. Letter to Tilden J. LeMell, 24 April 1973.

Turner, James. Letter to John Henrik Clarke, May 23, 1969.

Wang, Arthur. Letter to John Henrik Clarke, 4 December 1970.

X, Malcolm. Letter to Diallo Telli, 28 July 1964.

Statements, Reports, Minutes, and Remarks

"African Liberation Fund Rejected by African Studies Association." *African Heritage Newsletter* 2, nos. 1–2 (January–February 1971): 8.

"African Studies Association and African Liberation." *African Heritage Newsletter* 1, nos. 1–2 (November–December 1970): 9.

"Statement of the Black Caucus." In "Confrontation at Montreal: The Fight to Reclaim African History," by John Henrik Clarke. First Report to the African Heritage Studies Association, n.d.

Ad Hoc Committee – Black Caucus, 18 October 1968.

Clarke, John Henrik. "Confrontation at Montreal: The Fight to Reclaim African History." First Report to the African Heritage Studies Association, n.d.

———, "The Ideological Framework of AHSA," Draft version, 12 October 1970.

———, "The Ideological Framework of AHSA." *African Heritage Newsletter* 1, no. 1–2 (November–December 1970): 2.

Hansberry, William Leo. "W. E. B. Du Bois: His Influence on African History." Unpublished remarks, n.d.

Harding, Vincent. "Towards a Black Agenda." Institute of the Black World, Atlanta, Georgia, 1 May 1970.

Painter, Nell. "Abridged Minutes of the Black Caucus Meeting of 18 October 1968."

———, "Summary of the Meeting of the African Studies Association Board and the Black Caucus, Los Angeles, 19 October 1968."

Onwuachi, P. Chike. "Ideological Perspectives of the African Heritage Studies Association." *African Heritage Newsletter* 2, no. 1–2 (January–February 1971): 1–4.

Organizing Meeting of the Association of Black Scholars, n.d.

Statement of the Black Caucus to the African Studies Association, 19 October 1968.

X, Malcolm. "The 2nd African Summit Conference." Cairo, Egypt, 21 August 1964.

News Releases

"Afro-American Troops for Congo-Malcolm X." News release from the OAAU Information Bureau, Accra, Ghana, n.d.

News Release. Public Relations Office, University of Denver, 6 June 1970.

Memoranda

Clarke, John Henrik. Memorandum to Elizabeth Gardner, 27 November 1967.

———, Memorandum to De Hostos and Toussaint L'Ouverture Student Organizations and their Representatives, 18 March 1970.

———, Memorandum to the class of "A Survey of African History," New School for Social Research, n.d.

Biographical Documents

Clarke, John Henrik. "RE: Curriculum Guide to the Study and Teaching of African and Afro-American History; An Account of Applicant's Career as a Writer and a Teacher," 1966.

———, Hunter College Staff Personnel Record, 25 June 1969.

———, "A selected list of my most important works from 1939 to the present time," n.d.

———, "Contemporary Authors," Biographical Form, n.d.

———, Curriculum Vitae.

———, "Who'sWho in America 38ᵗʰ Edition," Galley Proofs.

News Articles

Clarke, John Henrik. "Israel and South Africa: The Unholy Alliance Against African People." *The Globe*, 18 March 1981, 3, 5–6, 11.

———, "Black Pseudo-Scholars Are 'In' with White America, but They Deserve to Be 'Outed,' Says Historian." *The City Sun*, 26 August–1 September 1992, 8, 37–38.

———, "Arthur Schomburg, Teacher: A Memoir." *The Black American* 18, no. 34, p. 20.

Cyrs, Eric, Benjamin P. Bowser, Herbert Parker, and Elder James Cage. "A World Libertarian: John Glover Jackson."

Huggins, Willis N. "How Wrong Is Hitler? On the History of Jews, Black Folk and 'Aryanism'?" *The Chicago Defender*, Saturday, 28 January 1939, 13.

Jackson, James E. "John Henrik Clarke: Advises CIA and Joins 'Beat the Russians' Band." *Daily World*, 12 November 1982.

New York Amsterdam News, 29 March 1969.

Queens Voice, 14 March 1969.
The Columbus Times, 9, no. 16, 5th week of January 1980.

Unpublished Papers

Hansberry, William Leo. "Africa in Stone Age Times, in Historical Antiquity, and in the Middle Ages." Hansberry Files, n.d., 1–4.

Unpublished Editorials

Clarke, John Henrik. "Response to James E. Jackson's Article in the November 12, 1982 Issue of the Daily World," 2 December 1982.
Wilkins, Roy. 5-page draft letter to the editor, n.d.

Special and Research Projects

"Syllabus of Black Heritage: A History of Afro-Americans." Office of Radio and Television, Columbia University, n.d.
Clarke, John Henrik. Statement of Plans for Research; Reference: "Africa without Tears," n.d.

Brochures, Bulletins, Newsletters, and Other Documents

"Africanism: Toward a New Definition." Brochure for the second annual conference of the African Heritage Studies Association.
"History of HARYOU-ACT."
Brochure of the African Heritage Studies Association.
Heritage Bulletin, nos. 9 and 10 (Weeks March 18 and March 25, 1965).
Schedule of the Heritage Program, Community Action Institute, HARYOU-ACT, Inc., 9 August 1965.
September 1969 brochure for the Department of Black and Puerto Rican Studies, Hunter College, City University of New York.

Published and Other Primary Sources

Books

Clarke, John Henrik. *Rebellion in Rhyme: The Early Poetry of John Henrik Clarke.* Trenton, NJ: Africa World Press, 1991; originally *Rebellion in Rhyme.* Prairie City, IL: Decker Press, 1948.

——, *The Lives of Great African Chiefs.* Pittsburgh: Pittsburgh Courier Publishing Company, 1958.

——, *History and Culture of Africa.* Hempstead, NY: Aevac Inc. Educational Publishers, 1969.

——, *Notes for an African World Revolution: Africans at the Crossroads.* Trenton, NJ: Africa World Press, 1991.

——, *Christopher Columbus and the Afrikan Holocaust: Slavery and the Rise of European Capitalism.* Brooklyn, NY: A&B Publishers Group, 1992.

——, *Who Betrayed the African World Revolution? And Other Speeches.* Chicago: Third World Press, 1994.

——, *My Life in Search of Africa.* Chicago: Third World Press, 1999.

——, ed. *Harlem: A Community in Transition.* New York: Citadel Press, 1964.

——, ed. *Harlem U.S.A.: The Story of a City Within A City.* Berlin, West Germany: Seven Seas, 1965.

——, ed. *American Negro Short Stories.* New York: Hill and Wang, 1966.

——, ed. *William Styron's Nat Turner: Ten Black Writer's Respond.* Boston: Beacon Press, 1968.

——, ed. *Malcolm X: The Man and His Times.* Trenton, NJ: Africa World Press, 1990; originally New York: Collier Books, 1969.

——, ed. *Social Studies: African American Baseline Essays.* Portland, OR: Portland Unified School District, 1987.

——, ed. *New Dimensions in African History: The London Lectures of Dr. Yosef ben-Jochannan and Dr. John Henrik Clarke.* Trenton, NJ: Africa World Press, 1991.

Clarke, John Henrik, and Amy Jacques Garvey, ed. *Marcus Garvey and the Vision of Africa.* New York: Vintage Books, 1974.

Huggins, Willis N. and John G. Jackson. *Introduction to African Civilizations with Main Currents in Ethiopian History.* Baltimore: Inprint Editions, 1999; originally New York: Avon House, 1937.

Seifert, Charles C. *The Negro's or Ethiopian's Contribution to Art*. Baltimore: Black Classic Press, 1991; originally New York: The Ethiopian Historical Pub. Co., 1938.

Book Chapters

Clarke, John Henrik. "Black Americans: Immigrants Against Their Will." In *The Immigrant Experience in America*, edited by Frank J. Coppa and Thomas J. Curran, 172–191. Boston: Twayne Publishers, 1976.

———, "African-American Historians and the Reclaiming of African History." In *African Culture: The Rhythms of Unity*, edited by Molefi Kete Asante and Kariamu Welsh Asante, 157–171. Trenton, NJ: Africa World Press, 1990; originally Westport, CT: Greenwood Press, 1985.

———, "African Cultural Response to Slavery and Oppression in the Americas and the Caribbean." In *African Presence in the Americas*, edited by Tanya R. Saunders and Shawna Moore, 73–95. Trenton, NJ: Africa World Press, 1995.

———, "Our Black Seminarians: An Introduction." In Yosef A. A. ben Jochannan. *Our Black Seminarians and Black Clergy Without a Black Theology*. Baltimore: Black Classic Press, 1998.

Schomburg, Arthur A. "The Negro Digs Up His Past." In *The New Negro: An Interpretation*, edited by Alain Locke, 231–237. New York: Arno Press and The New York Times, 1968; originally New York: Albert and Charles Boni, 1925.

Stewart, Maria W. "Lecture, Delivered at the Franklin Hall, Boston, Sept. 21, 1832." In *Spiritual Narratives*, edited by Henry Louis Gates, Jr., 1–84. New York: Oxford University Press, 1998.

Journal Essays

Boyd, Herb. "In Memoriam: Dr. John Henrik Clarke (1915–1998)." *Black Scholar* 28, no. 3/4 (2001): 50–52.

Clarke, John Henrik. "La célébration d'une veillée funèbre dans la tribu Ga du Ghana." *Présence Africaine* (December 1958–January 1959): 107–112.

———, "Ancient Nigeria and the Western Sudan." *Présence Africaine* nos. 32–33 (1960): 11–18.

————, "Africa and the American Negro Press." *Journal of Negro Education* 30, no. 1 (Winter 1961): 64–68.

————, "The Morning Train to Ibadan." *Journal of Negro Education* 31, no. 4 (Autumn 1962): 527–530.

————, "Third Class on the Blue Train to Kumasi." *Phylon* 23, no. 3 (3rd Quarter 1962): 294–301.

————, "The Search for Timbuctoo." *Journal of Negro Education* 33, no. 2 (Spring 1964): 125–130.

————, "A Search for Identity." *Social Casework* 51, no. 5 (May 1970): 259–264.

————, "The Black Family in Historical Perspective." *Journal of Afro-American Issues* 3, no. 3/4 (Summer/Fall 1975): 336–342.

————, "African-American Historians and the Reclaiming of African History." *Présence Africaine* no. 110 (2nd Quarterly 1979): 29–48.

————, "Pan-Africanism: A Brief History of an Idea in the African World." *Présence Africaine* no. 145 (1st Quarterly 1988): 26–56.

————, "The Influence of Arthur A. Schomburg on My Concept of Africana Studies." *Phylon* 49, nos. 1, 2 (Spring/Summer 1992): 4–9.

Clarke, John Henrik and Sylvester Leaks. "Malcolm X: His Grandeur and Significance." *Présence Africaine* no. 62 (2nd Quarterly 1967): 77–83.

X, Malcolm. "The Black Struggle in the United States," *Présence Africaine* 26, no. 54 (2nd Quarterly 1965): 8–24.

Pamphlets

Crowe, Larry F. "Reflections on the Life of Dr. John Henrik Clarke: January 1, 1915 to July 16, 1998." Chicago: Kemetic Institute, 1998.

Magazine Articles

"In Memoriam. John Henrik Clarke 1915–1998." *Journal of Blacks in Higher Education* no. 21 (Autumn 1998): 14.

Boyd, Herb and Sharon Fitzgerald. "The Powerful Legacies of Two Giants." *American Visions* 13, no. 5 (October–November 1998): 30–33.

Braxton, Gloria J. "John Henrik Clarke: A Doyen of African History." *African World* 1, no. 1 (November/December 1993): 33–34.

Clarke, John Henrik "Old Ghana." *Negro History Bulletin* 23, no. 5 (February 1960): 116–117.

———, "New Ghana." *Negro History Bulletin* 23, no. 5 (February 1960): 117–118.

———, "The New Afro-American Nationalism." *Freedomways* 1, no. 3 (Fall 1961): 285–295.

———, "African Studies in the United States, An Afro-American View." *Africa Today* 16, no. 2 (April–May 1969): 10–12.

———, "The Fight to Reclaim African History." *Negro Digest* 19, no. 4 (February 1970): 10–15, 59–64.

———, "The Growth of Racism in the West." *Black World* 19, no. 12 (October 1970): 4–10.

———, "The Meaning of Black History." *Black World* 20, no. 4 (February 1971): 27–36.

———, "The Afro-American Image of Africa." *Black World* 23, no. 4 (February 1974): 4–21.

———, "Towards Pan-Africanism: Report from Addis Ababa, Ethiopia, December 1973, the Third International Congress of Africanists." *Black World* (March 1974): 71–76.

———, "Marcus Garvey: The Harlem Years." *Transition* no. 46 (1974): 14–15, 17–19.

———, "On 'The Cultural Unity of Africa.'" *Black World* 26, no. 4 (February 1975): 12–26.

Kelley, Robin D. G. "Dr. John Henrik Clarke, The Peoples' Scholar." *Black Issues Book Review* 1, no. 5 (September/October 1999): 15.

Newman, Richard. "John Henrik Clarke." *Transition* no. 77 (1998): 4–8.

Painter, Nell. "John Henrik Clarke, 1915–1998." *Crisis* (September/October 1998): 40.

Taped Lectures and Speeches

Clarke, John Henrik. "The Cultural Unity of African River Valley Civilizations." 17 March 1989, CD, available from Men of Respect Historical Society, New York, New York, http://www.menofrespect.com.

———, "Black People Need to Listen." Address to New York community audience, circa the early 1990s, DVD, available from the Nubian Network, http://www.blackconsciousness.com.

———, "The Preservers of Afrikan World History," address to New York community audience, circa 1990s, DVD, available from the Nubian Network, http://www.blackconsciousness.com.

———, "Global White Supremacy: From the End of the Nineteenth Century to the Middle of the Twentieth Century and the Afrikan Independence Explosion." Symposium on Global White Supremacy, United Afrikan Movement, Slave Theatre, Brooklyn, New York, 22 January 1992, DVD, available from http://www.tapvideo.com.

———, "The Search for the African State of Mind and Being through African Liberation," 16 January 1993, available from Men of Respect Historical Society, New York, New York, CD, http://www.menofrespect.com.

———, "Can Afrikan People Save Themselves?" Address to northern New Jersey community audience hosted by Afrikan Echoes, circa 1995, DVD, available from the Nubian Network, http://www.blackconsciousness.com.

———, "The Meaning of Malcolm X.," Video recording of a speech delivered in Harlem, New York City, unknown date.

Interviews, Questionnaire, and Oral Histories

Abdur-Raazaq, Abdullah. Oral Histories, The Malcolm X Project at Columbia University, http://www.columbia.edu/cu/mxp/araazaq.html.

Adams, Barbara Eleanor. *John Henrik Clarke: Master Teacher.* Brooklyn, NY: A&B Publishers, 2000.

Clarke, John Henrik. Questionnaire response to James Naazir Conyers, 18 September 1992.

Conyers, James E. Interview with Ahati N. N. Toure, 21 March 2003.

Davis, Ossie. Oral Histories, The Malcolm X Project at Columbia University, http://www.columbia.edu/cu/mxp/odavis.html.

Ferguson, Herman. Oral Histories, The Malcolm X Project at Columbia University, http://www.columbia.edu/cu/mxp/hferguson.html.

———, Telephone interview with Spartacus R, Global African Peoples' Radio, London, England, 2 August 2006.

Person-Lynn, Kwaku, ed. "On My Journey Now: The Narrative and Works of Dr. John Henrik Clarke, The Knowledge Revolutionary." *The Journal of Pan African Studies: A Journal of Africentric Theory, Methodology and Analysis* Special Issue, 1, no. 2 (Winter–Fall 2000) and 2, no. 1 (Spring–Summer 2001): 101–279.

Smith, Jimmi. Interview by Institute for Ethnic Studies, "The History of the Institute for Ethnic Studies," 7 June 2001, IES Archives.

Stanford, Max. Oral Histories, The Malcolm X Project at Columbia University, http://www.columbia.edu/cu/mxp/mstanford.html.

Swanston, Anna, ed. *Dr. John Henrik Clarke: His Life, His Words, His Works.* Atlanta, GA: I AM Unlimited, 2003.

Newspaper Articles

"Administration Meets with Black Candidate." *Daily Nebraskan*, 21 April 1969, 3.

"Afro Society's Twelve Demands to Bring University Response." *Daily Nebraskan*, 21 April 1969, cover.

"Black Students Skeptical, Will Adopt Wait-and-see Attitude – Williams." *Daily Nebraskan*, 23 April 1969, cover.

"Departments Join, Offer Negro History Course." *Daily Nebraskan*, 7 October 1968.

"Obituary: John Henrik Clarke." *New York Times*, 22 July 1998, A17.

A Constant Reader. "For Freedom's Journal." *Freedom's Journal*, 5 December 1828.

Boyd, Herb. "Clarke and Williams Solidify Union in Marriage." *New York Amsterdam News*, 25 September 1997, 3.

——, "Father History Passes." *New York Amsterdam News*, 23 July 1998, cover.

——, "Series of Special Programs Marks the Anniversary of Historian's Death." *New York Amsterdam News*, 15–21 July 1999, 9.

——, "Dr. Clarke Remembered." *New York Amsterdam News*, 20–26 July 2000, 8.

——, "137th Street to Be Renamed for John Henrik Clarke." *New York Amsterdam News*, 19–25 October 2000, 5.

——, "Harlem Scholar Remembered." *New York Amsterdam News*, 23–29 November 2000, 4.

——, "Hundreds Pay Tribute to Clarke." *New York Amsterdam News*, 19–25 July 2001, 6, 30.

——, "A Revered Elder at the Center of Controversy." *New York Amsterdam News*, 30 January–5 February 2003, 4, 30.

Bibliography

Clarke, John Henrik. "We See Ourselves in New Ways." *New York Times*, 15 June 1969, D19–20.

Dinkins, David N. "John Henrik Clarke's Legacy Will Continue to Enrich Us." *New York Amsterdam News*, 23 July 1998, 13.

Dvorak, John. "NU students protest administration's inability to provide relevant programs." *Daily Nebraskan*, 16 April 1969, cover.

———, "Black Students, Administration Meet; Regent Talk Scheduled for Saturday." *Daily Nebraskan*, 18 April 1969.

Gates, Henry Louis, Jr. "Black Demagogues and Pseudo-Scholars." *New York Times*, 20 July 1992, A15.

Horsford, Victoria. "John Henrik Clarke Royal Treatment at Movie Gala Preview." *New York Amsterdam News*, 7 June 1997, 5

Johnson, Rudy. "Parley Stresses African Heritage." *New York Times*, 10 May 1970, 59.

Johnson, Thomas A. "Blacks Interrupt Parley on Africa." *The New York Times*, 19 October 1969.

———, "Blacks Present Views on N. E. T." *New York Times*, 1 December 1970, 73.

Karriem, Bruce. "John Henrik Clarke: A Man for All Seasons." *New York Amsterdam News*, 23 July 1998, 12.

Katz, William Loren. "A Giant in Our Time." *New York Amsterdam News*, 23 July 1998, 12.

Kelley, Robin D. G. "Self-Made Angry Man." *New York Times Magazine*, 3 January 1999, SM17.

Labbe, Theola. "A Legacy Hidden in Plain Sight: Iraqis of African Descent Are a Largely Overlooked Link to Slavery." *Washington Post*, 11 January 2004, http://www.washingtonpost.com.

Pedersen, Jim. "Interdisciplinary course status of 'Negro culture' questioned." *Daily Nebraskan*, 21 February 1969, cover.

Scott, J. H. "Who Are We?" *The Christian Recorder*, 30 December 1880.

Sharpton, Al. "Dr. John Henrik Clarke." *New York Amsterdam News*, 23 July 1998, 13.

Stuckey, Sterling. "Black Studies and White Myths." *New York Times*, 13 February 1971, 27.

Thomas, Robert McG., Jr. "John Henrik Clarke, Black Studies Advocate, Dies at 83." *New York Times*, 20 July 1998, A13.

Turner, Henry McNeal. "A Great Book. Ought to be Read by Everybody – Only Those Blind to Their Interests Will Fail to Get It." *The Christian Recorder*, 30 September 1880.

Waddell, Bob. "Popular Black Studies Course Dropped Because of a 'Lack of Coordination.'" *Daily Nebraskan*, 6 July 1971, 4.

Websites

African Studies Association Presidents, http://www.africanstudies.org/ASA%20 Pres.htm.

Bradley, Michael. "The Iceman Inheritance: A Frightening Publication History of Jewish Media Suppression," http://www.michaelbradley.info/books/iceman/ iceman_promo.html.

Fordham University, http://www.fordham.edu/general/Orientation/Fordham_ at_a_Glance1625.html.

Global African Presence, http://www.cwo.com/~lucumi/runoko.html.

Kemetnu Productions, http://www.kemetnu.com/.

Nubian Network. "The Initiation Into Eternity for Dr. John Henrik Clarke, View 2." 21 July 1998, http://www.blackconsciousness.com/sshop/clark.html.

———, "The Initiation Into Eternity for Dr. John Henrik Clarke, View 3." 21 July 1998, http://www.blackconsciousness.com/sshop/clark.html.

———, "The Initiation Into Eternity for Dr. John Henrik Clarke, View 4." 21 July 1998, http://www.blackconsciousness.com/sshop/clark.html.

Person-Lynn, Dr. Kwaku, http://www.drkwaku.com/.

The Global Afrikan Congress (GAC), http://www.globalafrikancongress.com/ about/protocol.htm#Footnote.

Secondary Sources

Books

Anderson, James D. *The Education of Blacks in the South, 1860–1935*. Chapel Hill: The University of North Carolina Press, 1988.

Ani, Marimba. *Yurugu: An African-Centered Critique of European Cultural Thought and Behavior*. Trenton, NJ: Africa World Press, 1994.

Appleby, Joyce, Lynn Hunt, and Margaret Jacob. *Telling the Truth About History*. New York: W. W. Norton, 1994.

Aptheker, Herbert. *Afro-American History: The Modern Era*. New York: Carol Publishing Group, 1971.

———, ed. *A Documentary History of the Negro People in the United States, 1910–1932*. Vol. 3, *From the N.A.A.C.P. to the New Deal*. Secaucus, NJ: The Citadel Press, 1973.

———, ed. *A Documentary History of the Negro People in the United States*. Vol. 1, *From Colonial Times through the Civil War*. New York: Citadel Press, 1979.

Armah, Ayi Kwei. *Two Thousand Seasons*. Popenguine, Senegal: Per Ankh, 2000; originally Nairobi, Kenya: EAPH, 1973.

Asante, Molefi Kete. *Afrocentricity: The Theory of Social Change*. Buffalo, NY: Amulefi Publishing Company, 1980.

———, *The Afrocentric Idea*. Philadelphia, PA: Temple University Press, 1987.

———, *Kemet, Afrocentricity and Knowledge*. Trenton, NJ: Africa World Press, 1990.

———, *Afrocentricity: The Theory of Social Change*. Revised and expanded. Chicago: African American Images, 2003.

Bailey, James. *God-Kings and Titans: The New World Ascendancy in Ancient Times*. New York: St. Martin's Press, 1973.

Ball, Charles. *Slavery in the United States: A Narrative of the Life and Adventures of Charles Ball, A Black Man, Who Lived Forty Years in Maryland, South Carolina, and Georgia as a Slave*. Mineola, NY: Dover Publications, 1970; originally New York: John S. Taylor, 1837.

Bearden, Romare and Harry Henderson. *A History of African-American Artists: From 1792 to the Present*. New York: Pantheon Books, 1993.

Bell, Howard Holman, ed. *Minutes of the Proceedings of the National Negro Conventions, 1830–1864*. New York: Arno Press and The New York Times, 1969.

ben Jochannan, Yosef A. A. *African Origins of the Major "Western Religions"*. Vol. 1 of *The Black Man's Religion*. Baltimore: Black Classic Press, 1991; originally New York: Alkebu-lan Books Associates, 1970.

———, *Black Man of the Nile and His Family*. Baltimore: Black Classic Press, 1989; originally New York: Alkebu-lan Associates, 1970, 1972.

———, *Africa: Mother of Western Civilization*. Baltimore: Black Classic Press, 1988; originally New York: Alkebu-lan Book Associates, 1971.

———, *A Brief Chronology of the Development and History of the Old and New Testament: From Its African and Asian Origins to Its European and European-*

American Revisions, Versions, Etc. New York: Alkebu-lan Books Associates, 1973.

———, *Cultural Genocide in the Black and African Studies Curriculum*. New York: Alkebu-lan Books Associates, 1973.

———, *The Myth of Genesis and Exodus and the Exclusion of Their African Origins*. Vol. 2 of *The Black Man's Religion*. New York: Alkebu-lan Books Associates, 1974.

———, *The Need for a Black Bible*. Vol. 3 of *The Black Man's Religion*. New York: Alkebu-lan Books Associates, 1974.

———, *Understanding the African Philosophical Concept Behind "The Diagram of the Law of Opposites"*. New York: Alkebu-lan Books Associates, 1975.

———, *Our Black Seminarians and Black Clergy Without a Black Theology: The Tragedy of Black People/Africans in Religion Today*. Baltimore: Black Classic Press, 1998; originally New York: Alkebu-lan Book Associates, 1978.

———, *The Saga of the "Black Marxists" Versus the "Black Nationalists": A Debate Resurrected, Vol./Book 1–3*. New York: Alkebu-lan Books and Education Materials, 1978.

———, *In Pursuit of George G. M. James' Study of African Origins in "Western Civilization"*. New York: Alkebu-lan Books and Education Materials Associates, 1980.

———, *They All Look Alike! All of Them?* 4 vols. New York: Alkebu-lan Books and Education Materials Associates, 1980–1981.

———, *We the Black Jews*. Vols. 1–2. New York: Alkebu-lan Books and Education Materials Associates, 1983.

———, *Abu Simbel-Ghizeh: Guidebook/Manual*. New York: Alkebu-lan Books and Educational Materials, 1986.

———, *Influence of Great Myths of Contemporary Life: Or, The Need for Black History in Mental Health: A Sociopolitical and Anthropological Student's and Researcher's Edition*. New York: Alkebu-lan Books Associates, 1986.

———, *The African Mysteries System of Wa'Set, Egypt, and Its European Stepchild: "Greek Philosophy"*. New York: Alkebu-lan Books and Educational Materials, 1986.

———, *From Afrikan Captives to Insane Slaves: The Need for Afrikan History in Solving the "Black" Mental Health Crisis in "America" and the World*. Richmond, VA: Native Sun Publishers, 1992.

ben Jochannan, Yosef A. A. and George E. Simmonds. *The Black Man's North and East Africa*. New York: Alkebu-lan Books Associates, 1971.

Blassingame, John W. *The Slave Community: Plantation Life in the Antebellum South*. New York: Oxford University Press, 1972, 1979.

Bloom, Allan David. *The Closing of the American Mind: How Higher Education Has Failed Democracy and Impoverished the Souls of Today's Students*. New York: Simon & Schuster, 1987.

Blyden, Edward Wilmot. *Christianity, Islam and the Negro Race*. 2nd ed. Baltimore: Black Classic Press; originally London, W. B. Whittingham & Co., 1888.

Bolden, Tonya. *Strong Men Keep Coming: The Book of African American Men*. New York: John Wiley and Sons, 1999.

Bowser, Benjamin P. and Louis Kushnick, with Paul Grant, ed. *Against the Odds: Scholars Who Challenged Racism in the Twentieth Century*. Amherst and Boston: University of Massachusetts Press, 2002.

Bradley, Michael. *The Iceman Inheritance: Prehistoric Sources of Western Man's Racism, Sexism and Aggression*. New York: Warner Books, 1978; originally Toronto: Dorset, 1978.

Brent, Linda. *Incidents in the Life of a Slave Girl, Written by Herself*. In *The Classic Slave Narratives*. Edited by Henry Louis Gates, Jr. New York: Mentor, 1987.

Brown, William Wells. *The Black Man: His Antecedents, His Genius, and His Achievements*. New York: Thomas Hamilton, and Boston: R. F. Wallcut, 1863.

————, *The Negro in the American Rebellion: His Heroism and His Fidelity*. Boston: Lee Shepard, 1867.

————, *The Rising Sun; or, The Antecedents and Advancement of the Colored Race*. Boston: A.G. Brown and Company, Publishers, 1874.

Burgess, John W. *Reconstruction and the Constitution, 1866–1876*. New York: C. Scribner's Sons, 1902.

Cabral, Amilcar. *Return to the Source: Selected Speeches of Amilcar Cabral*. Edited by Africa Information Service. New York: Monthly Review Press, 1973.

Campbell, Mavis Christine. *The Maroons of Jamaica, 1655–1796: A History of Resistance, Collaboration and Betrayal*. Granby, MA: Bergin & Garvey, 1988.

Churchill, Ward and Jim Vander Wall. *The COINTELPRO Papers: Documents from the FBI's Secret Wars Against Dissent in the United States*. 2nd ed. Boston: South End Press, 2002.

Conyers, James L., Jr., ed. *Charles H. Wesley: The Intellectual Tradition of a Black Historian*. New York: Garland, 1997.

————, ed. *Carter G. Woodson: A Historical Reader*. New York: Garland, 2000.

————, ed. *Black Cultures and Race Relations*. Chicago: Burnham, 2002.

————, ed. *Afrocentricity and the Academy: Essays on Theory and Practice.* Jefferson, NC: McFarland, 2003.

Conyers, James L., Jr., and Julius E. Thompson, ed. *Pan African Nationalism in the Americas: The Life and Times of John Henrik Clarke.* Trenton, NJ: Africa World Press, 2004.

Dallas, Robert Charles. *The History of the Maroons, from Their Origin to the Establishment of Their Chief Tribe at Sierra Leone, including the Expedition to Cuba for the Purpose of Procuring Spanish Chasseurs and the State of the Island of Jamaica for the Last Ten Years with a Succinct History of the Island Previous to that Period.* London: Cass, 1968.

Danquah, Joseph Boakye. *The Ghanaian Establishment: Its Constitution, Its Detentions, Its Traditions, Its Justice and Statecraft, and Its Heritage of Ghanaism.* Edited by Albert Adu Boahen. Accra: Ghana Universities Press, 1997.

de Graft-Johnson, John Coleman. *African Glory: The Story of Vanished Negro Civilizations.* London: Watts, 1954.

de Groot, Silvia W. *From Isolation Towards Integration: The Surinam Maroons and Their Colonial Rulers: Official Documents Relating to the Djukas, 1845–1863.* The Hague, Netherlands: Nijhoff, 1977.

de Tocqueville, Alexis. *Democracy in America.* Edited by J. P. Mayer and Max Lerner and translated by George Lawrence. New York: Harper & Row, 1966.

Delany, Martin R. *The Origin of Races and Color.* Baltimore: Black Classic Press, 1991; originally *Principia of Ethnology: The Origin of Races and Color, with an Archeological Compendium of Ethiopian and Egyptian Civilization, from Years of Careful Examination and Enquiry.* Philadelphia: Harper & Brother, Publishers, 1879.

Diamond, Jared. *Guns, Germs, and Steel: The Fates of Human Societies.* New York: W. W. Norton, 1999.

Diop, Cheikh Anta. *African Origin of Civilization: Myth or Reality.* Edited and translated by Mercer Cook. New York: Lawrence Hill Books, 1974.

————, *Black Africa: The Economic and Cultural Basis for a Federated State.* Translated by Harold J. Salemson. Westport, CT: Lawrence Hill Books, 1978.

————, *The Cultural Unity of Black Africa.* Chicago: Third World Press, 1978.

Douglass, Frederick. *Narrative of the Life of Frederick Douglass, an American Slave, Written by Himself.* Edited by Houston A. Baker, Jr. New York: Penguin Books, 1982.

Du Bois, W. E. B. *Black Reconstruction in America: An Essay Toward a History of the Part Which Black Folk Played in the Attempt to Reconstruct Democracy in America, 1860–1880.* New York: Russell and Russell, 1962; originally 1935.

———, *The Education of Black People: Ten Critiques, 1906–1960.* Edited by Herbert Aptheker. New York: Monthly Review Press, 2001.

———, *The Negro.* Philadelphia: University of Pennsylvania Press, 2001; originally New York: Henry Holt, 1915.

Dubois, Laurent. *Avengers of the New World: The Story of the Haitian Revolution.* Cambridge, MA: The Belknap Press of Harvard University Press, 2004.

Dubois, Laurent and John D. Garrigus, ed. *Slave Revolution in the Caribbean 1789–1804: A Brief History with Documents.* Boston/New York: Bedford/St. Martin's, 2006.

Ernest, John. *Liberation Historiography: African American Writers and the Challenge of History, 1794–1861.* Chapel Hill: The University of North Carolina Press, 2004.

Evanzz, Karl. *The Judas Factor: The Plot to Kill Malcolm X.* New York: Thunder's Mouth Press, 1992.

Falade, Fasina. *Ifa: The Key to Its Understanding.* Lynwood, CA: Ara Ifa Publishing, 2002.

Falola, Toyin. *Yoruba Gurus: Indigenous Production of Knowledge in Africa.* Trenton, NJ: Africa World Press, 1999.

Finkelstein, Norman G. *Beyond Chutzpah: On the Misuse of Anti-Semitism and the Abuse of History.* Berkeley and Los Angeles: University of California Press, 2005.

Foner, Philip S., ed. *Frederick Douglass: Selections from His Writings.* New York: International Publishers, 1945.

Franklin, John Hope and Albert A. Moss, Jr. *From Slavery to Freedom: A History of African Americans.* 7th ed. New York: Alfred A. Knopf, 1994.

Frazer, Sir James George. *Folk-lore in the Old Testament: Studies in Comparative Religion, Legend and Law.* London: Macmillan, 1918.

Frederickson, George M. *The Black Image in the White Mind: The Debate on Afro-American Character and Destiny, 1817–1914.* New York: Harper Torchbooks, 1971.

Garrow, David J. *Bearing the Cross: Martin Luther King, Jr., and the Southern Christian Leadership Conference.* New York: William Morrow, 1986.

Gomez, Michael A. *Exchanging Our Country Marks: The Transformation of African Identities in the Colonial and Antebellum South*. Chapel Hill: The University of North Carolina Press, 1998.

Gould, Julius and William L. Kolb, ed. *A Dictionary of the Social Sciences*. New York: UNESCO and The Free Press, 1964.

Gould, Stephen Jay. *The Mismeasure of Man*. New York: W. W. Norton, 1981.

Graves, Robert and Raphael Patai. *Hebrew Myths: The Book of Genesis*. New York: McGraw-Hill, 1964.

Greene, Harry Washington. *Holders of Doctorates Among American Negroes: An Educational and Social Study of Negroes Who Have Earned Doctoral Degrees in Course, 1876–1943*. Boston: Meador Publishing Company, Publishers, 1946.

Griffith, Cyril E. *The African Dream: Martin R. Delany and the Emergence of Pan African Thought*. University Park: The Pennsylvania State University Press, 1975.

Harris, Joseph E., ed. *Pillars in Ethiopian History: The William Leo Hansberry African History Notebook*. Vol. 1. Washington, DC: Howard University Press, 1974.

———, ed. *Africa and Africans As Seen by Classical Writers: The William Leo Hansberry African History Notebook*. Vol. 2. Washington, DC: Howard University Press, 1977.

Hegel, Georg Wilhelm Friedrich. *Philosophy of History*. Translated by J. Sibree. New York: P. F. Collier and Son; London: The Colonial Press, 1900.

Hilliard, Asa G. *The Maroon Within Us: Selected Essays on African American Community Socialization*. Baltimore: Black Classic Press, 1995.

———, *African Power: Affirming African Indigenous Socialization in the Face of the Culture Wars*. Gainesville, FL: Makare Publishing, 2002.

Hine, Darlene Clark, ed. *The State of Afro-American History: Past, Present, and Future*. Baton Rouge: Louisiana State University Press, 1986.

Holloway, Joseph E. and Winifred K. Vass. *The African Heritage of American English*. Bloomington and Indianapolis: Indiana University Press, 1993.

Hornsby, Alton, ed. *Essays in African American Historiography and Methodology*. Acton, MA: Copley, 2004.

Huntington, Samuel P. *The Clash of Civilizations and the Remaking of the World Order*. New York: Touchstone, 1996.

———, *Who Are We?: The Challenges to America's National Identity*. New York: Simon & Schuster, 2004.

Jackson, John G. *Was Jesus Christ a Negro? and, The African Origin of the Myths and Legends of the Garden of Eden: Two Rationalistic Views.* New York: published by the author; Wilson [printer], 1933.

———, *Christianity Before Christ.* New York: Blyden Society, 1938.

———, *Ethiopia and the Origin of Civilization: A Critical Review of the Evidence of Archaeology, Anthropology, History and Comparative Religion, According to the Most Reliable Sources and Authorities.* New York: Blyden Society, 1939.

———, *Pagan Origins of the Christ Myth.* New York: Truth Seeker Co., 1941.

———, *Introduction to African Civilizations.* New York: Kensington Publishing, 1970.

———, *Man, God, and Civilization.* New Hyde Park, NY: University Books, 1972.

———, *Black Reconstruction in South Carolina.* Austin, TX: American Atheist Press, 1987.

———, *Hubert Henry Harrison: The Black Socrates.* Austin, TX: American Atheist Press, 1987.

———, *The Golden Ages of Africa.* Austin, TX: American Atheist Press, 1987.

———, *Ages of Gold and Silver and Other Short Sketches of Human History.* Austin, TX: American Atheist Press, 1990.

———, *The Mysteries of Egypt.* Chicago Heights, IL: L & P Enterprises, 1990s.

James, C. L. R. *The Black Jacobins: Toussaint L'Ouverture and the San Domingo Revolution.* 2nd ed. New York: Vintage Books, 1963.

Jennings, La Vinia Delois. "Chancellor Williams." *Dictionary of Literary Biography.* Vol. 76, *Afro-American Writers, 1940–1955*, edited by Trudier Harris, 196–199. The Gale Group, 1988.

Jordan, Winthrop. *The White Man's Burden: Historical Origins of Racism in the United States.* New York: Oxford University Press, 1974.

July, Robert W. *A History of the African People.* 5th ed. Prospect Heights, IL: Waveland Press, 1998.

Karenga, Maulana. *Odu Ifa: The Ethical Teachings.* Los Angeles: University of Sankore Press, 1999.

———, *Introduction to Black Studies.* 3rd ed. Los Angeles: University of Sankore Press, 2002.

———, *Maat, The Moral Ideal in Ancient Egypt: A Study in Classical African Ethics.* New York: Routledge, 2004.

Karenga, Maulana and Jacob H. Carruthers, ed. *Kemet and the African Worldview: Research, Rescue and Restoration*. Los Angeles: University of Sankore Press, 1986.

Keita, Maghan. *Race and the Writing of History: Riddling the Sphinx*. New York: Oxford University Press, 2000.

King, Martin Luther, Jr. *Where Do We Go from Here: Chaos or Community?* Boston: Beacon Press, 1967.

Kinshasa, Kwando M. *Emigration vs. Assimilation: The Debate in the African American Press, 1827–1861*. Jefferson, NC: McFarland, 1988.

Kotkin, Joel. *Tribes: How Race, Religion, and Identity Determine Success in the New Global Economy*. New York: Random House, 1992.

Lewis, R. B. *Light and Truth: Containing the Universal History of the Colored and Indian Race, from the Creation of the World to the Present Time*. Boston: Published by a Committee of Colored Gentlemen, Benjamin F. Roberts, Printer, 1844.

Martin, Tony. *Race First: The Ideological and Organizational Struggles of Marcus Garvey and the Universal Negro Improvement Association*. Westport, CT: Greenwood Press, 1976.

———, *The Pan-African Connection: From Slavery to Garvey and Beyond*. Dover, MA: The Majority Press, 1983.

Massey, Gerald. *A Book of the Beginnings: Containing an Attempt to Recover and Reconstitute the Lost Origines of the Myths and Mysteries, Types and Symbols, Religion and Language, with Egypt for the Mouthpiece and Africa as the Birthplace*. London: Williams & Norgate 1881.

Meier, August, and Elliott Rudwick. *Black History and the Historical Profession, 1915–1980*. Urbana and Chicago: University of Illinois Press, 1986.

Miller, John J. *Alternatives to Afrocentrism*. Washington, DC: Center for the New American Community, Manhattan Institute, 1994.

———, *Alternatives to Afrocentrism*. 2nd ed. Washington, DC: Center for Equal Opportunity, 1996.

———, *The Unmaking of Americans: How Multiculturalism Has Undermined the Assimilation Ethic*. New York: Free Press, 1998.

Mitchell, B. R., ed. *International Historical Statistics, The Americas, 1750–1988*. New York: Stockton Press, 1993.

Moore, Richard. *The Name Negro: Its Origin and Evil Use*. New York: Afroamerican Publishers, 1960.

Nell, William C. *The Colored Patriots of the American Revolution: With Sketches of Several Distinguished Colored Persons: To Which Is Added a Brief Survey of the Condition and Prospects of Colored Americans.* Boston: Robert F. Wallcut, 1855.

Ochsner, David, ed. *A Century of Achievement: One Hundred Years of Graduate Education, Research, and Creative Activity.* Lincoln: University of Nebraska, 2001.

Omer-Cooper, J. D. *History of Southern Africa.* 2nd ed. Portsmouth, NH: Heinemann, 1994.

Painter, Nell Irvin. *Exodusters: Black Migration to Kansas after Reconstruction.* New York: W. W. Norton, 1976, 1986.

Pennington, James W. C. *A Text Book of the Origin and History, etc., etc. of the Colored People.* Hartford, CT: L. Skinner, Printer, 1841; reprint Detroit: Negro History Press, n.d.

Person-Lynn, Kwaku, ed. *First Word: Black Scholars, Thinkers, Warriors, Knowledge, Wisdom, Mental Liberation.* New York: Harlem River Press, 1996.

Price, Richard. *The Guiana Maroons: A Historical and Bibliographical Introduction.* Baltimore: Johns Hopkins University Press, 1976.

———, ed. *Maroon Societies: Rebel Slave Communities in the Americas.* 3rd ed. Baltimore: The Johns Hopkins University Press, 1996.

Quarles, Benjamin. *The Negro in the Making of America.* New York: Macmillan, 1969.

———, *Black Mosaic: Essays in Afro-American History and Historiography.* Amherst: The University of Massachusetts Press, 1988.

Rogers, J. A. *As Nature Leads: An Informal Discussion of the Reason Why Negro and Caucasian are Mixing in spite of Opposition.* Chicago: Printed by M.A. Donohue & Co., 1919.

———, *The Ku Klux Spirit: A Brief Outline of the History of the Ku Klux Klan Past and Present.* New York: Messenger Pub. Co., 1923.

———, *From "Superman" to Man.* New York: Lenox Pub. Co., 1924.

———, *The Real Facts About Ethiopia.* New York: J.A. Rogers Publications, 1936.

———, *Sex and Race: Negro-Caucasian Mixing in All Ages and All Lands.* Vol. 1, *The Old World.* New York: J. A. Rogers Publications, 1940.

———, *Your History from the Beginning of Time to the Present.* Pittsburgh, PA: The Pittsburgh Courier, 1940.

————, *Sex and Race: A History of White, Negro, and Indian Miscegenation in the Two Americas*. Vol. 2, *The New World*. New York: J. A. Rogers Publications, 1942.

————, *Sex and Race: Why White and Black Mix in spite of Opposition*. Vol. 3. New York: J. A. Rogers Publications, 1944.

————, *World's Great Men of Color*. Vol. 1. Edited by John Henrik Clarke. New York: Touchstone, 1996; originally New York: J. A. Rogers Publications, 1946.

————, *Nature Knows No Color-Line: Research into the Negro Ancestry in the White Race*. New York: J. A. Rogers Publications, 1952.

————, *100 Amazing Facts about the Negro: With Complete Proof: A Short Cut to the World History of the Negro*. New York: H. M. Rogers, 1957.

————, *Africa's Gift to America: The Afro-American in the Making and Saving of the United States*. New York: J. A. Rogers Publications, 1959.

————, *The Five Negro Presidents: According to What White People Said They Were*. New York: Helga M. Rogers, 1965.

————, *World's Great Men of Color*. Vol. 2. New York: Macmillan, 1972.

Sales, William W., Jr. *From Civil Rights to Black Liberation: Malcolm X and the Organization of Afro-American Unity*. Boston: South End Press, 1994.

Sanneh, Lamin O. *Abolitionists Abroad: American Blacks and the Making of Modern West Africa*. Cambridge, MA: Harvard University Press, 1999.

Schlesinger, Arthur M., Jr. *The Disuniting of America: Reflections on a Multicultural Society*. New York: W. W. Norton, 1991, 1998.

Scott, William R. *The Sons of Sheba's Race: African-Americans and the Italo-Ethiopian War, 1935–1941*. Bloomington and Indianapolis: Indiana University Press, 1993.

Sinnette, Elinor Des Verney. *Arthur Alfonso Schomburg: Black Bibliophile and Collector: A Biography*. New York: The New York Public Library and Detroit: Wayne State University Press, 1989.

Some, Malidoma Patrice. *Of Water and the Spirit: Ritual, Magic, and Initiation in the Life of an African Shaman*. New York: Arkana, 1995.

Stuckey, Sterling. *Slave Culture: Nationalist Theory and Foundations of Black America*. New York: Oxford University Press, 1987.

T'Shaka, Oba. *Return to the African Mother Principle of Male and Female Equality*. Vol. 1. Oakland, CA: Pan Afrikan Publishers, 1995.

Takaki, Ronald. *Iron Cages: Race and Culture in 19th Century America*. New York: Oxford University Press, 1990.

Thompson, Alvin O. *Flight to Freedom: African Runaways and Maroons in the Americas*. Kingston, Jamaica: University of West Indies Press, 2006.

Thorpe, Earl E. *Negro Historians in the United States*. Baton Rouge, LA: Fraternal Press, 1958.

———, *The Central Theme of Black History*. Durham, NC: Seeman Printery, 1969.

———, *Black Historians: A Critique*. New York: William Morrow and Company, 1971.

Toynbee, Arnold J. *A Study of History*. Vols. 1–6, abridged. New York: Oxford University Press, 1947.

Trevor-Roper, Hugh. *The Rise of Christian Europe*. New York: Harcourt, Brace & World; London: Thames and Hudson, 1965.

Turner, Lorenzo Dow. *Africanisms in the Gullah Dialect*. Chicago: University of Chicago Press, 1949.

Vaillant, Janet G. *Black, French, and African: A Life of Leopold Sedar Senghor*. Cambridge, MA: Harvard University Press, 1990.

Vass, Winifred Kellersberger. *The Bantu Speaking Heritage of the United States*. Los Angeles: Center for Afro-American Studies, University of California, 1979.

Von Wuthenau, Alexander. *The Art of Terracotta Pottery in Pre-Columbian Central and South America*. New York: Crown Publishers, 1970.

Walker, Clarence E. *We Can't Go Home Again: An Argument about Afrocentrism*. New York: Oxford University Press, 2001.

Walters, Ronald W. *Pan Africanism in the African Diaspora: An Analysis of Modern Afrocentric Political Movements*. Detroit: Wayne State University Press, 1993.

Washington, James M., ed. *A Testament of Hope: The Essential Writings and Speeches of Martin Luther King, Jr.* New York: HarperSanFrancisco, 1986.

Weinstein, Brian. *Eboue*. New York: Oxford University Press, 1972.

Wiener, Leo. *Africa and the Discovery of America*. Philadelphia: Innes and Sons, 1920–1922.

Williams, Chancellor. *The Destruction of Black Civilization: Great Issues of a Race from 4500 B.C. to 2000 A.D.* Chicago: Third World Press, 1987; originally Dubuque, IA: Kendall-Hunt, 1971.

Williams, George Washington. *A History of the Negro Race in America from 1619 to 1880. Negroes as Slaves, as Soldiers, and as Citizens; together with a Preliminary Consideration of the Unity of the Human Family, an Historical Sketch of Africa, and an Account of the Negro Governments of Sierra Leone and Liberia*. 2 vols., vol. 1. New York: G.P. Putnam's Sons, 1883.

————, *A History of the Negro Troops in the War of the Rebellion, 1861–1865, Preceded by a Review of the Military Services of Negroes in Ancient and Modern Times.* New York: Harper Brothers, 1888.

Wilson, Amos N. *The Falsification of Afrikan Consciousness: Eurocentric History, Psychiatry and the Politics of White Supremacy.* Brooklyn, NY: Afrikan World InfoSystems, 1993.

————, *Blueprint for Black Power: A Moral, Political and Economic Imperative for the Twenty-First Century.* Brooklyn, NY: Afrikan World InfoSystems, 1998.

————, *Afrikan-Centered Consciousness versus the New World Order: Garveyism in the Age of Globalism.* Brooklyn, NY: Afrikan World InfoSystems, 1999.

Wilson, Joseph T. *The Black Phalanx: A History of the Negro Soldiers of the United States in the Wars of 1775–1812, 1861–'65.* Hartford, CT: American Publishing Company, 1888; reprint New York: Arno Press, Inc. and The New York Times, 1968.

————, *Emancipation: Its Course and Progress, from 1481 B.C. to A.D. 1875, with a Review of President Lincoln's Proclamation, the XIII Amendment, and the Progress of the Emancipation Monument.* Hampton, VA: Normal School Steam Press Print, 1882; reprint New York: Negro Universities Press, 1969.

Woodson, Carter Godwin. *The Miseducation of the Negro.* New York: AMS Press, 1977; originally Washington, DC: The Associated Publishers, 1933.

————, *The African Background Outlined; or, Handbook for the Study of the Negro.* Washington, DC: Association for the Study of Negro Life and History, 1936.

Wright, W. D. *Black History and Black Identity: A Call for a New Historiography.* Westport, CT: Praeger, 2002.

Book Chapters

Aldridge, Delores P. "Womanist Issues in Black Studies: Towards Integrating Africana Womanism into Africana Studies." In *Africana Studies: A Disciplinary Quest for Both Theory and Method,* edited by James L. Conyers, Jr., 143–154. Jefferson, NC: McFarland, 1997.

Asante, Molefi K. "Afrocentricity and the Quest for Method." In *Africana Studies: A Disciplinary Quest for Both Theory and Method,* edited by James L. Conyers, Jr., 69–90. Jefferson, NC: McFarland, 1997.

Conyers, James L., Jr. "John Henrik Clarke and Africana History: A Bibliographical Essay." In *Pan African Nationalism in the Americas: The Life and Times of*

John Henrik Clarke, edited by James L. Conyers, Jr., and Julius E. Thompson, 21–34. Trenton, NJ: Africa World Press, 2004.

Donaldson, Shawn R. "'Feminist' or 'Womanist'? A Black Woman Defining Self." In *Africana Studies: A Disciplinary Quest for Both Theory and Method*, edited by James L. Conyers, Jr., 175–179. Jefferson, NC: McFarland, 1997.

Gordon, Vivian. "Black Women, Feminism, and Black Liberation: Which Way?" In *Africana Studies: A Disciplinary Quest for Both Theory and Method*, edited by James L. Conyers, Jr., 155–174. Jefferson, NC: McFarland, 1997.

Harris, Joseph E. "Profile of a Pioneer Africanist." In *Pillars in Ethiopian History: The William Leo Hansberry African History Notebook*. Vol. 1, edited by Joseph E. Harris, 3–30. Washington, DC: Howard University Press, 1974.

Holloway, Joseph E. "Africanisms in African American Names in the United States." In *Africanisms in American Culture*. 2nd ed., edited by Joseph E. Holloway, 82–110. Bloomington and Indianapolis: Indiana University Press, 2005.

Huggins, Nathan I. "Integrating Afro-American History." In *The State of Afro-American History: Past, Present, and Future*, edited by Darlene Clark Hine, 157–168. Baton Rouge: Louisiana State University Press, 1986.

Inikori, Joseph E. "Slavery in Africa and the Transatlantic Slave Trade." In *The African Diaspora*, edited by Alusine Jalloh and Stephen E. Maizlish, 39–72. College Station: Texas A & M University Press, 1996.

Laurence, Ken. "Academics: An Overview." In *Dirty Work 2: The CIA in Africa*, edited by Ellen Ray, William Schaep, Karl Van Meter, and Louis Wolf, 80–86. Secaucus, NJ: Lyle Stuart, 1979.

Mayfield, Julian. "Into the Mainstream and Oblivion." In *The American Negro Writer and His Roots*, edited by American Society of African Culture, 29–34. New York: American Society of African Culture, 1960.

Mazama, Ama. "The Afrocentric Paradigm." In *The Afrocentric Paradigm*, edited by Ama Mazama, 3–34. Trenton, NJ: Africa World Press, 2003.

Mazrui, Ali A. Introduction to *UNESCO General History of Africa*. Vol. 8, *Africa Since 1935*, edited by Ali A. Mazrui and C. Wondji, 1–25. Berkeley: The University of California Press; Oxford: James Currey; Paris: UNESCO, 1993, 1999.

Opoku, Agyeman. "Pan-Africanism Versus Pan-Arabism: A Dual Asymmetrical Model of Political Relations." In *The Middle East Reader*, edited by Michael Curtis, 21–46. New Brunswick, NJ: Transaction, 1986.

Patterson, Raymond R. "John Henrik Clarke's Rebellion in Rhyme." In *Pan African Nationalism in the Americas: The Life and Times of John Henrik Clarke*, edited by James L. Conyers, Jr., and Julius E. Thompson, 35–40. Trenton, NJ: Africa World Press, 2004.

Rabaka, Reiland. "W. E. B. Du Bois and/as Africana Critical Theory: Pan-Africanism, Critical Marxism, and Male Feminism." In *Afrocentricity and the Academy: Essays on Theory and Practice*, edited by James L. Conyers, Jr., 67–112. Jefferson, NC: McFarland, 2003.

Rashidi, Runoko. "Notes on Black Scholars of the Moors in John G. Jackson's Life." In *Golden Age of the Moor*, edited by Ivan Van Sertima, 89–92. New Brunswick, NJ: Transaction, 1992.

———, "Dedication and Tribute: The Passing of Giants: John G. Jackson and Chancellor Williams." In *African Presence in Early Asia*, edited by Runoko Rashidi and Ivan Van Sertima, 19–20. New Brunswick, NJ: Transaction, 1995.

———, "William Leo Hansberry (1894–1965): Hero and Mentor of Dr. Chancellor Williams." In *Egypt: Child of Africa*, edited by Ivan Van Sertima, 25–26. New Brunswick, NJ: Transaction, 1995.

Toure, Ahati N. N. "On the Myth of Male Supremacy: Adam and Eve and the Imperative of a New Afrikan-Centered Epistemology of Gender." In *Africana Studies: A Disciplinary Quest for Both Theory and Method*, edited by James L. Conyers, Jr., 180-192. Jefferson, NC: McFarland, 1997.

———, "Nineteenth Century African Historians in the United States: Explorations of Cultural Location and National Destiny." In *Black Cultures and Race Relations*, edited by James L. Conyers, Jr., 16–50. Chicago: Burnham, 2002.

———, "John Henrik Clarke and Issues in Afrikan Historiography: Implications of Pan Afrikan Nationalism in Interpreting the Afrikan Experience in the United States." In *Pan African Nationalism in the Americas: The Life and Times of John Henrik Clarke*, edited by James L. Conyers, Jr., and Julius E. Thompson, 1–19. Trenton, NJ: Africa World Press, 2004.

Journal Essays

"Vital Signs: The Statistics That Describe the Present and Suggest the Future of African Americans in Higher Education." *The Journal of Blacks in Higher Education* no. 15 (Spring 1997): 73–79.

Bibliography

Abdel-Rahman, Mohamed E. "Interactions Between Africans North and South of the Sahara." *Journal of Black Studies* 3, no. 2 (December 1972): 131–147.

Ajayi, J. F. Ade. "The Place of African History and Culture in the Process of Nation-Building in Africa South of the Sahara." *Journal of Negro Education* 30, no. 3 (Summer 1961): 206–213.

Akpan, M. B. "Liberia and the Universal Negro Improvement Association: The Background to the Abortion of Garvey's Scheme for African Colonization." *Journal of African History* 14, no. 1 (1973): 105–127.

Alford, Kwame Wes. "The Early Intellectual Growth and Development of William Leo Hansberry and the Birth of African Studies," 30, no. 3 *Journal of Black Studies* (January 2000): 269–293.

Anderson, Robert Nelson. "The Quilombo of Palmares: A New Overview of a Maroon State in Seventeenth-Century Brazil." *Journal of Latin American Studies* 28, no. 3 (October 1996): 545–566.

Asante, Molefi Kete. "The Ideological Significance of Afrocentricity in Intercultural Communication." *Journal of Black Studies* 14, no. 1 (September 1983): 3–19.

———, "The Afrocentric Idea in Education." *Journal of Negro Education.* 60, no. 2 (Spring 1991): 170–180.

———, "A Discourse on Black Studies: Liberating the Study of African People in the Western Academy." *Journal of Black Studies* 36, no. 5 (May 2006): 646–662.

Baur, John Edward. "Mulatto Machiavelli, Jean Pierre Boyer, and The Haiti of His Day." *Journal of Negro History* 32, no. 3 (July 1947): 307–353.

Bell, Howard H. "The Negro Emigration Movement, 1849–1854: A Phase of Negro Nationalism." *Phylon Quarterly* 20, no. 2 (2nd Quarter 1959): 132–142.

Bellegarde, Dantes. "President Alexandre Petion." *Phylon* 2, no. 3 (3rd Quarter 1941): 201–202, 205–213.

Bilby, Kenneth. "Swearing by the Past, Swearing to the Future: Sacred Oaths, Alliances, and Treaties among the Guianese and Jamaican Maroons." *Ethnohistory* 44, no. 4 (Autumn 1997): 655–689.

Bittle, William E. and Gilbert L. Geis. "Alfred Charles Sam and an African Return: A Case Study in Negro Despair." *Phylon* 23, no. 2 (2nd Quarter 1962): 178–194.

Blackett, Richard. "Martin R. Delany and Robert Campbell: Black Americans in Search of an African Colony." *Journal of Negro History* 62, no. 1 (January 1977): 1–25.

———, "Return to the Motherland: Robert Campbell, a Jamaican in Early Colonial Lagos." *Phylon* 40, no. 4 (4th Quarter 1979): 375–386.

Brock, Lisa. "Questioning the Diaspora: Hegemony, Black Intellectuals and Doing International History from Below," *Issue: A Journal of Opinion* 24, no. 2 (1996): 9–12.

Brooks, George E., Jr. "The Providence African Society's Sierra Leone Emigration Scheme, 1794–1795: Prologue to the African Colonization Movement." *International Journal of African Historical Studies* 7, no. 2 (1974):183–202.

Bruce, Dickson D., Jr. "The Ironic Conception of American History: The Early Black Historians, 1883–1915." *Journal of Negro History* 69, no. 2 (Spring 1984): 53–62.

Burrow, Rufus, Jr. "The Afrikan Legacy in Personalism." *Western Journal of Black Studies* 26, no. 2 (Summer 2002): 107–118.

———, "Martin Luther King, Jr.'s Doctrine of Human Dignity." *Western Journal of Black Studies* 26, no. 4 (Winter 2002): 228–239.

Butchart, Ronald E. "'Outthinking and Outflanking the Owners of the World': A Historiography of the African American Struggle for Education." *History of Education Quarterly* 28, no. 3 (Fall 1988): 333–366.

Cannon, J. Alfred. "Re-Africanization: The Last Alternative for Black America." *Phylon* 38, no. 2 (2nd Quarter 1977): 203–210.

Coleman, Edward M. "William Wells Brown as an Historian." *Journal of Negro History* 31, no. 1 (January 1946): 47–59.

Cruz-Carretero, Sagrario. "Yanga and the Black Origins of Mexico." *Review of Black Political Economy* 33, no. 1 (Summer 2005): 73–77.

Debo, Annette. "Signifying *AFRIKA*: Gwendolyn Brooks' Later Poetry." *Callaloo* 29, no. 1 (2006): 168–181.

Diggs, Irene. "Zumbi and the Republic of Os Palmares." *Phylon* 14, no. 1 (1st Quarter 1953): 62–70.

DjeDje, Jacqueline Cogdell. "Remembering Kojo: History, Music, and Gender in the January Sixth Celebration of the Jamaican Accompong Maroons." *Black Music Research Journal* 18, no. 1/2 (Spring 1998): 67–120.

Dove, Nah. "African Womanism: An Afrocentric Theory." *Journal of Black Studies* 28, no. 5 (May 1998): 515–539.

————, "Defining a Mother-Centered Matrix to Analyze the Status of Women." *Journal of Black Studies* 33, no. 1 (September 2002): 3–24.

Ennes, Ernesto. "The Palmares 'Republic' of Pernambuco Its Final Destruction, 1697." *The Americas* 5, no. 2 (October 1948): 200–216.

Erhagbe, Edward O. "African-Americans and the Defense of African States Against European Imperial Conquest: Booker T. Washington's Diplomatic Efforts to Guarantee Liberia's Independence, 1907–1911." *African Studies Review* 39, no. 1 (April 1996): 55–65.

Ferguson, Herman. "The Price of Freedom," *Souls* 7, no. 1 (2005): 84–106.

Franklin, John Hope. "George Washington Williams, Historian." *Journal of Negro History* 31, no. 1 (January 1946): 60–90.

Goines, Leonard. "Africanisms among the Bush Negroes of Surinam." *The Black Perspective in Music* 3, no. 1 (Spring 1975): 40–44.

Guzman, Jessie P. "W. E. B. Du Bois -- The Historian." *Journal of Negro History* 30, no. 4 (Autumn 1961): 377–385.

Hall, N. A. T. "Maritime Maroons: 'Grand Marronage' from the Danish West Indies." *William and Mary Quarterly* 42, no. 4 (October 1985): 476–498.

Harris, Robert L., Jr. "Coming of Age: The Transformation of Afro-American Historiography." *Journal of Negro History* 67, no. 2 (Summer 1982): 107–121.

————, "In Memoriam: Dr. John Henrik Clarke, 1915–1998." *Journal of Negro History* 83, no. 4 (Autumn 1998): 311–312.

Henriksen, Thomas H. "African Intellectual Influences on Black Americans: The Role of Edward W. Blyden." *Phylon* 36, no. 3 (3rd Quarter 1975): 279–290.

Jackson, John G. "Egypt and Christianity." *Journal of African Civilizations* 4, no. 2 (November 1982): 65–80.

————, "Krishna and Buddha of India: Black Gods of Asia." *Journal of African Civilizations* 7, no. 1 (1985): 106–111.

————, "The Empire of the Moors: An Outline Based on Interview and Summary." *Journal of African Civilizations* no. 11 (Fall 1991): 85–92.

Johnson, Tekla Ali. "Colonial Caste Paradigms and the African Diaspora." *The Black Scholar* 34, no. 1 (Spring 2004): 23–33.

————, "The Enduring Function of Caste: Colonial and Modern Haiti, Jamaica, and Brazil." *Comparative American Studies* 2, no. 1 (March 2004): 61–73.

Kamara, Gibreel M. "Regaining Our African Aesthetics and Essence through Our African Traditional Religion." *Journal of Black Studies* 30, no. 4 (March 2000): 502–514.

Kent, R. K. "Palmares: An African State in Brazil." *Journal of African History* 6, no. 2 (1965): 161–175.

Klingberg, Frank J. "Carter Godwin Woodson, Historian and his Contribution to American Historiography." *Journal of Negro History* 41, no. 1 (January 1956): 66–68.

Kopytoff, Barbara Klamon. "The Early Political Development of Jamaican Maroon Societies." *William and Mary Quarterly* 35, no. 2 (April 1978): 287–307.

———, "Colonial Treaty as Sacred Charter of the Jamaican Maroons." *Ethnohistory* 26, no. 1 (Winter 1979): 45–64.

Langley, J. Ayo. "Chief Sam's African Movement and Race Consciousness in West Africa." *Phylon* 32, no. 2 (2nd Quarter 1971): 164–178.

Legum, Colin. "The Organization of African Unity -- Success or Failure?" *International Affairs* 51, no. 2 (April 1975): 208–219.

Lewis, Linden. "Richard B. Moore: The Making of a Caribbean Organic Intellectual." *Journal of Black Studies* 25, no. 5 (May 1995): 589–609.

Lockett, James D. "The Deportation of the Maroons of Trelawny Town to Nova Scotia, then Back to Africa." *Journal of Black Studies* 30, no. 1 (September 1999): 5–14.

Lynch, Hollis R. "Edward W. Blyden: Pioneer West African Nationalist." *Journal of African History* 6, no. 3 (1965): 373–388.

Mazama, Ama. "The Áfrocentric Paradigm: Contours and Definitions." *Journal of Black Studies* 31, no. 4 (March 2001): 387–405.

———, "Afrocentricity and African Spirituality." *Journal of Black Studies* 33, no. 2 (November 2002): 218–234.

Mazrui, Ali A. "Africa Between Nationalism and Nationhood: A Political Survey." *Journal of Black Studies* 13, no. 1 (September 1982): 23–44.

Miller, M. Sammye. "Historiography of Charles H. Wesley as Reflected through the Journal of Negro History, 1915–1969." *Journal of Negro History* 83, no. 2 (Spring 1998): 120–126.

Mixon, Gregory. "Henry McNeal Turner Versus the Tuskegee Machine: Black Leadership in the Nineteenth Century." *Journal of Negro History* 79, no. 4 (Autumn 1994): 363–380.

Ogunleye, Tolagbe M. "The Self-Emancipated Africans of Florida: Pan-African Nationalists in the 'New World.'" *Journal of Black Studies* 27, no. 1 (September 1996): 24–38.

————, "*Aroko, Mmomomme Twe, Nsibidi, Ogede, and Tusona*: Africanisms in Florida's Self-Emancipated Africans' Resistance to Enslavement and War Stratagems." *Journal of Black Studies* 36, no. 3 (January 2006): 396–414.

Okonkwo, R. L. "The Garvey Movement in British West Africa." *Journal of African History* 21, no. 1 (1980): 105–117.

————, "Orishatukeh Faduma: A Man of Two Worlds." *Journal of Negro History* 68, no. 1 (Winter 1983): 24–36.

Pérez, Berta E. "The Journey to Freedom: Maroon Forebears in Southern Venezuela." *Ethnohistory* 47, no. 3–4 (Summer 2000): 611–634.

Perkins, Eugene. "Literature of Combat: Poetry of Afrikan Liberation Movement." *Journal of Black Studies* 7, no. 2 (December 1976): 225–240.

Reed, Pamela Yaa Asantewaa. "Africana Womanism and African Feminism: A Philosophical, Literary, and Cosmological Dialectic on Family." *Western Journal of Black Studies* 25, no. 3 (2001): 168–176.

Reviere, Ruth. "Toward an Afrocentric Research Methodology." *Journal of Black Studies* 31, no. 6 (July 2001): 709–728.

Rogers, Ben F. "William E. B. Du Bois, Marcus Garvey, and Pan-Africa." *Journal of Negro History* 40, no. 2 (April 1955): 154–165.

Sanneh, Laming. "Prelude to African Christian Independency: The Afro-American Factor in African Christianity." *Harvard Theological Review* 77, no. 1 (January 1984): 1–32.

Semmes, Clovis E. "Foundations of an Afrocentric Social Science: Implications for Curriculum-Building, Theory, and Research in Black Studies." *Journal of Black Studies* 12, no. 1 (September 1981): 3–17.

————, "Foundations in Africana Studies: Revisiting *Negro Digest/Black World*, 1961–1976." *Western Journal of Black Studies* 25, no. 4 (2001): 195–201.

————, "Existential Sociology or the Sociology of Group Survival, Elevation, and Liberation." Journal of African American Studies 7, no. 4 (2004): 3–18.

Shepperson, George. "Notes on Negro American Influences on the Emergence of African Nationalism." *Journal of African History* 1, no. 2 (1960): 299–312.

Smith, John David. "A Different View of Slavery: Black Historians Attack the Proslavery Argument, 1890–1920. *Journal of Negro History* 65, no. 4 (Autumn 1980): 298–311.

Snipes, Wesley. Foreword to "On My Journey Now: The Narrative and Works of Dr. John Henrik Clarke, The Knowledge Revolutionary," edited by Kwaku Person-Lynn. *The Journal of Pan African Studies: A Journal of Africentric*

Theory, Methodology and Analysis Special Issue, 1, no. 2 (Winter–Fall 2000) and 2, no. 1 (Spring–Summer 2001): 107–111.

Thompson, Vincent Bakpetu. "Leadership in the African Diaspora in the Americas Prior to 1860." *Journal of Black Studies* 24, no. 1 (September 1993): 42–76.

Turner, Diane D. "An Oral History Interview: Molefi Kete Asante." *Journal of Black Studies* 32, no. 6 (July 2002): 711–734.

Veney, Cassandra R. "The Ties That Bind: The Historic African Diaspora and Africa." *African Issues* 30, no. 1 (2002): 3–8.

Vinson, Ben, III. "Fading from Memory: Historiographical Reflections on the Afro-Mexican Presence." *Review of Black Political Economy* 33, no. 1 (Summer 2005): 59–72.

Wesley, Charles H. "The Reconstruction of History." *Journal of Negro History* 20, no. 4 (October 1935): 411–427.

———, "Racial Historical Societies and the American Heritage." *Journal of Negro History* 37, 1 (January 1952): 11–35.

———, "Creating and Maintaining an Historical Tradition." *Journal of Negro History* 49, no. 1 (January 1964): 13–33.

———, "W. E. B. Du Bois -- The Historian." *Journal of Negro History* 50, no. 3 (July 1965): 147–162.

———, "The Need for Research in the Development of Black Studies Programs." *Journal of Negro Education* 39, no. 3 (Summer 1970): 262–273.

Winters, Clyde Ahmad. "Afrocentrism: A Valid Frame of Reference." *Journal of Black Studies* 25, no. 2 (December 1994): 170–190.

Woodson, Carter G. "Ten Years of Collecting and Publishing the Records of the Negro." *Journal of Negro History* 10, no. 4 (October 1925): 598–606.

Dissertations and Theses

Alford, Kwame Wes. "A Prophet without Honor: William Leo Hansberry and the Discipline of African Studies, 1894–1939." Ph.D. diss., University of Missouri-Columbia, 1998.

Ball, Jared A. "Still Speaking: An Intellectual History of John Henrik Clarke." M.A. thesis, Cornell University, 2001.

Crowder, Ralph L. "John Edward Bruce and the Value of Knowing the Past: Politician, Journalist, and Self-Trained Historian of the African Diaspora, 1856–1924." Ph.D. diss., University of Kansas, 1994.

Ogunleye, Yvonne Tolagbe. "An African Centered Historical Analysis of the Self-Emancipated Africans of Florida, 1738 to 1838." Ph.D. diss., Temple University, 1995.

Encyclopedia Entries

Toure, Ahati N. N. "Rogers, Joel Augustus." In *Encyclopedia of the Harlem Renaissance*. Vol. 2, edited by Cary D. Wintz and Paul Finkleman, 1070–1072. New York: Routledge, 2004.

Magazine Articles

Hansberry, William Leo. "W. E. B. Du Bois' Influence on African History," *Freedomways* 5, no. 1 (Winter 1965): 73–82.

Popoola, S. Solagbade. "Pilgrimage to Ile-Ife." *Orunmila* 1 (July 1985): 6–14.

Thompson, Clifford. "St. Clair Bourne: Documenting the African-American Experience." *Cineaste* 26, no. 3 (Summer 2001): 34–35.

Bulletins

Bulletin of the Association of Concerned Africa Scholars no. 46 (Winter 1996).

Websites

Barbados. CIA World Factbook, http://www.cia.gov/cia/publications/factbook/geos/bb.html#Intro.

Contemporary Authors Online, Gale, http://www.galenet.com/servlet/GLD/form?origSearch=true&o=DataType&n=10&l=1&locID=txshracd2588&secondary=false&u=CA&u=CLC&u=DLB&t=KW.

French Guiana. CIA World Factbook, https://www.cia.gov/cia/publications/factbook/geos/fg.html.

Index

Mozambique 259, 260
Mphahlele, Ezekiel 6, 27
Muhammad Speaks 228
Muslim 80, 173, 174, 222, 223, 226,
   229, 267, 268, 288
Muslim Mosque, Inc. 222
myth 14, 27, 64, 109, 135, 158, 174,
   175, 202, 268, 288

Namibia 126
Napata 75, 79
Nasser, Abdel 225
Nation of Islam 27, 161, 222
National Association for the
   Advancement of Colored People
   (NAACP) 25, 97, 198, 199, 282,
   286
National Association of Television
   and Radio Announcers 97, 98
National Council for Black Studies
   (NCBS) 270
nationality 11, 12, 14, 15, 185-190,
   192-199, 205, 206, 221, 242, 243,
   252, 287
negritude 239, 291
Negro Digest/Black World 4, 6, 27, 132,
   290, 291
Negro History Bulletin 44, 108
Negro Society for Historical Research
   (NSHR) 29, 32, 33, 35
Negroid 60, 77, 78
Nell, William Cooper 29, 189
neocolonialism 176, 223, 224, 235
New School for Social Research/New
   School University 66, 70, 99, 124

New York City Board of Education
   66, 126, 127
New York Public Library 3, 5, 30, 37
Nigeria 26, 27, 37, 42-44, 64, 71, 94,
   133, 171, 225, 257, 259, 260, 262,
   267
Nile Valley 3, 14, 62, 68, 124, 127,
   148, 150, 162, 164
Nkrumah, Kwame 26, 28, 37, 42, 43,
   64, 225
Noble, Gil 25
Nubia 62, 79
Nyasaland (Malawi) 64
Nyerere, Julius 225

Obatala 172, 234
Obote, Milton 225
Odu Ifa 172
Ogunleye, Tolagbe 253, 254
Olokun 172
Olympio, Sylvanus 43
Omer-Cooper, J. D. 190
Onwuachi, P. Chike 230, 234, 237,
   291, 293
oppression 8, 11, 14, 31, 134, 135,
   137, 159, 161, 165, 175, 176, 193-
   195, 202, 205, 224, 225, 256, 264,
   267, 283
oral history 4, 5, 156
Organization of African Unity
   (OAU) 27, 61, 222-224, 226, 228,
   229
Organization of Afro-American
   Unity (OAAU) 6, 14, 15, 27, 221-
   230, 242